LEARNING AS DEVELOPMENT

Learning is the foundation of the human experience. It is the common thread across cultures and geographies and forms a continuous and malleable link across the life stages of human development. Disparities in learning access and outcomes around the world have real consequences for income, social mobility, health and well-being. This book traces the path of international development from its pre-colonial origins, through the rise of economics, to the emergence of a learning equity agenda. Today's unprecedented environmental and geopolitical challenges compel us to invest in learning—our most renewable resource. *Learning as Development* asks us to rethink international education in a changing world.

Daniel A. Wagner (Ph.D. University of Michigan) is the UNESCO Chair in Learning and Literacy, and Professor of Education at the University of Pennsylvania. He is Founding Director of the International Literacy Institute and Director of Penn's International Educational Development Program. A former Peace Corps Volunteer and Fulbright Scholar, he has served as an advisor to UNESCO, UNICEF, World Bank, USAID, DFID and other agencies, governments, and civil society organizations. He was elected Fellow of the American Educational Research Association and was the recipient of the 2014 UNESCO Confucius International Literacy Prize. He is the author or editor of more than 25 books and many other publications. See www.danwagner.org.

"This book greatly advances our knowledge and understanding of how to improve learning for all—especially for those who have been most marginalized, such as the poor, girls and women, indigenous populations, migrants and those impacted by climate change. It is especially welcome as the world moves towards implementing the United Nations 2030 Sustainable Development Goals."

—Irina Bokova, Director-General, UNESCO

"Dan Wagner's magnum opus covering learning and development (both international and life course development) is unparalleled in scope and depth and with case material from numerous cultures in the Middle East, Africa and Latin America. The book is full of new ideas to improve education, and reduce poverty and inequality in low-income countries. Its comprehensive treatment of issues in international development guarantees its permanent value to experts or novices alike. This is a long-awaited book on educational development."

—Robert A. LeVine, Roy E. Larsen Professor Emeritus
Harvard University, USA

"*Learning as Development* is a great read. The depth of discussion and the literature it draws on has a wealth of resources. My students really need this in order to critically reflect on what we can (and cannot) achieve through the SDGs. Thumbs up for this excellent book!"

—Moses Oketch, Professor, Institute of Education,
University College London, UK

"As Pope Francis has stated, the fate of the world today depends on how we support the needs of the most disadvantaged among us, particularly those affected by migration and climate change. Dan Wagner has written a well-researched and comprehensive volume with critical insights on improving education that will help make a difference in the world today and tomorrow."

—Archbishop Marcelo Sanchez Sorondo, Chancellor,
Pontifical Academy of Sciences, The Vatican

"This is a refreshing, accessible volume that combines scholarship with thoughtful descriptions of learning from many cultures; it humanizes and broadens the discussion of education and development."

—Marlaine Lockheed, World Bank and
Center for Global Development

"Excellent! It is time to walk the talk! The time has come for rethinking and rebuilding the learning process worldwide. This incisive and thoughtful book strikes an important balance between research and practice, and should be read by policy makers as well as those who engage in the everyday critical work of education and development."

—Adama Samassekou, Minister of Education, Mali

LEARNING AS DEVELOPMENT

Rethinking International Education in a Changing World

Daniel A. Wagner

Routledge
Taylor & Francis Group

NEW YORK AND LONDON

First published 2018
by Routledge
711 Third Avenue, New York, NY 10017

and by Routledge
2 Park Square, Milton Park, Abingdon, Oxon, OX14 4RN

Routledge is an imprint of the Taylor & Francis Group, an informa business

Library of Congress Cataloging-in-Publication Data
Names: Wagner, Daniel A., 1946– author.
Title: Learning as development : rethinking international education
    in a changing world / Daniel A. Wagner.
Description: New York, NY : Routledge, 2018. | Includes bibliographical
    references and index.
Identifiers: LCCN 2017026751| ISBN 9781848726062 (hb : alk. paper) |
    ISBN 9781848726079 (pb : alk. paper) | ISBN 9780203115305
    (ebook : alk. paper)
Subjects: LCSH: Education—Economic aspects—Developing countries. |
    Learning—Developing countries. | Economic development—
    Developing countries.
Classification: LCC LC67.D44 W34 2018 | DDC 370.116—dc23
LC record available at https://lccn.loc.gov/2017026751

ISBN: 978-1-84872-606-2 (hbk)
ISBN: 978-1-84872-607-9 (pbk)
ISBN: 978-0-203-11530-5 (ebk)

Typeset in Bembo
by Apex CoVantage, LLC

For Mary

CONTENTS

FOREWORD

Solving problems associated with learning and the quality of education has never been so important. Education stands at the heart of the 2030 United Nations Agenda for Sustainable Development, as a transformational force for overall human development.

Since its founding in 1945, UNESCO has placed educational advancement at the center of all its action, as a universal human right and an imperative for sustainable development and lasting peace. Enormous strides have been made toward universalizing education, but exclusion remains the harsh reality for over 160 million children and youth, while illiteracy is holding back over 700 million adults from full participation in their societies—with girls and women carrying the heaviest burden. The message of the 2030 Agenda is clear: it will not be achieved without putting education first, and new approaches and strategies are required to empower every learner with the competences and skills to navigate and leverage 21st century opportunities.

This new agenda calls for a better understanding of the complexities of educational provision, based on evidence, lessons learned, taking into account national contexts.

With this volume, *Learning as Development: Rethinking International Education in a Changing World*, I am deeply grateful to Professor Dan Wagner, UNESCO Chair in Learning and Literacy at the University of Pennsylvania, for his comprehensive research and guidance in seeking solutions to the problems we face in securing educational opportunities for people around the world. Professor Wagner has been a longstanding and dynamic contributor to the spirit and practice of UNESCO's work over many years, beginning with his first UNESCO publication during the 1990 International Literacy Year entitled "Literacy—Developing the Future" (published in five languages). More recently, the International Literacy Institute, of which Dr. Wagner is founding Director, was the co-recipient of the 2014 UNESCO Confucius International Literacy Prize for its innovative work using technology to support early literacy for South African school children.

In this volume, Professor Wagner brings together the latest research findings from around the world, drawing from specialists representing a wide range of social science disciplines. This book greatly advances our knowledge and understanding of how to improve learning for all—especially for those who have been most marginalized, such as the poor, girls and women, indigenous populations, migrants, and those impacted by climate change. His book provides a source of relevant findings along with a way of understanding the inherent problems in improving education among these populations that is especially welcome today, as the world moves to implement the 2030 Agenda.

Professor Wagner is well known for his scientific approach to educational problems. With considerable dedication, he has spent a lifetime pursuing a rigorous examination of educational interventions, policies, and methods. Through his efforts, and the efforts of others like him, we are better able to solve the real-world problems facing us. For these reasons, we at UNESCO, and I personally, welcome this new book by an esteemed university colleague.

Irina Bokova
Director-General of UNESCO

PREFACE

It is human nature to be preoccupied with the lives of others. And it is our capacity for empathy that leads people in one part of the world to seek to help those in another. The variation in our collective circumstances—combined with the visibility we now have into that variation through all forms of media—has created a growing awareness of the divides between rich and poor, sick and well, and safe and at-risk communities all around the world. Professionals who work on such issues (in government service, academia, foundations, etc.) employ the term *international development* to refer to a field dedicated to addressing and overcoming these divides.

Over my career, I've been continuously inspired by the advancements we've made in how to approach and address international development. Yet, I've also been frustrated at times by a discourse that seems compressed or locked into silos by academic discipline or subject matter. When we're asked what makes individuals and societies thrive, there is much insight and creativity to be found at the intersections among different fields and the experts representing them. Learning across the disciplinary divides has been at the core of my approach to solving social and educational problems.

Thus, it is no coincidence that this book is about learning, education, and international development, and, in particular, on how narrowing the gap in learning can change lives for the better. Learning is the fundamental thread of human development, preparing us for a multitude of life pathways. It is also a powerful proxy for determining societal success and resilience. For the purpose of this book, I have tried to bring together perspectives from across disciplines that represent what is known in the field today, in order to inform new directions for improved policy and practice for learning.

The world faces unprecedented challenges—from civil conflict to pandemics, along with mass migration, youth unemployment, and climate change—that can only be effectively addressed by a knowledgeable citizenry. Thus, our collective ability to advance learning and well-being for children, youth, and adults has never been more important, especially among the poor and marginalized. The potential to address these challenges is also unprecedented. We know more than we ever have about what it takes to bridge inequities in learning and education. This volume makes the claim that, with the right learning equity agenda and our capacity for human engagement and empathy, we can build a substantially better future.

ACKNOWLEDGMENTS

I am grateful to my teachers in engineering at Cornell University who, with pains-taking rigor, taught me how to build things in the real world. I am also indebted to the Peace Corps in Morocco and Moroccan friends from whom I first learned to deeply appreciate how different peoples and cultures connect and learn to adapt to one another. I am grateful as well to those in many other parts of the world with whom I participated in conversations and projects large and small, and from whom I continuously learned how all development is local.

My interest in the social sciences and education grew during my graduate stud-ies at the University of Michigan, where I had the enormous good fortune to be mentored by Harold W. Stevenson. Later, I benefitted greatly from a post-doctoral fellowship at Harvard University under the wise guidance of Robert A. LeVine. Over four decades, many other colleagues and friends have been generous with their thoughts, counsel, and patience, especially within my long-term home at the Graduate School of Education at the University of Pennsylvania.

For this volume, I received excellent comments and criticism from a number of colleagues and friends, including: Alejandro Adler, Bob Boruch, Julian Cristia, Luis Crouch, Amy Jo Dowd, Peter Easton, Elliot Friedlander, Steve Heyneman, Iddo Gal, Amber Gove, Ameena Ghaffar-Kucher, Priya Joshi, Steve Klees, Robert A. LeVine, Joshua Muskin, Michelle Neuman, Scott Paris, Ben Piper, Sidney Strauss, Tim Unwin, and Sharon Wolf. Also, a special thanks goes to several long-time partners, including: C. J. Daswani, Masennya Dikotla, Wadi Haddad, and Mohamed Maamouri. Their willingness to share time and critical thinking was vital, not only with regard to this book, but also for their encouragement and friendship over many years.

My two children deserve special shout-outs: Jonah, for his tireless efforts in challenging some of my most cherished yet erroneous beliefs, and for strategiz-ing ways to conceptualize key issues in this book; and Claire, for steadily driving home the importance of practical, real-world applications from scientific research, especially for the poor and disenfranchised. Also, I owe a huge thanks to my wife, Mary, who read, re-read, critiqued, and re-critiqued the entire book project.

Those of us lucky enough to be teachers are aware of the countless ways that students influence and challenge our thinking. They, too, provided inspiration for this book. Some who offered specific feedback included: Nathan Castillo, Anna Drabek, Kimberly Fernandes, Gareth Smail, and Fatima Tuz Zahra.

I had help with editing and document preparation from several talented individuals: Jennifer Moore, Cecelia Cancellaro, and especially Elizabeth Baird who helped greatly in the final stages of book preparation.

Naturally, all errors of fact and interpretation are the sole responsibility of the author, and are not intended to represent the views of the above individuals or any agency or organization.

Earlier in my life, my parents provided steady encouragement and were, themselves, gracious examples of lifelong learners. In more recent decades, the support received from my wife and children has been a constant reminder of how much learning and growth takes place in one's own home. In so many ways, their encouragment, patience, and love were the bedrock of this endeavor, shaping the broad contours of the book, and my life.

ABBREVIATIONS AND ACRONYMS

CWPM	Correct words per minute (oral reading fluency)
ECD	Early childhood development
EGRA	Early grade reading assessment
HDI	Human Development Index
ICT	Information and communications technology
L1, L2	First language (mother tongue), second language
LFP	Low-fee private schools
LSEA	Large-scale educational assessment
MDGs	Millennium Development Goals
NFE	Non-formal education
NGO	Non-governmental organization
OECD	Organization for Economic Cooperation and Development
PISA	Program for International Student Assessment
RCT	Randomized control trials
ROI	Return on investment
SQC	Small, quicker, cheaper (approaches to assessment)
SDGs	Sustainable Development Goals
UN	United Nations
UNDP	United Nations Development Program
UNESCO	United Nations Educational, Scientific, and Cultural Organization
UNICEF	United Nations Children's Fund
UIS	UNESCO Institute for Statistics
USAID	US Agency for International Development

INTRODUCTION

Toward a New Understanding of Development

Lessons From a Spring Day in Al-Kataba

Over 40 years ago, on a warm spring day in the small town of Al-Kataba, Morocco, I observed a young man rocking back and forth while sitting on the porch of the local mosque. He held a foot-long stick in his right hand that he slid over a smooth, rectangular-shaped board. On further inspection, it became clear that he was using the stick to tap out a rhythm over a set of Arabic words written on the board. While startling and perplexing to me, the purpose of the activity was quite obvious to a Moroccan friend with whom I was traveling. This system of tapping out words was a typical method of studying the Quran in many mosques in Morocco.

At that time, I was a graduate student in psychology. Nothing I had studied had given me the background needed to decipher this experience. Though I was specializing in the study of cognition and learning, this type of practice in Morocco was nowhere to be found in my courses or textbooks. I read about experiments undertaken mainly on American "human subjects" who were undergraduates recruited for studies of the "ways humans think." For example, researchers studied how many nonsense syllables could be learned in a short period of time and repeated back without error. Memorizing lists of nonsense syllables would have been as strange an activity to the young man in Morocco as tapping on a board would be to American college sophomores. Yet, if my textbooks were truly about how (all) humans learn, why had I not been exposed to the kind of variations that I discovered during my travels?

This question, and others that followed, led me to invest many years in observing and studying how people learn around the world. From young children to adult learners, with a considerable emphasis on children in school, I have sought to understand the full spectrum of why and how people learn, and what impact learning (and failing to learn) has on life beyond the classroom. With a global lens, I have delved deeply into how learning prepares people for their futures.

Concurrently, I have sought to understand how countries around the world prepare for the future, and measure themselves against other nations. Typically, we call this area of inquiry *international development*. Discussions on this topic often revolve around economic development, and more specifically the comparisons of, say, the gross national product (GNP) of different countries. Considered on a global scale, many professionals and the public at large think of international development—or simply "development"—as synonymous with improving GNP or GNP per capita. In other words, national or individual income has become the primary indicator of "successful" development.

Yet there are substantial limitations to this economics-centric view of development. First, a perspective that focuses on measurements like GNP puts large-scale blinders on our view of people on the ground; vital resources may or may not "trickle down" to fulfill the needs and values of ordinary individuals. The gaps between the rich and poor within most countries are increasing, creating inequities in important societal functions such as schooling, health, and well-being. Additionally, the forces of globalization and climate change—and their impacts on urbanization and environmental sustainability—are putting major pressures on the most fragile populations, increasingly leading to civil conflict and mass migration. For these reasons and others, it seems unwarranted in today's world to maintain our concentration solely, or even primarily, on economic growth.

This book focuses on what international development would look like if economics were not the primary yardstick for measuring national success. Specifically, what would international development become if viewed through the prism of *human development*? How humans grow, adapt, create, and seek well-being and happiness—the central concern of people in all cultures—is what is meant by the term human development. At its core is *learning*, since learning is the very process through which individuals progress or develop from one stage of life to the next. Learning is a complex, necessary, and ubiquitous human behavior—something we do every day of our lives, in both formal and informal contexts. And, as readers will come to see, opportunities for learning are not equally distributed. The variations in what people learn are as wide and deep as the distinctions between individuals and societies the world over. Through this book I've endeavored to pull together new research and real-life examples that support this alternative, learning-focused view on how to measure, interpret, and promote international development.

Much like my early impressions of Morocco, what has struck me over the years is that most of the research on education and international development has paid only peripheral attention to learning and its variations in distinct cultural contexts. Among professionals and the public alike, the science of learning is commonly perceived to be the result of robust evidence and standardized measurement techniques. But we now recognize that the scientific basis for understanding the who/what/where/why/when/how of learning has been based mainly on research undertaken with middle-class children and college sophomores in wealthy countries.

To fully understand learning across the world and how it impacts human development—especially in poor and marginalized communities—we must broaden our awareness of cross-cultural variation. Doing so will allow us to answer puzzling questions that plague development efforts, such as: Why do teachers trained in Uganda show little evidence of using what they have studied to improve their students' learning? Why do minority language children struggle to learn to read the national language in some countries, but not in others? Why do people in some adult literacy programs learn more about their peers than they do about reading? We will address the above questions, and others of this type, in this volume.

Learning and Society

Learning is the glue that holds families and societies together. An essential part of what we learn in the home is transferred cultural knowledge that is cumulative over time. This is the cornerstone of maintaining coherent and meaningful social groups, and preparing children for the future. In conjunction, formal settings like schools seek to ensure that fundamental skills like reading and writing are inculcated in each successive generation. In a world that is increasingly at risk from civil strife, resource limitations, and environmental degradation, citizens need to be well-informed and constantly learning to adapt and to cope.

When learning improves so does the quality of life. Yet crafting the most effective interventions to support learning presents a constant challenge for development professionals, given that learning opportunities and contexts vary so widely across the world. Generally speaking, we know that a great deal of this variation can be attributed to differences in socioeconomic class, language, and gender. Further, learning is influenced by factors like access to schools, the presence of trained teachers, and classroom size. But, there are specific policies and approaches that lead directly to better learning across the life span, and across domains of society. Research shows, for instance, that early education for young children has a long-term payoff of about ten times the investment, in terms of reduced social costs. Multiple studies show that when teachers understand how reading skills are acquired, school achievement goes up and student dropout rates go down. When adult women in low-income countries learn to read, rates of HIV/AIDS go down. If appropriately designed, programs that put mobile phones and tablets directly in the hands of children can have remarkably positive consequences for learning in and out of school.

These promising outcomes show us that learning is both a useful way to measure success in international development, and a critical guarantor for the future of the world's children. While reflecting on the nature of *learning as development* in this book, we must focus on how to rethink education, broadly defined, and its relationship to international development. Using this lens, we can advance the scope of development theory, policy, and practice by not limiting ourselves to the sterile and misleading notion that equates national economic development with personal fulfillment. We also open up a new conversation about development that can be understood not only by statisticians and government technocrats, but also by the multiple stakeholders that they serve.

Structure of This Book

The chapters in this book are divided into four main sections. Following the Introduction, Part I is devoted to examining the interrelationships between international development, human development, and learning as development—culminating in new ways to think about education and international development. Chapter 1, "International Development," looks at the historical role of colonialism in international development, and how agencies and researchers have taken diverse disciplinary approaches to define and implement development strategies over the years. Chapter 2, "Human Development," describes a life-span human development approach advocated in this volume, its value to revised thinking about international development, and its role in the establishment of the 2030 United Nations Sustainable Development Goals. Chapter 3, "Learning as Development," provides a framework for examining the multiple roles of learning in everyday life and in cultural contexts, as well as the central position of learning in international development.

In Part II, three broad chronological stages of learning are examined. Chapter 4, "Learning in Early Childhood," considers the remarkable growth of interest in early childhood interventions and preschool programs, and why more investments are being made than ever before in this area. Chapter 5, "Children and Basic Skills," reviews how school-aged children learn the fundamentals such as reading and math, and why these skills have become the gateway to further socioeconomic advancement. Chapter 6, "Youth and Adult Learning," examines learning outside of schools, including youth and adult literacy programs, and non-formal education in the sectors of agriculture and health. These chapters, taken together, are designed to present an overview of the differing ways and contexts in which humans learn throughout their lives, from birth through adulthood.

Part III considers two core educational institutions, each of which has held a prominent historical position in supporting learning. Chapter 7, "Schools and Schooling," describes the large role that schools have played over many centuries. Schools in many poor contexts struggle to provide a modicum of quality teaching and learning, especially in light of increased enrollments and urbanization in developing countries. While public schools still dominate this landscape, both private and religious schools have grown as well, and offer new challenges and opportunities. Chapter 8, "Teachers and Pedagogies," recognizes the pivotal role that formal instruction, and those who provide it, play in all schools. While training and paying teachers constitute the largest fiscal share of the costs of formal schooling, teachers receive widely varied quality of training, with concomitant results. Teachers and their instructional pedagogies are mainly regulated by national authorities who therefore constitute a key leverage point for improving children's learning. Taken together, schools and teachers often dominate conversations about educational development, especially among policymakers and international agencies. In this book, we consider how these educational institutions are implicated in learning outcomes.

In Part IV, dramatic changes are described that are already beginning to shake up the world of learning and development. Chapter 9, "New Technologies," provides a critical analysis of the use of innovative digital tools that can (but do not always) support substantially increased learning both in and out of the classroom. Chapter 10, "Globalization and the Environment," considers how the pressures of climate change, globalization, civil conflict, and migration will impact the sustainability of our planet and the role that learning will play in what we do about it. Chapter 11, "Measurement of Learning," explores the methodological and empirical considerations of trying to interpret and extend findings in educational development, particularly in the area of learning assessments. Chapter 12, "Learning Equity," offers alternative ways to think about global metrics, and how to narrow the gap between the haves and have-nots in learning. It also lays out a set of five priorities for establishing a learning equity agenda. Finally, in the Epilogue, I provide some reflections on problems and possibilities of international development in a progressive and sustainable world.

Evidence

On a topic as broad and deep as that covered in this volume, evidence must be drawn from a multitude of sources—from historical and ethnographic accounts to international surveys and experimental designs. Other resources include primary reports and publications from fieldwork, as well as secondary analyses undertaken by statisticians. To achieve a comprehensive synthesis, I have had to impose a subjective process of selecting research for citation. Several of my selection preferences follow.

First, this volume is focused primarily on individual learners and their contexts; comparative educational systems and the history of policymaking—topics of considerable importance—are referenced at various points (especially in Part I), but they are not the center of the present discussion. A second preference concerns geography and demography. This book focuses on poor and marginalized people in low-income developing countries. It does not seek to be balanced or representative in terms of geographical coverage, nor does it examine the relatively well-off students in secondary or higher education. Third, by emphasizing the poor in low-income countries, there are consequences both in terms of scientific and policy generalizations. This book challenges the notion that scientific findings about learning and education can, with only modest adaptation, be applied universally. Conversely, the notion that context specificity necessarily negates the applicability of findings from other places is also contested. This duality complicates arguments as well as renders them more applicable over time and space. Fourth, where possible, the focus here is on the doable and the practical—what people have done, rather than what might exist in an idealized world. It also means that topics such as neuroscience and genetics—over which societies have very little control—are seldom touched upon. Fifth, the evidentiary claims offered in this book may be interpreted in multiple ways—by discipline, methodology, or ideological persuasion; I have tried, as much as possible, to be clear on the evidence lens employed.

Finally, stories have been included at the beginning of each chapter to provide a contextual background for the specific topic addressed—to give the reader a feel for each topic in a localized setting. Most are from direct or indirect observations by the author. To preserve anonymity, these are sometimes composites taken from more than a single instance or location, and personal and location names have been changed. A few of the stories have been adapted from other writers, as indicated in the endnotes. With respect to endnotes, these have been used liberally so that the reader can find further sources of research as well as additional comments on them. Hopefully, this in-depth commentary will be useful for readers who wish to pursue topics in greater depth.

Advancing the Social Good

In the chapters that follow, I argue that human development in general, and learning in particular, should be a much higher priority in international development than it is today. To make this argument, I combine perspectives from multiple social sciences; the history of international development and international education; the study of life-span human development and human learning; and changing trends such as globalization and new technologies. One of the major goals of this book is to unify and synthesize these perspectives in ways that support the argument that learning is, in many important respects, the elemental ingredient for international development—an approach I call *learning as development.*

This book is written for those who care about improving the lives of people around the world, in particular those who live in low-income countries. It is also about the nature of human transformation across the life span, from infancy through adulthood. Even though people in all countries take learning and education seriously, educational systems often underperform, especially so in developing countries. This result has political, social, individual, and moral consequences.

Finally, this book is about aspirations. It represents a way to support the hopes of peoples around the world for a better life; the hope that our global engagement will improve children's lives; and the hope that if we know more about improving learning, we can advance the social good.

PART I
Development

1

INTERNATIONAL DEVELOPMENT

Izel: The Legacy of Colonialism in Yucatan

Twenty-five-year-old Izel grew up during a time of high hope in central Yucatan. In his grandparents' time, the area was still recovering from the "Caste Wars," a 50-year rebellion for Yucatan's independence. The Mayans lost that war, but Izel's parents, hoping to give their children a better life than previous generations had known, worked hard to educate Izel and his five siblings. They supplemented their peasant farming income by making hammocks that his mother sold in the nearby town of Ticul, accessible by motorcycle on a rutted road. His father had some schooling and learned enough Spanish to eventually get a job as an assistant garage mechanic. Izel managed to graduate from high school, and his hopes were understandably high when rumors began circulating that wealthy businessmen were coming to Yucatan to build deluxe hotels on the Caribbean shore—what would eventually become known as the Riviera Maya, near some of the great ruins that are now major international tourist sites. Many young men with high school educations, like Izel—especially those who spoke good Spanish—expected to find hotel jobs and make enough money to buy homes in their villages. When Izel traveled to the area in search of work, he discovered that the full-time jobs were instead taken by Spanish-speaking *mestizos* who had come from big cities in Mexico, could speak English, and were familiar with the ways of the *gringos* who frequented the hotels. With his hopes dashed, Izel remained in Ticul, despondent, taking odd jobs and hoping for other economic development projects that might favor Mayans.

———————

Contemporary international development originated with European colonization, a reality that has influenced economic development efforts for centuries, both directly and indirectly. For Izel, the results are direct and visible. The skills he learned in high school were helpful, but clearly not sufficient. Local jobs are scarce, and those created by international investments (such as the Riviera Maya resorts) have passed him by, much as they did for his parents and grandparents. While Izel can use his skills to make hammocks or buy and sell products in the local market, his options are limited as long as more lucrative jobs are given to outsiders.

A complex web of forces is responsible for the barriers that Izel faces. Job opportunities are influenced by social class, race, and geographical location—a foundation that was laid partly through a history of domination and colonization, and partly due to the limits of a rural Yucatecan education. One of the biggest challenges in international development work today is trying to understand the weight of this colonial history and its bearing on people around the world. There are real forces of social and economic power that benefit some and oppress others. History shows us that one of the best ways to combat these discriminatory and oppressive forces is through learning and education—in other words, a more knowledgeable citizenry.

Colonialism and Early International Development

Christopher Columbus, Vasco da Gama, and other legendary global explorers of the 15th century were among the first European practitioners of international development. Through their famous voyages, these early explorers exposed indigenous peoples to European ways—to their values and conventions, and also to their diseases, military arms, and global politics. Those who followed the early explorers added profit, power, and religious faith to the numerous motives for their colonial conquests.

Over the next several centuries, colonial empires—most prominently British, French, Spanish, and Portuguese, but also Russian, Japanese, Turkish, German, American, and others[1]—sought to carve up the world's land masses and impose their will and economic systems upon local populations. These pre–World War II powers were deeply involved in what was often explicitly referred to as "development work." This primarily involved the imposition of Western norms while extracting both natural and human resources.[2] The original empire builders thought they were bringing the benefits of "civilization" to ignorant "savages" in traditional societies.[3] They were conquerors and colonizers by design (see Box 1.1), seizing land and people. At the same time, the colonizers attempted to replace what they viewed as pagan beliefs and superstitions with their own religious and cultural heritage, in order to reproduce the "civilized world" in a foreign land. A classic example is that of the British Raj—one of the many legacies of the British rule in India, Pakistan, and Bangladesh.[4] This practice would later be termed the "white man's burden,"[5] or the presumed responsibility of Europeans.

From the start, empire building was fraught with conflict and social turbulence. Even today, many of our global and regional conflicts stem directly from these endeavors.[6] For the most part, the colonizers failed (or chose not) to understand and legitimize local beliefs, values, and ways of life. The moral views of the conquerors were framed and supported by the notion that privileged and technologically advanced societies had a right, and even a duty, to dominate the less fortunate around the world.

BOX 1.1   WHAT IS COLONIALISM?

Colonialism is the subjugation by physical and psychological force of one culture by another—a colonizing power—through military conquest of territory. . . . Colonialism has two forms: colonies of settlement, which often eliminate indigenous people (such as the Spanish destruction of the Aztec and Inca civilizations in the Americas), and colonies of rule, where colonial administrators reorganize existing cultures to facilitate their exploitation (such as the British use of *zamindars* to rule the Indian subcontinent). The outcomes are, first, the cultural genocide or marginalization of indigenous people; second, the extraction of labor, cultural treasures, and resources to enrich the colonial power, its private interests, and public museums; and third, the elaboration of ideologies justifying colonial rule, including notions of racism and modernity.

Source: McMichael (2011, p. 17)

Following World War II, liberation movements rose up to throw off the mantle of colonialism, but often left in place the colonial organization and ideologies that allowed local elites to continue exploiting the poor.[7] In this way, some of the most harmful aspects of the colonial era were carried over to post-independence governments. Even with the increases in global economic development over the last half-century, there remain significant inequities across many dimensions of life in the developing world.[8]

Given this troubled past, several questions arise. To what extent are current development policies free from these earlier historical actions, or rather based upon them? Can Western countries, which still provide the bulk of international development aid today, be trusted with designing development activities? How do current development practices compare with the quests for political power from decades and centuries past? Although there are no perfect answers, these questions are addressed throughout this volume. For now, it is important to remember that international development today bears significant legacies from its colonial past.

Bretton Woods and the Origins of Economic Development

Contemporary development efforts can be traced to the Bretton Woods Conference in July of 1944. This historic gathering, formally known as the United Nations Monetary and Financial Conference, laid the groundwork for the establishment of the International Monetary Fund and the World Bank in the wake of World War II (see Figure 1.1). Delegates from the 44 Allied nations[9] attending

FIGURE 1.1   John Maynard Keynes (right) and Henry Morgenthau, the US Treasury Secretary, at Bretton Woods Conference in 1944, to Lay the Foundation of the International Monetary System

Source: Alfred Eisenstaedt/Time & Life Pictures/Getty Images

this landmark meeting used terms such as "economic prosperity" and "economic take-off" to indicate how the rich nations of the world should help other nations prosper economically (especially those recently devastated by the war; and later on, those that remained poor).[10] Ingrained in this mandate was the assumption that poor nations should become more like the countries that were represented by the attending delegates.[11]

The views of economic historian Walter Rostow can be discerned in the decisions made that fateful summer in New England. Rostow argues, in *The Stages of Economic Growth: A Non-Communist Manifesto*, that in order for countries to become "developed," they must move beyond their traditional economies and adopt a modern economic framework—one necessarily connected to a globalized economy. As the subtitle of his book makes clear, Rostow was writing at a time of decolonization and national liberation movements, which the US government perceived as potential Communist threats.

Rostow identified five main stages of economic growth: (1) traditional society; (2) pre-conditions to economic take-off; (3) take-off; (4) the drive to maturity; and (5) developed society (or society of high mass consumption).[12] Development moves linearly, in his view, toward an end state in which all people of the world presumably share the resources and advancements that development made possible.

This theoretical and prescriptive framework gained strong support during the half-century following WWII, and played a role in the establishment of a new world order. The economic engines of the time, the drive to rebuild after a crippling world war, and the nascent optimism at the war's end, gave rise to impressive economic growth in some parts of the world. The nations that "took off"—Rostow's notion that countries' economies can take off like airplanes with the aid of outside forces, then, once "in the sky," manage on their own—eventually included the so-called "Asian tigers." These are the economic powerhouses of Hong Kong, Singapore, South Korea, and Taiwan—to which were added Brazil, Russia, India, and China (also known as the BRICs).[13] Economists with this mindset view economic growth as a rising tide that lifts all boats.[14]

More than a half-century later, Rostow's theory remains a strong influence in the development field. This is not so much because the data support Rostow's stages, but rather because there seem to be few good alternatives, other than to assume that hard work and good investments will eventually lead both individuals and nations to better futures.[15] In reality, however, Rostow's views are less definitive than ever before. Most developing countries have not reached the final "developed" stage even after decades of development efforts. Further, some advanced economies have begun to stagnate in growth, while numerous developing economies are affected by turbulence in global markets.

Nor is there a defined development end point that all countries share. Indeed, various attempts at self-reliance have led countries as diverse as Tanzania, Cuba, Bhutan, and North Korea to push for a greater degree of economic independence. This has allowed them to pursue national development policies that are separate from the globalizing forces of development.[16] Efforts to create an alternative "Third World" perspective on development flourished in the 1970s and 1980s but eventually lost steam, with some saying that the era of development had come to an end.[17]

Even if Rostow's model is now considered somewhat *passé*, economists continue to dominate the conversation about development, with the World Bank acting as a major driver of development planning. The idea that international development stems from the economics of multinational trade still holds sway in many development circles, even as critics call it economic neo-imperialism. According to this more critical view, countries of the world will only be considered "integrated into the global economy" when international corporations can sell their products and services to poor people in poor countries (see Figure 1.2), while at the same time extracting raw materials (such as iron ore or oil) for refinement and/or manufacturing in industrialized countries. Such vestigial hegemony of the world's major economic powers is largely taken for granted in today's world under the term "globalization." Yet, as the gap between the economic haves and have-nots has widened over the decades, some have concentrated on trying to make sure that the poor don't fall further behind.

FIGURE 1.2   An Indictment of the Impact of Globalization on the Poor

Source: Sylver, courtesy of Worth1000/DesignCrowd

Culture and Poverty

Endeavoring to reduce or eliminate poverty,[18] international agencies have created programs and interventions within many sectors of development, including education, health, and agriculture.[19] Most international agencies claim to target investments at populations most in need—those in high or "extreme poverty," meaning those who live on less than US$1.25 per day (see Figure 1.3).[20] In 2011, people in extreme poverty comprised roughly two billion people, or about 36% of the current global population; by 2015, extreme poverty is estimated to have been halved to less than one billion people.[21] Clearly, the overall number of those living in extreme poverty has dropped substantially over the last 25 years; however, since the poverty decline is heavily influenced by the economic prosperity gains in a single country—China—it is misleading to claim (as some have) that poverty has been reduced across the developing world.[22] The absolute number of those remaining in poverty remains enormous,

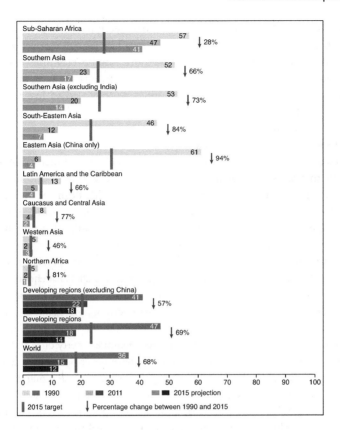

FIGURE 1.3 Proportion of People Living in Extreme Poverty on Less Than US$1.25 a Day 1990, 2011, and 2015 (Percentage)

Source: United Nations (2015a, p. 14)

and actual dollar levels, as we shall see, do not fully capture people's perception of poverty. These extremely poor groups are sometimes referred to as those at the "bottom of the pyramid," a term popularized in 2006 by C. K. Prahalad, a professor of global business.[23] He used the term to describe the large group of people living in developing countries who have been ignored by major corporations as potential consumers.[24]

Poverty generally replicates itself across generations, a phenomenon that tends to further entrench those at the bottom. People often fall into a "poverty trap,"[25] the cycle in which the factors that led to their initial poverty continue to hold them back over the course of their life. Among those who first popularized the notion of being "stuck" in poverty is Oscar Lewis, who published a groundbreaking book in 1959 entitled *Five Families: Mexican Case Studies in the Culture of Poverty*.[26] This work explored the inner workings of five very different Mexican families for an entire day, providing a close-up, insider view of their lives. The families represented a cross-section of Mexican society at the time the book was written, and each fit into Lewis's conceptualization of a "culture of poverty"—the notion that those born into poverty inherit a specific, self-perpetuating value system that profoundly impacts their aspirations and worldviews. According to Lewis, the families were forced to live within the "nagging, debilitating drudgery of penny existence" that he predicted would be maintained across time.[27]

Five Families was recognized as a major contribution to our understanding of what it means to be poor, that is to say, embedded below wealthier social strata in conditions that are self-perpetuating. However, there were also critiques of this view. Some argued that Lewis overgeneralized about Mexican society given the very small number of families he observed, that social mobility was more possible than he suggested, and that he overstated the case of "fatalistic" thinking by people who were just less ambitious about making changes.[28]

In any event, his ideas remained very influential,[29] and hit a corresponding nerve in the United States at the time. Poverty was beginning to receive national attention. President Lyndon Johnson's "war on poverty" was declared with great fanfare in January 1964, and its major goal was "not only to relieve the symptom of poverty, but to cure it and, above all, to prevent it."[30] Embodied in this initiative was the belief that with enough effort, funds, and expertise, the United States could eradicate poverty once and for all.

But the conditions and predictors of poverty have never been equivalent across societies, and such variations make combatting it a distinctly challenging goal. When considering how to craft development initiatives to alleviate poverty, substantial care needs to be taken when exploring what it means to be poor in specific cultural contexts. Having a mobile phone in India may make one feel rich, but in Japan it has little impact on perceived self-worth. There is a large body of evidence that suggests that culture contributes to making and breaking both the perception and experience of "cycles of disadvantage."[31] But what exactly do we mean by *culture*?

In the 1950s, anthropologists Alfred Kroeber and Clyde Kluckhohn reviewed more than 100 definitions of culture.[32] They came up with a synthesis that comprises the notion of both explicit and implicit patterns of beliefs and behaviors within and across groups—all of which necessarily have consequences for development interventions (see Box 1.2). Today, the term "culture" is thought to be

BOX 1.2 A DEFINITION OF CULTURE

Culture consists of patterns, explicit and implicit, of and for behavior acquired and transmitted by symbols, constituting the distinctive achievements of human groups, including their embodiments in artifacts; the essential core of culture consists of traditional . . . ideas and especially their attached values.

Source: Kroeber and Kluckhohn (1952, p. 181)

the ways in which knowledge, attitudes, and values distinguish one group from another. As Clifford Geertz later elaborated, culture is "semiotic" in nature—it's about people making meaning in local contexts.[33] Thus, cultural identities can also overlap. For instance, within a group of people from India, some might hail from the state of Andhra Pradesh while others from Gujarat. Some might speak Hindi while others speak Telugu. Some might inhabit urban areas while others reside in rural villages. Some might be relatively wealthy while others are quite poor. Such distinctions make a real difference in the lives of individuals who are part of these groups, communities, and regions. How people react to new ideas that are out of step with their cultural norms (e.g., educating girls in a traditional Muslim society) and new tools (e.g., using chemical fertilizers instead of traditional ones)—whether by informal diffusion or by the design of a development agency—can make a huge difference in the success of any development project.

Culture, globalization, demographics, migration, and urbanization interact with one another in myriad ways, and this complexity produces major variations in how groups perceive the inputs and outputs of development work. Cultural differences are among the most crucial challenges to the effectiveness of development work, and to alleviating poverty. Put simply, the mismatch between policymakers (and their policies) and the recipients of development assistance goes a long way toward explaining the many failures of development work over decades.

In 1995, akin to Lyndon Johnson's "war on poverty," but 30 years later, James Wolfensohn became President of the World Bank, and set an agenda "to reduce poverty and improve the quality of people's lives" across the globe. Now, nearly seven decades since Bretton Woods and 20 years since Wolfensohn announced his antipoverty agenda, there is a growing view that, although culture must be understood for development to take place, poverty is not a direct consequence of cultural stereotypes as Lewis first proposed.[34] Even so, it is not unusual for the media to portray poverty as the result of debilitating "backward traditions," "illiteracy," or simply a lack of "work ethic."[35] However, such biases are not only present in the popular press. Less than 12% of psychological science research focuses on populations in developing countries, despite the fact that more than 80% of the world's population lives there.[36] This imbalance between the primary emphasis of social science research versus where this research is applied in development is a major problem, and is indicative of how social scientists have viewed development over the years.

The Social Sciences of Development

Economists, sociologists, political scientists, psychologists, and anthropologists typically see the field of development (and the role of education in development) quite differently. By tracing the history of each social science's conceptualization of development, we can discern the varied ways that specialists have approached development work, based on their chosen methodological tools. For example, economists use national income data, psychologists use surveys, and anthropologists engage in ethnographic case studies. These tools necessarily drive the kinds of outcomes found.[37] Since economists have played the dominant role in driving development discourse, that is where our discussion begins.

Development Economics

In its *Human Development Report* of 1990, the United Nations stated that "the link between economic growth and human progress is not automatic."[38] Even so, in the half-century following the founding of the World Bank in 1944, raising the GNP of low-income countries was and still is the primary aim of most of the major development agencies.[39] This form of development emphasizes the creation of economy-boosting infrastructure, such as roads, bridges, and dams that would facilitate the building of markets and the flow of goods and services.[40] While advances have been made in some developing countries (such as the BRICs, mentioned previously) over recent decades, many countries' economies have leveled off or declined (see Figure 1.4). Some economists have focused on the measurable "gap" in GNP per capita between different segments of populations within countries—termed the Gini coefficient, used to measure societal economic inequalities.[41]

Naturally, development economists thought more broadly than just bridges and dams—*human capital* was also on their minds.[42] The human capital approach posits that growth in human potential "accelerates economic growth, enhances personal incomes, reduces social inequalities, improves health and nutrition, and helps to

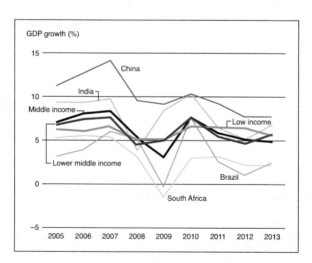

FIGURE 1.4 Gross Domestic Product (GDP) Growth, 2005–2013

Source: World Bank (2015a)

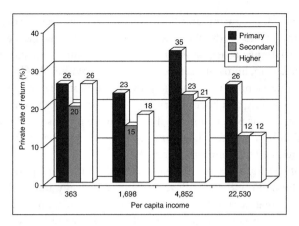

FIGURE 1.5 Private Returns on Investment (ROI) in Education by Income

Source: Psacharopoulos and Patrinos (2004)

reduce high rates of population growth and of infant mortality."[43] And, when economists thought about the importance of human capital, they also thought nearly exclusively about access to education, at least in part because building schools was a component of their fiscal portfolio.

Thus, following Rostow's stages model, economic "take-off" required certain "minimum levels" of education. Some claimed, for example, that at least four to six years of primary schooling was the intellectual floor upon which solid national economic growth must be built.[44] More recent versions of this required threshold can be seen in the current focus on levels of skill attainment across nations as predictors of economic growth, the research basis of which has come under serious criticism.[45]

Though it may be impossible to determine a precise return on investment (ROI) of education, most economists and policymakers—and nearly every parent—can see a strong correlation between more education and greater prosperity.[46] Otherwise, why would parents from New York to New Delhi, as well as those in the slums of Rio de Janeiro and Lagos, spend large portions of their incomes on sending their children to the best schools possible?[47] Such educational investments at the individual or family level are part and parcel of the perceptions of people the world over, and they are mirrored in the data collected on private economic ROI of increasing years of education at varied income levels in developing countries (see Figure 1.5).[48]

Sociology of Development

Sociologists study the systems, organizations, and institutions that govern individual and societal outcomes. For example, we need only read a newspaper to see how the terms "development" and "democracy" are often seen as co-existent and self-reinforcing, at least in the West. Western notions of social justice—including gender and racial equality as well as other forms of non-discrimination—are today intimately linked to humanitarian goals embedded within development work. Other goals of development—such as improved education, health, reduced fertility, lower infant mortality, and better nutrition—have become part of the mission of many development agencies. Historically, it's been the job of sociologists to examine the relationships between these institutional goals and the ways that different populations respond to them across time.

As one of the founders of modern sociology, Karl Marx posited that economic development and social development were really one and the same.[49] Marx believed that without a revolution in the ownership of the means of production, the gap between the rich and the poor would only increase, and that the poor would only get poorer.[50] Building on Marx's perspectives, many sociologists have viewed both human capital theory and modernization as key reasons why poor countries (and poor people) remain poor in a world dominated by imperialism (see Figure 1.6).[51] Over the years, they have put forward the concept of "dependency theory"—the idea that the world consists of a group of wealthy countries that feed off poor countries' raw materials and cheap labor, while also making them increasingly dependent on expensive Western-manufactured goods. Later termed "neo-colonialism," this perspective suggested, as did "world-systems" theory, that there were powerful "core" nations that dominated "peripheral" nations, both in economic development

FIGURE 1.6 View of British Imperialism

Source: The Granger Collection

and in education.[52] In this line of thinking, education systems in developing countries are overly dependent on the ideas, curricula, and expertise of wealthy countries.[53]

Another way that sociologists have analyzed dependency is through the cultural dimension of contact within societies. Well-known for his research in this area was the French sociologist Pierre Bourdieu, who conducted his early work in Algeria.[54] He, and others who followed, posited the theory of "social reproduction"—the idea that societies tend to re-create themselves across generations, thereby establishing rigid class structures that strictly limit social mobility within nations. This outcome is due, Bourdieu posited, to the transmittal of "cultural capital" (such as social networks, language, literacy, and school-based learning) from one wealthy generation to the next. Thus, in countries like India or Peru, the dominant classes educate their children in the dominant (national or international) language(s). Children also learn both cognitive and "soft" (socio-emotional and interpersonal) skills, and have access to social networks that allow them to maintain their advantage over those who do not have the same resources. For sociologists, the notion of cultural capital remains a prominent explanation of socioeconomic differences between the rich and the poor. In contrast to Marx, Bourdieu preferred to invoke social reproduction as a more culturally sensitive and longer-term explanation of economic differences than that of material wealth.[55]

A further sociological analysis was introduced by Paulo Freire, a Brazilian educator who supported "liberation theology"—a derivative of Marxist thinking that proliferated mostly in Latin America, as an alternative approach to development. Freire criticized Western education, which he felt promoted the "banking" of facts and concepts—to pass national examinations, for example—that were alien to many students (both children and adults) in poor and indigenous societies. He was an early advocate of teaching literacy,[56] and promoting the idea of critical pedagogy as a form of empowerment to confront the hegemony of the upper classes of society.[57]

The sociological approach to development takes seriously both the cultures and institutions that help shape the attitudes and values of diverse populations, while at the same time positing structural obstacles to change (such as socioeconomic classes and the nature of the political economy) that must be addressed by development theorists.[58]

Political Science of Development

Political scientists view development largely through a lens of governmental agencies and the relationships between the actors and organizations that interface with these agencies. Naturally, political leadership plays a major role in development. In particular, considerable attention has been paid to the importance of the "political will" of national leaders. One notable empirical study of political will was undertaken in six African countries, where it was shown that the degree to which data (e.g., on infant mortality) was effectively utilized depended more on government agents than on the type and quality of data collected.[59] That is, political leadership (through these government agents) trumped the validity of the data itself—it mattered more that development projects had strong central governmental support. Such top-down trends are also seen in the media. Long-serving political leaders are often singled out for their successes (e.g., Paul Kagame in Rwanda for improving the national health system) or failures (e.g., Robert Mugabe in Zimbabwe for ruining its once-admirable agricultural system).[60]

In tandem with top political leaders, there are many other stakeholders engaged in development work, including national government ministers, policymakers, international donor representatives, community leaders, teachers, parents, and technical specialists. Most development efforts do not include all such stakeholders, and only rarely are the local beneficiaries truly part of decision-making processes. This means there can be substantial contention among stakeholders before, during, and after project implementation. Take, for example, the Three Gorges Dam in central China that is fed by the Yangtze River. With its 26 turbines that produce 18,000 megawatts of power, the dam holds back enough water to slow the rotation of the Earth. While the dam provides roughly 3% of the country's energy needs, it has come at enormous environmental and social costs, and has been the subject of local, national, and international protests—largely due to the top-down decision-making process that implemented it.[61]

Despite historical resistance, there are growing efforts to include local stakeholders in decision making.[62] In Chapter 11, for example, we review citizen-led learning assessments that provide parents with more detailed information about their children's schools. In this way, parents feel more empowered to hold government officials accountable for their children's progress in the classroom. Similarly, there is increasing support for community monitoring of teachers in classrooms.[63] Albert Hirschman, a Harvard and Princeton academic, recognized in the 1970s and 1980s that top-down "successful" development programs were almost always counter-productive in the longer term.[64] He argued that development efforts will necessarily be judged as a mixture of success and failure—and indeed that *failures* are often a required step to greater success.[65] During these same years, the most glaring and toxic aspects of imperial economic and political power began to recede, with greater "buy-in" from aid recipients and communities beginning to grow.[66]

Psychology of Development

Psychologists have posited that development is largely a cognitive and behavioral phenomenon fostered at the individual level. Their view has long been that "modernization" encompasses the kinds of attitudes and values that individuals (as well as groups and cultures) need in order to achieve economic growth. Nearly 50 years ago, cross-national psychological surveys revealed that countries characterized by stronger economic growth were those with citizens who were more ambitious, more persistent, more adaptable, and educated in Western-style schools.[67] In this view, traditional societies—and citizens' beliefs—need to become more modern in order for a population or country to become more economically developed. Contemporary versions of this idea can be seen in the recent emphasis on soft skills (such as "grit") in schools and the workplace, where such skills are said to be more predictive of success than the cognitive skills tested in school-based assessments.[68] Critical assessments of such universalistic psychological theory have come from many quarters over time, including from those who suggest that there are "multiple modernities" one can point to.[69]

The idea that some cultures are more psychologically advanced than others has had a long and sometimes infamous history. With the improved ability to measure skills at the individual level, psychologists became deeply embroiled in controversies associated with cultural, ethnic, or racial superiority.[70] This topic has at times had shameful consequences. In South Africa, for example, the *apartheid* era was partly reinforced by studies of racial inferiority in human intelligence, where results from cognitive tests were used to support the treatment of non-whites as second-class citizens.[71] In its *apartheid* years, the South African government used race as a determining factor of who could become "developed," based on the calculated use of data purporting to show that Africans were of limited intelligence.[72] Fortunately, this early racial intelligence "science" has now been debunked not only morally, but also scientifically.[73] Today, we know that communities are so variegated that simple dichotomies like intelligent versus unintelligent not only fail to capture the realities of the cultural practices of individuals, but also have unwarranted detrimental effects.

As researchers began to study the effects of modernization on indigenous peoples in diverse parts of the world, they also began to search for the causes of differences in learning, thought, perception, and logic. For example, Alexander Luria studied the impact of literacy campaigns on peasants during the Russian revolution.[74] His work, and that of others over the following decades, lent support to the notion of a "great divide" between the cognitive worlds of those who are literate and those who are not, and hence those who are modern or not.[75] Subsequent research found that the cognitive consequences of literacy are quite specific to the types of learning undertaken and skills acquired.[76] Still, the idea that the mental aptitudes of peoples in developing countries are somehow different than (and deficient to) those in the West continues to be invoked in development work.[77] We will see that such large-scale cultural claims have limited validity, and must be very specific in order to be useful.[78]

More recent work by psychologists has been much more positive. As we will see in the following chapters, psychologists have taken the lead in studying the social and cognitive development of children and adults—work that has had an important influence on how we understand the nature of change in the human development life-cycle. Psychologists have also been pioneers in the area of learning and instruction, a topic to which we will turn in Chapter 3 and beyond.

Anthropology of Development

Cultural anthropology is the comparative study of the ways different peoples make sense of their world. Anthropologists were among the first to describe the varieties of culture and poverty around the world, typically working in close proximity and support of their imperial compatriots. In the last half-century, however, anthropologists have been among the fiercest critics of development, claiming that it is an inherently hegemonic enterprise. As one such critic complained, development workers "disturbingly recycle, in the name of cultural sensitivity and local knowledge, conventional views of modernization, social change, and the Third World."[79] Today, anthropologists often advocate for the protection of traditional societies and local cultures from what they see as neo-colonial predators supported by capitalism and globalization.[80]

With respect to schooling, anthropologists study which subjects are taught, which textbooks are chosen, and what the resulting impact is on who gets ahead, and who's left behind. They also ask what decisions get made, and who has a seat at the decision table. With children in poor countries gaining increased access to schools, the transition between home and school has become an important focus of anthropologists as well. Research suggests that a student's ability to learn in a new context is challenged when there is a significant discordance between the home and school environments.[81] One consistent finding is that a teacher's supportive and respectful attitude toward the student's home language and culture can facilitate positive attitudes toward school and improved learning conditions.[82]

Anthropologists have also explored the ramifications of cultures in contact with one another, particularly in terms of migration. John Ogbu, a Nigerian anthropologist who taught for decades at the University of California at Berkeley, sought to understand why some minority groups succeeded in education while others often fell behind over multiple generations.[83] Ogbu proposed a distinction between "voluntary" versus "non-voluntary" migrants, and claimed that those who sought to migrate (i.e., traveled voluntarily) were much more likely to succeed than those who were forced to travel (either due to slavery, indentured servitude, or civil conflicts at home). Among his examples were Koreans who migrated largely for economic opportunity, as contrasted with Africans who were taken by force to North America.

Anthropologists often emphasize the need to be inclusive of others' localized views, and note that minority voices are often not part of development decision-making processes that impact schooling.[84] In addition, many anthropologists are concerned that development professionals will inevitably make mistakes because they lack an in-depth understanding of local culture and language. For example, one anthropologist stated, "[our] work can also degenerate into a simplistic anti-statism, which takes the form of a romanticism that suggests that the grassroots are virtuous and that if only the state were not there then everyone would be egalitarian and nature-loving."[85] The claim is that development "experts"[86] have a strong tendency to misjudge local contexts. Stories abound in the media about development agencies building power plants that have devastating environmental consequences, providing anti-malarial bed nets that are used for fishing, or importing textbooks in languages that children cannot read. In short, there exists a plethora of anthropological complaints about how local cultures have been misunderstood.

Interdisciplinary Approaches

What, then, is the right way to approach international development? Many anthropologists (and some economists) argue that top-down approaches to development necessarily lead to overly prescriptive and intellectually arrogant interventions.[87] Sociologists have noted how neo-colonial ideas are maintained by world systems and by intergenerational cultural transmission.[88] Psychologists, in the days of pre- and post-colonialism, became embroiled in pernicious Darwinian-inspired debates around superior intellect and eugenics. These are some of the cautionary remarks from differing disciplines, and are worth noting when projects do not work as intended.

On the positive side, each of these social sciences has offered opportunities to better understand individual lives in both global and local contexts. Together, in an interdisciplinary manner, broader and deeper knowledge can help guide development work.[89] One thing is certain: the full measure of how to define and predict the knowledge, attitudes, and values of different groups cannot be subsumed by one theorist, theory, or discipline. Changing lives and changing societies "for the better" is notoriously difficult—even the criteria of what constitutes "better" is continuously up for debate. Nonetheless, the challenge to improve international development remains.

The Arc of International Development

The field of international development has strong proponents and detractors. The former group generally consists of a large array of government and intergovernmental agencies, non-governmental agencies (NGOs), bilateral aid agencies, foundations, and the public. As one observer commented: "The strength of 'development' discourses comes from its power to seduce in every sense of the term: to charm, to please, to fascinate, to set dreaming, but also to abuse, to turn away from the truth, to deceive. How could one possibly resist the idea that there is a way of eliminating the poverty by which one is so troubled?"[90] Still, detractors are plentiful. Some are those who are on the "receiving end" of development (the so-called "beneficiaries"[91]), while others include, among others, development specialists and academics who are troubled by what they perceive as repeated failures.

Recall the discussion of Izel, who had missed out on a bigger and more ambitious life for himself—he was not a beneficiary of the major economic gains in Yucatan. Still, Izel's life is not one of massive deprivation and destitution. He is not among the one or two billion people today who are even more deeply locked in poverty. Even so, he exemplifies the difficulties of overcoming a history of poverty, discrimination, and life's limitations.

Development work is an ongoing and labor-intensive process. The ramifications of its centuries-old history still linger in those societies where colonization took place, something to which Izel would likely attest. Yet global levels of poverty, in terms of the average income per capita, have declined over recent decades, even while extreme poverty remains endemic and the gaps between the rich and the poor have grown. The various social science underpinnings of poverty and development suggest that our present world remains a very difficult place for the poor and the poorly educated.

If we look at the arc of international development, its earliest years were largely a story of cultural imperialism. Over the ensuing centuries, it has been transformed into something more consciously benign (though surely not always effective nor without flaw) with a focus on economic development and poverty reduction. Today, in an era in which we must, of necessity, be oriented to a sustainable world, we must seek new paths to support *human development and learning*.

Notes

1. Russia took territories in Central Asia and encroached into the Middle East; Japan took land from China; the Turks expanded the Ottoman Empire into Egypt, the Arabian Peninsula, and across North Africa; Germany established colonies in East and West Africa; the United States attained defacto-occupation of parts of Latin America and the Philippines. There were many other incursions, such as Italy into Libya and Ethiopia, Belgium into Congo, and others. Thanks to S. Heyneman (personal communication) for his views on colonization.
2. Easterly (2014).
3. Costantini (2008) states: La civilisation (opposée à l'état sauvage ou à la barbarie) [sont] . . . les peuples "civilisés" . . . , moins par tel ou tel trait défini que pour la supériorité de leur science et de leur technique, et pour le caractère rationnel de leur organisation sociale." *Translation*: Civilization (as opposed to a state of savagery or barbarism) . . . refers to "civilized" peoples, less by a specific trait or feature, but by the superiority of their science and technology, as well as by rational character and social organization.
4. In Arora and Goyal (1995). Thanks to F. Zahra for this example.
5. Kipling (1929).
6. For a recent review, see Loomba (2015).
7. While Latin American countries were no longer colonies well before WWII, they nonetheless were often beholden culturally and economically to their earlier colonizers and to the United States.

8. In this book, we use the word "developing" to refer specifically to low-income countries or regions that lag behind the economies of industrialized countries or regions. Much has been said about the use and misuse of the term "developing" country, and some view it as a pejorative word. The reader will note that this book tries to move beyond labeling countries and peoples only in terms of economic levels. Thus, the term "low-income" also has limitations. Hence, the book will at times use each of these terms where it seems most appropriate.

9. The Allied nations were those that fought and defeated the Axis countries (led by Nazi Germany and Japan) during World War II.

10. The World Bank's focus on development and poverty was not a primary aspect of the organization until the 1960s. By contrast, the International Monetary Fund was not conceived as a development institution, but rather a source of fiscal assistance. Thanks to S. Heyneman (personal communication) for his thoughtful comments.

11. In a review of the near-term events that followed Bretton Woods, Rist (2008, p. 71) pointed out the President Truman, in his Inaugural Address in 1949, included a major clause concerning "development"; namely that "[W]e must embark on a bold new program for making the benefits of our scientific advances and industrial progress available for the improvement and growth of underdeveloped areas. . . . For the first time in history, humanity possesses the knowledge and skill to relieve the suffering of these people."

12. Rostow (1960). Rostow's development model has since been challenged by scholars who claim that many developing countries have simply not followed this view of modernization; for example, see Seligson (1998), and in the work of Albert Hirschman as reviewed in Adelman (2013). The reference in Rostow to "high consumption" was intended to link his ideas to those of Ford Motor Company and other manufacturers that provided good wages and relatively cheap goods that could be sold to the masses—his definition of a developed society. Rostow apparently thought that his final stage would help developing countries resist the temptation of Communism (Rist, 2008, p. 99). Another critique, by Chang (2002), claimed rich countries were implicitly or explicitly involved in preventing poor countries from using the same strategies that rich countries themselves had used to get rich, thus "kicking away the ladder."

13. Some have noted that many of the "tigers" were countries with strongman leaders who paved the way for eventual entry into the China market. Thanks to S. Klees (personal communication) for this latter observation.

14. For example, Dollar and Kraay (2002) and Dollar et al. (2016).

15. As Rist (2008, p. 103) wrote: "Rostow's evolutionary schema became plausible—or rather, comforting—because it justified the dominant practices and made it seem likely that they would succeed. . . . [I]t was based on *faith* that the age of mass consumption would spread throughout the world."

16. In Tanzania this included President Nyerere's Arusha Declaration of 1967; Cuba's revolution and resistance to US "imperialism" in the 1960s; Bhutan's efforts at maintaining a Buddhist kingdom; and North Korea's resistance to nearly the entire global community with respect to human rights. S. Heyneman (personal communication) points out, however, that in the cases of both Cuba and Tanzania, each was a very large recipient of foreign assistance per capita when compared with other developing countries.

17. For example, Partant's (1982) *The End of Development* (in French: *La fin de developpement: Naissance d'une alternative?*). This time period also saw the World Bank's promotion of structural adjustment, where development was seen more as "living within national means," with the focus on budgetary constraints rather than faith in the Rostow's stages of development. See discussion in Rist (2008). The Third World was said to be those countries that were "non-aligned" with either the West or Socialism;

but with the fall of the Berlin Wall and the increase in globalization, the term has fallen out favor.

18. Poverty is a condition in which people live with a severe shortage of income and/ or material resources (such as housing, water, land, or cattle). It can be measured on both absolute and relative scales. For instance, poverty is measured across the globe by the presence of hunger, disease, forced migration, and environmental degradation, and the absence of income to address such problems. On the other hand, poverty may also be relative, in the form of discrimination by a majority culture based on (among other things) ethnicity, gender, disability, and material possessions ("my neighbor has a motorbike and I do not").

19. A "sector" refers to the general management categories used by governments to define an area of governmental interest and budgetary support, and usually involves the designation of a Minister or Secretary in charge—such as the Minister of Education.

20. See World Bank (2016a). In recent years, some agencies have increased the cutoff point of extreme poverty to US$1.90 per person per day.

21. The distribution of the poorest populations has now shifted, such that many are located in middle-income countries (such as China, India, Nigeria, and others), so that the preponderance of the poorest populations are no longer only in the poorest countries. See Kanbur and Sumner (2011); Sumner (2012, p. 1) also presciently states that: "One interpretation of the shift in global poverty is that extreme poverty is gradually changing from a question of poor people in absolute poor countries to questions about domestic inequality."

22. Radelet (2016), based on these same data, argued that extreme poverty is no longer a major issue, but his conclusions follow from the same misleading tendency to track global averages rather than particular groups. Similarly, see more on this sampling perspective in Chapter 11. Milanovic (2016) found that as inequality rises within countries, it is falling between countries—that is, a reduction in global inequality across nations.

23. The first use of the term "bottom of the pyramid" is attributed to Franklin D. Roosevelt in a 1932 speech called "The Forgotten Man," about the poor at the bottom of the economic pyramid. See further discussion on the bottom of the pyramid in Chapter 11.

24. Prahalad (2006). Prahalad counseled corporate leaders on how to improve marketing to the poor (and so reap greater profits), such as by designing miniature bars of soap for rural families who could not afford to purchase standard-size bars. Hence his notion was to make a *fortune* at the bottom of the pyramid, rather than focus on *assisting* those at the bottom. Yet the idea of tailoring marketing practices to particular groups of consumers has become a much ballyhooed course of action for the digital economy as giant corporations, such as Amazon and Google, increasingly try to shape their products and marketing to appeal to ever-more specific groups of consumers.

25. Sachs (2005). Also see Azariadis and Stachurski (2005) and Kraay and McKenzie (2014).

26. Lewis (1959, 1998).

27. Quotation from Birdwhistell (1960, p. 534).

28. McClelland (1961).

29. See, for example, the recent book by Putnam (2015) on poverty in the United States, and Sachs (2005) on the poverty trap.

30. Quotation is from President Johnson's 1964 State of the Union address, https://ows. edb.utexas.edu/site/jad2793edc370s/speeches-and-legislation.

31. Woolcock (2014, p. 5).

32. Kroeber and Kluckhohn (1952).

33. Geertz (1973). Geertz explained (p. 5): "Believing, with Max Weber, that man is an animal suspended in webs of significance he himself has spun, I take culture to be those webs, and the analysis of it to be therefore not an experimental science in search of law but an interpretative one in search of meaning. It is explication I am after, construing social expression on their surface enigmatical."

34. As Oscar Lewis (1959, 1998, p. 8) stated: "The people in the culture of poverty have a strong feeling of marginality, of helplessness, of dependency, of not belonging. They are like aliens in their own country, convinced that the existing institutions do not serve their interests and needs. Along with this feeling of powerlessness is a widespread feeling of inferiority, of personal unworthiness." For a contrasting view, see Small et al. (2010, pp. 10–11), who stated: "The literature on *poverty* and the literature on *culture* are too often produced in substantially different intellectual worlds, worlds that involve different interlocutors, theories of behavior, styles of thought, and standards of evidence. Traditionally, the former world has included not merely sociologists but also economists, political scientists, and demographers; favored quantitative evidence; placed a premium on clarity; and operated with an eye to solving social problems. The latter has included humanists, anthropologists, historians, and sociologists; favored interpretive or qualitative analysis; and rewarded the development of new theories. As a result, major works in one field have often had little impact in the other."

35. A second perspective on the culture of poverty is that some cultures are simply more attuned to development due to their native cultural traditions: for example, the collectivist values of Confucian societies (such as hard work and respect for education) help to explain the economic rise of the East Asian Tigers. Also, see Huntington's (1996) well-known book, *Clash of Civilizations*, and the results of PISA international comparisons showing the strong achievement and ambition of the peoples in East Asian nations. Others, such as Woolcock (2014, p. 2), have countered that development agencies should consider within-country ethnic variation—such as by caste in India, or by religion in the Mideast—in order to build development upon local cultural characteristics. He states that there is now "broad agreement that culture is more fruitfully understood as context-specific sources of identity, aspiration and meaning, and as repertoires (i.e., an array of normative behavioral and political 'tools') that members of particular groups deploy to construct, navigate and make sense of their world." Woolcock, in support of this, cites the work of Swidler (1986, p. 273) who states that: "[c]ulture influences action not by providing the ultimate values toward which action is oriented, but by shaping a repertoire or 'tool kit' of habits, skills, and styles from which people construct 'strategies of action.'" Woolcock (2014, p. 10) builds on Swidler's ideas by stating: "Far from celebrating or deploring 'culture' as a reified group characteristic, or dismissing it as an ethereal manifestation of more fundamental economic processes or interests, in this contemporary rendering culture is afforded a distinctive and central role in shaping the processes by which life is constructed, navigated and interpreted." Overall, that some societies are more able to adapt to change, are more education-friendly, and more able to move out of poverty, remains with us to the present day.

36. Arnett (2008).

37. See further discussion on methodologies in Chapter 11.

38. UNDP (1990). *Human Development Report.* NY: United Nations. Cited in Rist (2008, p. 206). More on the UNDP's view on development is highlighted in Chapter 2.

39. GNP (Gross National Product) is the estimated value of the total worth of production and services, by a nation's citizens within its national boundary *and on foreign land* (receipts from abroad), calculated over the course on one year. The figure uses Gross Domestic Product (GDP), which is an estimated value of the total worth of a nation's production and services, *within its national boundary,* by its citizens and

foreigners, calculated over the course on one year. Both GNP and GDP measure the size and strength of a national economy.

40. Critics have not been kind to this approach. See, for example, the work of Danaher (1994) who stated: "The unwritten goal of the IMF and World Bank was to integrate the elites of all countries into the capitalist world system of rewards and punishments. The billions of dollars controlled by the IMF and World Bank have helped to create greater allegiance of national elites to the elites of other countries than they have to their own national majorities."

41. Gini coefficient measures the statistical dispersion of income or wealth distributed across society and has been used as measure of inequality on income within countries. For further discussion, see Chapter 12.

42. Some of this discussion is drawn from Phillips and Schweisfurth (2014).

43. Colclough (2012, p. 136). He goes on to say: "[t]here are many subsidiary claims within the same paradigm [on human capital]—that it encourages more democratic politics, reduces war and civil strife, strengthens female autonomy and reduces discrimination." The human capital approach was initially built on the writings of Theodore Schultz (1961) and Gary Becker (1964).

44. Fagerlind and Saha (1983). Other economists suggested that attainment of literacy among 40% of a society's population is a necessary but not sufficient condition for economic growth, and that 70% to 80% is required for rapid economic expansion; see Anderson and Bowman (1965) and Azariadis and Drazen (1990). The fundamental supposition is that literacy is the indispensable building block for an informed and flexibly skilled citizenry in any country. See further discussion on literacy and development in Chapters 5 and 6.

45. See, for example, the work of Hanushek and Woessmann (2007, 2012, 2015) on the impact of cognitive skills on economic development (measured through international assessments). In this work, the authors state that their "[e]arlier research shows the causal relationship between a nation's skills—its knowledge capital—and its long-run growth rate, making it possible to estimate how education policies affect each nation's expected economic performance (Hanushek & Woessmann, 2015, p. 15). In a recent and persuasive review, Komatsu and Rappleye (2017) found important statistical inconsistencies in the Hanushek-Woessmann analyses.

46. Psacharopoulos (1985). In a recent critical review of human capital theory, Klees (2016) quotes Psacharopoulos and Patrinos (2004) as saying that "the concept of the rate of return to education is unassailable" (2004, p. 9), a point that Klees strongly disputes. Klees (private communication) suggests that it is nearly impossible to measure the *social* ROI (what's good for people) based on such economic ROI analyses.

47. There are exceptions as well. Some parents, for example, view the "data" they have on schooling and income in different ways, and thus come up with their own calculation as to how much school a family should have. See Banerjee and Duflo (2011).

48. The broadly held belief of the impact of education on income is not universally shared. In one recent review (Pritchett et al., 2013, p. 9), the authors state: "Evidence suggests that expanded educational opportunities do not translate into improved economic performance. At the country level, the average Kenyan over the age of 15 in 2010 had more years of schooling than the average French person in 1985. Sadly, Kenya's 2010 GDP per capita was only 7 percent of France's GDP per capita in 1985. Kenya represents a trend: massively increased enrollments even where incomes have stagnated in recent decades. More broadly, the link between schooling and economic growth in cross country analysis is fragile at best." Also, as discussed later in Chapter 3, many specialists think that it is the quality of education (rather than years of school) that is most predictive of national economic performance. In a recent review, Heyneman and Stern (2015) support the notion of quality of education, but they also point out some of the limitations of this argument. One is

that this work is correlational, such that better learning in schools might be due to higher economic performance, rather than the other way around. Another critique (see Stromquist, 2016) is that broad definitions of "quality" of education, when relying primarily on international assessments as the proxy variable, are inherently limited and misleading. Still others have suggested that individual skills and education have little to do with alleviating poverty or improving employment. Klees (2016, p. 648) provides four critiques of the theory of ROI on education: "the concept of economic efficiency that underlies them is unsound; earnings do not reflect productivity; even if it did, earnings, at best, is a partial and misleading measure of social benefits; and even if earnings were relevant, our ability to estimate the empirical effect of education on earnings is abysmal." He claims, rather, that it is "capitalist and other world system structures whose very logic makes poverty, inequality, and lack of employment inevitable" (p. 659).

49. Marx was trained in German sociology, but was also well-known as a philosopher, economist, politician, and journalist.

50. Marx (1887). See also Piketty and Goldhammer (2014) for a salient and contemporary update.

51. Figure is from an American cartoon (1888) depicting John Bull (England) as the "octopus of imperialism."

52. For more on world-systems theory, see Wallerstein (1992, 2004) and Clayton (1998).

53. See various related views in: Mazrui (1975), Carnoy (1974; 1999), Arnove and Torres (1999), Samoff and Carroll (2004).

54. Bourdieu (1977, 1986).

55. In the United States, see the work of Bowles and Gintis (1976) as just one example. Some (Harber, 2004) have argued that schooling itself can have very negative consequences, such as through punishment, gender bias, and so forth. More recently, with respect to the United States, see Lareau (2011).

56. A number of non-governmental organizations (NGOs), such as ActionAid, have developed literacy programs based on Freire's perspective. Before he died in 1997, Freire began to change his view about keeping education narrowly focused on indigenous cultures and languages, realizing that globalization was forcing a reconsideration of the value of multiple perspectives rather than only local empowerment (Freire & Macedo, 2005). A short video documentary on Freire's later views may be seen at: http://literacy.org/media.

57. See further discussion of Freire and literacy work in Chapter 6.

58. See Robertson and Dale (2015) on the obstacles related to the political economy.

59. See Nove et al. (2014) on the six-country study; and more generally Sumner and Mallett (2012).

60. Tepperman (2016), in his book *The Fix: How Nations Survive and Thrive in a World in Decline*, claims that political leaders need to be especially pragmatic, and give up on extremes that tend to follow when one political party overthrows another (he cites examples from Kagame's Rwanda to da Silva's Brazil). Tepperman notes that skilled leaders today must depend on technocratic solutions that can be implemented in real time, as opposed to a future what-if world. But he also says that the most effective leaders are those who benefit from extreme conditions (e.g., drought, civil conflict, or economic stagnation) and see a clear way to finding concrete and workable solutions.

Political will is a necessary factor in the politics of development, but it would be unwise to assume that it is sufficient on its own. The Nobel Prize–winning economist Herbert Simon coined the term *satisficing* to refer to the kind of decision-making strategies that can both "satisfy" and "suffice" when attempting to solve complex problems. Simon (1979) wrote that "decision makers can *satisfice* either by finding optimum solutions for a simplified world, or by finding satisfactory solutions for a more realistic world. Neither approach, in general, dominates the other, and both have continued to co-exist in the world of management science [italics added]." Simon also found that in such situations, we may try to simplify the problem to such an extent that an optimal-looking decision can be made; on the other hand, we may come up with a satisfactory (but not optimal) decision when dealing with a real-world (and highly complicated) problem. Trying to combine the two dimensions, by bringing to bear all available cross-disciplinary expertise, is what can produce a satisficing solution. The notion of satisficing has special salience in the sphere of international development.

61. Campbell-Hyde (nd).
62. Groves and Hinton (2013) and Fowler (2013).
63. This has also been termed "participatory action research"; see Rahnema (1990) for an early example.
64. Hirschman (1958) was an early dissenter from pure economic macro models of development. Later, Hirschman (1981) was even more critical, stating that the "decline of development economics cannot be fully reversed; our sub-discipline has achieved its considerable luster through the implicit idea that it could slay the dragon of backwardness virtually by itself or, at least, that its contribution to this task was central. We now know that this is not so." From Hirschman, p. 23; cited in Rist (2008, p. 219).
65. See discussion in a biography of Hirschman by Adelman (2013, pp. 388–394).
66. However, it also became clear that many former colonies began to rely heavily on economic, military, and development aid from their former imperial powers; for critical views, see Coyne (2013), Klees (2010), Moyo (2009), and Webster and Engberg-Pedersen (2002).
67. Lerner (1958), McClelland (1961), and Inkeles and Smith (1974). According to Eisenstadt (2000, p. 4) in a seminal review, "becoming 'modernized' [first contrasted] the awareness of a great variety of roles existing beyond narrow, fixed, local, and familial ones. The second [facet] recognized the possibility of belonging to wider translocal, possibly changing, communities."
68. See further discussion of soft skills in Chapter 5. Also: Heckman and Kautz (2012), Duckworth (2016), Duckworth et al. (2007), and Tough (2012). A half century after McLelland's work, the World Bank (2015b) published a review of how psychological and soft variables (similar to modernization) can be applied to economic development outcomes, particularly in terms of human decision making; see a critical review in Wagner et al. (2016). See also the recent work on the relationship between well-being and academic outcomes in Adler (2016).
69. See Eisenstadt (2000, p. 2) who stated: "The idea of *multiple modernities* (italics added) presumes that the best way to understand the contemporary world—indeed to explain the history of modernity—is to see it as a story of continual constitution and reconstitution of a multiplicity of cultural programs."
70. Wilhelm Wundt established the first experimental psychology laboratory in 1879 in Leipzig, and went on to study human psychological differences, resulting in a global perspective on *Folk Psychology* (Wundt, 1916).
71. Earlier, Rodney (1972) laid out his claim that it was Europe that caused the under-development of Africa. Also, it is well-known that Nazi Germany used such tests to advance insidious work on eugenics and sterilization. See D'Souza (1995).
72. Dubow (1995).
73. Collier (1994), Neisser et al. (1996), Nicolas et al. (2013), Sternberg et al. (2005), and Rakoff (2016).
74. Luria (1976). See further discussion in Chapter 2.

75. Goody and Watt (1968). A more negative view of the "great divide" gave rise to the claim that illiteracy and/or lack of formal schooling rendered traditional cultures different or inferior to Westerners.
76. Scribner and Cole (1981) in Liberia, and Wagner (1993) in Morocco.
77. The World Bank (2015b) described, for example, how rural farmers are overwhelmed by too much complexity in their lives at harvest time, and therefore make poor economic decisions.
78. See further discussion in Chapter 11.
79. Escobar (1991, p. 658).
80. Also, see Aikman (1999), Breidlid (2013), Coyne (2013), Dichter (2003), Maren (2009), and Mosse (2013).
81. Anderson-Levitt (2003); Dachyshyn and Kirova (2008); Moll (1990).
82. See further discussion of language of instruction in Chapter 5.
83. Ogbu (1978).
84. As Wali (2012, p. 12) states: "What value can be attributed to literacy that comes from walking in the forest and learning from your parents the names, shapes, and utilities of a myriad diversity of life forms? Should health only be defined as being able to live as long as you can, or are relatively shorter life spans that are packed with meaningful experiences also acceptable for health measurement? And is wealth only to be attributed to monetary value, or can wealth also be assigned to accumulated ecological knowledge or memories of ancestral lore stored in collective memories passed on from generation to generation?"
85. Ferguson, writing about Lesotho, as cited in Gilman and Ticktin (2014, p. 250). See also Ferguson (1990).
86. See Easterly (2014) in *The Tyranny of Experts* for a broad critique of "development experts."
87. Hanlon et al. (2010); Easterly (2006, 2014).
88. Bourdieu (1977).
89. Banerjee et al. (2006); Cohen and Easterly (2010); Collier (2007); Kenny (2011); Ramalingam (2013).
90. Rist (2008, p. 1). See also Willis (2011).
91. The term *beneficiaries* is still widely used, particularly by philanthropic organizations. In light of the fact that many recipients do not benefit from development projects, the term is probably no longer very useful or accurate.

2

HUMAN DEVELOPMENT

A Life-Span Approach

Sangay: Well-Being in Bhutan

Twenty-eight-year-old Sangay grew up in a comfortably wealthy family in central Thimpu, the capital of Bhutan. After graduating from high school, he left for university in Calcutta, where he completed his degree in mathematics. Upon graduation, he was called back to Bhutan by his father, who had found him a job in the national education ministry. Though the ministry was a highly sought-after workplace in Bhutan, Sangay came to realize that his classmates who had stayed in India enjoyed a booming economy with higher-paying jobs (for those with college degrees in mathematics). They owned cars and homes and sent their children to private schools. But his friends also complained about difficult bosses, tough competition, and long commutes in a traffic system that was as chaotic and dangerous as it was slow. Sangay had seen similar scenes in comedy films set in the United States, with people screaming out of car windows. None of that, thought Sangay, occurred in Thimpu. Sangay had occasional daydreams about taking his family back to Calcutta, where he could earn more and occupational mobility was possible. Each time, however, he concluded that life was preferable—his well-being was better—in Bhutan.

Income is rarely the sole measure that guides a person's decisions, or what shapes the contour of her or his life. Humans are far more complex than that. For Sanjay, this meant sacrificing greater wages for what he viewed as a better life. His experience of well-being in Thimpu caused him to resist the temptation to live and work in Calcutta. As is the case with most people in most countries, many factors go into an individual's decision making, both conscious and unconscious. The term *human development* was coined to capture these multiple pathways in a person's life, from infancy through adulthood.

Bhutan is a Buddhist kingdom that has managed to keep its traditions, many of them ancient, in the face of global change. In one sense, it is a unique country and frequently held up to represent the notion of societal well-being. The national government (including King Wangchuck) has strongly promoted the idea of *Gross National Happiness*. Rather than determine Bhutan's success in terms of GNP per capita, the government introduced a metric in which human well-being (happiness) is measured instead.[1] One could argue that in a country as mountainous, isolated, and limited in natural resources as Bhutan, this makes sense. At the same time, elevating the importance of human development and well-being not only fits with Bhutan's cultural history, but also provides a broader and more natural picture of how all humans make complex decisions in their lives.

Defining Human Development

Around the world, universities teach courses on human development—generally framed as the study of how children grow from birth through adulthood and into old age. Humans everywhere grow physically, cognitively, and emotionally over time. Certain milestones are typically achieved based on our biology and genes, while others happen only due to our social and cultural milieu. As described in this chapter, children begin to learn immediately after they are born, and develop advanced thinking skills by adolescence. As they enter adulthood, people Sangay's age have reached a point in their development (late 20s) when they need jobs in order to thrive, if not survive.

Several conceptual approaches have provided windows into our understanding of human development, and each will contribute to a broader conversation about the nature of international development.

Ages and Stages

For more than a century, psychologists and other social scientists have been detailing and categorizing the acquisition and development of behaviors from birth through infancy, young childhood to adolescence, and adulthood into later life—what we now commonly call *life-span* human development. Some, such as the pediatrician Berry Brazelton, noticed how infants react to initial stimulation and develop coping mechanisms that are demonstrable in young children the world over. Others, such as the psychologist Jean Piaget, studied young children's cognitive development—how children moved from a stage of "concrete" thinking, for example, to more abstract "operational" thinking during adolescence. The psychoanalyst Erik Erikson famously sought to uncover universal stages of social development: from trust and competence to care, and later on to generativity and wisdom. These researchers, and many others, generally subscribed to the idea that human development was likely to be largely invariable across cultures.[2] In other words, social scientists, following their colleagues in the physical sciences, sought "rules" of behavior that would be consistent the world over.

Other experts recognized the need to study human development across chronological time, but also posited the critical importance that culture plays in how these stages develop.[3] For example, nearly a century ago, the anthropologist Margaret Mead published the influential book *Coming of Age in Samoa,* written in part to answer a key question that troubled social scientists. As Mead put it, "I have tried to answer the question which sent me to Samoa: Are the disturbances which vex our adolescents due to the nature of adolescence itself or to the civilization? Under different conditions does adolescence present a different picture?"[4] Simply stated: how much of human behavior is due to "nature," and how much to "nurture"? Sparked by Mead's and others' work, this enduring question became the catalyst for the serious scientific investigations that followed. Some researchers engaged in comparative studies of child rearing in diverse countries, while others collected data from detailed ethnographic accounts worldwide and put them into searchable databases.[5]

The growing belief in the significance of nurture in human development led to long-term interest in the roles of family, socialization, culture, environment, and nutrition in mediating children's growth. One of the fundamental questions was whether children from diverse cultures are similar at birth, before cultural inputs have a significant impact. With this question in mind, *Culture and Infancy: Variations in the Human Experience* was published in 1977, containing two dozen case studies of child rearing from around the world.[6] In countries as diverse as Uganda, Mexico, and the United Kingdom, researchers found that culture began to impact infants at birth, and sometimes even before birth through pregnancy practices. In particular, mother-infant "attachment" (or bonding) was studied in a rural Ugandan village.[7] Previously, attachment was thought to be a requirement for all young infants; without it they would suffer irreparable loss and depression later in life. Yet, in Uganda, researchers found that infants seemed to exhibit few if any negative consequences from being left alone for long periods, and could still be considered "well-attached" to their mothers or other adults.[8] It was concluded that attachment is not a simple dichotomy of attached or non-attached, but rather can vary with the frequency and intensity of the original bonding. This is only one example of work in a field that covers topics such as child caregiving in families, how different cultures value children, and how societies manage the acculturation of diverse groups that must live together or in proximity.[9]

Over the past half-century social scientists have traveled the world to study how children develop, and especially how this development intersects with schooling, a national priority in all countries. Among many other findings, we now know that infants begin to learn language as soon as they hear it, and that young children can learn multiple languages nearly simultaneously.[10] We know that adolescents require community support and make decisions that are sometimes counter-intuitive, and that older adults remain interested in learning long after they finish formal schooling. Each of these generally accepted findings is based on research within life-span human development, and each will have implications in later chapters in this book.[11] What we also know is that there is great variation in how societies manage and shape human behavior over the life course, and also that such behavior can be predicted from earlier observations much of the time (but not all of the time).

Continuities and Discontinuities

In his classic publication "The Contents of Children's Minds on Entering School," G. Stanley Hall, one of the founders of educational psychology, urged teachers to understand how prior learning—what children bring to the classroom—should influence what is taught. He wrote: "Every teacher on starting a new class or in a new locality, should make sure that his efforts along some lines are not utterly lost, should undertake to explore carefully, section by section, children's minds with all the tact and ingenuity he can command and acquire, to determine what is already known."[12] Similarly, the anthropologist Ruth Benedict found that the *coherence* in individual behaviors and attitudes is both historical and psychological—it comprises human intentions, values, and interpretations. According to Benedict, who wrote in the 1930s about the Kwakiutl Native Americans in the Pacific Northwest, customs take root only when they have passed through the "needle's eye of social acceptance."[13] As would be expected, most social scientists who study human development have gravitated toward explaining "what comes next" from their observations of "what came before." Such *continuities* over time align well with the ages and stages approaches described earlier.

Yet, as soon as scholars came to view human development as a continuous process, others began to question the accuracy of this picture. How can we account for large variations in behavior and values across cultures? What happens when the processes of human development are disrupted in one way or another, say by the death of a parent, a major environmental disaster, or civil conflict?

Variations in human development sometimes look like "discontinuities" when normative milestones and processes are shaped in cultural and life circumstances that vary markedly from Western social science. One example comes from some of my own early work on memory development in children. During doctoral fieldwork in Morocco in the 1970s, I planned to study the role of schooling and other social experiences in enhancing memory skills in children and adults.[14] Over the course of my research, I was told by a friend to investigate the "amazing" memory skills of some Moroccan rug sellers he knew. For over a millennium, merchants have sold rugs in the local carpet *souk* (market) in Marrakech. Rug selling, a serious and lucrative profession all over the Middle East, is done mostly by families who have passed along their buying and selling skills to their children over generations.

To be successful in their trade, expert rug sellers have to be able to quickly and accurately recognize the complex pattern of each rug so that it can be identified among the floor-to-ceiling piles that line the walls of their shops. Some are large, others are small, but each Moroccan rug has a unique hand-crafted design of colored geometric shapes and figures. The research findings showed that rug sellers had far better memory skills (for rug designs) than well-educated college sophomores at the University of Michigan (the basis for the comparative study). Moreover, the rug sellers' memory organization was fundamentally different than those of the college sophomores.[15] These results not only demonstrated that people can develop "domain-specific" cognitive skills built upon particular cultural experiences, but also that major variations in such skills may be altered by social inputs—such as intensive work with rug patterns in Morocco or attending school and studying with textbooks in America.[16]

These conclusions were surprising to some at the time, since memory skills and norms were thought to be more or less universal. Findings like these were part of a movement in cognitive psychology that advocated a new approach to learning, one that included both "expertise" and "social construction" components.[17] This differed from the prevailing paradigm that cognitive development was mainly endowed by nature and proceeded mostly in continuous stages.

A second strand of work on discontinuity has been termed "regressions" in development.[18] That is, sometimes the normative attainments of behaviors or attitudes not only do not happen as expected, but actually decrease over time. Such discontinuities were most obvious in stage theories of development (as discussed earlier) where sets of skills or emotions are expected to appear in a universal order. In Piaget's stage theory, for example, children are expected to show operational thinking[19] by about eight to ten years of age; but some researchers found that children could reach this stage only to then fall back on earlier stages of thinking.[20] Other studies, carried out cross-culturally, found that many children who do not attend school never reach this stage of operational thinking, or else fail to maintain it.[21] Such developmental regressions, including irregular progress through stages and lack of attainment of the final stage, led to growing disenchantment with Piaget's theory and other stage theories that did not take culture, schooling, and experience into account.[22]

Individual or collective crises can also disrupt the continuity of development. All people experience personal losses during their lifetimes, including the normative losses and disruption that occurs as a result of the death of a family member or close friend.[23] Crises also occur as the result of social disruption, such as a health emergency (e.g., the 2015 Ebola epidemic in West Africa), a dramatic weather event (e.g., the 2004 *tsunami* in Sri Lanka), or civil conflict (e.g., South Sudan). Sometimes short, sometimes lasting through generations, these crises impact the emotional development of individuals and communities.[24] In some sense, emotional crises represent not only disruptions that can force change and reversal (i.e., emotional regressions), but, since such crises are part and parcel of all lives, they can be seen as continuities as well. Either way, it is clear that cultural and familial experience shape human reactions to emotional stresses in everyone's lives.

Life-span human development thus provides an expansive way to view changes that take place over the life span of any one individual. While there are some obvious commonalities when we consider birth and infancy, it is easy to see that divergences begin to take place as a consequence of contact with the surrounding environment. Scientists have sought to build conceptual models to understand how context and culture shape human development, and none is more central than systems theory.

Systems Approaches and Feedback

Ludwig von Bertalanffy was born in 1901 in a small town near Vienna, in a family with ties to nobility going back three centuries. A precocious child, he was educated by private tutors and entered university in Vienna at age 17. Having studied biology and philosophy, von Bertalanffy posited the concept of a *general systems theory* as a way of thinking about "closed" versus "open" systems of biological (living) things.[25] His work was influential in many areas of the social and biological sciences, particularly for taking into account the simultaneous dynamics of both closed and open systems relationships, and the role of *feedback* loops in driving change. He claimed that classical laws of thermodynamics applied to closed systems, but that they did not apply to open systems (living things) that interacted with the environment. But in both closed and open systems, self-regulation was possible only through feedback that provided ways for the system to adjust to changes in inputs. Ideas such as systems thinking and systems engineering, cybernetics, and self-regulation through feedback (as seen in Piaget's developmental theory), can all be traced in one way or another to von Bertalanffy's general systems theory. We shall see later in this volume the importance of feedback when attempting to discern the utility of learning assessments and interventions in educational development work.[26]

Gregory Bateson, an anthropologist who was married to Margaret Mead, was greatly influenced by von Bertalanffy's work. Bateson asserted that cultures, too, have feedback loops within societies to maintain what he termed "homeostasis"— ways to regulate social problems (or self-regulate, in von Bertalanffy's terminology) and reduce conflict. For Bateson, this was the key way for any cultural group to survive.[27] Based on work in Indonesia and elsewhere, Bateson theorized that all humans are part of clusters of interlocking systems containing individuals, societies, and ecosystems. Both competition and dependency exist within each system (large or small), such that each must be adaptive to changes through feedback loops to maintain homeostasis or survival. In line with general systems theory, Bateson posited that all peoples and cultures are connected to each other and to the natural world, combined into an integrated macrosystem.

The idea of interlocking systems—or a macrosystem—was not entirely new. As mentioned earlier, Karl Marx was also a systems thinker on a global scale, writing a half-century earlier than von Bertalanffy and Bateson. One of his pioneering ideas was that the advent of industrialization would inevitably lead to a major conflict between the economic structure of capitalism and the poorer social classes. Termed *dialectical materialism*, Marx thought that industrialization would bring about a revolution leading to entirely new stages of human evolution and social transformation.[28]

Marx's view of systems showed up later in the work of the psychologist Lev Vygotsky and his student Alexander Luria, in the wake of the Communist revolution and the establishment of the Soviet Union. In 1929 and 1932, Luria, under Vygotsky's guidance,[29] traveled to Central Asia on a research expedition, the purpose of which was to uncover how pre-literate peasants developed, as compared to the educated and post-revolutionary workers in urban areas of the Soviet Union. Vygotsky claimed that education (and Communism) changed human thinking in fundamental ways, due to dialectical relationships established between the individual and society—what he called the "zone of proximal development." He further argued that a person's cognitive development was contingent upon inputs from more knowledgeable others (such as teachers or mentors). Ultimately, he was criticized by Soviet politicians for his so-called "negative" views of peasants' "traditional" thinking. Though he died at a relatively young age, Vygotsky's views on culture, mediated learning, and the *scaffolding* of learning (how learning is tailored by a more skilled person for a less skilled person), ultimately had a lasting influence in the West.[30] And these conceptual bridges helped to link universalistic psychological theories of learning to social and cultural change in diverse societies.

Putting the above conceptual and empirical pieces together into a comprehensive system became the goal of an American of Russian extraction, Urie Bronfenbrenner. A child psychologist who taught for many years at Cornell University, Bronfenbrenner sought to encapsulate these dynamics into a single "ecological systems model." His idea was straightforward: each individual (beginning at conception) is surrounded by multiple layers of input that affect his or her development. These combine to create each individual's unique path of human development.[31] In the first layer (*microsystem*), the child interacts with parents on a very proximal basis, while in the next layer (*mesosystem*), the child is influenced by larger groups consisting of other family members, friends, schools, and religious communities. He or she then interacts with socio-cultural and governmental institutions (*exosystem*) that are surrounded by the final layer of the *macrosystem*, that is, the larger culture of norms and values that surrounds all the other layers (see Figure 2.1). Due to its comprehensive logic, Bronfenbrenner's

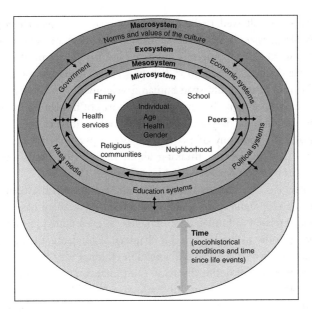

FIGURE 2.1   Bronfenbrenner Ecological Systems Model of Human Development

Source: Bronfenbrenner (1994)

multidimensional approach to life-span human development has inspired many researchers over the years.[32]

The progression of human development over the life span and across sociohistorical time—as understood through Bronfenbrenner's model—helps us understand the myriad possible inputs to an individual's life not only at the individual level, but also at a social, macrosystem level. While comprehensive in many ways, this model did not take into account the impacts of global change—there is no mention of factors such as civil conflict, global warming, natural disasters, forced migration, and disease. It is to this broader connection with international development that we now turn.

Human Development and International Development

Early in my career, while studying how children grow up in diverse countries, I was invited to a meeting at the United Nations to discuss an upcoming planned conference. I was pleased to be invited, but I was quite surprised to learn that among the organizers there was only one with advanced graduate research training in the field of child development. Somewhat perplexed, I pulled together a few colleagues to discuss how it could be that so few trained experts were part of an agency whose broad mission was to help children.

In the years that followed, I edited a small book entitled *Child Development and International Development*.[33] The main thesis was that there are two very different ways that the word "development" can be defined: first, in terms of international development as defined by economists (Chapter 1); and second, by psychologists, as reviewed above, in terms of life-span human development. And, when economists discuss human development, it is usually in the form of human *economic* capital— that is, how the number of years of formal schooling (or the skills acquired in school) impacts the economy of a country.[34] When psychologists discuss human development, they are usually thinking about maximizing human *psychological* capital, as in Bronfenbrenner's ecological model.[35]

Today, there are a number of reasons why the connection between these two meanings of development is increasingly important. First, there has been growth in global policy related to human development—as exemplified in the UN development goals (see discussion later in this chapter). Second, there is a growing recognition that cognitive and social differences in children vary enormously within and across countries. Third, this diversity—and increasingly evident inequities in development across cultures—can only be narrowed with well-researched, well-formed, and scalable interventions. We know more and expect more from our social interventions. Fourth, and more generally, professionals working in agencies that support international development have learned (the hard way) that progress requires a substantial knowledge of life-span human development—including how child rearing, cognitive development, beliefs, and values are shaped by culture and experience.

One seminal figure who brought human development to the forefront of international development is Amartya Sen. Born and raised in Dhaka and Calcutta, Sen received his Ph.D. from Cambridge University. He was the winner of the 1998 Nobel Prize in Economics, based on a distinguished career in philosophy, mathematics, and economic development. In 1981, Sen published *Poverty and Famines: An Essay on Entitlement and Deprivation*, in which he argued that famine occurs not only from a lack of food, but from inequalities built into the mechanisms of food distribution. He suggested that the historic 1943 famine in Bengal state was actually caused by an urban economic boom that raised food prices, causing millions of rural workers with low incomes to starve to death. Building on earlier work,[36] Sen posited a human "capabilities approach" for international development that considers positive freedoms—an individual's ability to be or do or choose something—rather than what he termed *unfreedoms*—the constraints and limitations that deprive individuals. Thus, in the Bengal famine, rural workers' unfreedoms to buy food remained in place. Millions starved because they lacked the positive freedom to undertake actions to help themselves. That is, they lacked the basic human capability to avoid death.

In a subsequent book entitled *Development as Freedom* (1999), Sen argued that what matters most in international development is not economic value *per se*, but rather how much control individuals have over their lives. He argued that "a person who is starving and a person who is fasting have the same type of functioning where nutrition is concerned, but they do not have the same *capability*, because the person who fasts is able not to fast, and the starving person has no choice."[37] According to Sen, such capabilities need to include: political freedoms and transparency in government; freedom of opportunity; and economic freedom from extreme poverty. In other words, human development is based on increasing human agency at all levels of society. Even though trained as an economist, Sen was among the first to oppose the narrow economic definition of development, by highlighting individual freedoms rather than income per capita.

Building on Sen's work, the United Nations Development Program (UNDP)[38] began to publish a series of annual reviews of development, entitled the *Human Development Report*. This publication ranked all nations on a single combined indicator—the Human Development Index (HDI). The HDI comprised a number of important economic and social indicators such as health, human security, environmental sustainability, and standard of living. In this distinctive work, the UNDP stated that "the defining difference between the economic growth and the human development schools is that the first focuses exclusively on the expansion of only one choice—income—while the second embraces the enlargement of all human choices—whether economic, social, cultural, or political."[39] In other words, "People are the real wealth of a nation. The basic objective of development is to create an enabling environment for people to live long, healthy and creative lives."[40]

In the years since UNDP began collecting global data, the world has seen positive trends overall in the HDI, due to improvements in health systems, access to schooling, and GNP per capita (see Table 2.1). Even so, large variations in the HDI exist due to extreme poverty in certain parts of the world, as discussed in the previous chapter. Looking at this through what UNDP terms "human deprivations," we can see that chronic hunger, illiteracy, and poor sanitation (among other factors) continue to afflict hundreds of millions of people worldwide (Figure 2.2). In addition to reducing such deprivations, UNDP also saw the merits of the Bhutan example discussed earlier, and prepared its own *World Happiness Report*.[41] This approach acknowledges the importance of supporting positive well-being in human development, an area of growing research.[42]

The HDI is similar in a number of ways to Bronfenbrenner's ecological systems model: both account for individual life-span human development and the socio-cultural conditions that impact people over time. Together, the two "developments"—human development and international development—have gained considerably more attention with the arrival of UN development goals adopted by the nations of the world.[43]

TABLE 2.1 Human Development Index and Components, 2010 and 2013

Human Development Group or Region	Human Development Index Value		Life Expectancy at Birth (Years)		Mean Years of Schooling (Years)		Expected Years of Schooling (Years)		Gross National Income Per Capita (2011 PPP US$)	
	2010	2013	2010	2013	2010	2013	2010	2013	2010	2013
Very High Human Development	0.885	0.890	79.7	80.2	11.7	11.7	16.2	16.3	38,548	40,046
High Human Development	0.723	0.735	73.9	74.5	8.1	8.1	13.1	13.4	11,584	13,231
Medium Human Development	0.601	0.614	67.1	67.9	5.5	5.5	11.3	11.7	5,368	5,960
Low Human Development	0.479	0.493	58.2	59.4	4.1	4.2	8.7	9.0	2,631	2,904
Arab States	0.675	0.682	69.7	70.2	6.2	6.3	11.7	11.8	15,281	15,817
East Asia and the Pacific	0.688	0.703	73.5	74.0	7.4	7.4	12.3	12.5	8,628	10,499
Europe and Central Asia	0.726	0.738	70.7	71.3	9.6	9.7	13.3	13.6	11,280	12,415
Latin America and the Caribbean	0.734	0.740	74.2	74.9	7.9	7.9	13.8	13.7	12,926	13,767
South Asia	0.573	0.588	66.4	67.2	4.7	4.7	10.6	11.2	4,732	5,195
Sub-Saharan Africa	0.468	0.502	55.2	56.8	4.8	4.8	9.4	9.7	2,935	3,152
World	0.693	0.702	70.3	70.8	7.7	7.7	11.9	12.2	12,808	13,723

Note: PPP is Purchasing Power Parity

Source: UNDP (2015, p. 64)

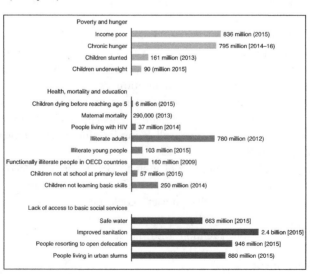

FIGURE 2.2 Extent of Human Deprivations in the World

Source: UNDP (2015, p. 62)

United Nations Development Goals

The most galvanizing events in the push toward improved human development and international development are the two consecutive sets of goals established by the United Nations. The first set, ratified in September 2000 by the UN member states under then-Secretary General Kofi Annan, included eight major *Millennium Development Goals* (MDGs; Table 2.2). The specific targets of the MDGs included cutting extreme poverty and illiteracy by 50%, achieving gender parity in primary schools, combatting HIV/AIDS, and improving environmental sustainability—all by 2015. Results from this 15-year initiative were significant. First, the UN and a diverse group of public and private agencies came together with one voice to acknowledge a responsibility to address the problems of the poor worldwide. This was in contrast to the closed-door approach of top-down decision makers who met at the Bretton Woods conference five decades earlier. Second, even though the MDGs began with the economic goal of reducing poverty, the remaining seven goals were largely about other aspects of human development, such as education, health, and gender parity.

Fifteen years after establishing the MDGs, the UN took stock of the progress toward the eight goals.[44] They found that global poverty had decreased, mostly due to major gains in GNP per capita in a few Asian countries, especially China. They also saw substantial improvement in maternal health (see Figure 2.3). Since 1990, the maternal mortality rate has been cut nearly in half, and most of the reduction has occurred since 2000. In 2014, nearly three-quarters of births worldwide were assisted by skilled health personnel, an increase from about 60% in 1990. Yet, in developing regions, large inequities continued. For example, only about half of births in rural areas were attended by skilled health personnel, compared with nearly 90% in urban areas. Also, only half of pregnant women in developing regions received the recommended minimum of four antenatal care visits. In sum, much was achieved in the area of maternal health, but a great deal remained to be done.

TABLE 2.2 The 2015 UN Millennium Development Goals (MDGs)

Goal category	Description
Poverty	Eradicate Extreme Hunger and Poverty
Education	Achieve Universal Primary Education
Gender	Promote Gender Equality and Empower Women
Children	Reduce Child Mortality
Health	Improve Maternal Health
HIV/AIDS	Combat HIV/AIDS, Malaria, and Other Diseases
Environment	Ensure Environmental Sustainability
Partnerships	Develop a Global Partnership for Development

Source: United Nations (2000). www.un.org/millenniumgoals/. Abridged by author.

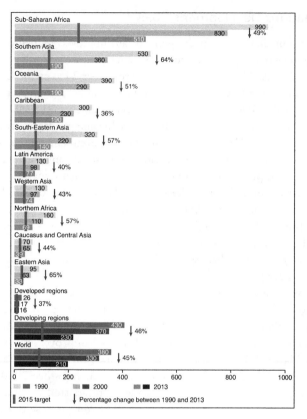

FIGURE 2.3 Maternal Mortality Ratio 1990, 2000, and 2013 (maternal deaths per 100,000 live births, women aged 15–49)

Source: UN (2015a, p. 38)

Thus, in September 2015, the UN body of nations came together again and agreed on a new and expanded set of goals—the *Sustainable Development Goals* (SDGs), to be achieved by 2030. This next set of 2030 UN goals—the 17 SDGs—broadens the range of targets for international development (see Table 2.3). The term "sustainable" is in reference to the increasingly perilous situation caused by climate change worldwide, as well as the inevitable constraints of a fixed planetary ecosystem. As discussed later (see Chapter 10), globalization and environmental constraints are now becoming increasingly central to the international development agenda.

The new 2030 SDGs also contain a specific goal on education, SDG #4, that includes a highlighted role for learning, namely to "Ensure inclusive and quality education for all and promote lifelong learning."[45] Within this goal, there is a set of specific educational targets (Box 2.1), several of which are directly

TABLE 2.3 The 2030 UN Sustainable Development Goals (SDGs)

Goal category	Description
Poverty	End Poverty in All Its Forms Everywhere
Food	End Hunger, Achieve Food Security
Health	Ensure Healthy Lives and Promote Well-Being
Education	Ensure Inclusive and Equitable Quality Education
Women	Achieve Gender Equality and Empower All Women and Girls
Water	Ensure Availability and Sustainable Management of Water and Sanitation
Energy	Ensure Access to Affordable, Reliable, Sustainable, and Modern Energy
Economy	Promote Sustained, Inclusive, and Sustainable Economic Growth
Infrastructure	Build Resilient Infrastructure
Inequality	Reduce Inequality Within and Among Countries
Habitation	Make Cities and Human Settlements Inclusive, Safe, Resilient, and Sustainable
Consumption	Ensure Sustainable Consumption and Production Patterns
Climate	Take Urgent Action to Combat Climate Change and Its Impacts
Marinosystems	Conserve and Sustainably Use the Oceans, Seas, and Marine resources
Ecosystems	Protect, Restore, and Promote Sustainable Use of Terrestrial Ecosystems
Institutions	Promote Peaceful and Inclusive Societies for Sustainable Development
Sustainability	Revitalize the Global Partnership for Sustainable Development

Source: United Nations (2015). www.un.org/sustainabledevelopment/sustainable-development-goals/. Abridged by author.

relevant to the three chapters that follow: ensuring access to quality early childhood development; ensuring primary and secondary education with effective learning outcomes; and increasing the number of youth and adults who have relevant skills. Attention to learning in a sustainable world is at the center of the SDGs, and it represents an important global policy shift toward human development.

Achieving the SDGs will require a much better understanding of the relationship between improved human development and the political impetus for global collective action by international agencies, national governments, community activists, the private sector, non-profits, academics, and others. The wealthier nations of the world have shown that they are aware of this responsibility. As shown in Figure 2.4, development assistance has grown substantially both in overall funding (a near-doubling over the past 15 years) as well as in the number of donor countries.[46] Estimates are that upwards of US$40 billion annually will

BOX 2.1   SPECIFIC TARGETS OF SDG #4 ON EDUCATION

   i. By 2030, ensure that all girls and boys complete free, equitable, and quality primary and secondary education leading to relevant and Goal-4 effective learning outcomes.

  ii. By 2030, ensure that all girls and boys have access to quality early childhood development, care and preprimary education so that they are ready for primary education.

 iii. By 2030, ensure equal access for all women and men to affordable and quality technical, vocational and tertiary education, including university.

 iv. By 2030, substantially increase the number of youth and adults who have relevant skills, including technical and vocational skills, for employment, decent jobs and entrepreneurship.

  v. By 2030, eliminate gender disparities in education and ensure equal access to all levels of education and vocational training for the vulnerable, including persons with disabilities, indigenous peoples and children in vulnerable situations.

 vi. By 2030, ensure that all youth and a substantial proportion of adults, both men and women, achieve literacy and numeracy.

 vii. By 2030, ensure that all learners acquire the knowledge and skills needed to promote sustainable development, including, among others, through education for sustainable development and sustainable lifestyles, human rights, gender equality, promotion of a culture of peace and non-violence, global citizenship and appreciation of cultural diversity and of culture's contribution to sustainable development.

viii. By 2030, build and upgrade education facilities that are child, disability and gender sensitive and provide safe, nonviolent, inclusive and effective learning environments for all.

 ix. By 2030, substantially expand globally the number of scholarships available to developing countries, in particular least developed countries, small island developing states and African countries, for enrolment in higher education, including vocational training and information and communications technology, technical, engineering and scientific programs, in developed countries and other developing countries.

  x. By 2030, substantially increase the supply of qualified teachers, including through international cooperation for teacher training in developing countries, especially least developed countries and small island developing states.

Source: United Nations, www.un.org/sustainabledevelopment/education/

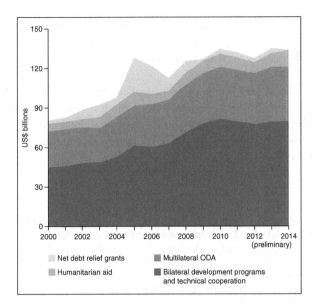

FIGURE 2.4 Official Development Assistance (ODA) From OECD-DAC Countries, 2000–2014

Source: United Nations (2015a)

be needed to achieve the SDGs by 2030, about a 25% increase in current annual development assistance.[47]

An Expansive View of Human Development

We have seen how two historically separate strands of "development" have been pulled together. On the one hand, economic theorists in international development thought that poor countries would follow Western trends toward economic take-off. On the other hand, other social scientists focused on how children and adolescents mature in similar or quite different cultures, and have sought to understand diverse variations in life-span human development. Taken together, we begin to see how combining these approaches can help us ensure a better quality of life for people the world over.

Sangay, the ministry official in the chapter's opening, was reflecting on his life in "small town" Thimpu, compared to the "fast lane" of Calcutta. Sangay's dilemma is not unique. In recent decades, some parts of the world have indeed "taken-off," to use economic development terminology. But take-off and quality of life are not the same thing, and so the advantages found in Thimpu were enough to keep Sangay in Bhutan. His story is one modest example of the movement away from the traditionally narrow view of economic development to an expanded consideration of human development.

With the advent of 17 development goals to be met by 2030, the United Nations has refocused world attention—our attention—on ways to improve the lives of children, families, and communities across the globe. Meeting these goals will be an enormous challenge. In the next chapter, we consider the specific role that learning will play.

Notes

1. The King of Bhutan, His Majesty Jigme Khesar Namgyel Wangchuck, stated: "Gross National Happiness (or GNH) has come to mean so many things to so many people but to me it signifies simply—Development with Values. Thus for my nation today GNH is the bridge between the fundamental values of kindness, equality and humanity and the necessary pursuit of economic growth. GNH acts as our National Conscience guiding us towards making wise decisions for a better future" (Gross National Happiness Centre, 2013).
2. Erikson, though known as a universalist, also engaged in cross-cultural research, mainly among the Sioux and Yurok at the Pine Ridge Reservation in South Dakota. One of Piaget's students, Pierre Dasen, also did cross-cultural work on Piaget's theory. Thus, cross-cultural research was not uncommon, but was mainly used, both then and often now, to confirm the breadth of a theory, rather than to challenge its fundamentals. Some were open to substantial change, however, as in the case of Brazelton's Neonatal Behavior Assessment Scale (Brazelton & Greenspan, 2001), which was altered to take into account cultural diversity, such as in the data on the Gusii that was collected by LeVine (1977); thanks to R. LeVine (personal communication) for this observation.
3. Bornstein (2010); Bruner and Greenfield (1966); Cole and Scribner (1974); Jahoda (1973); LeVine (1977); Wagner and Stevenson (1982).
4. Margaret Mead (1928).
5. Comparative child rearing was studied by Whiting and Whiting (1975). The data were collected at Yale University as part of the Human Relations Areas Files, available at http://hraf.yale.edu.
6. Leiderman et al. (1977).
7. This attachment necessity for good mental health derived from orphaned children who were in British foster homes as a consequence of WWII, and is based on the work of Bowlby (1969), who took an ethological perspective that compared children with birds and mammals.
8. See Ainsworth (1977).
9. LeVine et al. (1994); Bekman and Aksu-Koc (2009). On the matter of acculturation, see Berry (2009). Some argue that too many researchers claim universals in infant growth and development. "It is fair to say that claims about what human infants need—for their emotional and intellectual development, not just their health and physical growth—are more abundant than the cross-cultural evidence to support them. Many psychologists feel free to draw conclusions unqualified by consideration of population variability, especially when public concerns about mental health and educational achievement are involved. Psychiatric and educational problems are grounded in a particular

population's conceptions of the desirable. Terms like 'optimal development,' 'security of attachment,' 'developmentally appropriate,' and 'maternal competence' represent cultural preferences for developmental courses and outcomes, not the findings of empirical research on the human species as a whole" LeVine (2004, p. 153).

10. Mehler et al. (1998) found that infants make distinctions between sounds like "p" and "b" almost immediately after birth, reinforcing the idea that many early learning skills are likely to be universal. Thanks to S. Strauss for this example.

11. See, for example, the role of infant plasticity in Chapter 4, on language learning in Chapter 5, and on youth and adult learning in Chapter 6.

12. Hall (1891, pp. 154–155), cited in Pintrich (1994).

13. Benedict (1934/1989, p. 232); also Benedict (1938). Benedict based these writings on the fieldwork of her mentor and famed anthropologist, Franz Boas. See discussion of Benedict's work in Rosenblatt (2004).

14. Recall the opening vignette on Morocco in the Introduction.

15. Wagner (1978).

16. In the same Morocco study (Wagner, 1978, p. 25), I also reported findings in recognition memory that supported the following distinction, namely that the "structure of memory is a universal in cognition, while control processes [mnemonic strategies] seem to be more culture-specific, or a function of the particular experiences that surround each growing child." Feldman (1994) pursued similar issues in a book entitled *Beyond Universals.*

17. Chi et al. (2014).

18. See Bever (1982) for some early examples. Also Cocking (1994).

19. Operational thinking would often be tested by using Piaget's "conservation" problem, which involved knowing that mass or weight was conserved (or considered the same amount) regardless of the form of the liquid or mass when shown to children.

20. Strauss (1981) found that Piaget's concept of conservation in children was sometimes reversed when children were assessed in different ways, essentially amounting to a regression in developmental stage. Strauss and Stavy (1982) also made the distinction between regression and reversion. As they defined it, regression is going back to a former level and can be permanent. It is the result of trauma, drugs, brain damage, psychopathology, etc. Reversion is a temporary return to a former way of thinking. In this volume, we treat both as evidence of discontinuity.

21. For the original study in Senegal, see Greenfield and Bruner (1966); for a broader overview, see Greenfield and Cocking (2014). One of Piaget's students did work on similar issues in Ivory Coast; see Dasen (1984).

22. Thanks to S. Paris for comments on this section.

23. In her classic book *On Death and Dying*, Elizabeth Kubler-Ross (1969) wrote of the phases people usually go through after the loss of a loved one.

24. Belsky and Pluess (2013).

25. von Bertalanffy (1968).

26. See especially Chapter 11.

27. Bateson (1972/2000).

28. See Sperber (2013) for a broad-ranging rendition of Marx's view.

29. Proctor (2013) provides a fascinating account of this research. The fieldwork in 1929 focused a great deal on the variations among cognitive development in Soviet "minority" groups. However, Vygotsky was too ill to travel with Luria. On the later fieldwork in 1932 to Uzbekistan, Luria traveled with German gestalt psychologist, Kurt Koffka, who kept a detailed diary. Koffka's gestalt approach was universalist, while Luria's was more culturally focused; Luria refused to use the standardized testing instruments provided by Koffka.

30. Vygotsky (1978). For a recent review of Vygotsky and his link to Marxist theory, see Gielen (2016). On cultural psychology, see Cole (1998). Lave and Wenger (1991) built on Vygotsky's concept of the "zone of proximal development" to posit the notion of scaffolding of learning—the idea that a person can get assistance from someone more knowledgeable to build her/his own skills or knowledge. Vygotsky argued against the idea that learning happens "spontaneously" and haphazardly, but he also thought, like Piaget, that education cannot dramatically help learning unless the child was "ready" developmentally for what was to be learned. See also further discussion in Chapter 8, on how teachers should teach "at the right level."

31. Bronfenbrenner (1977, 1994).

32. Another way to look at Bronfenbrenner's systems approach is that he espoused a universal development model whose specifics were the life encounters or inputs that come with cultural socialization. Thanks to S. Strauss (personal communication) for this observation.

33. Wagner (1983b, 1986).

34. Becker (1964).

35. One limitation on the use of Bronfenbrenner's psychological model of human development has been the dearth of psychologists and child development specialists in international development work until fairly recently.

36. Sen (1979/2010).

37. Cited in Nussbaum (2011, p. 1); italics added. This again is the "capabilities approach," referring to the ability of an individual to make her/his own choices. See also a broader discussion in Stiglitz et al. (2009).

38. UNDP (1990).

39. Ul-Haq (1995, p. 14).

40. UNDP (2010, p. 11, from 1990 document). In the 1990 HDR, even Aristotle was cited: "Wealth is evidently not the good we are seeking, for it is merely useful and for the sake of something else" (UNDP, p. 9; cited in Rist, 2008, p. 206). See also the multidimensional poverty measurement work in the Oxford University Poverty and Human Development Initiative (Alkire et al., 2015).

41. Helliwell et al. (2015).

42. The field of positive psychology (Seligman, 2011; Seligman & Csikszentmihalyi, 2000) has grown in recent years. It now includes cross-national research on personal well-being and education. In a recent three-country study, Adler (2016) found that in Bhutan, Mexico, and Peru, intervention programs that enhanced both students' and teachers' awareness and skills in well-being had significant positive impacts on academic performance. See also: Adler and Seligman (2016), Diener and Seligman (2004), and Diener et al. (2013). Thanks to A. Adler (personal communication) for helpful observations on this topic.

43. In his critique of the economics of human capital, Klees (2016) cites Sen's work on capabilities, as well as Tikly and Barrett (2011) on capabilities and social justice.

44. For the official review, see UN (2015a).

45. Rose (2015) notes that this goal requires what she terms "clarity, measurability and equity." See further discussion on equity in Chapter 12.

46. A partial list of prominent agencies working in international (educational) development would include: (a) United Nations Specialized agencies: United Nations Children's Fund (UNICEF), United Nations Education Science and Cultural Organization (UNESCO), World Bank, World Health Organization (WHO); (b) Bilateral donor agencies: Agence Francaise pour Developpement (AFD), German Agency for International Development (GIZ), Japan International Cooperation Agency (JICA), UK Department for International Development (DFID), US Agency

for International Development (USAID); and (c) Foundations active in development: Bill and Melinda Gates Foundation, Ford Foundation, Hewlett Foundation, and Rockefeller Foundation. Part of this growth may be attributed to the UN goals, while others have suggested that at least some of this assistance increase may have resulted from the post-2001 (9/11) rush to defeat global terrorism (Easterly, 2016).

47. See International Commission on Financing Global Educational Opportunity (2016) for a broad overview and multiple scenarios; and Klees (2017) on global taxation.

3

LEARNING AS DEVELOPMENT

Naima: The Kuttab and the Souk in Morocco

Morocco is a country with a long and distinctive history. Indigenous Berbers,[1] Roman and Arab invasions, and colonial conquests by France and Spain all figure in its broad cultural composition. In Beni Hamdane, a small village in the foothills of the Middle Atlas Mountains, lives Naima, an 18-year-old woman who is engaged to be married. As the oldest child, she has worked hard to take care of her four siblings and a chronically ill father, who is unable to help financially. Her main chore, besides caretaking, is to bring firewood from the surrounding hillsides to her home on the edge of town. Her native language is Amazigh. Due to the many activities needed to support her family, Naima has never attended the town's modern public school. She did go to the local *kuttab* (Islamic school) for two years and learned how to recite Quranic verses, and to read and write rudimentary Arabic. She also learned to speak dialectic Moroccan Arabic from daily interactions with neighbors.

Beyond household and firewood duties, Naima also liaises with a range of contacts in the outside world. Such activities vary by the day. Sporadically, the mailman arrives in her neighborhood with letters. Naima helps him deliver the mail, often knowing simply by the handwriting to whom each letter belongs. Once a month, the "electric man" arrives to collect money for the family's electricity usage; Naima handles this swiftly and efficiently, drawing money from an earthenware jar kept in the kitchen, switching effortlessly among the several different currencies in use—*dirhams, francs,* and *rials*. Naima is known in Beni Hamdane for her ability to negotiate the lowest prices in the *souk* (market). To those of her social class, as well as those higher up on the social scale, Naima is a young woman worthy of respect. She will become, in all likelihood, a mother, a participant in the economy of her village, and a stalwart supporter of her children.

There are many regions of the world where girls and young women receive little or no education, especially if they, like Naima, are from ethno-linguistic minority groups. By the standards of the UN, and even the Moroccan government, Naima would be considered illiterate. And they are correct: Naima cannot read a prescription label on a box of medicine, nor a posting of election results on the wall of the marketplace. Yet anyone can see and appreciate Naima's competence, which is the result of years of active, informal learning. Her competence is also a result of her persistence, a soft skill that she will likely transfer to her children and others in her community. Naima shows us that learning is ubiquitous and inseparable from human development. But while her sophisticated skillset is well-adapted to the life she lives, Naima's lack of exposure to formal schooling puts her at a disadvantage should she ever want more choices in life, or to do more than provide a subsistence income for her family.

What Is Learning?

As the legendary wizard Merlin advises young Arthur (see Box 3.1), learning is the "only thing which the mind can never exhaust." Indeed, learning is fundamental to every infant, child, adolescent, and adult. Learning is how we reach our human potential, and it is codified in the myriad customs every culture uses to define what it means to be human. It is also central to a learning vision of development—the way that we adapt to life's experiences, manage challenges that arise, and find a sense of well-being. Human development depends on the unique ability of the brain to find ways to process—that is, to adapt to and manage—a wide array of complex daily activities, and thus become more competent every day.

For scientists, *learning* has meant many different things over the years. Its multiple definitions are too numerous to list, especially when taking into account linguistic variations of the term and its meanings in local contexts.

BOX 3.1 ON THE IMPORTANCE OF LEARNING

"The best thing for being sad," replied Merlin, beginning to puff and blow, "is to learn something. That's the only thing that never fails. You may grow old and trembling in your anatomies, you may lie awake at night listening to the disorder of your veins, you may miss your only love, you may see the world about you devastated by evil lunatics, or know your honour trampled in the sewers of baser minds. There is only one thing for it then—to learn. Learn why the world wags and what wags it. That is the only thing which the mind can never exhaust, never alienate, never be tortured by, never fear or distrust, and never dream of regretting. Learning is the only thing for you. Look what a lot of things there are to learn."

—T. H. White, *The Once and Future King*

In Western social sciences, learning is defined most commonly as a mental change—such as in knowledge, skills, attitudes, and values—based on experiences of some kind.[2] Thus, schooling is not the same thing as learning. While schooling is usually designed to foster curriculum-based learning in classrooms, research increasingly demonstrates that much of what we presume is learned in school isn't, and that a great deal of learning takes place outside of schools.

Our understanding of human learning has evolved significantly over many years. A decade after Darwin's 1859 publication *On the Origin of Species*, Sir Francis Galton, a half-cousin of Darwin, posited that much of our ability to learn was inherited, and his work eventually gave rise to intelligence testing.[3] Theories of learning were strongly influenced by psychologists Ivan Pavlov, Edward Thorndike, and B. F. Skinner, who showed the importance of conditioning, reinforcement, and incentives for changing behavior (largely using dogs, cats, and pigeons, respectively).[4] In the 1940s, American psychologist Abraham Maslow described learning as part of a person's self-actualization—the pinnacle of a hierarchy of universal human needs.[5] Modern learning scientists, beginning in the 1970s, sought to better understand how conceptual changes take place, how knowledge is integrated from multiple sources, and how irrelevant or redundant information can be safely ignored. In a major review, Harold Stevenson compiled more than 500 studies of how children's learning had been observed and categorized, and about skills that could be applied in educational settings. Unsurprisingly for that time period, Stevenson made no reference to cultural factors that affect learning. Yet, in the years that followed, Stevenson helped pioneer cross-cultural studies of children's learning and education, especially in East Asia.[6] More recently, neuroscientists have helped pinpoint the areas of the brain that are associated with specific learning activities, again highlighting the commonalities of certain dimensions of learning.[7]

Human learning is universal. With few exceptions, humans learn to speak, see well enough to avoid bumping into trees, and remember what they ate for dinner the evening before.[8] Moreover, learning develops in systematic and well-understood ways across the human life span—for example, from facial recognition in infancy to collaborative learning in adolescence.[9] Cognitive research clearly shows important commonalities in how humans develop the world over. Despite these similarities, however, there are great variations across individuals and societies with respect to how, when, and where learning takes place; what is learned; and the ways that societies recognize and support (or don't support) learning. Ultimately, our prodigious capacity to learn is in large part what separates humans from other living organisms. This global diversity in learning and its cumulative (rather than linear) nature is at the heart of new thinking about human development and international development.

Learning Contexts and Practices

Two broad dimensions of learning must be considered: first, how learning varies by *context*; and second, how learning skills are used in particular places for particular purposes, often referred to as *practices*. The term context is used here in the ethnographic sense, as a conceptualization that is culturally specific. As such, contexts can be general (a Western classroom), or local and specific (two parents and their child at home).[10] An example of a particular learning practice—a term stemming from the work of Vygotsky—might be how a young child repeats a phrase aloud in order to memorize it.[11] As described later, contexts and practices are always interwoven, as there is no practice that takes place independent of a context, and vice versa.

The idea that learning—whether in or out of school—varies significantly across cultural contexts is not new.[12] Examples of distinctive learning styles abound in the research literature, starting from decades ago.[13] We know, for example, that students in poor schools in developing countries often struggle to learn when the language of instruction is foreign to them. In such situations, children (and often their teachers) resort to rote learning and memorization.[14] Cross-cultural research has demonstrated the importance of factors like parental literacy, indigenous rites of passage, and even the shape of environmental landscapes on the skills that children and adults acquire over time.[15]

While learning must be understood within specific cultural contexts—whether in Peru or Samoa or Canada—important commonalities across cultures exist as well. For example, some contexts are designed explicitly to support *formal* systems of learning, such as schools across the world. Other learning contexts (most, in fact) are not consciously designed—for example, homes where children interact with family members and other children; or on streets that are marked by visual signs; or in markets filled with distinct smells, sounds, and material goods. These less-structured, *non-formal*, or *informal* learning contexts have a major impact on learning as well.[16] A concern, then, is how to conceptualize learning in a way that helps to achieve particular learning goals (such as those that governments or parents seek) while at the same time appreciating the diverse contexts in which learning practices occur in everyday life.

A Framework for Learning

One way to view the spectrum of learning is through a *learning framework* that considers the wide variety of possible learning experiences, and designates quadrants that describe the relationship between learning contexts and learning practices along two dimensions (see Figure 3.1a).[17] Each of the four quadrants represents the intersection of contexts and practices for learning. The "puzzle" style pieces are

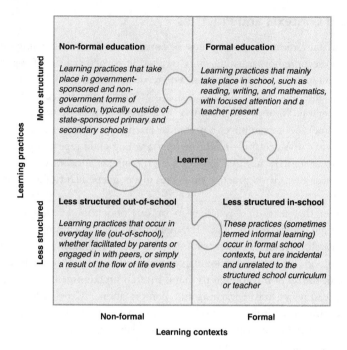

FIGURE 3.1a Learning Framework: Contexts and Practices (Definitions Are in Quadrants)

Source: Wagner (2014c, p. 8)

intended to suggest that the quadrants are interconnected and often overlapping—in real life these operate more like continua than separate boxes. Thus, contexts and practices may be applied in more than a single quadrant at the same time. Examples for each of these quadrants are provided next.

Formal Contexts—More Structured Practices

The top right quadrant of Figure 3.1a comprises learning practices that we most often think of as formal education or *schooling*. School directors, ministers of education, and most international agencies see the classroom as the learning context most under their control, through curriculum-based learning. As schools modernize, especially in urban areas, libraries and computer labs have also become places where formal and structured learning takes place. Teachers, teacher training, and textbooks are some of the tools that are put to use in highly structured contexts to improve learning. Development goals and budget allocations have largely targeted the measurable aspects of schooling, such as attendance, access, and persistence. The majority of learning research has taken place within this quadrant.

Non-Formal Contexts—More Structured Practices

Non-formal education (top-left quadrant) refers to both government-sponsored and non-government forms of education, typically found outside of state-funded primary and secondary schools. These include preschools and other early education programs,[18] private schools and tutoring outside of school hours, independent school programs, youth literacy programs for school dropouts, and adult education programs. Non-formal educational institutions represent a variety of learning contexts, some of which may be very similar to formal schools in terms of regulation, government control, certifications, and so on; others may occur outside controlled classroom contexts, such as in religious Islamic *madrasas* (as detailed in Chapter 7).[19] Also included in this quadrant is technical or vocational education because these programs are most often not subject to the systematic regulations usually found in formal schools.[20]

Formal Contexts—Less Structured Practices

As shown in the bottom-right quadrant, many less-structured learning practices actually occur inside schools and classrooms, in what we sometimes term *informal learning* contexts. These are typically incidental and unrelated to the structured discourse organized by the school, teacher, or curriculum.[21] Recent observational studies of time use have shown that a substantial fraction of class time, especially in poor and under-resourced classrooms, entails children interacting with other children (also termed peer-to-peer learning).[22] In wealthy countries especially, the growing use of social media on mobile phones and tablets in the classroom represents another example of informal learning in formal contexts.[23] In addition, there may be posters on walls and textbooks to peruse, even when the teacher is absent. Of course, *what* students learn may not be what the schools wish them to learn, as many teachers report.[24]

Non-Formal Contexts—Less Structured Practices

The bottom-left quadrant reflects learning that occurs in everyday contexts. Examples might include a parent telling a bedtime story to a child, a vendor describing her wares in the local markets of rural Mali, or the chants at a Balinese funeral.[25] The non-formal, less-structured learning quadrant is meant to represent the multitude of learning contexts that exist in everyday life, whether facilitated by parents, engaged in with peers, or simply resulting from life events. Casual television and Internet browsing would be considered part of this learning quadrant. It is probably fair to say that this learning quadrant contains most of an individual's daily waking hours of active learning. Given how much time in school is not spent on formal, structured learning activities, some have estimated that actual learning

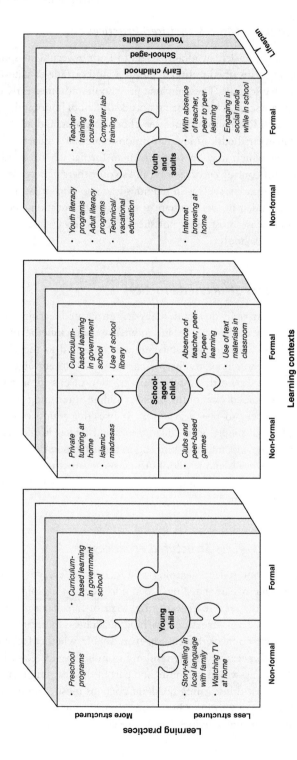

FIGURE 3.1b Learning Framework: Across Three Ages (Examples of Practices Are in Quadrants)

time (say, for reading practice) could be more than tripled during available out-of-school time.[26] For example, one recent study in Rwanda found that only about 14% of a child's waking hours were spent learning in school over a calendar year, leaving the remaining 86% open for potential learning in non-formal settings.[27] Research on this type of learning, especially in developing countries, remains quite limited.[28]

The learning framework outlined here provides a systematic way of thinking about clusters of specific settings and practices—the *where* and the *how* of learning. Its purpose is to signal where learning takes place and in what form, and to highlight places and types of learning that have largely been overlooked—and understudied—by researchers and practitioners in education. Although labeled here as distinct quadrants, it is important to reiterate that these should be viewed as dynamic influences on learning that overlap and intersect.[29]

The four quadrants also develop across an individual's life span, with changes occurring as a function of diverse cultural, environmental, and social influences that may also change with time.[30] Thus, the contexts and practices for learning may be quite different for a young child when compared with a school-aged child, or with youth and adults. Examples of learning practices at each of these life stages are provided in Figure 3.1b.

Learning Curves: Time, Responsive Environments, and Opportunity

Learning takes time, and is highly dependent on experiential contexts. One of the first researchers to study these two facts was Hermann Ebbinghaus, a German experimental psychologist. At the end of the 19th century, his research demonstrated how adults learned lists of words over time, based on difficulty of the task[31]—what eventually became known as the *learning curve*.[32] The term has become part of the contemporary lexicon, and whether steep or shallow it refers to the difficulty of learning a particular task.[33]

Accumulated skill, as Ebbinghaus and later researchers found, is certainly a function of time and effort. The more individuals persist and repeat a word list over time, for example, the greater number of words they accurately remember. He also found that interruptions and lengthy periods of intervening experiences could greatly decrease the extent and accuracy of list memory.[34] This finding is well-known to anyone trying to learn a foreign language, where interruptions and other intervening language experiences make for a much steeper learning curve and cause one to forget what was previously learned.

While learning contexts also matter a great deal, *responsive* environments matter as well. Vygotsky's concept of the "zone of proximal development" refers to the degree of expertise that an individual is capable of mastering in relation to the mentoring provided (formally or informally) by a more knowledgeable person.[35]

In other words, an individual learns best when the environment responds to particular learning needs in real time. For example, there is a great deal of research on language learning in the early years of life, and the tailored way that parents use their own language so that it fits and supports the child's language acquisition. Termed "motherese," this designer-style of parental language input has been shown to have direct and positive outcomes for children's language acquisition.[36] In the classroom, the same notion may be seen in what has been called "reciprocity" in teacher-learner interaction.[37]

Responsive environments, whether planned or unplanned, exist at all ages of the life span—and some have a greater impact than others. In Figure 3.2, four learning curves over ages 7–11 years are shown for children in rural India, based on gender, parents' wealth, and schooling. These latter factors produce radically different outcomes for basic skills, even for children who are in school. While detailed ethnographic descriptions of the home are not provided, it is reasonable to make the assumption that the contexts in which the rich children live (boys and girls) have a cumulative positive impact on their learning of reading and math. These learning curves (or trajectories) show that when such supportive and responsive contexts are not available, children fall further and further behind—creating a growing learning gap between groups.[38]

Most learning is not nearly so structured as that of Ebbinghaus's word lists. Many children do not go to school, or if they do, the teacher may be absent or unprepared—and thus they are deprived of a supportive learning context. These children have not had a sufficient *opportunity to learn*[39] in a formal school setting, since they didn't have textbooks or a capable teacher. In other words, opportunity

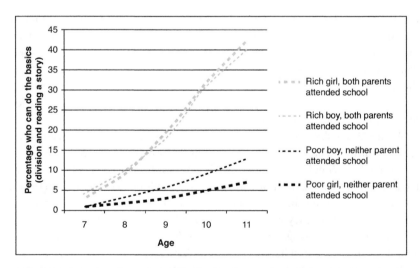

FIGURE 3.2 Learning Curves in India for Reading and Math (Division) Under Four Conditions, School Children Ages 7–11 Years

Source: P. Rose data using ASER-India data, in https://blogs.unicef.org/blog/achieving-the-education-sdg-start-early-and-stay-the-course/

to learn can be operationally defined based on empirical inputs and learning outcomes. In supportive school environments (mainly in wealthy countries), a great deal is known about the normal progression of learning in the areas of mathematics and science.[40]

Education and Learning

In 1968, Philip Coombs published *The World Educational Crisis*.[41] In his book (and an update that followed nearly two decades later), Coombs alerted development specialists to what he called a "shocking reality"—namely, that even with all the progress that was being made in economic development and the growing number of schools being built, huge swaths of children still lacked a good quality education. He drew attention to a growing, multifaceted "disparity" between educational systems and their environments, referring to it as a "worldwide crisis in education."[42]

A few years later, Robert McNamara, then-President of the World Bank, emphasized this same problem by calling attention to the severe poverty of 800 million people (nearly 40% of the developing world at that time), and the role that "basic education" must play.[43] These numbers are much larger today, even though in the intervening years there has been a significant expansion of access to schooling. Poor countries were not the only contexts of crisis, however. Within a decade, the United States was justifiably alarmed about educational disparities among its own children, upon the 1983 publication of the influential report *A Nation at Risk*.[44] Over these several decades, nearly all nations developed strategies to accommodate what Coombs aptly called the "social demand" for more and better education.

But universal education was not always an accepted international goal. Only with the 1946 Universal Declaration of Human Rights was UNESCO charged with putting basic education and literacy at the top of its policy agenda. In the decades that followed, many development agencies and donors supported the view that education is "a fundamental human right."[45] Yet it was not until 1990 that the United Nations and its partners brought this world crisis to a head with the ground-breaking International Conference on Education for All, held in Jomtien, Thailand. This gathering focused the world's attention on both increasing *access* to education and increasing the *quality* of that education, asserting that education should support the "basic learning needs of every person . . . child, youth and adult."[46]

The 1990 Jomtien conference, and a second Education for All conference held in 2000 in Dakar, Senegal, established a set of six educational goals that were subsumed into the broader set of UN MDGs described in the previous chapter.[47] These efforts led not only to a substantive upsurge in international development assistance for education, but also greater awareness of the importance of children's education on a global scale.

Even before such UN goals were established, however, it was clear that expanded school enrollments would not ensure higher levels of learning, particularly in low-income countries. Rather, poorer learning outcomes might result from raised enrollments, due to larger class sizes, insufficient numbers of trained teachers, and greater pressure on available educational infrastructure. In one notable example, a 1999 World Bank survey found that three years of schooling in rural Bangladesh had approximately zero value in terms of learning achievement.[48] In other words, the effort of getting larger numbers of children into school could have little or even negative impact.

Today, nearly three decades after Jomtien and with substantially more investment in education development, children are still learning only a fraction of the taught curriculum. They are still dropping out of school at alarming rates. Even so, the goal of universalizing access to primary schooling was one of the most important successes of the 2015 MDGs.[49] As shown in Figure 3.3, the number of students in schools has grown steadily even in the poorest countries. Such expansion in enrollment is a major achievement, but does not resolve the serious question of what children are actually learning in schools.

Despite the inclusion of the educational goals in the MDGs and SDGs, education has received a far lower proportion of official development resources than other sectors, such as health and infrastructure.[50] This trend is shown in Figure 3.4, where one can see that development aid for health over the past 40 years increased from 5% to 20%, while aid to education dropped from 10% to about 6% (in constant dollars). Importantly, even though the relative spending of development aid for education decreased over time, actual education spending as a share of national

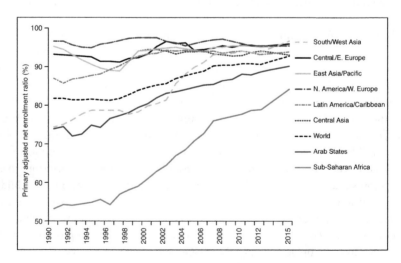

FIGURE 3.3 Growth in Primary Net Enrollment Rates, 1990–2012 and 2015 (Projection)

Source: UNESCO (2015a, p. 6)

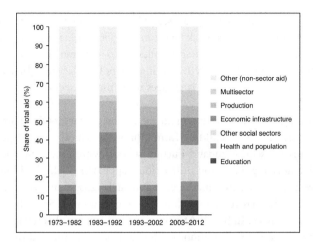

FIGURE 3.4 Share of International Donor Aid Going to Various Sectors, Including Health and Education

Source: UNESCO (2015a, p. 25)

income (GNP) increased in most developing countries over the past two decades (from about 4% to about 6%).[51] Nonetheless, national education systems in many developing countries face major challenges in the form of increasing cultural and linguistic heterogeneity, as well as in terms of internal and external migration, civil unrest, and more.[52]

Language and Learning

Language, ethnicity, and culture are, as tourists like to say, what makes the world go round. At the same time, within-country heterogeneity often poses one of the most important challenges to national education authorities. In 1959, the anthropologist George Peter Murdock published the influential monograph, *Africa: Its Peoples and Their Culture History*.[53] In a single volume, Murdock described the incredible variety of peoples, ethnic groups, and languages across the African continent. He and others pointed out that the national boundaries of newly independent African countries often bore little relationship to the diversity of the peoples residing in them. Typically, these geographical boundaries were decided by colonial powers that had other motivations in mind, such as political control rather than ethnic or linguistic continuity or homogeneity.[54] Many specialists accurately predicted that politically motivated national boundaries would inevitably come into conflict with this ethno-linguistic diversity.[55]

There are an estimated 7,000 spoken languages in the world today. Sub-Saharan Africa alone has 1,200 to 2,000 languages.[56] Some countries have hundreds of languages and dialects: Cameroon has more than 200 languages, of which 38 are written; Thailand has over 70 languages, and Indonesia more than 730, while Latin America's indigenous peoples speak an estimated 550 different languages.[57] Often, social and political (including military) forces try to help resolve the problems that language diversity creates, usually by opting for policy decisions that result in a hierarchy of officially recognized languages to be used in schools and governance structures.

Increased migration and displacement are among the factors that have led to an escalation in the mixing of children from ethno-linguistically varied populations into classrooms and schools today.[58] Further, schools within the same country may have varied language policies and instructional approaches.[59] In the United States, where there is no officially sanctioned national language, massive immigration from Latin America has resulted in a *de facto* recognition of Spanish as a second (non-official) language. In South Africa, there are 11 national languages taught in different ways in different communities, but English is considered the "prestige" language amongst most people in the country.

In contexts of poverty, the uptick in language heterogeneity has often led to very low educational attainment in ethno-linguistic minority groups.[60] As shown in Figure 3.5, such populations are nearly twice as likely to be in the bottom quintile of educational attainment compared with majority language populations. This situation is particularly evident where both implicit norms and explicit policies of

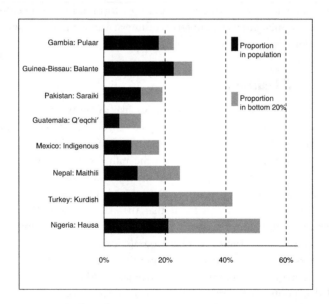

FIGURE 3.5 Percent of Selected Language Groups in the Bottom 20% of the Education Distribution, in Selected Countries

Note: The bottom 20% is the 20% of 17- to 22-year-olds with the fewest years of education.

Source: UNESCO (2010, p. 152)

language and ethnic discrimination impact children's economic and social status, as well as learning in school.

Over 200 million school-age children speak languages at home that are not recognized in their schools or official settings. In indigenous populations, many such languages remain without an accepted written form.[61] This diversity has given rise to two opposing policy directions. The first supports the adoption of colonial languages—particularly English, French, Spanish, and Portuguese—so that economies of scale in textbook and curriculum production, teacher training, and economic globalization can be promoted. Up until around the year 2000, this was the dominant view of national and international policymakers, even if some remarked on its cultural unfairness.[62] The second view is that bilingual or multilingual educational programs should be supported, since they validate local culture, build on cognitive and linguistic strengths, and can generate more local support for education, particularly among the poor.[63]

Each of these two policy perspectives faces an additional challenge: cultures and languages evolve over time. To understand which groups use which languages, how these languages have spread or have been constrained, and how usage has changed with increasing globalization, is central to any serious policy proposal about language and education. Such a review has recently been undertaken in Africa, where language use and change in more than 30 countries was recently analyzed.[64] One of the most striking findings was the current low usage of European colonial languages in contemporary Africa, even in those countries that have a centuries-long history of colonial language education. Less than 20% of the adult populations in former British and French colonies actually speak their colonial languages, despite many decades of language instruction.[65] Counter-intuitively, this research also found that the instructional use of colonial languages had a negative impact on the spread of these languages. It seems that the explicit teaching of these *lingua francas* as elite languages worked against their spread amongst the broader population.

Consider South Africa, for example. During the *apartheid* era (1948–1994), Blacks[66] were forced to live in homelands where schooling was undertaken in a prescribed set of local languages. During this time, the national government was predominantly controlled by Whites who spoke *Afrikaans*, a Dutch dialect. With the ratification of the post-*apartheid* South African constitution, 11 languages were declared to be "official," and were to be taught in schools and used by government institutions. Nine of these were Black African languages, and the other two were English and Afrikaans. Sociolinguists estimate that in 1994, roughly half of Blacks who spoke a second language spoke either Afrikaans or English.[67] Yet, about a decade later, researchers found a huge language shift among Black South Africans. Many had decided that English was the language of the future, while Afrikaans was tainted as the old *apartheid* language. Hence, large numbers of Black young adults stopped using Afrikaans and voluntarily stopped speaking Afrikaans to their children—so much so that the number of Blacks who spoke

Afrikaans diminished by nearly half, resulting in one of the most rapid major language shifts on record.[68]

There are varied motivations for teaching languages beyond one's mother-tongue. From a top-down perspective, it is clear that many national governments and international development agencies promote language learning that conforms to national policy priorities, including the choice of official languages. Some agencies, such as UNESCO, have taken the view that language is essentially a human rights issue (see Box 3.2), and support mother-tongue instruction where possible.[69] Others have pointed out how the linguistic practices of children who can communicate across a variety of languages and contexts may have greater future opportunities in the global marketplace.[70] Also at issue is the identity formation of children who may feel that their home language is less valuable than the language they hear in school, on television, or digitally on the Internet.[71]

Conflicting views on language policy in the classroom underscore an even broader role of language in defining national policy. Wars have been—and still are—fought over the language rights of peoples in many parts of the world. Leaders of insurrections of all kinds have used the right to speak and teach in their own language as a central principle of freedom. Language conflicts range from relatively modest social movements, such as advocating the use of the *Breton*

BOX 3.2   THE RIGHT TO CHOOSE THE LANGUAGE OF LEARNING

The 1989 ILO Convention 169 concerning Indigenous and Tribal Peoples in Independent Countries . . . states:

- Children belonging to the peoples concerned shall, wherever practicable, be taught to read and write in their own indigenous language or in the language most commonly used by the group to which they belong.
- When this is not practicable, the competent authorities shall undertake consultations with these peoples with a view to the adoption of measures to achieve this objective.
- Adequate measures shall be taken to ensure that these peoples have the opportunity to attain fluency in the national language or in one of the official languages of the country.
- Measures shall be taken to preserve and promote the development and practice of the indigenous languages of the peoples concerned.

Source: UNESCO (2005, p. 137)

language in western France, to internecine and long-term struggles, such as those fought in South Africa before the end of *apartheid*, and in southern Mexico, where the use of local languages has been a rallying cry for revolution for more than a century.[72] Language can also be thought of as a matter of survival, both cultural and political. In the Amazonian jungle of Peru, for example, the use of the *Arakmbut* language—maintained by local leaders to counter what they see as the cultural encroachment of Spanish-speakers—is thought to be one of the few remaining ways of preserving indigenous culture.[73] The same is true for Tibetans in China today.[74]

Overall, people's motivations for learning languages beyond their mother-tongue are quite variable. Attitudes may also change over time, based on the multiple experiences and contexts within which people grow up and enter the workforce. Given the variability in motivating factors, designing better educational support is one of the central challenges to pedagogical policy.[75]

We also know that local values, customs, and languages must be more carefully understood and respected. If they are, the field of development will have new opportunities to rectify some of the mistakes of the past, and also contribute to better futures by building on a greater sensitivity to ethno-linguistic variation.[76] Women, and especially mothers with young children, are the principal conveyors of mother-tongue use and early learning across generations. For these and other reasons, issues of gender-based discrimination over the centuries have given way in recent years to a much greater emphasis on gender parity and educational equity more broadly.

Gender and Learning

Until the Industrial Revolution, schools were open mainly to boys, and usually boys from wealthier families. When public schooling in Europe began in the mid- to late 19th century, girls began to enter in greater numbers, but it was only in the early 20th century that gender parity in education was achieved in industrialized countries. By contrast, in most low-income countries, progress in gender parity has been much slower, even though educational access for girls and women has been a longstanding priority for the United Nations.

The UN MDGs included a goal to "eliminate gender disparity in primary and secondary education."[77] Major donors and national authorities invested in establishing more schools, hiring more female teachers, building hygienic facilities geared toward girls and young women, and other such investments. Progress toward this goal, especially at the primary school level, is another success of the UN MDGs. According to UNESCO, of the 161 countries with data for 1999 and 2012, the number that reached gender parity rose from 83 in 1999 to 104 in 2012.[78] The poorest nations, however—those that began with low gender parity in 1999—mostly failed to reach parity in primary or secondary schools (Figure 3.6).

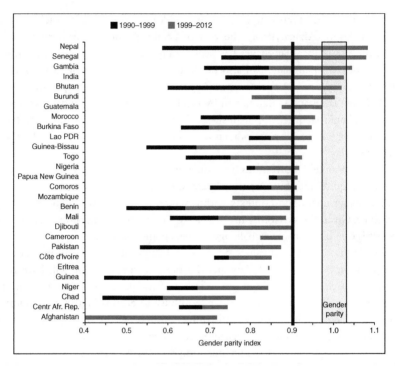

FIGURE 3.6 Gender Parity Index (GPI) of the Primary Gross Enrollment Ratio, Countries With GPIs Below 0.90 in 1999, 1990–1999, and 1999–2012

Source: UNESCO (2015a, p. 158)

Furthermore, girls who do attend secondary school often earn lower scores on national assessments compared with boys. They are also more likely to marry and have children at a younger age, and are more susceptible to health threats such as HIV/AIDS.[79]

Even with global increases in gender parity, discrimination is acutely visible on the ground, especially in low-income countries. A typical example was described by ethnographers in Mali, where longstanding cultural values keep girls at home, burdened with major domestic responsibilities that preclude regular school attendance. They state that, in pastoral communities, girls' school attendance is as low as 30% due to early marriage; excessive domestic work; and there is an "assumption that girls and women are inferior to men in intellect."[80] Especially in the traditional areas of poor nations, there are extreme aspects of this form of gender discrimination.[81] Data from Guatemala, for example, reveals that indigenous Quechua-speaking females have far lower school enrollment rates as they reach adolescence (Figure 3.7).[82] These findings demonstrate that socially excluded girls and women are subjected to stigmatization that directly impacts their life chances, and also how gender and language can interact to create even greater disadvantage in learning.

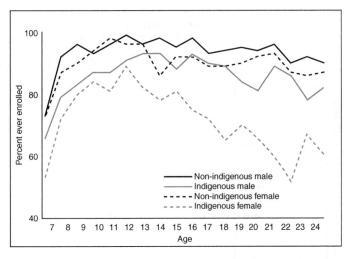

FIGURE 3.7 School Enrollments by Ethnicity and Gender in Guatemala, 2000

Source: Lewis and Lockheed (2007)

The Education Crisis Is a Learning Crisis

For nearly half a century, development agencies and national governments have focused on what they saw as an "educational crisis." In reality, however, education is just a proxy for learning. Over time, as Coombs correctly forecast, the demand for education has increased, resulting in some positive outcomes (more children in school), but also a number of serious problems. The first of these is a dramatic shortage of experienced teachers. There has been only modest success in training a sufficient number of qualified teachers to match the large increase in student enrollment, especially at the primary school level. Many teachers are drafted into service, often without sufficient preparation. Many even lack a high school diploma.[83] There are also shortages of lavatories, textbooks, and other educational supports, exacerbated by the gender and language issues just discussed.[84]

What most worried Coombs was how to maintain the quality of learning as schooling expanded. In this, too, he was quite prescient. While the initial UN MDGs aimed to get children into school, far less attention and funds were given to ensure that adequate learning took place. Thus, it came as no surprise that studies began to show that many children in low-income contexts were learning only a small fraction of their school's curriculum. Many of these students could not read a single word *in any language* after two or three years of schooling (Figure 3.8). Put more succinctly: creating more access to schooling is a good thing, but these efforts do not guarantee better learning outcomes.

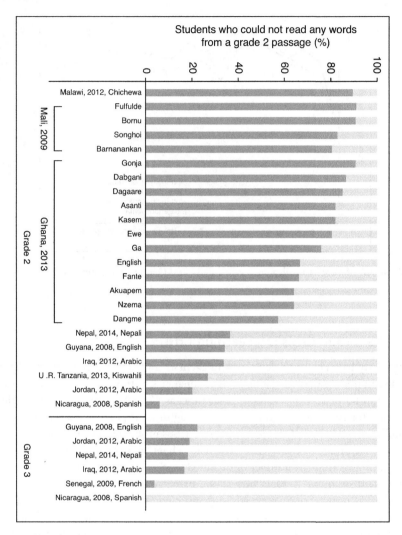

FIGURE 3.8 Percentage of Students Who Could Not Read a Single Word After Two or Three Years of School, 2009–2014

Source: Research Triangle Institute (2015), adapted from UNESCO (2016a, p. 196)

In the opening vignette, Naima provides an example of the challenges we face with improving education in low-income countries, but also the varied nature of learning. Some might see her as an archetype of the world's education crisis, but she's actually doing quite well in the life she is leading. Her problem is that she will have few opportunities for advancement when Beni Hamdane inevitably becomes more connected with the larger Moroccan marketplace. Additionally, she will have limited skills to pass on to her children. Using the learning framework described in this chapter, it is clear that Naima has taken considerable advantage of less-structured learning in non-formal contexts. She has not, however, been able to engage much, if at all, in the other three quadrants of learning.

The good news is that we know a lot more about learning today than we did when Coombs predicted a global education crisis. National and international agencies are gathering data on more children each year, using a variety of methods that help to identify areas of need as well as productive ways of making a difference. Still, we need to pay far more attention to people—young and old alike—who are most in need.

Learning—the central measure of the quality of education—is the principal challenge of the new United Nations goals for the year 2030. By investing as early as possible in promoting children's learning, major gains can be made.

Notes

1. In current terminology, people of Berber heritage are called *Amazigh*, which is also the name of their indigenous language. The Amazigh people long pre-dated the Roman and Arab invasions. In more recent decades, Amazigh has been given official linguistic status in Morocco, and is taught in an increasing number of schools (Boutieri, 2016).
2. For a discussion of the origins of learning theory, see the historical overview of behaviorism, gestalt, and cognitive psychology given by de Corte (2010). By contrast, economists tend to view learning as a phenomenon reflected in an individual's rational choices, which change in response to a product's perceived value, increases or decreases in the market price, or availability of alternatives (cf. World Bank, 2015b).
3. Galton's (1869) work also led to the infamous rise of eugenics, the idea that the world should control for intelligence by selective reproduction, which more or less led directly to the racist ideas propagated in Europe in the first half of the 20st century.
4. de Corte (2010).
5. Maslow (1943).
6. Stevenson (1972) provided a comprehensive state-of-the-art review that helped to launch a decades-long expansion of research on children's learning. Later on, Stevenson devoted considerable effort to studying how societies helped to shape learning and schooling (e.g., Stevenson & Stigler, 1982; Wagner & Stevenson, 1982).
7. Brain research has led to fascinating advances in our understanding of learning processes, including how young infants unlearn various linguistic patterns through probabilistic practices, allowing them to become native speakers of the dominant language(s) in their environment; see Kuhl (2010).
8. Of course, there are interesting counter-examples to these generalizations. For example, considerable cross-cultural research has shown that there are both universals and cultural specificities in human memory, from childhood to adults (Wagner & Paris, 1981).
9. On collaboration, constructivism, and socio-constructivism, see Brown et al. (1989), de Corte (2010, p. 41), and Rogoff and Lave (1984).
10. The origin of the term learning *context* can probably be traced to Wundt's (1916) massive global work on "folk psychology" in the late 19th century. More contemporary versions can be seen in the cross-cultural work of Cole et al. (1971). In a recent

example, Schneider and Stern (2010, p. 84) state that "good learning environments: stimulate learners to be mentally active; address prior knowledge; integrate fragmented pieces of knowledge into hierarchical knowledge structures; balance concepts, skills and meta-cognitive competence; provide expedient structures in the environment that help learners to develop well-organized knowledge structures; and present information adequately for efficient processing in the human mind given its inherent limitations for processing."

11. Vygotsky called this "private speech" as way of guiding mental behavior Vygotsky (1978). The term cognitive *practice* also has a long history; see Luria (1976, 1987) and earlier discussions in Chapter 2. Later work by Heath (1983) and Street (1984)—in the language and literacy sub-disciplines, respectively—also contributed through the notions of literacy "events" and "practices." In terms of cognitive psychology, more broadly speaking, the term "cognitive process" is most often used, since it has a more universal definition (Neisser, 1967/2014).

12. Pioneering work was done by Wilhelm Wundt, cited earlier, in psychology, and Franz Boaz in anthropology.

13. Kagan et al. (1963); Witkin et al. (1977).

14. See further discussion on rote learning in Chapter 8.

15. In the area of cross-cultural psychology, see Cole and Scribner (1974), Wagner (1993), Wagner and Stevenson (1982), and Gielen (2016). One of the early findings in this domain is that of the environmental impact of "carpentered worlds" (that is, urban landscapes) on human perception (Segall et al., 1966; also Wagner, 1977; Wagner & Heald, 1979).

16. One related cross-cultural study compared "intentional" learning with what was termed "incidental" learning, comparing the skill levels of children in and out of school in rural Yucatan (Wagner, 1974).

17. The idea of comparing contexts and practices, as pointed out earlier, is not new. However, the increasing interest in what happens outside of formally structured experiences has become more central to learning research. See a recent in-depth discussion in Britto et al. (2014). The present learning framework was originally described in Wagner et al. (2012), revised in Wagner (2014c), and further adapted here.

18. As noted in Chapter 4, the dramatic growth in preschools in developing countries has led to a mix of those with support from non-governmental as well as governmental agencies. Even so, they are still part of the non-formal category in most countries by virtue of their relative independence from the teaching and instructional systems (i.e., curricula) that are central to most ministries of education.

19. *Madrasas*—Islamic or Quranic schools that teach the basics of Islam to children beginning at a young age, and sometimes continuing into young adulthood—are often labeled as non-formal education systems (as in Morocco), while in other countries may be part of the formal system (as in Indonesia).

20. Technical and vocational training programs (TVET) are occasionally listed as part of formal education in some reviews (Oketch, 2007). However, it is important to note that not all non-formal contexts would fit neatly into the top-left quadrant. For example, BRAC schools (in Bangladesh) or the Escuela Nueva model schools (in Colombia) are designed to include informal learning practices, but they also receive state support in terms of regulation, oversight, and certification.

21. "*Informal learning* takes place in homes, playgrounds, museums, among peers and in other settings where a designed and planned educational agenda is not authoritatively sustained over time" (Bransford et al., 2000, p. 216), cited by de Corte (2010); italics in the original.

22. DeStefano and Elaheebocus (2009); Britto et al. (2014).

23. Foehr (2006).
24. Topping (2005).
25. Bransford et al. (2000) called this *implicit* learning, where "information is acquired effortlessly and sometimes without someone being aware of having acquired it"; cited by de Corte (2010).
26. See Dowd et al. (2014) on "opportunity to learn," and in further discussion in this chapter.
27. See also Friedlander and Goldenberg (2016). See further discussion of this study in Chapter 5.
28. With the advent of better early reading measures (Wagner, 2011a), there is now considerably more research on the home determinants of reading, much of it focused on what has been called "literate environments," building on early work by Hess and Holloway (1984) and Wagner (1993), and more recently field studies in Malawi, Ethiopia, and Nepal (Dowd, 2011).
29. Western-trained education specialists have often studied within a universalistic methodology in psychology and linguistics, epitomized by such major thinkers as Piaget and Chomsky. This has led to a tendency to view research findings as representative of larger truths. It is argued here that such tendencies must be resisted to some extent, especially when the focus is on population samples that vary from the social science norm.
30. See Bronfenbrenner (1977) and his "ecological model" (mentioned earlier) for an early effort to take life chronology into account.
31. In word list learning, difficulty is judged by words that are more or less distinctive from one another.
32. Ebbinghaus (1913).
33. In the present discussion, we may think of learning curves over the human life span as an individual's level of accumulated knowledge or skills. In school children, such a learning curve might refer to the level of reading skill that is demonstrable over years of studying.
34. Technically, these interruptions were known as "interference."
35. Vygotsky (1978) was also discussed in Chapter 2.
36. Gleitman et al. (1984).
37. Alexander (2015). See further discussion of teacher-student interactions in Chapter 8.
38. As discussed in the next chapter, this gap is sometimes termed the Matthew effect (Stanovich, 1986).
39. DeStefano and Elaheebocus (2009). Similarly, Abadzi (2009) has described the importance of instructional time loss in poor communities.
40. Work on "learning progression" refers to the purposeful sequencing of teaching and learning expectations across multiple developmental stages, ages, or grade levels. The term is most commonly used in reference to learning standards that are concise, clearly articulated descriptions of what students should know and be able to do at a specific stage of their education. See Duncan and Rivet (2013) in science education. See also the discussion of curricular pace in Chapter 8.
41. See Coombs (1968, 1985).
42. Cited in Coombs (1985, p. 5).
43. McNamara (1973).
44. Gardner (1983).
45. UNESCO (1975; cited in UNESCO, 2006, p. 136).
46. UNESCO (1990; cited in UNESCO, 2006, p. 136), italics added.
47. United Nations (2000). For a recent policy review of the institutional agency roles in defining and selecting skills as part of EFA, MDGs, and the Global Monitoring Reports, see King (2011).
48. Greaney et al. (1999).

49. Mass education did not result from the establishment of the UN goals, but has been growing for more than a century. It accelerated due to a considerable number of factors. As stated by Meyer et al. (1992, p. 146): "Both the rates of appearance of mass education and the rates of expansion accelerated sharply around World War II, probably affected by both the intensification of the nation-state principle and the increased centrality of mass education within the model of the national state."

50. A UNESCO report states that: "In assessing *whether political commitment to EFA was reaffirmed and sustained* throughout the [15-year] period, it is clear that the EFA movement suffered once the MDGs became the dominant development agenda. The result was excessive emphasis on universal primary education." And that: "UNESCO proved cautious in its approach to high-level political engagement, so the forum of choice for global policy actors in education shifted away from the High-Level Group. The assumption that global and regional conferences are powerful enough to hold countries and the international community to account has not proved to be valid" (UNESCO, 2015a, pp. xiv–xv).

51. UNESCO (2015a), p. 244. Given that nearly 90% of national education budgets are spent on teacher and administrative salaries, these increases mainly reflect the expansion of increased primary school net enrollment rates, most likely influenced by MDG national commitments. Net enrollment rate is the ratio of school-age children who are enrolled in school to the population of the corresponding official school age.

52. See Chapter 10.

53. Murdock (1959).

54. As discussed in Chapter 1.

55. Kapil (1966) and Murdock (1959). See also later discussion in Chapter 10 of the work by Kaplan (1994).

56. Alidou et al. (2006).

57. UNESCO (2010); Cortina (2014).

58. Issues of migration and globalization are a focus of Chapter 10.

59. See further discussion on language of instruction in Chapter 5.

60. In Figure 3.5, the indigenous language category in Mexico consists of those who speak indigenous languages only and do not speak Spanish.

61. UNESCO (2010, p. 173); Dutcher (2004).

62. Albaugh (2014, pp. 224–225) writes: "Colonial rule, particularly in Francophone Africa, left a legacy of teacher directed education. . . . This is exacerbated when an unfamiliar language is used, and children become twice disadvantaged—not proficient in their own *or* the foreign language. . . . Teachers talk and children listen silently. Learning must be passive, rote and repetitious."

63. UNESCO (1953) was the first international agency to come out in support of indigenous languages and bilingual education. More recent support has come from mainly academic researchers such as: Bialystok et al. (2005), Brock-Utne (2012), Cummins (2000), and Heugh (2006).

64. Albaugh (2013, 2014). See further discussion on global change in Chapter 10.

65. Albaugh (2014) provides a detailed description of how actual language use and skill were estimated in English, French, and other colonial languages.

66. The use of "Black" and "White" as descriptive terms were adopted by countries and scientific communities for varied reasons, and have been used in prejudicial ways over many years. For example, the *apartheid* regime in South Africa, used these two terms along with "mixed" to create discriminatory social policies. These terms are used here advisedly, and only for making distinctions that relate to the scientific and historical literature.

67. Chick (2002).

68. Babson (2010); Chick (2002).
69. By contrast, French development agencies have been promoting local language use as a better bridge to learning French (a colonial language), under their policy of linguistic *rayonnement*. *Rayonnement* is the promotion of the French language as a *lingua franca*. See Albaugh (2014, pp. 232–233) for a particularly lucid political analysis of who is for or against local language policies. She makes an astute contrast between the reason why the education systems of English-speaking former colonies seem to work much better than the French-speaking former colonies (where school dropout is nearly twice as high).
70. This has been termed "trans-languaging"—where the multiple languages are used in a blended fashion. Cited in Heugh (2015, p. 281); see also Garcia and Wei (2014) and Kerfoot and Simon-Vandenbergen (2014).
71. Norton and Toohey (2011). See also the vignette of Illa, in rural Peru, in Chapter 4.
72. Reed (2001).
73. Aikman (1999, pp. 76–77) writes: "Formal education denies Arakmbut knowledge and the legitimacy of their way of life. Not only do educators teach and preach a hegemonic discourse, but the school as an institution has colonized Arakmbut space and time. . . . The school timetable and calendar force Arakmbut time into the rigid strictures of institutionalized learning. . . . A brief look at the [secondary school] curriculum displays not only its divergences from Arakmbut learning practices but its alienation of Arakmbut agricultural knowledge and skills through an emphasis on technology-biased market-oriented rationale."
74. Postiglione (2013).
75. For an early volume on the role of ethnicity, language, and literacy, see Wagner (1983b).
76. In support of localizing development, Woolcock (2014, p. 16) points out "the importance of identifying and disseminating successful *indigenous* responses—as opposed to advocating the adoption of 'best practice solutions' as determined by external 'experts.' . . . Forging detailed scholarly and experiential knowledge of local contexts is also important for discerning the generalizability (or 'external validity') of claims regarding the efficacy of policy interventions."
77. MDG goal 3 is on gender parity.
78. UNESCO (2015a, p. 155). Gender parity index (GPI) is considered met if the index falls between 0.97 and 1.03.
79. UNESCO (2015a, p. 169).
80. Sanou and Aikman (2005, p. 182).
81. See Aikman and Unterhalter (2005) and Heward and Bunwaree (1999).
82. Lewis and Lockheed (2007) show what is widely recognized worldwide—namely that indigenous peoples are often discriminated against, especially females within those groups. The gender dimension of this problem is also linked to ethno-linguistic groups. Women speaking local or "tribal" languages are much more likely to be monolingual than men in the same communities; the latter have had more access to schooling and are more likely to be in contact with other linguistic groups due to work, travel, and schooling.
83. See Chapter 8.
84. Hanushek (1995); Michaelowa (2001); UNESCO (2005); Berry et al. (2015). For a useful review of experimental studies related to textbooks, teacher incentives, and class size, see Kremer et al. (2013).

PART II
Learning

4

LEARNING IN EARLY CHILDHOOD

Illa: Early Learning in Peru

Four-year-old Illa lives with her family on the outskirts of mountainous Cuzco, Peru. Her story is typical of Peruvian families who seek to maintain traditional values while also providing opportunities for their children. Illa is bright and expressive. She developed strong oral competencies in Quechua through interaction with her parents and extended family. However, her Spanish language skills are very limited—based on what she has overheard in the marketplace where her parents sell blue potatoes grown on their steeply positioned plot of land, a 40-minute bus ride from central Cuzco.

From a learning perspective, the shape of Illa's life will greatly depend on the opportunities she has in the next few years. Her parents want her to carry on their traditional values and continue to speak Quechua, but they also want her to go to school and, perhaps someday, university. To achieve this, Illa will need to develop competencies in Spanish that are much more extensive than those of her parents, cousins, aunts, and uncles. She will need to learn how to comprehend, speak, read, and write Spanish at an academic level—the gateway to formal education and the world beyond her village.

For Illa, the pathways to achieving these goals are actually quite limited, but will likely include the bilingual preschool programs that have sprung up in Cuzco and its periphery. There is one such preschool in a nearby village that uses Quechua as its principal language of instruction. Spanish is taught as a second language and is used daily in songs and stories, along with beginning literacy instruction. Illa's parents, along with many friends and neighbors, are counting on this early contact with Spanish to help their children *hacer mas* (do better) when they get to primary school, and not become one of the many children and adolescents who drop out and return to farm potatoes with their parents.

Illa's case represents an important focal point in international development that was touched on in the previous chapter: children growing up within minority language communities often struggle to learn in school. Opportunities to be upwardly mobile are limited. With family and community support (emotional, cognitive, and financial), Illa might gain entry into the bilingual preschool, though access to these services in rural areas is far from universal, and their quality varies. With luck and hard work, along with a combination of effective parental and institutional support, Illa might make it through primary and secondary school and, perhaps, beyond.

More than two millennia ago, Plato (360 BC) described infancy as a time when children "are taking shape and when any impression we choose to make leaves a permanent mark."[1] In the 18th century, philosopher John Locke spoke about the "tabula rasa," where children's experiences are imprinted on a so-called blank slate.[2] Thus, understanding how and what children learn, from shortly after conception onward, has always been a critical part of a life-span approach to human development.[3] Further, the links between early learning and later learning are clear across cultures, and have major consequences for children both in and out of school.

Therefore, it is surprising that support for early childhood education has taken so many years to take root. There are three main reasons why national and international agencies largely neglected this issue until recently. First, up until the 1970s, the welfare and development of children under school age was largely left up to the family. Parenting norms around the world—in particular the notion that mothers would be the primary caretakers—privileged the home as the place where early learning would naturally occur.[4] Second, when international agencies eventually began to promote early childhood development it was the health-oriented institutions (e.g., WHO and UNICEF) that were given most of the responsibility. The central focus of these agencies was to provide health care, improve nutrition, and ensure that children arrived at school safely. At the time, the thinking was that, once children were in school, teachers and other education authorities would take responsibility for them. Third, when such agencies considered supporting centers and preschools for young children in developing countries, existing programs tended to cater to the wealthier urban communities.

Thus, the prevailing thought at that time was that early childhood development programs were a luxury for the rich rather than a necessity for the poor. This view has been turned on its head with more recent findings that demonstrate how such programs are an important way children can actually catch up to their better-off peers.

Early Child Development Programs

Early childhood is generally defined as the period from birth to the time a child enters formal schooling (around the world, schooling typically begins around six to eight years of age). Thus, UNESCO defines early childhood care and education

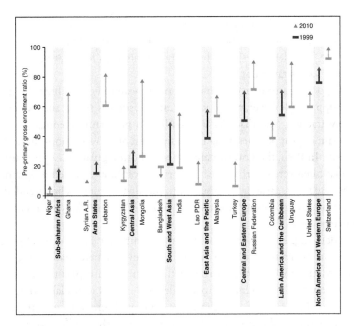

FIGURE 4.1 Enrollment in Pre-Primary Education Varies Widely Between and Within Regions, Between 1999 and 2010

Source: UNESCO (2012b, p. 51)

programs as those providing health, nutrition, security, and learning from infancy through preschool or pre-primary education.[5]

Although participation in early childhood development (ECD) programs has grown dramatically in recent years, there is significant variability both across countries and regions (Figure 4.1). For example, Ghana and Mongolia have doubled and tripled (respectively) their enrollments of children in pre-primary programs over a decade, while in Bangladesh this number has remained stagnant or dropped slightly.[6] Diversity is found within countries as well: the wealthiest urban quintile of Nigerians are more than five times as likely to have children in pre-primary programs as the poorest rural quintile.[7] Overall, ECD participation over the past decade has grown about 54% in wealthy countries, but only about 17% in low-income countries.[8]

Faith-based organizations also play a major role in providing ECD programs. Often housed within a place of worship, these organizations offer nearly 25% of all ECD programs in developing countries.[9] Private for-fee ECD programs are also growing quickly, but appear to increase national inequalities due to their fee structures, as evidenced in such countries as India and Ethiopia.[10] Where no government services are provided, these private ECD programs are in high demand.[11]

Parents who think their children will be high achievers and thus better prepared for formal schooling may also choose private sector programs.[12] Faith-based programs are considered desirable by many parents who feel that these programs replicate the values taught at home.

For the poor, equity in access to preschooling can only be achieved with government support. However, many poor countries, such as Nepal and Niger, spend only a tiny fraction (less than 0.1% of GNP) on pre-primary education.[13] Even with government support, learning inequities exist due to variations in the quality of provision. In Peru, the government supports both regular ECD programs with professional caregivers in urban areas, and rural, community-based programs with volunteer caregivers. Evaluation research found that children who attended ECD programs with the professional caregivers were 10% more likely to attend school at the correct age.[14]

These data suggest that parental and community demand for ECD programs is growing in many contexts, but certainly not everywhere. Part of the growth is related to the increased importance that families are placing on learning, and their view that schooling—broadly defined—leads to social and economic advancement. Nonetheless, some families are more hesitant to give their young children structured educational experiences at an early age.[15] This may derive in part from differences in cultural values, an issue that we will delve into next, or, as in Illa's story, the fact that the availability of quality programs may be quite limited.[16]

Cultural Differences in Child Rearing

Children's homes are the first places where they begin to absorb the lessons and values that will shape them for the rest of their lives, and such environments vary widely across cultures. In *Culture and Infancy: Variations in the Human Experience,* Herbert Leiderman and colleagues wrote about the many ways that children are brought up around the world:

> From the moment of birth, human infants are dependent on others for biological survival. . . . Despite the sometimes heroic efforts of children to resist the pressures of family and society, the process of acculturation continues generation after generation. This process, commonly termed socialization . . . , is actually a form of adaptation.[17]

Robert LeVine, a psychological anthropologist, and one of the contributors to Leiderman's book, further describes the role of culture in child rearing from his work in Africa:

> Cultural evolution within human populations . . . produces standardized strategies of survival for infants and children, strategies reflecting

environmental pressures from a more recent past, encoded in customs rather than genes and transmitted socially rather than biologically.[18]

Clearly, there is sizable heterogeneity in the ritualized approaches to child rearing across the globe. Some are positive (e.g., the praising of "good" behavior), while others are considered by many to be negative (e.g., corporal punishment) or destructive (e.g., female genital cutting[19]). One useful way to think about the shaping of early behavior is with the term "developmental niche," which describes three key components of a child's environment: the physical and social settings they inhabit; culturally regulated customs and child-rearing practices; and beliefs or "ethnotheories" of parents, teachers, and others responsible for their care.[20] Due to such culturally embedded practices, there are many views about what constitutes "appropriate" socialization in societies today, especially in light of global change.[21]

Cigdem Kagitcibasi, a child psychologist, studied how context affects child rearing in Turkey.[22] She found that self-described "modern" Turkish parents tended to put a high value on individualism, and children's independence from their parents. By contrast, she found that Turkish parents in "traditional" agrarian contexts emphasized obedience training, prohibited play, and restricted the exploration of ideas and beliefs. She determined that there is no single approach to early child rearing from a Turkish perspective. Rather, within Turkish society there are multiple accepted ways of supporting children, with varying degrees of extended family involvement and respect for parental authority.[23]

While there are numerous valid and diverse opinions with respect to positive practices in child rearing, there is much greater cross-cultural consensus regarding the dangers to children's health and well-being. Child mortality rates (under five years), for example, are one way to measure health threats to children (Figure 4.2).

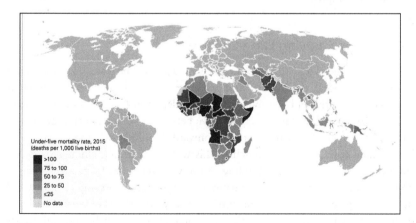

FIGURE 4.2 Under-five Mortality (Deaths per 1000 live Births), 2015
Source: UNICEF (2015, p. 5)

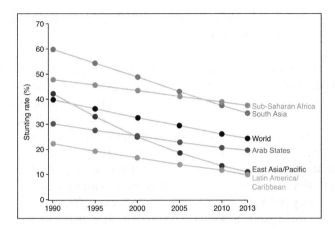

FIGURE 4.3 Childhood Malnutrition (and Stunting) by Region of the World, 1990–2013

Source: UNESCO (2015a)

The highest rates are in sub-Saharan Africa and in South Asia. This finding is mirrored by regional statistics on children at risk of malnutrition and stunting, which have generally declined from higher levels in 1990 (see Figure 4.3). While infant mortality and malnutrition statistics have improved over recent decades in each region, they still pose a particular challenge for Africa and South Asia, where the rates are nearly double those of other regions. According to some estimates, more than 200 million young children under the age of five are currently living in poverty and will fail to reach their full potential.[24] The links between education and health in children have increasingly been the subject of research as assessment methods have improved.

Methods for Studying Early Childhood

Following on the work of Mead, Leiderman, and LeVine, social scientists have learned a great deal about how young children learn and develop in different corners of the world, and the strategies that are deployed by each culture to "raise a child." Out of such research, we now have better tools for measuring growth in cognitive and social behavior from birth onward. Until recently, the international development community tied much of this work to fostering children's survival and health, with substantial funding from UN specialized agencies such as UNICEF and certain major foundations.[25] In one such example, nutritional supplements given to infants (from birth to two years of age) in Guatemala were found to result in improved schooling outcomes, better adult health, and higher wages even 30 years later.[26] Overall, nutritional and health interventions are known to have a positive impact on physical growth, cognitive functioning, and school achievement.[27]

Neuroscience, or the brain-based study of human behavior, also lends an important dimension to the study of these topics. In international development, neuroscientific research has concentrated most on infancy and early childhood, largely due to the cognitive and social consequences of poverty-related health risks, such as poor nutrition. Neuroscience models posit that the central nervous system is critical to the child's functions, leading to a number of possible ramifications in terms of sensorimotor coordination, cognitive and language processing, and social-emotional outcomes.[28] Tools for measuring risk factors include physiological predispositions and health, along with cultural (e.g., ethnotheories) and social (e.g., child-rearing methods) inputs. In high-poverty contexts, when accompanied by lower psycho-social stimulation, there is considerable risk for delays in growth and development. In one well-known study, young children born in Romanian orphanages who were adopted and raised in Great Britain were found to have significantly lower IQ scores than similarly adopted children who were born in Great Britain. However, if children were adopted and supported before the age of two (as opposed to a later age), most caught up with the other children—thus showing that earlier interventions were essential.[29]

Whether there is a *critical period* by which time interventions must happen, or whether there remains considerable resilience in the face of early deprivation, loss, and/or trauma, is still a matter of debate.[30] Consider a widely cited study by Betty Hart and Todd Risley that measured conversational word frequency spoken by parents of different social classes to their children, from one to four years of age.[31] Using this methodological approach, the authors reported a projected "30 million word gap" by the time children were two years old, as shown in Figure 4.4. What this suggests is that if a child falls behind in early language inputs, the disparities will grow much larger over time, as seen by the extrapolation of vocabulary growth. Although this study claimed that differences in children's vocabulary inputs were attributable mainly to differences in income or social class (as shown in the figure), further research has revealed that the differences were likely due to distinctive styles of parental interaction.

Indeed, recent studies have found that interventions to bridge vocabulary gaps must extend beyond focusing on word input and instead foster parent-child dyadic interactions that build word exposure and word learning.[32] A recent reanalysis of the Hart-Risley findings determined, using their same data, that the differences were more likely attributable to differences in parental education and language interactions with children rather than simply differences in income level.[33] Finally, a study in Ecuador of productive vocabulary among children of different

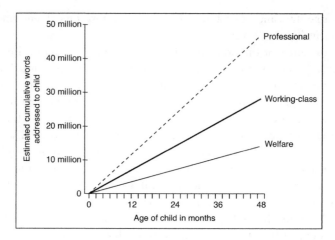

FIGURE 4.4 The 30 Million Word Gap: The Number of Words Addressed to Children Differs Across Income Groups (in the United States)

Source: Hart and Risley (2003)

socioeconomic groups found similar gaps, but these were not linked to parents' linguistic inputs to children.[34]

What can we learn from these findings? Evidence to date suggests that gaps in both parental vocabulary and children's vocabulary seem to vary by social class and education of the parents, but they also may be due to cultural influences and language interactions as mediated by social class. Still, we do not know whether these findings will be maintained over time, or if they impact other social and cognitive skills that are directly linked to learning outcomes in school.[35]

Overall, new methods for studying young children have allowed us to start building a substantial knowledge base. Results show that differences in early development depend on social and cultural differences in child rearing, such as parenting, language use, and socialization.[36] Such categories of behavior may be divided broadly into either cognitive or socio-emotional caregiving activities that vary by national levels of the Human Development Index.[37] As shown in Figure 4.5, socio-emotional measures of caregiving (e.g., parents playing with their children) as well as cognitive caregiving (e.g., parents reading books and telling stories to their children) may vary quite widely both within and across countries.[38] These differences, and the methods to study them, have laid the foundation for our ability to better measure and understand the impact of ECD on school readiness, as well as longer-term education, employment, and behavioral outcomes.[39]

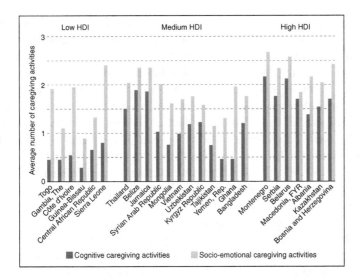

FIGURE 4.5 Variation in Cognitive and Socio-Emotional Caregiving in Low-, Medium-, and High-HDI Countries

Source: World Bank (2015b), based on Bornstein and Putnick (2012)

Intergenerational Learning and the Home-School Transition

Across all cultures, families and home environments play a crucial role in early learning and preparedness for later life.[40] In an era of increased globalization, we know that ever-greater burdens of childcare will be placed on single parents, elderly family members, non-parental relatives, older siblings, and peers.[41] Economic pressures are already requiring parents to work longer hours outside the home, leaving them with less available time to care for their children or serve as resources for learning.[42]

Thus, intergenerational learning—how family or community members directly influence a child, and vice versa—differs today in important ways from behaviors and values observed by cultural anthropologists of the past. The increase in girls' access to schooling, as one example, has led to a sharp increase in women's literacy in recent decades.[43] This, in turn, has had significant consequences for children's learning and health outcomes, both positive (in terms of learning support) and potentially negative (mothers may travel away from home and are less available to their young children).[44] These factors are complex, with sizeable variability across families and cultures. Nonetheless, trends point to increased roles (if not always increased time) for parents and families with respect to children's learning in the home.

Today's changes in family life are also forcing us to reconsider the opportunities for informal learning in and out of school, as discussed in Chapter 3. Beyond family support, the growth of school access has led to young people becoming peer resources for learning and language in low-income countries. There is evidence that these youths are serving as intermediaries for reading medical prescriptions and helping with school assignments for younger and less educated siblings and peers.[45] Research indicates that over a third of children under three years of age are in the care of older siblings under ten years of age. Some "child-to-child" programs, such as in Ethiopia, have found that it is possible to build positive outcomes from this trend.[46] Intergenerational exchanges, whether intentional or not, constitute a prime source of informal learning for young children, and will impact their ability to learn in school.[47]

From these findings and others, we know that a smooth "home-school transition" should be encouraged as much as possible in order to ensure an optimal learning path for children.[48] Further research suggests that this transition can be enhanced by emphasizing three aspects of early childhood development programming:[49]

- *Participative:* Families, community partners, and school leaders share decision-making responsibilities, maintain open communication, and use evaluation information to improve educational programming.
- *Holistic:* Children's needs are considered and responded to holistically, including health, education, and social well-being.
- *Linguistically, culturally, and developmentally appropriate:* Educational services are designed to respect and respond to children's home language, culture, and developmental level.[50]

Broadly speaking, the development of robust social relationships between peers, families, and educational institutions is critical for a child's successful transition from home to school. Some transitions come naturally as part of community traditions in contexts where all children are expected to progress more or less smoothly to school. In other circumstances, where children's transitions to school are troubled, policymakers are increasingly turning to specific intervention programs.

Interventions in Early Childhood

Early childhood development interventions—programs that support the upbringing of children at home or in community settings—are one of the major ways that development agencies have sought to improve learning from an early age. The increased emphasis on ECD interventions is due to the fact that they are cumulative: the earlier the intervention, the greater the learning (and other consequences) over time.

From the 1970s onward, there have been a growing number of ECD interventions in international contexts. The early studies were undertaken in the United States and Europe, and later in developing countries. In an influential review of 20 intervention studies, Patrice Engle and colleagues concluded in *The Lancet* that by supporting basic health and nutritional services, more than 200 million children under the age of five could avoid what they termed "developmental loss" of potential in cognitive development and education.[51] Published in 2007, it caught the attention of many policymakers around the world, and set in motion a new and much stronger interest in supporting ECD interventions in developing countries.

Economists who have become involved in ECD interventions tend to look at this domain as one of investment in human capital, as discussed in Chapter 1. They examine the rate of return (ROI) on investing in young children for their income productivity over the life course.[52] As shown in Figure 4.6, the hypothetical ROI of interventions are posited to be cumulative over time, and highest when begun early. The ROI ratios are considerably lower when investments are made later in life.[53] Support for this perspective has come from a variety of research studies initially undertaken in the United States. The best known are those of the Perry Preschool and Chicago Child-Parent-Center projects, where the average

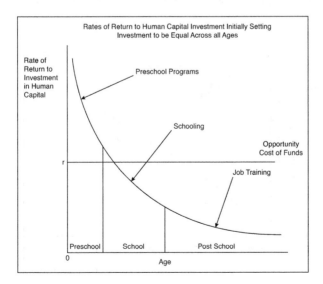

FIGURE 4.6 Rates of Return on Investment (ROI Curve) to Human Capital Investment

Source: World Bank (2011), based on Carneiro and Heckman (2003, p. 93)

ROI ratio is about 8 or 9 to 1,[54] when the benefits of the early preschool programs are weighed against social and other costs.[55] These findings have been frequently cited when policymakers support popular programs like Head Start in the United States.

In developing countries, one of the best-known longitudinal interventions was undertaken in Colombia, where the effects on children's cognitive development were found to be directly proportional to the amount of social and educational support provided (Figure 4.7). In addition, a 20-year longitudinal study undertaken in Jamaica showed that a two-year intervention on physically stunted toddlers increased their earnings in adulthood over a control group by about 25%.[56] At present, studies in the United States show much higher ROI than in developing countries, and this may be due in part to the social costs "saved" when the target groups (that is, those who received the intervention) show lowered rates of American social services (such as incarceration and drug treatment services). By contrast, the value of such social costs may be lower in developing countries where the relative price of prison, drug treatment, and so forth may be much lower.[57] Thus, the hypothetical ROI curve described earlier needs to be understood in light of varying cultural contexts and costs.

ECD interventions show the importance and utility of investing in young children, especially those who are poor, malnourished, or who live in societies where life circumstances are very unstable.[58] Research support for ECD's impact has grown in recent years. In Bangladesh, for example, children who participated in rural preschool programs improved their reading and math

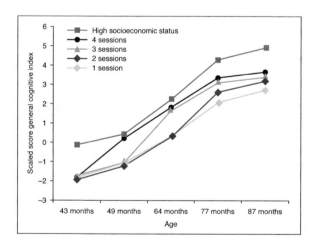

FIGURE 4.7 Change in Cognitive Development as a Function of Length and Type of Intervention in Colombia

Source: Engle et al. (2007)

skills and were better equipped to enter primary school.[59] An impact evaluation of ECD in rural Mozambique found that children's cognitive, fine motor, and socio-emotional skills increased, along with primary school enrollment rates, in communities that received early intervention programs.[60] Beyond the (obvious) moral imperative to help young children, there is mounting evidence from many countries that high-quality ECD interventions, including home visiting and parenting programs, can help to produce strong human development gains.[61]

New Directions in Early Childhood Policy

In 1989, the United Nations Convention on the Rights of the Child (UNCRC) was signed by nearly all nations in the world.[62] The UNCRC is a human rights treaty that sets out the civil, political, economic, social, health, and cultural rights of children.[63] It states that children everywhere should be treated "without discrimination of any kind, irrespective of the child's or his or her parent's or legal guardian's race, color, sex, language, religion, political or other opinion, national, ethnic or social origin, property, disability, birth or other status."[64] This powerful statement led many national governments and development agencies to take a closer look at how children are valued and supported, especially children who are the most disadvantaged. The UNCRC contains four "general principles" that build a case for greater investments in young children, including the right to: (1) survival and development; (2) non-discrimination; (3) respect for views and feelings; and (4) the best interests of the child.[65]

The growing interest in ECD programs is evident in a variety of policy statements and conventions (see Table 4.1) that can be directly traced to the UNCRC. Unfortunately, early childhood development was not included among the MDGs in 2000 due in large part to the view at that time that early childhood development was not critical to children's access to schooling. Over the past 20 years, research has clearly demonstrated the benefits of ECD interventions.[66]

Today, the policy landscape, public interest, and increased provision of ECD have changed significantly. ECD is now directly referenced in SDG 4.2: "By 2030, ensure that all girls and boys have access to quality early childhood development, care and pre-primary education so that they are ready for primary education."[67] Achieving this goal for all children in low-income countries will be one of the most challenging dimensions of the SDGs. This is all the more difficult because of the funding disparities between ECD and other sectors. To take one example, huge resources in development aid are spent on higher education, rather than on young children where the need and potential is so much greater (see Figure 4.8).

TABLE 4.1 Sample of International Policy Statements on Early Childhood Protection

Policy statement	Year
Declaration of Alma-Ata (Health for All Declaration)	(1978)
Ottawa Charter for Health Promotion	(1986)
The Convention on the Rights of the Child	(1989)
World Declaration on Education for All	(1990)
Framework for Action to Meet Basic Learning Needs	(1990)
Education for All: Achieving the Goal—The Amman Affirmation	(1996)
Jakarta Declaration on Leading Health Promotion Into the 21st Century	(1997)
Optional Protocol on the Sale of Children, Child Prostitution, and Child Pornography	(2000)
Optional Protocol on the Involvement of Children in Armed Conflict	(2000)
UN Millennium Declaration	(2000)
Millennium Development Goals	(2000)
The Dakar Framework for Action—Education for All: Meeting Our Collective Commitments	(2000)
Expanded Commentary on the Dakar Framework for Action	(2000)
NGO Declaration on Education for All	(2000)
Regional Frameworks for Action:	(2000)
• Education for All—A Framework for Action in Sub-Saharan Africa: Education for African Renaissance in the Twenty-First Century • Education for All in the Americas: Regional Framework of Action • Education for All in the Arab States: Renewing the Commitment—The Arab Framework for Action to Ensure Basic Learning Needs in the Arab States in the Years 2000–2010 • Asia and the Pacific Regional Framework for Action: Education for All—Guiding Principles, Specific Goals, and Targets for 2015 • Regional Framework for Action—Europe and North America • Recife Declaration of the E-9 Countries	
General Comment no. 7: Implementing Child Rights in Early Childhood	(2005)
Rio Political Declaration on Social Determinants of Health	(2011)
SDG 4.2. Access to quality ECD, care and pre-primary education	(2015)

Source: adapted from Britto et al. (2013, p. 72)

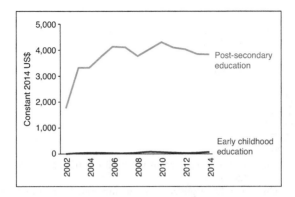

FIGURE 4.8 Direct Aid From Donors (in US Millions) to Early Childhood Care and Education and Post-Secondary Education, 2002–2014

Source: UNESCO (2016a, p. 139)

Preparing for the Future

In a small village in highland Peru, Illa's parents are aware of the significant stakes associated with getting their daughter into a preschool program that will help her learn Spanish and prepare her for future studies. At the policy level, the Peruvian government and the United Nations also have a stake in Illa's success.

But Illa's learning depends on many antecedent factors, such as: whether her parents speak to her in whole sentences rather than simple commands; whether they read to her; whether there are appropriate reading materials in her home; whether Illa feels respected and socially confident; and whether she can resist childhood diseases that could interfere with her learning and cognitive development. Crucially, Illa's life trajectory will largely depend on whether she is able to get into a preschool that will prepare her for subsequent learning opportunities.

One thing is certain. Parents, communities, and both national and international agencies all agree that Illa, and the many millions like her, represent the future. Countries—both rich and poor—can adopt early childhood policies that will help children engage in better learning opportunities, including the acquisition of preliminary skills for reading, mathematics and socio-behavioral competencies that will be needed in primary school. Learning these "basic skills" for school will be Illa's next big challenge.

Notes

1. Cited in Clarke and Clarke (2000, p. 11).
2. Quotations from Woodhead (2007, p. 6).
3. See, for example, Zeiders et al. (2016).
4. See, for example, Leiderman et al. (1977), discussed later in this chapter.

5. UNESCO website (nd).
6. These data may have various origins, but it seems that government support is one of the key reasons why Ghana and Mongolia have made positive strides.
7. UNESCO (2012b, p. 52).
8. For an early review, see Myers (1995); a recent policy review may be seen in Bernard van Leer Foundation (2016).
9. Britto et al. (2014). See also Bartlett et al. (2013).
10. Woodhead and Streuli (2013).
11. UBS Optimus Foundation (2014).
12. Britto et al. (2014).
13. UNESCO (2012b, p. 54).
14. Beltrán and Seinfeld (2010); reported in UNESCO (2012b, p. 56); for broad review, see Neuman et al. (2015).
15. As noted in Chapter 3, ECD preschool programs, even if structured and assisted by government and non-governmental agencies, are often considered to be "non-formal" education. This is largely because most ECD programs do not meet the criteria of having a formal curriculum that is supported by a trained core of professional teachers. As noted, however, as ECD programs become strengthened over time, they may become a bigger part of the formal educational system.
16. E. Friedlander (personal communication) found that children and parents reported about 75% of children attended ECD programs in one rural district in Rwanda, even though official government rates across the country were around 15%. They found, as discussed in Chapter 11, that serious discrepancies in government data collection are frequent.
17. Leiderman et al. (1977, p. 1).
18. LeVine (1977, p. 16).
19. Also known as female genital mutilation (FGM).
20. Super and Harkness (1986), and summarized in Woodhead (2007).
21. The term "appropriate" has been used in the notion of "developmental appropriate practices" (DAP) by childcare workers and teachers; see Woodhead (2007, p. 17). On globalization changes, see Chapter 10.
22. Kagitcibasi (1996).
23. See also Woodhead (2007, p. 19).
24. Grantham-McGregor et al. (2007) and McCoy et al. (2016).
25. Such foundations include, for example, Van Leer, Bill and Melinda Gates, and the William and Flora Hewlett.
26. Behrman et al. (2009a); wage effects were on adult men only.
27. Pollitt (1990).
28. Engle et al. (2007). Others, for example, Shonkoff (2010), Abadzi (2014), and Gabrieli (2009), have made the broader claim that neuroscience is a key constraint on learning in education. While interest in the connections between neuroscience and education have been growing, there is much debate about social versus "hardwired" difference in learning. Serious criticisms of the neuroscience approach have come from many sources (e.g., Bowers, 2016). Broadly speaking, this is not a new issue, and links back to some discussions mentioned in Chapter 1 on the biological versus social dimensions of intelligence testing and cognitive function. In other words, how much of the variance in a particular behavioral outcome may be explained by social versus biological/neuroscience variation. An interesting case in point is the work of Lyubomirsky et al. (2005), who proposed that "adult well-being" is 50% genetically based and limited by neurophysiological development; yet the authors' claims were based largely on findings of one- to two-year-old infant twins (not a useful basis to predict adult behavior), and a survey of twins from a secondary data analysis of twins (for whom the authors have little or no control over how temperament or well-being

was measured). In other words, the temptation of social scientists to invoke neurobiological hardwiring is a serious matter, and claims, as with the area of intelligence testing, need to be very carefully evaluated. A simpler—and more credible—explanation of the well-being results is that cognitive skills are learned through social interaction without some type of universalistic bio-behavioral theory.

29. Rutter and O'Connor (2004). A delay in a learning trajectory, while not desirable (especially for school-aged children), does not imply that catching up is unlikely or impossible. Arguments about impaired brain function, for *otherwise normal children*, in reading, language, or other cognitive activities seem, at present, to be exaggerated in the public press, and have only limited support within the scientific literature. What can be said is that early learning is helpful in that there is more time to learn a skill and progress within typical norms. See discussion on reading and dyslexia in Wagner (2011a, p. 97).

30. Woodhead (2007, p. 11), in a comprehensive review, states: "Fortunately for the species, and the future of children facing adversity and trauma, the young human brain does not normally 'shut down', and development does not normally 'stall', either literally or metaphorically, except in the short term or in the most extreme circumstances for the most vulnerable children. Evidence abounds on multiple adverse effects on children's well-being from material deprivations, disrupted, distorted and abusive relationships, conflict, displacement and forced migrations. Yet, increasingly, researchers have argued that generalised evidence offers an incomplete picture of the impact of adversities in children's lives, by overlooking significant numbers of young children who appear to thrive—despite adversity."

31. Hart and Risley (2003). Their findings are based on a sample of young (mainly African American) children in the United States. It should be noted that these researchers measured the amount of *adult* speech directed to young children. In later and more technically sophisticated research, Fernald et al. (2013) found parallel findings in children's produced speech, measured in real time. Again, higher social class children produced both qualitatively and quantitatively superior speech than that of lower social class children. By 24 months of age, infants from the higher social class families were six months ahead of the infants of the lower-class families. Fernald et al. (2013, p. 244) state: "One interpretation of these findings is that having the opportunity for rich and varied engagement with language from an attentive caretaker provides the infant not only with models for language learning, but also with valuable practice in interpreting language in real time." The figure shown from Hart and Risley (2003) actually extrapolates data to age four years, even though data collection ended at year three (36 months).

32. Golinkoff et al. (2015); Hirsh-Pasek and Golinkoff (2012).

33. Rindermann and Baumeister (2015). See also, Wasik and Hindman (2015) on some limits of vocabulary as a tool for assessment.

34. Paxson and Schady (2005, 2007) used a Spanish language version of the Peabody Picture Vocabulary Test to measure children's vocabulary from ages three to five in Ecuador.

35. The Hart and Risley (2003) original work is not without its serious critics. For example, Dudley-Marling and Lucas (2009, pp. 366–367) claim that Hart and Risley, by taking the language practices of the middle- and upper-SES families in their sample as the standard, transformed the linguistic differences they found among the welfare families in their study into linguistic "deficiencies." For instance, the tendency of welfare families to prefer more direct request forms of speech is presented as an illustration of what Hart and Risley deem the "prevailing negative tone" (p. 177) in welfare families that will take "thousands of hours . . . to overcome. . . . [T]he tremendous influence of Hart and Risley's research on vocabulary and social class exemplify the willingness—even eagerness—of many educators and educational policy

makers to accept explanations for academic failure that implicate the language and culture of poor children and their families as the cause of their academic struggles" (p. 188).

36. See Wagner and Stevenson (1982) for an early set of studies on this topic.

37. On HDI, see discussion in Chapter 2.

38. Socioeconomic level is represented in the figure by the Human Development Index (HDI).

39. There is some controversy around the conflation of "soft" socio-emotional skills and their cultural variations. Levin (2014) argues that socio-emotional (non-cognitive) measures add important value to understanding individual differences in educational achievement. By contrast, Camfield (2015, p. 78) suggests that non-cognitive skills are inadequate "explainers" of cultural difference, noting that there is a "tendency of measurement to decontextualize and individualize social and structural problems (for example, stalled social mobility in the UK and growing inequality in South Africa) and the solutions to these, and shift the responsibility for them onto the individuals who are experiencing them." He states that soft-skill measures serve to take "what is essentially a political problem, . . . and [recast] it in the neutral language of science."

40. Henderson and Berla (1994); Forget-Dubois et al. (2009); Gertler et al. (2012); Ball et al. (2014).

41. Nsamenang (2011). See also see Chapter 10.

42. Li et al. (2014).

43. The gains in women's literacy are largely due to the increase in enrollment of girls in primary schools, providing at least some literacy skills. As shown in the next chapter, however, many girls (and boys) are not able to read well even after multiple years at school. Still, they have better reading skills than previous generations that did not have access to school, and children can, in adult literacy programs, support parental literacy learning (see Chapter 6; and UNESCO-UIL, 2015).

44. See LeVine et al. (2012) for a discussion of the effect of maternal literacy on health outcomes. Other research (e.g., Strickland & Barnett, 2003) suggests that the exposure to print at home, and parents' engagement in conversation and reading activities with the child are correlated with children's oral language skills at school entry and their later reading outcomes. Clearly, fathers play an enormous role in many societies, but when women's literacy is far lower than men's, the impact of maternal literacy tends to stand out.

45. Wagner (2010a). See also the work of Save the Children in their Literacy Boost program (Dowd, 2011).

46. Heymann (2006) and UNICEF (2012); on Ethiopia, see: www.unicef.org/evaldatabase/index_80717.html.

47. Anderson-Levitt (2003); Dachyshyn and Kirova (2008); Johnson and Welsh (2000); Moll et al. (1992); UNESCO (2003, p. 14).

48. While the term "home-school transition" is widely used in the research literature, it has been pointed out that this should not be unidirectional. That is, there is not simply a hand-off by parents to teachers, but mostly a bi-directional relationship between families and educational institutions. Thanks to E. Friedlander (personal communication) for this observation.

49. Drawn from Mangione and Speth (1998). For a broad discussion of African childhood transitions, see Nsamenang and Tchombe (2011).

50. See Chapter 5 for further discussion of the importance of home language (mother-tongue) as the language of instruction.

51. Engle et al. (2007, p. 239). Engle states: "The most effective early child development programs provide direct learning experiences to children and families, are targeted toward younger and disadvantaged children, are of longer duration, high quality, and

high intensity, and are integrated with family support, health, nutrition, or educational systems and services" (p. 229). A later series of *Lancet* papers was published in Lake (2011) and Richter et al. (2016). Nores and Barnett (2010) conducted a meta-analysis of early childhood intervention programs in developing countries, and found that interventions that incorporated a component of education, childcare, or cognitive stimulation had the largest impact on young children's cognitive development compared to pure cash transfers or solely nutritional interventions. Thanks to S. Wolf (personal communication) for pointing out this last reference.

52. ROI was also discussed in Chapter 1.
53. This widely cited figure (Carneiro & Heckman, 2003; Heckman, 2006; Heckman, 2011) is mainly hypothetical; it is only roughly based on estimated ROI for real projects along the trajectory shown, an important limitation of the configuration. See Mustard and Young (2007); and for more specificity by geographical region, see the systematic review by Tanner et al. (2015).
54. In other words, this would be a return of eight to nine dollars for each dollar invested.
55. The World Bank has published estimates that are even higher, with a ROI at about 17 to 1; see Sayre et al. (2015, p. 2). More detail on the Perry Preschool may be seen at: www.highscope.org/content.asp?contentid=219; while Chicago CPC may be seen at: http://cps.edu/Schools/EarlyChildhood/Pages/Childparentcenter.aspx. Other ECD intervention studies undertaken in the United States have shown both higher and lower cost to benefit ratios, and have employed home visiting, parental education, and early stimulation within ECD programs (Karoly et al., 2005).
56. Gertler et al. (2014).
57. In other words, the costs of welfare, unemployment benefits, and incarceration may be a much larger proportion of the national budget in the United States than in most low-income countries.
58. Support on the value of ECD comes from a number of analytical studies, such as Crouch (2015), Sayre et al. (2015), and Yoshikawa et al. (2015). Unstable contexts would include, for example, conflict zones, as discussed in Chapter 10.
59. Aboud (2006).
60. Martinez et al. (2012).
61. Britto (2015); also Behrman et al. (2005, 2009b). However, as noted by Woodhead (2007), some caution is required as to long-term benefits of ECD across different cultures, largely because of the myriad of individual and cultural pathways that children can take.
62. UN General Assembly (1989). See www.unicef.org/crc/.
63. The Convention defines a "child" as any human being under the age of 18 years.
64. See www.crin.org/resources/treaties/CRC.asp?catName=International+Treatie.
65. See Woodhead (2007, p. 24) and reference to UNCRC Articles 2, 3, 6, and 12; and General Comment 7.
66. Young (2002).
67. See Chapter 2 for a broader discussion of the SDGs.

5

CHILDREN AND BASIC SKILLS

Assiatou: Aspiring to Read in Guinea

It is early Monday morning in Kahalé village, about 45 kilometers from the capital city of Conakry. It's raining again, and the water is flowing off the corrugated tin roof of the one-room schoolhouse in the center of the village. The rain makes it difficult for Monsieur Mamadou, the teacher, to get to school, as the rural taxi keeps getting stuck in the mud, forcing him and the six other passengers to help the driver get back on the road. Once at school, Monsieur Mamadou waits for his students to arrive. At 9 a.m., the room is only half full, which is probably not a bad thing—a full classroom would mean 65 children, and there are only enough benches to seat 50. Eight-year-old Assiatou sits in the back row. She has her pencil out and carefully copies into her notebook each word the teacher has written on the blackboard. While going to school is better than staying home, Assiatou has a sense that she is not making good use of her time. She can copy the text but doesn't understand it. She can only read a few French words on the street signs and wall advertisements in her village. She feels bad about this, and wonders how it is that her classmates in the front rows seem to already know some French. She also wonders why Monsieur Mamadou only calls on those front-row pupils to work on the blackboard and not her. She's heard that there is a school she can attend after primary school, but only the kids who sit in the front rows seem to ever enroll there. What is the point of studying and staying in school, she wonders. Perhaps she should reconsider and follow in the footsteps of her older sister, who dropped out of school and was recently married at age 14. Is that a better path to follow?

_____

Young children like Assiatou will not learn to read and, as a result, are likely to drop out of school. They will not make it to secondary school, will not go to university, and will not get a job in the global economy. This year or next will probably be Assiatou's final year in school. She will eventually marry when she reaches puberty and begin a similar cycle of inadequate education for her own children.[1]

There is nothing remarkable about Monsieur Mamadou or Assiatou. Rather, their experiences are all too common in countries around the world, and mainly go unnoticed. Although dysfunctional classrooms exist in all nations, their consequences are exacerbated when resources for learning are already very limited—as they are in rural Guinea.

In today's globalizing world, we have made great progress toward getting all children into primary school. Well over 90% of children in most countries have access to schooling. But Assiatou shows us that merely having access isn't enough. It turns out that many children are not even learning the basics of reading, writing, and mathematics in their five years of primary school. This chapter focuses on what is being done to ensure that children actually learn these skills once they enter the classroom—and the obstacles that must be overcome.

Learning the Basics

UNESCO was charged with putting basic education at the top of its policy agenda as part of the Universal Declaration of Human Rights in 1946. In the decades that followed, UNESCO, the World Bank, and other agencies and donors supported "basic education as a fundamental human right," mainly referring to primary schooling from six to ten years of age.[2] As we have seen, most children begin to develop basic reading, writing, and mathematics skills early in life, well before schooling begins. For example, touching on the quadrants we explored in Chapter 3, reading skills are built upon informal language interactions that begin shortly after birth and are reinforced through a family's oral stories. Math skills also begin to take shape in infancy, and are solidified with activities like counting at home, and perhaps later through bargaining in local markets. Through exposure to these informal learning experiences, all children learn to discriminate sounds in their mother-tongue, one of the principle reasons why phonological awareness at an early age forms an essential foundation for reading.[3]

Yet children around the world do not have equal opportunities to develop the early skills upon which school-based learning takes place. For example, considerable research, mainly from Western countries, has shown the importance of parents reading storybooks to children in the early years before schooling. Through reading aloud, children typically learn to broaden their vocabulary, play language games, recognize print, and start to scribble and write. In wealthy countries, it is often assumed that the average child grows up with parents who can read and write. We often assume, rightly or wrongly, that these children have multiple age-relevant and language-relevant books in the home, and, nowadays, multimedia available via the Internet.[4] These emergent reading practices are common in high-income countries and among middle-class families in low-income countries, but occur far less often in poor and marginalized communities.[5]

Research has shown that primary school children in well-supported learning contexts build strong skills that are both sociolinguistic (in terms of oral language interactions) and psycholinguistic (in terms of cognitive component skills).[6] By contrast, children in poor and unsupportive contexts, especially in low-income countries, often are much weaker in one or more of these dimensions, as well as in writing development. These deficiencies lead to serious problems in learning to read and understand text.[7] In Figure 5.1, we can see that only a small fraction of children in grade 2 in a half-dozen African countries have mastered how to read with comprehension.[8] Such research, buttressed by studies in many low-income countries, has played an important role in convincing the international community, and national governments as well, how critical it is to improve the quality of primary schooling.

The origins of reading success or failure are often apparent early in a child's life. Important differences in parent-child language interactions (such as the extent of expansive language dialogue) are measurable during the first two years of life, and may grow over time.[9] Children who acquire these linguistic skills earlier gain more over time than those who start slowly—what is sometimes called the "Matthew effect," the phenomenon where "the rich get richer and the poor get poorer."[10] Though impact seems to vary by testing instrument and by context, the further behind a child falls in reading, the more difficult it is to make up for such losses.

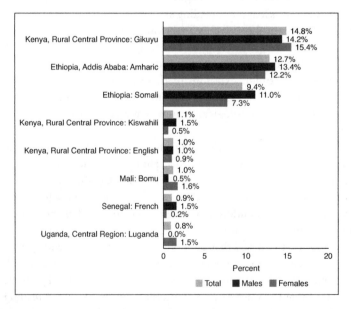

FIGURE 5.1 Percentage of Students Reading With at Least 80% Comprehension in Grade 2, 2008–2010 in Selected Countries

Source: Gove and Cvelich (2011, p. 14)

In terms of learning mathematics, the trajectory differs from reading in some important ways. During their early years, children universally develop an understanding of numbers based on counting, which provides them with a powerful tool for learning about addition and subtraction, as well as developing a familiarity with larger numbers. Cross-cultural research has shown that young children often have an impressive mastery of number sense, beginning in early childhood.[11] At the same time, everyday cultural contexts have been shown to have a significant impact on math skills. Take, for example, the case of Brazilian children who work as street vendors; they were found to have quite advanced math skills, well beyond what schools thought they could accomplish.[12] Nevertheless, with age and schooling, children's mathematical skills are increasingly mediated by language and symbol systems that are fostered by formal school instruction.[13] In poorly supported schooling contexts, children often show limited mastery of mathematical competencies beyond everyday counting and simple arithmetic skills. Further, mathematics taught in schools in poor communities is often learned in rote memory fashion that may work against the development of analytic skills needed to solve multi-step problems, and determine estimations and probabilities.[14]

Research conducted on math acquisition in low-quality schools shows findings similar to those found with respect to reading: that is, children fall further behind the stated curriculum benchmarks with each passing year of instruction. In India's state of Andhra Pradesh, for example, we see in Figure 5.2 that in grade 2, a competency like "two-digit addition without carry," has been attained by only 40% of children; while only 70% have attained it by grade 5. Thus, of the 60% of children who did not already master addition by grade 2, fewer than 50% gained

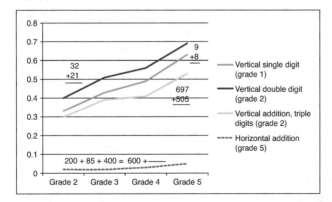

FIGURE 5.2 Mathematics Profiles From Andhra Pradesh (India) at End of Grades 2 and 5

Note: The y axis refers to the proportion of children in each grade that answer correctly.

Source: Data from Muralidharan as cited in Prichett and Beatty (2012, p. 2)

the skill during the additional three years of schooling—a remarkably low figure that indicates the limits of school effectiveness. Overall, 30% of all children could not do simple addition by grade 5, while less than 10% could do more complex addition at the same age.[15] Results like these reinforce the importance of supporting children like Assiatou, who was concerned that her learning was not going very well.

Early Grade Reading

Long before it became a popular topic, John Downing, an educational psychologist, published a number of works on the importance of learning to read in different languages and cultures. With his 1973 publication of *Comparative Reading: Cross-National Studies of Behavior and Processes in Reading and Writing*, Downing started a movement that was at first an academic program of research, and has today become a major enterprise in dozens of nations across the world. Initially, Downing sought to survey how children learn to read in a variety of major languages and orthographies.[16] Then, in conjunction with other researchers, he identified stages through which children progress on the path to becoming skilled readers, ranging from word decoding to reading comprehension.[17]

Skilled reading is considered to be the core achievement goal of schooling the world over. Primary school systems that fail to meet this universal benchmark after five years are considered to have not met their fundamental purpose—which is one reason why there is such concern today about reading problems in low-income countries. Up until 10–15 years ago, our understanding of reading was limited to research undertaken mainly in the industrialized world. This research has put an emphasis on the relation between cognitive skills, such as perception and memory, and specific reading component skills, such as decoding and comprehension.[18] Furthermore, much of this work was carried out with school-age children who were learning to read in English, or a handful of other languages.[19]

During the last decade or so, our knowledge base in this area has grown rapidly. Work done in both the United States[20] and in developing countries[21] has boosted interest in early reading, setting the stage for the development and use, in 2006, of the Early Grade Reading Assessment (EGRA) in developing countries. Later, in 2011, the US Agency for International Development (USAID) announced an All Children Reading initiative "to seek solutions to improve reading skills for children in the early grades," with the "goal of getting 100 million children reading by 2015."[22] This literacy initiative catalyzed the involvement of numerous additional agencies and donors at the international and regional levels, along with a wide variety of NGOs that expanded their work into early grade reading.

EGRA (and its various adaptations) has been employed in more than 65 countries and in more than 100 languages, and continues to expand.[23] When trying to develop a standardized instrument that could be adapted to all alphabetic languages, researchers focused on reading skills that could be easily measured. EGRA consists of five main domains: phonological awareness, alphabetic principle, vocabulary, fluency, and comprehension. These broad categories are then segmented into specific measurable skills.[24] For example, in the stage of emergent literacy, children do not yet understand the alphabetic principle that speech sounds can be represented by written language or print. Instead, they tend to memorize words, associate meaning with pictures and environmental print, and identify words by their unique shapes. Children at this stage notice the phonological features of spoken words (e.g., word length) and may learn to navigate a book (such as the direction of the page, or the purpose of pictures).

EGRA has provided a useful basic measurement tool for understanding children's acquisition of reading skills across diverse backgrounds, languages, and cultures.[25] And it has contributed to new policy options based on insights about which skills require additional support in differing contexts and languages, how to help teachers improve the teaching of reading, and how to create improved means for school systems to implement better reading instruction.[26]

A number of significant school-level interventions have been built around the EGRA instrument. One large project undertaken in Kenya involved more than 1,300 primary schools, comparing students in regular classes with others who were taught a specific curriculum based on the key subskills of EGRA.[27] In this intervention (in grades 1 and 2), teachers who received EGRA-supported materials and specialized training had much greater success: nearly double the number of children could read at grade level compared to those who had teachers without such materials or training. These positive consequences were about the same in both mother-tongue Kiswahili and in second language reading in English.[28] The strong results of this program were so well-received by the Kenyan government that the approach has been expanded nationwide.[29]

In sum, there is growing evidence that reading can be significantly improved in very poor contexts in developing countries.[30] As shown in the Kenyan example, assessment tools can make a major difference in helping to improve reading, and more broadly supporting the learning of children. The success of these measures to detect and intervene in early reading is paving the way for better evidence-based interventions by governments and development agencies who are now much more aware of early reading deficits.

Language of Instruction

While early grade reading assessments have helped to measure literacy at a young age, they have also shed light on a key policy issue that has troubled the field of education around the world: that is, in multilingual societies, which language should be used for instruction? In low-income countries, large numbers of children (sometimes the majority in marginalized communities) come to school not knowing the language of instruction in the classroom.[31] On the one hand, this complex learning context requires practical solutions that confront political realities—such as the need for proficiency in national and official languages—and an education system's ability to adapt to different languages and effective ways of teaching. On the other hand, we must acknowledge the cognitive realities of how children learn to read. As discussed in the case of Illa in Peru,[32] evidence strongly suggests that children from minority language groups do the least well in school, irrespective of which languages are already spoken and which must be learned. The longstanding discrimination experienced by minority language speakers may be found in nearly all countries, but is exacerbated by a multitude of historical and cultural factors in many developing countries.[33]

Is there a best way to implement a language of instruction policy? There are no easy answers to this question, due to variations in national histories and traditions as well as uncertainties about the nature of globalization, language change, and language preferences.[34] But there is mounting evidence that teaching children to read in their mother-tongue (or first) language is a crucial building block for effective learning.[35] Education practitioners in a growing number of countries have attempted to take a more inclusive approach to the use of children's mother-tongues and cultures through policies of multilingual education.[36] In recent years, there has been a strong movement toward recognizing the importance of the child's first language (L1) as contrasted to a second language (L2), especially when considering children in disadvantaged communities who are ethno-linguistic minorities. There are many factors that must be taken into account in language planning for the classroom, such as access, equity, gender, cost, language choice, and learning outcomes.[37] The complexity of these issues in specific contexts has made it difficult to generalize about optimal global strategies (see key variables in Figure 5.3).

In some countries, there is strong resistance to mother-tongue education for a variety of practical reasons. If there is a multitude of languages (for example, Papua New Guinea has an estimated 850 languages), and a limited number of teachers capable of teaching children in these languages, and if localized textbooks are not available, then education officials have often made the decision to support one or several official languages, rather than the mother-tongue of each separate language group. In another example, the South African government—following the fall of *apartheid*—opted for 11 official languages to be taught in primary school classrooms.[38] Thus, even if mother-tongue instruction is desirable, there are serious questions about whether the approach is feasible in heterogeneous multilingual contexts of many low-income schools.[39]

I had an unusual opportunity to study the problems associated with language of instruction in Morocco in the 1980s. Following Independence in 1956, Morocco was known mainly for three national languages—Arabic,[40] Amazigh,[41]

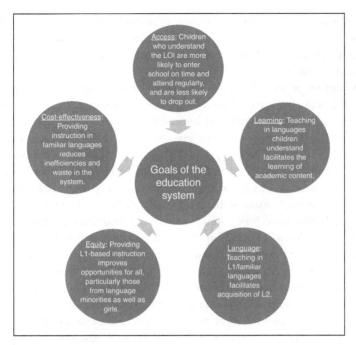

FIGURE 5.3   Inputs for Instructional Decision Making Based on Language Use on the Goals of National Education System

Note: LOI refers to language of instruction.

Source: Pflepsen (2015, p. 15)

and French.[42] After much national debate, the government chose Arabic as the principal language of primary school instruction. Such language planning issues are often quite difficult. In the case of Morocco, this decision was problematic because the French language was used in the city and for commerce, while the rural dwellers were often monolingual Amazigh speakers. The national linguistic compromise was Arabic for primary schooling. This choice had some positive features, including research that demonstrated that Amazigh-speaking children who attended Quranic preschools (in Arabic) learned more quickly to read in Arabic—catching up to the reading ability of native Arabic-speaking children by third grade in primary school.[43]

Overall, research evidence tends to support the "additive" notion that mother-tongue language (L1) reading skills enhance (or transfer to) second language (L2) reading skills.[44] The understanding of lessons in school is nearly always improved when children can learn in a language they already know.[45] Still, language contexts are often highly dependent on local cultural variables so that, in some contexts (such as in Morocco), learning in a second language first does not always produce inferior results.

Some key questions remain unresolved, however: When should teaching of L2 reading begin if it is a nationally required language? Should L2 reading instruction co-occur with curricular content in L2? What are the best ways to support the transfer of reading skills from one language to another, and when should the transition occur from L1 to L2?[46] Further, there are many settings (such as Morocco and Kenya, mentioned earlier) where there are three languages used: international, regional, and local.[47]

Skills transfer between L1 and L2 is a complex issue involving oral language and reading skills, background knowledge in each language, linguistic processing strategies, vocabulary skills, and motivation to learn. Words that appear in similar forms (even if pronounced differently) in both L1 and L2 also influence the process of L1 and L2 language and reading acquisition—a complex process indeed! In most situations, it seems that children can build on their L1 oral and written skills to learn in L2, but there are a great many social and contextual variables that matter.[48] Even in mathematics, L1 and L2 skills are potent factors in learning. In Suriname, for example, researchers found that children in grade 4 had improved mathematics skills in Dutch (L2) when compared with Saamaka (L1), but the reverse was true when mathematics skills were tested in word problems.[49] In South Africa, researchers found that students using English (L2) in grades 4–6 profited from mother-tongue (L1) instruction in grades 1–3 when compared with students who were required to learn in English-only classrooms in grades 1–3.[50] In another study in South Africa, research using census data indicated that the use of L1 in early instruction seems to have positive long-term economic outcomes.[51]

In sum, children seem better equipped to acquire bilingual (i.e., both L1 and L2) reading skills if they already have basic reading skills in their L1. Specifically, unless children already have automatic word identification skills and early reading comprehension in L1, learning to read in L2 remains a huge challenge. Learners who start to read in L2 might catch up to L1 learners in word-level reading skills, but usually not in reading comprehension.[52] Since skilled reading comprehension is dependent on oral language skills (and related knowledge and concepts), it is difficult for L2 learners with low oral L2 skills to catch up to L1 reading children. Indeed, one of the limitations of the EGRA for measuring early reading is its emphasis on reading fluency, especially when oral skills in L2 are weak.[53]

One way to think about the language transfer issue is to consider the distance between the two languages and their contexts for learning in schools. In Figure 5.4, a "distance theory" approach shows three generic contexts. Model A shows an "ideal" balance among the language(s) used by the child in the home and school: that is, where there is strong language overlap. Model B suggests a relatively greater distance (or discrepancy) between home L1 and school L2: that is, where the home language use (L1) is greater than the school language (L2) use. In Model B, in order to reduce this distance, an appropriate approach could be non-formal education or parental literacy programs to increase the use of L2 at home. Model C describes a situation where the greater distance is between the child and the school. In Model C, if the child's mother-tongue

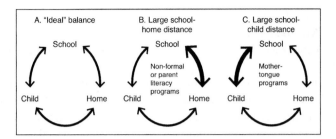

FIGURE 5.4 A "Distance Theory" Approach to Bilingual Education Programs

Note: Bolded arrows are intended to indicate greater distance (see explanation in text).

Source: Wagner (2011a)

(L1) is different from the school's (L2), the appropriate intervention would focus on supporting a bilingual education, built first on increased L1 usage in the school. Although these models may not be so easy to distinguish from one another in real life, they are a way to initiate discussion about how L1 and L2 should be approached.[54]

Teachers are a key component of any language-sensitive education program. Often, teachers are not sufficiently trained to actually implement mother-tongue (L1) reading policies because they were trained by government-run institutions in an official language (L2).[55] In other words, the ability of schools and their teachers to implement a bilingual policy is necessarily limited by teachers' own language competencies. Also, teachers' actual use of the school-mandated language of instruction may vary widely in practice, resulting in highly significant differences in children's language mastery by region and by instructor.[56] Large numbers of teachers may not be willing or able to teach either in mother-tongue (L1, when prescribed) or in a national language (L2, when prescribed). As such, even when a curriculum seems well-constructed and appropriate, its implementation can remain problematic.[57] And, in many countries, teacher deployment policies (that is, putting teachers with particular language skills where they are most needed) often do not match the national language of instruction policy.[58]

One additional dimension is a phenomenon that has been termed teachers' "linguistic insecurity" in classrooms where students use more than a single language.[59] Research has found that teachers sometimes maintain their classroom authority through the use of L2, even when children cannot comprehend it. Such teachers choose to use the national or international language (such as English or French) to maintain authority over students, and tamp down classroom interaction—from the instructors perspective, this can make the situation "safe" by not allowing students to feel empowered to speak.[60] It is little wonder that in such schools, a focus on rote learning becomes one of the ways that students can cope with a curriculum that they cannot understand.[61] And, as in Assiatou's situation, it helps to explain why children who speak the language of the teacher's instruction (usually L2) usually sit in the front rows of the class.

Overall, research supports the notion that bilingualism and bilingual reading can be additive and positive if the learner is allowed (via a good curriculum, an adequately trained teacher, appropriate textbooks in the right languages, and a supportive environment) to build L2 skills upon an L1 foundation.[62] While such felicitous conditions are often not met in developing countries, there is clearly a move toward providing children with materials for learning (and reading) in languages that they can better understand—namely, in their mother-tongue. This approach clearly carries the most promise for most children in the early grades.

Learning Environments and Resources

As discussed in Chapter 3, no learning takes place in isolation. Supportive and responsive environments make a major difference in how children learn, both inside and outside of school. In schools, textbooks are the government's principal way to engage and build children's knowledge and skills.[63] Yet in many schools in developing countries, students have little or no access to textbooks or they must be shared. In Tanzania, for example, only 10% of all grade 6 pupils had sole use of a reading textbook, and about 20% of sixth graders in Zimbabwe had their own reading texts. Further, textbook availability varies considerably within countries as well. In the case of Mali, French language textbooks are much more available in the capital, Bamako, than in rural parts of the country.[64] Finally, as shown in Figure 5.5, in various African countries most children must share their textbooks—meaning that their textbooks cannot be taken home for study after school hours. The ratio in Cameroon was about 11 school students in grade 2 for each reading textbook and 14 for each mathematics textbook.[65] To remedy the obvious problems associated with such uneven textbook availability, some international agencies are financing major initiatives to publish local language (L1) textbooks.[66]

In everyday life outside the classroom, informal learning can also support reading. The presence of written materials (e.g., books, textbooks, newspapers, and digital materials), as well as access to literate parents, siblings, and community members, creates a stronger *literacy ecology* that recursively encourages more reading.[67] This is evidenced by the highly publicized creation of "book floods" where schools and local libraries were provided with large quantities of books.[68] The literacy ecology concept has contributed to efforts by numerous donor agencies and NGOs to support the provision of books to homes and libraries in poor

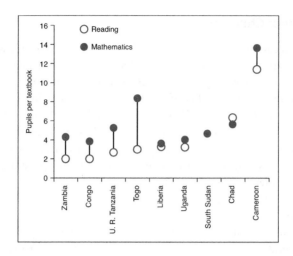

FIGURE 5.5   Textbook Availability Ratio in Selected Sub-Saharan African Countries

Note: Ratios refer to the number of pupils who need to share a single textbook, in reading and mathematics in grade 2 in latest available year.

Source: UNESCO (2016b, p. 2), see http://data.uis.unesco.org/

communities in developing countries.[69] The number of books in homes varies widely in countries and communities. One African survey reported that about 45% of school children in Zanzibar (Tanzania) had no books in their home, while in Kenya the figure was only 10%.[70] These differences are large though there remains uncertainty over which specific inputs—the presence of books, the types of books, the language used in the books, or the literacy support from family members—best support reading acquisition.[71]

Some have argued for a more holistic approach to improving the literacy ecology in a child's life. One in-depth study considered the relative influence of two interventions on reading outcomes in Rwandan primary school children: teacher training alone, and teacher training combined with community support of reading activities.[72] Findings showed that when compared with control groups of same-aged children, each intervention helped children improve their reading after two years, but that the combination of community support and teacher training had the largest overall impact. The study also found that three literacy ecology factors (reading habits and interactions, reading materials, and child interest/engagement) were significantly linked to reading outcomes. In sum, a growing and consistent body of research shows a strong relationship between the literacy ecology and community support for learning and improved outcomes in basic skills.

Out-of-School Children

Despite the success over the last three decades in providing children with greater access to primary school, more than 55 million children of primary school age are not in school today (Figure 5.6).[73] As is evident, substantial progress has been made to reduce the number of children leaving school, but the decline has mainly stopped in recent years. When added together with other children and adolescents, the total number of out-of-school children is estimated today at more than 100 million.[74] From the learning framework in Chapter 3, we know that there are many ways that learning out of school can help children to stay in school, or help them get back to school or perhaps into non-formal education programs.[75] Of course, a crucial way to reduce out-of-school rates is to increase school quality.

After initial enrollment, children's persistence in schooling in low-income countries often declines sharply after the first few years. Rather than "dropping out" (the usual term), it may be more appropriate to say that these children are subtly pushed out of school by systems and contexts that have not provided sufficient quality instruction.[76] In other words, there are many reasons that children stop attending school, including the constraints on parents who may need their

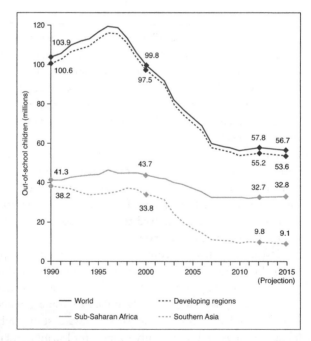

FIGURE 5.6 Number of Out-of-School Children of Primary School Age, Selected Regions, 1990–2015

Source: United Nations (2015a, p. 25)

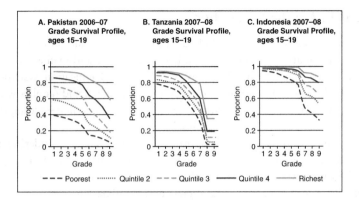

FIGURE 5.7   Comparison of Youth Aged 15–19 Who Have Completed (or Survived Until) a Given Grade, by Income Quintile, Various Years

Source: World Bank (2011, p. 18)

children at home, a lack of trained teachers, poor facilities, and so forth. As shown in Figure 5.7, countries like Pakistan, Tanzania, and Indonesia lose a significant portion of their class cohort by grade 9; and within countries, this appears highly related to the family income quintile. Children whose families are in the lowest income quintile are much more likely to leave school early than those at the middle or upper quintiles.[77]

Recent evidence suggests that trends of school leaving can be reversed through thoughtful interventions. In a recent study of primary school children in Kenya, researchers found that a combination of teacher training and text messages sent to the homes of children—both in support of early reading practices and of the inherent value of staying in school—found that reading skills improved and that the dropout rate for these children was cut in half.[78]

Today, most education systems in developing countries exhibit a fairly steep educational pyramid—where fewer and fewer students make it to each successive level of education. Not long ago these trends were seen as a socially positive measure of the selectivity of schooling, where the most skilled survive. Internationally, views have changed about the importance of selectivity for two main reasons. First, there is a greater sense—exemplified in the UN SDGs—that all children need to learn at least basic reading and math before moving into the workplace, where there are fewer and fewer unskilled employment opportunities. Second, when a child enters into a schooling cycle, an investment has been made in having the child enroll, be taught, and potentially take the place of another child who has dropped out. In other words, there are substantial costs or inefficiencies to the education system when children are not enrolled and learning. These two points converge to support the idea that children's learning in poor contexts remains a major problem, even when children have initial access to schooling.

Basic Skills Are the Foundation

A large proportion of school-aged children (between 25% and 50%) who live in low-income countries do not learn the basics of reading and mathematics. This situation creates massive inefficiencies within national education systems and national budgets, and ever-greater problems for the children and families who are mired in ineffective schools or who have left school altogether—adding to the 100 million children already out of school.

At the outset of this chapter, eight-year-old Assiatou was left wondering about her learning and her future. She was concerned that she was not part of the group of children who would succeed in school and in life. She was right to be concerned. If she doesn't learn to read in French, she will have little chance to move on to secondary school in Guinea or get a decent job. She might also be obliged to accept a marriage offer from one of her distant cousins in just a few short years.

Fortunately, there is hope with respect to improving the basic skills of children like Assiatou. Better assessments of learning have created new possibilities for detecting and reducing the chance of school failure. Creative interventions—both inside and outside of the classroom—have demonstrated how to best support children's basic skills before it is too late. A better understanding of the use of languages of instruction is leading the way to more informed and responsive approaches that take home culture and national policy into account. Much remains to be done to help children of primary school age, but good pathways are now beginning to open for children at risk. A revolution in learning is happening—building on early learning, laying a basic skills foundation, and expanding into learning in adolescence and beyond.

In today's world, however, too many children do not stay in school, and need alternatives for further education. This is the main focus of the next chapter.

Notes

1. In many cases, poor communities will not perceive "failure" because they have known nothing else but failure in schools. They often have never seen a well-performing school and excellent teaching staff. This is unfortunately true in poor schools in wealthy countries, such as in the United States.
2. UNESCO (1975; cited in UNESCO, 2005, p. 136). While six to ten years is about the median age of primary school children, it is not unusual in developing countries to start school one or two years later, and to remain in school two or more years beyond the age of ten; the latter extension is often due to the school's decision to have some children repeat one or more grades due to low achievement.
3. Ball et al. (2014); Adams (1990). See also, earlier discussion of infant cognition in Chapter 2.
4. Ferreiro and Teberosky (1982); Sulzby and Teale (1991); Ball et al. (2014). Additionally, as noted in Chapter 9 of this volume, there are increasing technological inputs ranging from "Sesame Street" on television to tablet-based games. See also the rising gap between populations in rich countries like the United States, and the earlier discussion of Putnam (2015).

5. Ball et al. (2014).
6. Snow et al. (1998); National Reading Panel (2000). Of course, there are also variations on the extent to which each of these component skills come into play while learning to read, and these may range from orthography to spelling-sound correspondences. For example, in languages with high regularity of spelling to sound correspondence, phonemic awareness may be a less critical component skill. For reviews, see Gove and Wetterberg (2011), Reddy and Koda (2013), and Wagner (2011a).
7. Wagner (2011a). Recent research is increasingly focusing on the home learning environment, where "reading habits in the home" are found to be critical factors in support of reading acquisition (Dowd, 2012). B. Piper (personal communication) has noted that, in Kenya, the poor acquisition of writing skills can actually impede reading acquisition. See also the discussion of the literacy ecology in Chapter 7 of this volume.
8. See the work on EGRA described by Gove and Wetterberg (2011), Gove and Cvelich (2011), and Piper and Korda (2011).
9. See the work of Hart and Risley (2003), discussed in Chapter 4.
10. The Matthew effect was popularized in reading research by Stanovich (1986), based on the parable of the talents in the biblical Gospel of Matthew, from Merton (1968). This also is related to similar phenomena in other cognitive skills, such as in vocabulary gaps discussed in Chapter 4. In reading acquisition, this has been taken to mean that those that fall behind in reading continue to fall further behind. See findings by Duff et al. (2015) as a recent example. B. Piper (personal communication) has observed that it is not surprising that children who score low on initial testing remain lower on later testing; but the gap does not always widen into a Matthew effect. Recent longitudinal studies in the United States have called into question the long-term consequences of early reading failure; see Blachman et al. (2014). A comprehensive review and meta-analysis (28 suitable studies out of 4,000 references) by Pfost et al. (2014) found a mixed set of findings that were heavily dependent on the type of measurement outcome used (vocabulary, decoding, etc.). They cite the work of Paris (2005) that shows that different developmental patterns may result as a function of the constraints of measurement tools. In other words, the choice of skill measurements may directly affect the pattern of outcomes measured over time. As Pfost et al. (p. 232) state: "[T]his particularly comprises measures of prereading skills such as letter-naming tasks, concepts about print, and so forth as well as measures of decoding accuracy due to their measurement restrictions (e.g., the percentage of reading errors is a highly skewed distribution with many students achieving zero errors). . . . Just one single result was found showing a Matthew effect in reading when it was based on measures of decoding accuracy or prereading skills, whereas a compensatory pattern [catching up pattern] was found five times." However, no studies from low-income countries were included in the Pfost analysis.
11. On universal counting skills, see Gelman and Gallistel (1978), Ginsburg et al. (1998), and Baroody and Dowker (2003). Also see some cultural variations in the work of Miller et al. (1995). A recent study of 10- to 18-year-olds in Bangladesh, however, found that the increase in mathematics learning in school was far below curricular expectations (Asadullah & Chaudhury, 2015).
12. For the Brazil research, see Schliemann et al. (1998). Earlier ethnographic math learning research was done in Papua New Guinea in the 1990s; see Saxe and de Kirby (2014). More recent work has been undertaken by Sitabkhan (2015) on marketplace learning of math and economic skills.
13. As noted in this chapter, mother-tongue and local language policies are becoming more popular in developing countries. However, relatively few local/indigenous languages have the complex terminology available for mathematics, so teachers are

more likely to teach it in English, French, or Arabic, when the concepts might be not be available in the local language. This can cause serious confusion in the instruction of mathematics in multilingual contexts. Thanks to B. Piper (personal communication) for this observation.

14. See Wagner (1983a), on rote memorization and reading, and also Chapter 7. For work on Early Grade Mathematics Assessment (EGMA), see Rubens and Crouch (2009), Nag et al. (2014), and RTI/USAID (2012); also see www.eddataglobal.org/documents/index.cfm?fuseaction=showdir&ruid=5&statusID=3. Mathematics instruction accounts for nearly 20% of weekly time in grades 1 through 5; this is less than reading, but still significant (Benavot, 2008). See Mayer (2002) for a review of rote learning in teaching and assessments in the United States.

15. Pritchett and Beatty (2012). See Uwezo (2014) for a description of difficulties in math learning in Ugandan classrooms.

16. Downing (1966, 1973). For comparative research on the orthographies of European languages, see Seymour et al. (2003).

17. This was followed and importantly expanded by Chall (1983). Mastery of the spoken language is a typical prerequisite for fluent reading comprehension in a language, although many exceptions exist. The issue of reading acquisition has been the subject of what was called a "great debate" in the United States (in particular), with specific abilities (such as the "phonics" approach to decoding of text) thought by some to be at the center of cognitive growth in reading. Research reviews have generally provided support for a more phonics- and skill-based approach to literacy acquisition as an optimal pathway for children's reading in alphabetic scripts (National Reading Panel, 2000; Snow et al., 1998; Snow & Kang, 2006; August & Shanahan, 2006). Additional support for this perspective has come from a variety of other languages, such as Spanish (Dickenson et al., 2004), Turkish (Oney & Durgunoglu, 1997), and Arabic (Abu-Rabia & Siegel, 2002). However, this empirical conclusion does not undermine the importance of cultural variables; rather, when these can be controlled within, say, a homogeneous sample of learners, phonics skill learning proves to be a crucial part of school-based instruction.

18. Kamil et al. (2000).

19. A recent Google search of scholarly publications in the field of reading/literacy reveals more than two million articles, books, and chapters. The vast majority of these are largely contained within a dozen major languages of the world. This statistic would leave the remaining 2,000 to 3,000 languages most commonly used with little research as to how reading is acquired or utilized. See further discussion about the imbalance of culturally appropriate research methodologies in Chapter 11.

20. In the area of reading disabilities, the work of Dynamic Measurement Group (2008) with the advent of DIBELS, a measurement tool, has had an international impact.

21. Wagner (1993) in Morocco; and in a later review, Wagner (2011a).

22. See www.usaid.gov/news-information/press-releases/feb-3-2015-all-children-reading-grand-challenge-development-announces-round-2.

23. For a review, see Dubeck and Gove (2015), in which there is also useful discussion of the possible misuse and misinterpretation of the EGRA instrument. For the current EGRA assessment instruments, see: http://static1.squarespace.com/static/55c4e56fe4b0852b09fa2f29/t/56e0633545bf213c2b5269e5/1457546040584/EGRA+Toolkit+Second+Edition_March_8_2016+.pdf. Also see the work of Save the Children's "Literacy Boost" approach in Dowd (2011) and Dowd et al. (2017).

24. See Gove and Cvelich (2011, p. 5). It should be noted that these domains or stages are somewhat arbitrary; as with stage theories discussed in Chapter 2, the components of one stage can be incomplete or overlap with another stage. However, one gets a sense from such stages of what to expect a child to achieve at certain points, even though there may be important variations by culture, language, and context.

25. No assessment is perfect, and EGRA has its critics, mainly among those who view (with some justification) strictly timed tests as much too narrowly constrained to be useful for teaching purposes. One of EGRA's limitations is that each subskill is measured on the number of letters, for example, that a child can identify in 60 seconds; yet one usually does not know which letters they find difficult to learn, or if this disaggregation would be helpful for teaching. The point is that teachers and researchers are limited in what they can glean from the data using EGRA. See Bartlett et al. (2015) for other critiques. Thanks to E. Friedlander for his comments on this matter.

26. Dubeck and Gove (2015, p. 6).

27. Piper et al. (2014). This intervention consisted of the following inputs to a quality improvement program aimed at grade 1 and 2 teachers in formal government and low-cost, non-formal private schools serving slum communities (p. 14): "The literacy arm of the program included 150 structured lessons in both Kiswahili and English. The design of the program allowed pupils to learn letter sounds in Kiswahili before the English letters, so that in English, teachers could point out which letters sounded similar to or different from Kiswahili. Teachers received modest instructional aids, including pocket charts and flashcards with letters on them, and students received low-cost student books that aligned with the scripted lessons." When USAID-funded and UK (Department for International Development)-funded work was combined, a total of 1,384 primary schools were in the Primary Mathematics and Reading (PRIMR) project. Also, a key dimension of the PRIMR project is that the training and classroom support was done by the government officers so that any effect of the intervention identified in the pilot work could plausibly be thought to continue in a similar magnitude when done at larger scale (B. Piper, personal communication).

28. While the effects on reading comprehension were roughly equivalent for Kiswahili and English, gains were somewhat higher than expected for English, and especially in the private non-formal schools. In this study, it would have been helpful to know the degree to which students spoke Kiswahili as a mother-tongue language or as a second language.

29. In the international work using EGRA, positive outcomes (e.g., moving from one to five words per minute on an oral reading fluency test to, say, 30 words per minute) may not only be statistically significant, but may also have a large effect size, indicating a substantial difference in mean scores. However, the credibility of this large impact also depends on the nature of the assessment itself. EGRA's use of fluency (correct words per minute) seems to be a highly malleable score, especially since many children in poor communities perform so poorly at the outset of using this measure. With other measures, such as reading comprehension, the research evidence suggests a much longer gradient to achieve a high effect size. See Paris and Paris (2006) for an overview of reading measurement trajectories. A related critique of EGRA concerns the prevalence of "floor effects" on statistical results, especially on correlations between key variables; see Hoffman (2012), who also provides a broad-based critique of EGRA's use in low-income countries.

30. There are other types of "thermometers" to measure reading levels at the low end of the spectrum, sometimes called "citizen-led assessments." See Chapter 11 for more detail on these assessments and their limitations.

31. The demographics on language skills of children and that of their classroom are very difficult to verify internationally, since neither governments nor international agencies have made this a priority. However, there is a growing body of in-depth ethnographic accounts, such as Hornberger (2003, Hornberger & Vaish (2009); see also the earlier discussion of ethnicity and language in Chapter 3, and the story of Illa in highland Peru in Chapter 4.

32. See Chapter 4.

33. See discussion in Chapter 1 on colonial and post-colonial education.

34. Ladson-Billings (1995); Osborne (1996); Valdiviezo (2013).
35. Hélot and Laoire (2011); Hornberger (2003).
36. Ball (2010); Ball et al. (2014); Canagarajah (2005); Benson (2004); Trudell (2016).
37. See useful overviews, see Pflepsen (2015) and Smits et al. (2008).
38. As in many countries, the trajectory of language choice may vary across levels of education. In Morocco, for example, French is widely used in secondary and higher education. In South Africa, English and (to a lesser extent) Afrikaans are used in secondary and higher education; there is a continuing devaluation of indigenous languages in South Africa when compared to English and Afrikaans (Tshotsho, 2013).
39. See Mufanechiya and Mufanechiya (2011) for the case of Zimbabwean junior primary schools. Also, Piper et al. (2016) found substantial resistance from communities and teachers to mother-tongue instruction in Kenyan primary schools.
40. Modern standard Arabic was chosen for schools, rather than the Moroccan dialect, spoken by most Moroccans.
41. See earlier discussion on Amazigh in Chapter 3.
42. French was the official language of the French colonial protectorate. Spanish was also used in some areas of northern Morocco that were controlled by Spain.
43. See Wagner et al. (1989); the explanation for this particular case example was that the Amazigh-speaking children also attended Quranic schools taught in Arabic that gave them an early start on the language.
44. See Cummins et al. (1984) on early work in this area, and later, Bialystok et al. (2005). Also see Koda and Reddy (2008) for a more nuanced approach that differentiates transfer through specific components that appear most liable to transfer.
45. Research in the Philippines showed that children taught through their mother-tongue scored higher in both mathematics and English than comparison classes in which the children were taught in a second language (either English or Filipino; Walter & Dekker, 2011), while a separate study found that grade 1 children who were taught science in a familiar language made fewer content errors overall, and transferred their knowledge to perform on par with English-instructed peers when tested in English. For a helpful review on mother-tongue and second language education in African countries, see Heugh (2006).
46. One area of current debate in sub-Saharan Africa is centered on whether pupils need three versus six (or other) years of primary schooling in L1 to benefit from transfer to L2. See Alidou et al. (2006). There is little consensus on this issue as yet. Recent reviews on language of instruction may be seen in Benson and Wong (2015) and Peyton (2015).
47. In Morocco, many children speak Amazigh at home, speak Arabic in primary school, and must learn French in secondary school; in Kenya, there are multiple local languages spoken at home, Kiswahili in primary school, and largely English in post-primary education. With the additional social, political, and cognitive dimensions, adding a third language to policy decisions makes the planning issues even more complicated. Of course, with a globalizing world, focusing only on the challenges of learning in a first, second, or third language is to miss out on the huge opportunities (indeed, necessities) of learning multiple languages, where multilingual interactions are increasingly important (including digitally). In wealthier contexts, such multilingualism is often encouraged. One of the ironies, as is apparent in the present discussion, is how multiple languages can negatively impact the learning of poor children, while positively enhancing the lives of children in well-off educational contexts.
48. See discussion in Bernhardt (2005) and Valdiviezo (2013) on ethnographic approaches in Peru.
49. In Platas et al. (2016), the EGMA assessment was used with children in grades 3 and 4. As noted in the text, performance on word problems was higher in the local language L1 (Saamaka), most likely because they could better understand the problems in mother-tongue rather than in L2 (Dutch).

50. Taylor and Coetzee (2013).
51. Eriksson (2014). The author cautions however that: "[I]t seems that mother-tongue instruction in this context might have had positive effects on school quality as evidenced through the increases in literacy of men and women. This cannot be disentangled from the relative benefits of teaching in English versus teaching English as a subject, as was done after the reform. The estimates presented in this paper most likely overstate the effects of simply changing the language of instruction, since they include effects on instructional quality and the ability of parents to help their children with homework" (p. 334).
52. See Lesaux and Geva (2006), Lesaux et al. (2006), and Koda (2007).
53. There is evidence to suggest that when some children try to read too quickly, especially in L2, their comprehension declines markedly. Some teachers trained in the EGRA reading assessments feel obliged to focus on number of words read correctly in a minute (the main test for reading fluency). In other words, the EGRA inherently emphasizes reading speed, as noted; see Crosson et al. (2008) and Droop and Verhoeven (1998). See also Crosson and Lesaux (2010) on the importance of text-reading fluency for language minority (L2) learners reading in English, implying possible limits to the application of the EGRA fluency measure when applied to second language learners. Some evidence (from the RTI EGRA Barometer, http://www.earlygradereadingbarometer.org/files/EarlyGradeReading-Barometer.pdf) from children in the Philippines, when comparing Tagalog (L1) and English (L2) speakers in EGRA showed the following results: ORF is more highly correlated with comprehension in L1 than in L2, suggesting that using EGRA in L2 is a less useful both for measurement and instruction. More recently, research has shown that many children can comprehend text even at fluency rates that are much lower than the Western norms (Dowd et al., 2016); see further discussion in Chapter 11.
54. These models mainly refer to oral language skills. They do not take into account issues of emergent reading, nor the differentiation that exists between different orthographies. Thanks to B. Piper (personal communication) for his observation on this point.
55. This is a very common situation in multilingual developing countries. Piper and Miksic (2011) found that when teachers have a strong capacity to teach language well, learning is improved. But, as with the Wagner et al. (1989) study in Morocco, Piper and Miksic (2011, p. 36) found in Kenya and Uganda that: "The cross-national analysis does not seem to support the notion that more mother-tongue instruction automatically leads to higher outcomes on assessments carried out in the mother-tongue. Neither does it offer evidence that reading skills in the mother-tongue automatically transfer over into efficient reading outcomes in English, as some mother-tongue advocates argue."
56. See Ball et al. (2014); also, Muthwii (2004) in Kenya and Uganda; and Commeyras and Inyega (2007) in Kenya.
57. Of course, issues related to teachers' ability to implement a given curriculum are not restricted to issues of language, as discussed further in relation to teacher preparedness in Chapter 8. In a recent report on the Kenya PRIMR project mentioned earlier, Piper et al. (2016) found positive results for teaching in mother-tongue on reading in mother-tongue, but they also noted that mother-tongue instruction did not seem to improve learning outcomes in English or other subjects. In other words, the transfer issue remains illusive, though see one ICT-based study on the transfer issue in South Africa (Castillo, 2017). A major concern in the Kenya research was the apparent resistance of teachers to the use of mother-tongue rather than Swahili or English, both of which were viewed by teachers as more "progressive." See further discussion of implementation science in Chapter 11.
58. See Chapter 8 for more on this point.

59. Maamouri (1998). Linguistic insecurity also appears in children's insufficient mastery of the classroom language, as described by Boukous and Institute Royal de la Culture Amazighe (Rabat) (2012, p. 182).
60. Hornberger and Chick (2001). This is not unlike the earlier example where the curriculum exceeds the skill level of the child, but is defended because the teacher "followed the curriculum."
61. See Chapter 8 for further discussion of rote learning.
62. Good bilingual education programs can also result in cost efficiencies (e.g., Patrinos & Velez, 2009).
63. Studies on the role of textbooks cannot be easily separated from the question of language of instruction (see Chapter 7); thus, some studies have found little impact of textbooks; see Glewwe et al. (2007), Kremer et al. (2013), and Kuecken and Valfort (2013). Also, see Braslavsky (2006). The problem of predicting the impact of a single factor, such as textbooks, is that it leads to further questions about how measurements are done, and the baselines for data collected. Still, it seems, as evidence suggests, that appropriately developed textbooks in the child's language of literacy would have positive consequences.
64. UNESCO-Pole de Dakar (2014, p. 215).
65. Based on reported data in UNESCO (2016b).
66. See discussion of new efforts to expand locally published textbooks (UNESCO, 2016b), and see https://en.unesco.org/gem-report/sites/gem-report/files/References%20 Textbooks%202016.pdf. Also see the Global Book Alliance, http://globalbookalliance. org. Textbook policies also need to reduce inefficiencies and centralize the production chain so that larger print runs can achieve lower prices per book.
67. Literacy ecology has also been called "literate environment," though the latter term tends to refer mainly to written materials. For example, Easton (2014, p. 33) states, citing UNESCO, that "a rich literate environment is a public or private milieu with abundant written documents (e.g. books, magazines, newspapers), visual materials (e.g. signs, posters, handbills), or communication and electronic media (e.g. radios, televisions, computers, mobile phones). Whether in households, neighborhoods, schools or workplaces, the quality of literate environments affects how literacy skills are acquired and practiced."
68. Elley (2000). Book floods were implemented at a time when the use of mother-tongue for instruction and for book publishing was just beginning. Thus, their impact seems to have been modest, and was not rigorously evaluated.
69. Among NGOs in this area working to support libraries, see the work of Room to Read, www.roomtoread.org.
70. UNESCO (2005, p. 208).
71. As pointed out by Kellaghan et al. (2009, p. 42): "Although access to books may be important, student learning is likely affected not directly by the availability of books but by characteristics of an environment that cherishes books, such as one in which parents place a high value on scholastic achievement, provide academic guidance and support for children, stimulate children to explore and discuss ideas and events, and set high standards and expectations for school achievement." See earlier meta-analysis study by Snow et al. (1998).
72. Friedlander and Goldenberg (2016, pp. 19–20); community support in this study primarily included reading activities such as "reading camps" that were village-based gatherings for children and "story time," which involved villagers telling stories to children. See also Friedlander (2015).
73. United Nations (2015a). These data are likely to be underestimated due to the dramatic increase in both internal and external migration (see Chapter 10).
74. UNESCO (2015a, p. 7) is a source for out-of-school numbers of lower secondary school age. There are also serious measurement issues on "out-of-school" statistics.

Carr-Hill (2012, 2013) points out that calculations need to include children who may be: employed by rich families as servants; moving around as part of mobile (migrant) populations; homeless; and in institutions (e.g., refugee camps, religious orders, etc.).

75. See earlier section on this topic, and also Chapter 6. See also the increase in low-cost private schools, as discussed in Chapter 7.

76. Thanks to C. J. Daswani for his early insights on this issue in rural India (Daswani, 2001). In the Rwanda study of Friedlander and Goldenberg (2016) described earlier, students who were tracked over two years were found to have annual repetition rates of as high as 44% in primary grades 1 and 2.

77. For an analysis from early childhood to primary school departure, see Crouch (2015).

78. Jukes et al. (2016). The dropout rate for intervention schools in Kenya in the control group was 5.3%, and in the intervention group it fell to 2.1%.

6

YOUTH AND ADULT LEARNING

Beyond the Classroom

Zeynep and Azra: Women's Literacy in Turkey[1]

In a quiet village in Gümüşhane Province in northeastern Turkey, a group of women are chatting in the sunshine of a late winter afternoon. The town's primary school is visible through the trees in the distance. School is over for the day and the children have come home, abandoning their books and bags to play outside. Zeynep (a university doctoral student researcher) approaches the group of women, who have been waiting for their children to get out of class. She sits down next to Azra, a woman of about 30, who she has met during a previous visit to the village and asks her about her daughter, who is ten years old and in grade 4 at the local school. When Zeynep asks Azra how her daughter is doing at school, Azra replies that she doesn't really know, other than that she seems to like school and does her homework early each evening. She says that since she sends her daughter to school, she assumes she must be learning. Zeynep then calls over to Azra's daughter to join them. Zeynep asks the daughter if she can read from the school storybook that she's carrying. As she stares at a page of the book, it's immediately apparent that the young girl is unable to read.

Once the girl resumes playing with her friends, Zeynep asks Azra if she was aware that her daughter isn't able to read her schoolbook. Azra, slightly irritated, asks how it is she could know whether her daughter is able to read since she herself had never learned. Zeynep then asks whether Azra would know if her daughter was ill—to which Azra responds that, yes, of course she'd know that because "all mothers know when their child is sick." Azra continues by saying that she feels her daughter's head to see if she has a fever—if her head is hot then she knows that her child is sick, and if the fever doesn't go down in a couple of days, she would take her to see the doctor.

At the risk of offending Azra, Zeynep asks: "Why is it that you know exactly what to do when your daughter has a fever, but when it comes to what she is learning in school you don't know?" Azra is ready with her answer. She says that some mothers do know how their children are doing because they've attended the local women's literacy program in the neighboring village and they can now read. With obvious regret, Azra continues, "I have to leave it to the teacher to teach my daughter. Someday, I hope that both my daughter and I will be able to read together."

___

Every person should have the right to *lifelong learning*, as stated in the UN SDG #4. For youth and adults in developing countries, this often refers to education outside of, or in addition to, public schools. Such programs may cater to young mothers like Azra in Gümüşhane Province, or to youth and adults in or out of the workforce. In Chapter 3, these were termed non-formal education programs. Though they consume only a small fraction of national educational resources, such programs fill an important gap in educational support for the poor and educationally disadvantaged. Such efforts not only improve the overall education, skills, and engagment of a country's citizens, but also, as in Zeynep's observations, impact society as a whole.

As noted earlier, many millions of children drop out of school, and there are many adults who have never gone to school. This has led to current renewed emphasis on youth and adult non-formal education programs. According to a UNESCO global report, among the 49 countries with data, adults (classified as people over 15 years of age) made up 4% of those enrolled at the primary education level, with the highest levels in Thailand (5.2%), Brazil (5.3%), and India (6.5%), where a total of more than nine million adults were enrolled in such programs.[2] A Latin American regional survey (see Figure 6.1) found

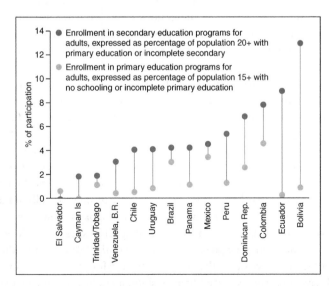

FIGURE 6.1 Adult Participation Rate in Primary and Secondary Education Programs as Percentage of the Population Without the Respective Qualifications, Selected Latin American and Caribbean Countries, 2010

Source: UNESCO (2016a, p. 237)

that in Mexico, 3.5% of adults with less than a primary education participated in adult primary school completion programs that include employment skills and citizenship training. In Bolivia, 13% of adults with less than a secondary school education participated in secondary school completion programs, typically comprised of vocational training and a qualification employment certificate. Though non-formal education programs represent only a small part of most national education systems, they tend to focus primarily on marginalized populations, making these programs ever more important for accomplishing the SDGs.

In this chapter, we explore the two main types of non-formal education programs for out-of-school populations: adult literacy programs that teach basic skills to those who have had little or no schooling, and youth education programs that are often tied to vocational and technical skills. Subsequently, we review programs that are embedded in the agriculture and health sectors as well as those oriented toward employment skills and "21st-century" skills.[3]

Literacy, Adult Education, and Empowerment

Typically, we think of literacy as the core cognitive achievement of what children acquire over the course of their formal education. Yet, over the centuries, literacy was often transmitted outside of what we now call formal schooling.[4] As early as the 16th century, reading was widespread within homes in Sweden as a function of family and church efforts to teach the Bible. In 19th-century Liberia, the Vai people created an indigenous script and have used it ever since for written communication.[5] Likewise, the Native American Cree of Northern Canada maintain the use of their syllabic script as a source of cultural identity.[6]

These several examples point to the fact that literacy (seen more broadly than the narrower confines of reading acquisition discussed in the previous chapter) is a cultural phenomenon that is practiced in a wide variety of contexts. Thus, while children are taught to read in classrooms today, achievement levels are often determined as much by out-of-school factors (such as the country's language policy and parents' education) as they are by in-school factors (such as teacher training or textbook quality). In-depth explorations in Morocco, Iran, and Liberia have shown, for example, that literacy and its practices can only be fully understood in relation to how (and how many) languages are spoken, how they are used, and how written language fits with its use in specific societies.[7] More spoken languages become written languages each year, with the related scripts, dictionaries, textbooks, and newspapers that support them. More individuals throughout the world have increasingly varied literacy skills, including a dramatic expansion in the use of new information technologies (see Chapter 9). The world is no longer a place, as it was in colonial times, where a small literate elite dominates the unschooled, illiterate masses. Today's world has multiple "literacies" and many types of competencies.[8]

Further, even though there are today relatively few illiterates (i.e., those who know nothing about scripts, numbers or reading), there are many individuals with limited literacy skills, such that their own governments might list them as illiterate for census purposes. International agencies have long been concerned about literacy from an economic productivity perspective, as noted in Chapter 1. In order to create worldwide statistical comparisons, UN agencies have relied primarily on data provided by their member countries. According to the most recent UNESCO statistics, world literacy rates have been increasing slowly over the last several decades, mainly due to the growth in primary school enrollment (see Table 6.1). It was once assumed that intensified efforts to achieve universal primary schooling would lead to a major decline in adult illiteracy around the world, but population growth and the poor quality of many schools (as noted in the previous chapter), have continued to fill the global ranks of the low-literate or illiterate youth and adult populations.

The term *literacy* typically connotes the ability to read and write, though some specialists would add basic math and digital skills to that list. Where major definitional debates about literacy continue, they often concern which specific abilities count most, and what levels should be defined as standards in a given society. While working in Zimbabwe early in my career, I was informed that the government defined a citizen as "literate" if he or she could recite a few lines from one of President Robert Mugabe's speeches to the nation. Perhaps this story was only anecdotal rather than official (I never found out for certain), but it gives a sense of the diversity of measures (or half-measures) that characterized some of the findings on literacy rates in various countries.

According to UNESCO, which has devoted substantial resources to promoting literacy, "a person is functionally literate when he has acquired the knowledge and skills in reading and writing which enable him to engage effectively in all those activities in which literacy is normally assumed in his culture or group."[9] While functional literacy has appeal because of its implied appropriateness to a given cultural context, the term is inadequately defined for measurement purposes. For example, it is unclear in an industrialized nation like the United States what level of literacy should be required of all citizens: does a coal miner have functionally different literacy needs than a lawyer? Similarly, in a developing country, at what level does an illiterate woman, as in Azra's case discussed earlier, need to learn to read and write in order to take on meaningful roles in her village, including being able to know whether her daughter is learning to read in school?

Not all literacy programs achieve their initially intended goals. In one in-depth study in Mali, research was undertaken to measure the outcomes of an

TABLE 6.1 Adult Literacy, 1985–2011

	Illiterate Adults		Women		Adult Literacy Rates Total		Gender Parity Index	
	Total							
	2005–2011 (000)	Change since 1985–1994 (%)	1985–1994 (%)	2005–2011 (%)	1985–1994 (%)	2005–2011 (%)	1985–1994 (F/M)	2005–2011 (F/M)
World	**773 549**	**-12**	**63**	**64**	**76**	**84**	**0.85**	**0.90**
Low-Income Countries	183 552	23	60	60	51	61	0.69	0.79
Lower-Middle-Income Countries	470 164	2	61	65	59	71	0.71	0.78
Upper-Middle-Income Countries	112 671	-57	67	67	82	94	0.86	0.96
High-Income Countries	: :	: :	: :	: :	: :	: :	: :	: :
Sub-Saharan Africa	181 950	37	62	61	53	59	0.68	0.74
Arab States	47 603	-8	63	66	55	77	0.62	0.81
Central Asia	290	-69	77	63	98	100	0.98	1.00
East Asia and the Pacific	89 478	-61	69	71	82	95	0.84	0.95
South and West Asia	407 021	2	60	64	47	63	0.57	0.70
Latin America and the Caribbean	35 614	-16	55	55	86	92	0.97	0.99
North America and Western Europe	: :	: :	: :	: :	: :	: :	: :	: :
Central and Eastern Europe	4 919	-59	79	78	96	99	0.96	0.99

Note: Data are for the most recent year available during the period specified. Gender parity is reached when the gender parity index is between 0.97 and 1.03.

Source: UNESCO (2014a, p. 70)

adult literacy education program for illiterate women in four rural villages.[10] Data were collected through interviews with women learners, home observations, literacy class observations, as well as through reading assessments. It turned out, after a six-month intervention, that very few women had learned how to read and write. However, the women in the literacy program were strongly influenced by the social organization of the program, which gave them time to leave their homes (and some of the drudgery of domestic work), engage in activities without their husbands' supervision, and form new types of social relationships with their non-familial peers. This adult literacy program did not achieve its stated goal of teaching literacy skills for subsequent economic productivity, but it did lead to something just as important, many would argue—the empowerment of women in their own life circumstances.

Paulo Freire, referenced in Chapter 1, is one of the best-known educators associated with literacy, and he, too, was interested in empowerment.[11] He served as a state minister of education in Brazil but is probably best known for his book *Pedagogy of the Oppressed*. Freire proposed that consciousness raising was not only the optimal form of adult learning but could also support social and economic goals (see Box 6.1). His views were proudly ideological. It was a stance in opposition to what Freire derisively called the Western "banking" pedagogy— the mere collection and storage of information found in books and in schools, rather than critical thinking. His conceptual approach to literacy, popular in post-revolutionary environments, was adopted by national campaigns in Cuba, Nicaragua, and Mozambique.[12]

Over time, Freire adapted his vision of educational liberation theology in order to grapple with the dynamics of changing economies worldwide. For most of his career, Freire vociferously supported the importance of mother-tongue instruction in adult literacy programs. Yet, in his later years, and after work in Guinea Bissau, Freire changed into an advocate for the use of Portuguese as the national (though L2) language of instruction, so that national coherence and economic development could be advanced. Thus, in the face of unemployment, aggressive downsizing and outsourcing, globalization, and the impact of

BOX 6.1 PAULO FREIRE ON ADULT EDUCATION

Education either functions as an instrument which is used to facilitate integration of the younger generation into the logic of the present system and bring about conformity or it becomes the practice of freedom, the means by which men and women deal critically and creatively with reality and discover how to participate in the transformation of their world.

—Paulo Freire, *Pedagogy of the Oppressed* (1972/1996)

climate change, the pressures on the poor to be more skilled led to a waning of Freire's original approach and growth in the establishment of more job-oriented, non-formal education programs discussed in this chapter. As we will see, there remain very serious questions about which skills are adequate and can be taught to assure employment, whether in wealthy countries or poor countries. Even so, Freire deservedly earned a reputation as a champion of literacy programs and human rights.

The adult literacy education movement is longstanding, and is directly part of the SDGs.[13] In 1995 the first International Adult Literacy Survey was published, surprising many lawmakers and the public by showing that large numbers (perhaps as high as 25% or more) of adults in industrialized countries like Great Britain, Germany, and the United States had inadequate literacy skills.[14] The advent of adult literacy skills assessments went a long way toward dispelling the notion that industrialized countries were fully literate, and therefore superior (in terms of educated citizenry) to other countries in the world. More recent surveys, such as one conducted by the OECD in 2013, showed similar trends (see Figure 6.2). Among other results, it was determined that about one-quarter of the national literacy averages in OECD countries were in the lower two skill levels (Levels 0–2

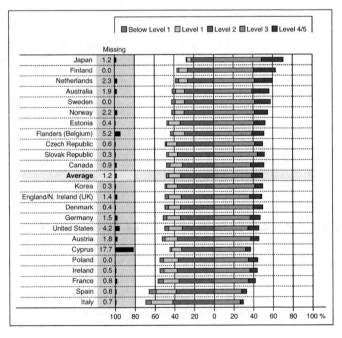

FIGURE 6.2 Literacy Proficiency Rates in Selected OECD Countries in the PIAAC

Source: OECD (2013, p. 9)

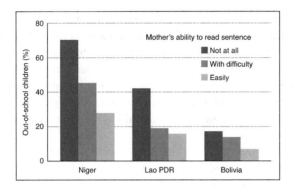

FIGURE 6.3 Mother's Literacy and Schooling Status in the Niger, the Lao PDR, and Bolivia, 2000

Source: UNESCO (2005, p. 130)

out of 5), though setting precise benchmarks for what it means to be literate remains contentious.[15]

Researchers have also attempted to investigate how adult literacy is related to social and economic outcomes. To take one example, multiple studies have confirmed the important role of a mother's literacy in the academic success of her children. Indeed, maternal education has been shown to be one of the most powerful determinants of how long children remain in school—as may be seen in countries like Niger, Laos, and Bolivia (Figure 6.3).[16] As with Azra in the opening vignette, it is not clear how a mother actually transmits skills, attitudes, and values to her children if she herself is poorly schooled and functionally illiterate. Yet, even in Azra's village, it seemed obvious that literate mothers have a better grasp on their children's progress in school, and probably a more expansive (and more optimistic) sense of life's opportunities.

Youth Education Programs

As described earlier, learning occurs through diverse practices and contexts over the life span. For young people, especially those who are not in school, achieving employment and self-development often requires alternative means of instruction. And nearly all countries have non-formal and informal programs that provide such assistance.[17] Most of these are designed for people between 10 and 20 years of age, and they tend to take three forms described next.[18]

Compensatory programs help to make up for inadequate or missed learning experiences in school. These are often community-based programs that help children and youth with limited or no access to government-provided schooling obtain educational outcomes equivalent to students in regular public schools. In many countries, these programs are designed for those who may have dropped out of primary or secondary school but wish to improve their skills (usually reading and math). Some are then able to re-enter school in order to obtain their primary or secondary certificates. One well-known example is that of the "bridge" programs in India, where students are supported by educational NGOs with government financing, in order to learn about computers and technology.[19] For children with disabilities, compensatory programs are designed to eliminate exclusionary educational practices and discriminatory attitudes.

Complementary programs provide enrichment beyond schooling, such as after-school or supplementary programs.[20] These add value to formal education, and the number of such complementary programs is on the rise. Many parents employ the latter to help ensure that their children will be able to pass the often rigorous examinations for entry into secondary or tertiary education. India and Pakistan are two countries in which tutoring has grown rapidly across ages and all income strata (Table 6.2), for example. A variant of complementary programs is termed "shadow education"—which refers to supplemental learning opportunities for children and youth in after-school or weekend programs. In South Korea, this includes "cram" after-school programs, individual tutoring, group tutoring, home-visit corresponding courses, and more recently, Internet-based tutoring.[21]

TABLE 6.2 Proportions of Children Age 3–16 Years Receiving Private Tutoring by Income Quintile, Rural India (2007–2008) and Rural Pakistan (2010)

Income Quintile	Proportion of Children Receiving Tutoring	Expenditure on Tutoring per Child (Indian/Pakistani Rupees per Month)
India		
1 = poorest	18.1	68.9
2	20.0	70.4
3	21.1	72.8
4	25.2	75.5
5 = richest	31.8	90.2
Pakistan		
1 = poorest	5.5	287
2	9.6	233
3	14.0	241
4	19.9	292
5 = richest	27.6	352

Source: Bray and Lykins, (2012, p. 15)

Alternative schooling refers to multigrade schools, mobile classrooms, and new online distance education classes. The methods for delivery are typically adapted to the specific needs of the learners. Multigrade schools often exist in rural and sparcely populated areas where students of varying ages and grades share the same instructor and classroom. Mobile classrooms are those that are organized around populations that are engaged in seasonal migration (such as nomads) or those who may be refugees.[22] Online schools and programs have begun to spring up where affordable broadband Internet is becoming available.[23]

In sum, the demand for learning beyond the school walls will continue to grow, driven by parents who wish to have their children receive a formal school certificate or degree, or enrich their children's education more generally. This trend is facilitated on the supply side by multiple stakeholders trying to promote new venues for learning. However, beyond education ministries, there are numerous initatives in other sectors—such as agriculture and health—that seek to promote learning through non-formal education.

Learning and Agriculture

Agriculture is a critical economic activity in every society—to put it simply, people need to eat. Roughly 20% of the world's population remains directly engaged in farming, but across individual countries the percentage of the population that farms varies widely. Only about 2% of the working population in the United States is involved in farming, while the figure exceeds 50% in India and varies between 30% and 70% in most of the world's low-income countries.[24]

Policymakers have often asked whether farmers in low-income countries would be more productive if they had more education. Research addressing this question has accumulated in recent years, and shows that indeed they do. In Kenya, for example, it was found that unschooled farmers' lack of literacy skills inhibited their effective use of fertilizers.[25] Another study, undertaken in Malawi, found that unschooled farmers are often unable to accumulate savings due to unpredictable expenses caused by weather and other factors; yet when such farmers were required to have savings accounts, they were better able to save for the planting season and generate more profits. Additional research in Tamil Nadu (India) similarly found that uneducated, low-income sugarcane farmers made substandard investment decisions during the so-called "high-stress" harvest season.[26] The general implication of such findings is that education (which was used as a proxy for learning[27]) is an important way to enhance farmers' productivity.

Literacy skills appear to offer farmers an increased capability to accomplish tasks like decoding labels on fertilizers and comparing prices. Research has shown that such skills also lead to the adoption of new, more sustainable farming technologies, such as organic fertilizers and enhanced water conservation methods.[28] In a comparative study in Cambodia, Egypt, and Ethiopia, researchers found that farmers who observed agricultural extension workers in the field showed improved productivity.[29] Finally, in a large-scale study of critical thinking skills, farmers with more schooling could better weigh the pros and cons of various decisions, and which crops to plant to optimize output.[30] Such abilities were found to be related to a growth in agricultural productivity of over 3% per annum.[31] In sum, farmers in low-income countries appear more productive if they have been to school.[32]

Over the years, and given the above evidence, various approaches have been proposed in order to boost the knowledge and skills of farmers. One of the most prominent is a non-formal education program called the Farmer Field Schools, where groups of volunteer farmers participate in hands-on activities that try to solve agricultural problems pertinent to local culture and geography.[33] This program, which is active in 27 African countries, consists of workshops in which farmers work on developing technical skills and feelings of self-empowerment (reminiscent of Freire's literacy work described earlier). The topics include how to take collective action in marketing produce, or how to elect leaders to represent farmers at larger convocations. Research on learning in Farmer Field Schools in Tanzania, Kenya, and Uganda has demonstrated a significant increase in both productivity and the farmers' sense of self-improvement.[34]

Learning and Health

Whether in wealthy or low-income countries, it is widely understood that higher GNP per capita is a strong predictor of better health, lower infant and maternal mortality, and improved access to quality medical care.[35] But to what degree do learning and literacy contribute to good health?

One of the most comprehensive and systematic reviews—covering more than 3,000 studies in the United States—found that low literacy skills were directly related to adverse medical outcomes.[36] Elsewhere, the findings are roughly the same. In India, researchers found that literacy produced stronger effects on improved health outcomes than did levels of household income.[37] More broadly, research has found that maternal education has especially strong impacts on children's health, such as a consistent decline in under-five mortality rates for each additional year of a mother's education (see Figure 6.4).

Yet, despite a growing body of evidence documenting the positive effects of education on health, the mechanisms by which this happens has remained unclear. What is it about a mother's education level that leads to better health outcomes? Possible explanatory variables include: more informed communication; improved critical thinking skills; a greater sense of empowerment (assuming a greater role in household decision making); improved knowledge of modern medical practices; or attitudinal changes from fatalism (believing that an illness is predestined) to greater rationalism (understanding the role of modern medicine). One multi-year study—conducted in Mexico, Nepal, Venezuela, and Zambia—found compelling evidence that maternal education led to communication and literacy skills that

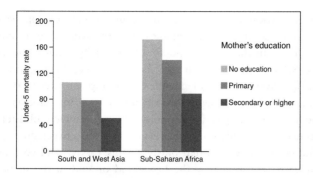

FIGURE 6.4 Under-Five Mortality Rate, Regional Weighted Average, by Mother's Education, 2004–2009

Source: UNESCO (2011, p. 35)

improved both mothers' understanding of key health messages and health outcomes among their children.[38]

Overall, research supports the claim that gains in learning and literacy have a positive impact on health outcomes for adults and their children. There is a strong likelihood that helping mothers' literacy skills, in particular, is a useful investment for improving health outcomes in children.[39]

Learning and Employment

Youth and adult learning (often measured by economists in terms of years of schooling attained) is thought to be the key to future employment. Indeed, this view is largely taken as axiomatic by economists and major international agencies as well as by national governments. And, a substantial body of data supports this belief, as discussed in Chapter 2. Even with this broad relationship confirmed in many countries, the actual degree of the correlation between schooling, skills, and employment can vary significantly by country.[40] In one recent study, for example, it was found that in Chile the attainment of a university degree was nearly twice as important to enter the workforce as it was in Argentina.[41]

However, many policymakers worry that the kinds of skills that young people learn—including those made available at considerable cost in secondary schools—may not guarantee improved income in the long run.[42] For one thing, there is a growing global "disconnect" between educational attainment on the one hand, and employment opportunities on the other; the two factors actually have only a modest statistical relationship across countries.[43] Furthermore, the challenge to the schooling-equals-employment nostrum may have more to do with specific types of skills and knowledge learned and particular types of employment.

Thus, youth and young adults leaving secondary school may not be a good fit with what industries seek in terms of an appropriate skill set. In this regard, non-formal and vocational education programs provide the opportunity for individuals trying to enter or stay employed in the workforce to attain high-relevance skills.[44] But the norm in poor and (especially) rural contexts, such as those in sub-Saharan Africa, is still what has been called "occupational pluralism"—that is, a diversification of income-generating activities in the informal employment sector. In an in-depth study in rural Ghana, respondents were asked to name income-generating activities and the degree to which subsistence farming was practiced. The study found that the distinction between crops grown for cash sale and consumption is often blurred: yams, cassava, and corn are grown and can either be consumed by the household or sold in the market.[45] This example—of which there are many variants—serves as an indication of just how difficult it is to know what kinds of employment skills need to be taught and learned, particularly in low-income societies.

In both rich and poor countries, the public and policymakers are becoming more aware that there is a complex and non-linear relationship between learning and employment, especially for those at the bottom of the pyramid.[46] What then constitutes the right kind of learning for those in poor contexts? How much and what types of learning are necessary for future employment, and for which types of jobs? These are much more difficult questions to answer than they appeared several decades ago when continued economic growth seemed assured.

21st Century Skills

At the other end of the scale, for those with the potential of upward mobility in a context of globalization, the demand for different types of skills—what are termed *21st century skills*—has begun to grow in both depth and breadth in low, middle, and high-income populations.[47] The OECD defines this skillset as largely comprised of soft skills—such as effective management, cooperation, creative thinking, and conflict resolution competencies—that are valued in the global labor markets worldwide, as in an Australian example (see Figure 6.5). Some of these skills can be defined with precision (such as literacy and numeracy), but others (such as ethical understanding and social capability) are difficult to define and even more challenging to teach. Another question is whether this set of skills would be similarly valued in developing countries.[48] The skills in the Australian example are mostly fostered through informal learning via everyday social and professional interactions. Instruction of these skills is a serious challenge in formal contexts for learning.

Thus, while teachers may be trained to teach academic skills that will be measured for further educational advancement, they are rarely prepared (or encouraged) to teach such soft skills.[49] This mismatch between the skills that are prioritized in formal schooling and those that are increasingly valued in certain parts of the labor market may have important consequences. For example, research

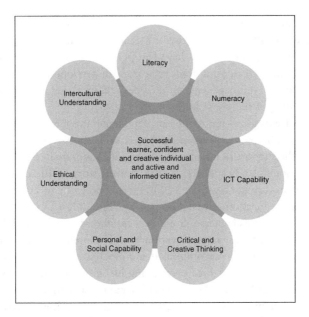

FIGURE 6.5   General Capabilities and Soft Skills as Part of the Education Curriculum of Australia

Source: UNESCO (2013b, p. 9)

on youth employment in sub-Saharan Africa has revealed persistent trends suggesting that schools are not adequately preparing students for the labor force.[50] Overall, and as noted above, these findings demonstrate an increasingly tenuous connection between the knowledge and skills that are emphasized in formal schooling and the real-world economic requirements of the labor market.[51]

There is little question that OECD industrialized countries, with their rapidly growing service and information economies, are moving toward training 21st century skills, and away from the memorization skills and fixed content knowledge that have characterized formal learning practices over the past century and more.[52] In low-income countries, however, the question of how, when, and even whether such 21st century skills should be prioritized in the present economic climate—given that basic learning skills are still wanting and a pool of globalized employment opportunities seems lacking—remains unanswered.[53]

Building Support for Lifelong Learning

Youth and adult learning is a cornerstone upon which lifelong learning is built, much as stated in UN SDG #4. While ministries of education in low-income countries often consider these endeavors only at the margin of their core school-based responsibilities (which are principally primary and secondary schooling), youth and adult non-formal education programs broaden the range of opportunities for individuals who have had poor, little, or no schooling experience. Though much more work needs to be done in developing countries, lifelong learning in OECD countries—which includes technical and vocational training and the upgrading of skills—is clearly on the rise.

Non-formal education programs can complement, reinforce, or update previous learning. The provision of more diverse skills should be seen as a natural expansion of the support of learning that individuals require in an ever-changing social and economic landscape. To take the opening story in Turkey, Azra still has a chance, perhaps through a women's adult literacy program, to make a difference in her daughter's education as well as in her own life.

In the previous three chapters—from early childhood through adult learning— a life-span approach to learning, education, and development was put forth. It is evident that much has been accomplished and much more remains to be done to improve learning over these three overlapping life stages. Fortunately, we already have many of the tools at hand to support learning as a central focus of development. As described in the next chapter, schools were created hundreds of years ago expressly for this purpose.

Notes

1. Based in part on notes by R. Banerji (by author's permission).
2. UNESCO (2016a, p. 237).
3. As noted in Chapter 3, the learning environment framework includes non-formal education, as well as preschool and early education programs. In Chapter 4, it was further noted that the growth in preschooling, especially with the advent of the SDGs, has led to its closer alignment with the formal schooling systems in many developing countries. In the present chapter, the focus is primarily on the non-formal education programs that cater to youth and adults.
4. Johansson (1987).
5. Scribner and Cole (1981).
6. Bennett and Berry (1987).
7. See Wagner (1993, 2010a) on Morocco; Street (1984, 1999, 2001) on Iran; and Scribner and Cole (1981) on Liberia.
8. Street (1999) coined the term "literacies" that has grown in popularity to include digital literacy, multimedia literacy, as well as the culturally specific literacy that he studied earlier in Iran.
9. Gray (1956, p. 19); also Venezky et al. (1990). The gender bias in the quotation from 1956 stands out strikingly in today's world.
10. Puchner (2001).
11. See earlier discussion of Freire in Chapter 1.
12. Wagner (1989b).
13. SDG 4.6 states: "By 2030, ensure that all youth and a substantial proportion of adults, both men and women, achieve literacy and numeracy." While the precise proportional goal for adults remains vague, efforts are underway to further clarify this target. See UNESCO-UIL (2016).
14. OECD/Statistics Canada (1995). This problematic finding in OECD countries is mirrored on developing countries as well—actual literacy levels are often found to

be far lower than governments have proclaimed. Agencies, such as UNESCO, which have played major roles in supporting literacy (especially adult literacy) seem to have based their programs more on advocacy than on research-based solutions (Wagner, 2015b).

15. OECD (2013). PIAAC is the Programme for the International Assessment of Adult Competencies. Below Level 1 and Level 1 are considered to be equivalent to being functionally illiterate, while Level 2 is a borderline but unacceptable level for European countries. See also: Durgunoglu and Oney (2002) and Greenberg et al. (2002). Also: Tuijnman et al. (1997), Wagner and Venezky (1999), and Lesgold and Welch-Ross (2012).

16. UNESCO (2005); also, see Easton (2014) for a recent review on adult literacy in Africa.

17. These are the types of learning practices described in the two left quadrants of Figure 3.1a.

18. Adapted from Britto et al. (2014).

19. See Wagner et al. (2010). Also see bridge programs of Andhra Pradesh at: www.ashanet.org/projects/state-view.php?s=28.

20. On types of supplementary programs, see Park et al. (2016).

21. Bray and Lykins (2012). These types of educational opportunities often make use of the very same teachers as those in public school, but offer additional financial compensation.

22. Transhumance generally refers to herders who move livestock from one grazing ground to another in a seasonal cycle (Aderinoye et al., 2007). See further discussion of refugees in Chapter 10.

23. See Chapter 9.

24. See http://data.worldbank.org/topic/agriculture-and-rural-development.

25. Duflo et al. (2008).

26. Malawi and India research (World Bank, 2015b). Based on Mani's work (Mani et al., 2013), the World Bank (2015b, p. 14) states that: "Farmers perform worse on the same series of cognitive tests before receiving their harvest income than after receiving their earnings. . . . In this sense, poverty imposes a *cognitive tax*." For a broader look at the impact of "scarcity" on poverty, and its cognitive consequences, see Mullainathan and Shafir (2013). Wagner et al. (2016) provides a critique of Mani's work and some aspects of this World Bank (2015b) report.

27. In most studies that consider the impacts of learning on farmer productivity and health, the proxy variable for learning has been number of years of education. This is largely because of the greater ease of data collection, including the administrative data collected by government agencies. Increasingly, data on learning and literacy—collected from the population samples—indicates that outcomes are better explanatory variables than number of years of schooling. This is because, as noted earlier, years of schooling are only moderately related to learning outcomes.

28. Zahra (2017).

29. Robinson-Pant (2016).

30. As reviewed in Reimers and Klasen (2013), some researchers have argued that the relationship between literacy and productivity would be larger in somewhat more advanced economies, since the impact of advanced farming techniques would be more "sensitive" to increased farmer skills. The authors provide a number of studies that support this claim (p. 134).

31. Reimers and Klasen (2013) based their analysis on a 95-country study.

32. See Asadullah and Rahman (2009), Jamison and Lau (1982), Asfaw and Admassie (2004), and Robinson-Pant (2016).

33. Larsen and Lilleør (2014).

34. See Friis-Hansen and Duveskog (2012, p. 416): "[The Farmer Field School] uses a learner-centered, problem-based approach to teaching involving field observations, the relating of these observations to the ecosystem, and applying previous experience

through group discussions. . . . A group of farmers who meet regularly (usually weekly) in the field form the field school, while plants or animals at the learning site form the main study materials. The learning takes place under the guidance of a trained facilitator, who helps promote active participation, group dialog, and reflection."

35. See, for example, Pritchett and Summers (1996).
36. DeWalt et al. (2004). One recent study in Mozambique found that HIV/AIDS knowledge was strongly related to both basic reading and math skills (Ciampa et al., 2012).
37. Rajan et al. (2013, p. 104) state that: "Standard policy prescriptions for improving public health in less developed countries focus on raising average income levels since it is widely accepted that 'wealthier is healthier.' Our analysis [in India] suggests it is low poverty and high literacy rather than wealth per se that improves public health. . . . Expanding economic output improves public health not by raising average income but by reducing poverty and increasing literacy—undermining the dominant pro-market liberalization position and supporting the pro-poor position. Moreover, of the two predictors, literacy has a markedly stronger effect than poverty."
38. See LeVine et al. (2012). This research, undertaken in four countries, showed that young women internalize teacher-pupil interactions in two ways: they act like pupils in health clinics and like teachers with their infants and toddlers. This was, in LeVine's view (personal communication), a way of explaining the widespread impact of schooling on health. In a cross-national systematic study with 175 countries, Gakidou et al. (2010) also found a strong relationship, over 40 years, between women's education and reductions of child mortality.
39. See more on the intergenerational transfer of cognitive skills in Sticht et al. (1992).
40. Hanushek and Woessmann (2012) provide a global synthesis, mainly based on international large-scale assessments.
41. Bassi et al. (2012).
42. Bassi et al. (2012, p. 13) states: "In a globalized, knowledge-based economy, education has become the linchpin of competition. . . . Facing the accelerated changes in the world economy—a dynamic exacerbated by the recent economic crisis—young people do not believe that they are being adequately equipped with the skills they need for their transition into the workforce."
43. UNDP (2013a, p. 93).
44. Adams (2008); Bennell (1999); Muskin (1997, 2012); McGrath (2012).
45. The Ghana example is from Palmer (2007).
46. The links between more schooling and the global common good were raised in an important report by Jacques Delors (1996) and recently reprised in UNESCO (2015c). The complex relationship between schooled skills and employment has become more obvious in wealthy countries as well, as described in a recent report by Beaudry et al. (2016), showing that high-skilled jobs in the United States have been falling over the past decade or so—what the authors term the "great reversal."
47. Levy and Murnane (2007); Dobbs et al. (2012).
48. There is an overlap between the current drive for *21st-century skills*, oriented specifically toward the workplace, and *higher-order skills*, that is, ones based on taxonomies of cognitive tasks (from low-complexity tasks of simple comprehension to higher-complexity tasks of application and critique). See Bloom et al. (1956) and Pellegrino and Hilton (2012). Higher-order skills encompass meta-cognition, interpersonal abilities (self-regulation, motivation), and intrapersonal skills (cross-cultural communication, teamwork); also see Ball et al. (2014), Marzano (2001), and Winthrop and McGivney (2015). For the case of socio-emotional soft skills in Latin America, see an in-depth discussion of results in Bassi et al. (2012, p. 138). Also, see the earlier discussion of socio-emotional skills (Duckworth et al., 2007; Adler, 2016).

49. In a World Bank report, Wang (2012, p. 23) wrote that "PISA claims that it assesses students' skills and competencies to fully participate in and contribute to a successful modern society. The Trends in International Mathematics and Science Study (TIMMS), on the other hand, measures students' achievements in mathematics and science in school. Yet neither of these assessments assesses important skills that are critical to success in the contemporary global economy—namely, communication, leadership, and teamwork."

50. In one study, 8 of the 13 countries demonstrated that the average duration of the school-to-work transition was five years or longer, "suggesting young people in these countries are faced with substantial labour market entry problems upon leaving the school system" Guarcello et al. (2007, p. 29). See also the work of Allais (2012) in South Africa. Of course, this claim is not unique to developing countries. American researchers have consistently worried about whether there is a glut of degrees relative to the growth of national economies; see also earlier cited study by Beaudry et al. (2016). In a complaint against the notion of an "education gospel" that more education will necessarily lead to more jobs, historians Lazerson and Grubb "contend . . . that this faith in the individual, social, and economic benefits of education is 'overblown.'" While they admit that there are private and public gains from schooling, they argue that the individual benefits have been "exaggerated," that "education now plays only a small role in major sectors of the economy," that "about 35 to 40 percent of those in the labor force . . . may have too much schooling for their jobs," and that "the status effects of schooling have declined." They advocate that "we all need to revise our claims for education" (cited in Keller, 2005, pp. 171, 205, 167, 263).

51. Pellegrino and Hilton (2012, p. 5) state that high educational attainment in the United States is crucial for such skills, and further note that "development of the full range of 21st century competencies within the disciplines will require systematic instruction and sustained practice."

52. Manyika et al. (2017) provides an overview of the role of automation and robotics in light of the future of employment.

53. UN SDG Goal #4 on education includes the following sub-goal SDG #4.4: "By 2030, substantially increase the number of youth and adults who have relevant skills, including technical and vocational skills, for employment, decent jobs and entrepreneurship." The specific issue of 21st-century skills is not addressed. A review by Care et al. (2016) considers trends toward 21st-century skills by national ministries of education. The authors found that, in the order of priority attributed to such skills, communication skills came out on top with somewhat less priority put on creativity, critical thinking, and problem solving.

PART III
Educational Institutions

7

SCHOOLS AND SCHOOLING

Salah: Dreaming of City Life in Tunisia

Hbira, a town with about 4,000 inhabitants, sits in the semi-desert plains of rural Tunisia, about 150 kilometers south of Tunis. Salah, age 12, is en route to his primary school. Founded in 1957, the school's most impressive feature is a large, shady central playground where students gather whenever classes are not in session. By the time Salah arrives, dozens of his classmates are milling around outside the school gate, some buying penny candy or sunflower seeds from the vendor stationed outside. There are 33 children in Salah's class, the larger of two fifth grade classes in the school. Wooden desks, each with two seats, are arranged in four columns facing the blackboard in his classroom. Sunlight brightens the space on the side with windows, and four bare light bulbs hang from the ceiling. The walls are decorated with pictures cut from magazines—a soccer team, several individual players, a smiling girl petting a white horse, two men doing karate, and hunters on a hillside.

Si Mustafa, Salah's teacher, instructs the class in history, geography, civics, and Arabic language arts. He is proud of his own fluency in Standard Arabic and tries to instill a similar love and respect for the language in his students. As the children jostle in their seats on this clear spring morning, Si Mustafa greets them. He chooses three students to write their brief compositions on the blackboard and three others to read them aloud for corrections. When a reader comes to an error, the rest of the students jab their hands into the air, pleading loudly for the teacher to call on them, until he designates one student to answer. At the end of the class, Si Mustafa begins a discussion on the relative merits of city versus village life. Salah dreams of his future in the big city, with cafes and cinemas and wide, paved streets, but other students counter that cities are expensive, too big, and confusing.

Salah's primary school in Hbira reflects the type of schools found in many poor regions of the world. Resources are limited. Materials—such as textbooks, wall posters, and so forth—may be hand-me-downs that schools have inherited over the years, or may be absent altogether. The infrastructure—such as electricity, bathrooms, and windows that open and close—may be decaying or non-functional. And the teachers—even the well-educated and motivated ones like Si Mustafa—may have been trained years earlier with pedagogies that are now viewed by education specialists to be outdated or even counterproductive. Yet schools are one of the main places where children like Salah are introduced to the idea of their future, their aspirations, and the larger world.

Indeed, from a national and international perspective, it is in schools—from primary and secondary schools in childhood through universities in adulthood—where huge investments have been made to foster learning and knowledge acquisition. In addition, a host of other pre-employment, socio-emotional, and attitudinal skills have been woven into national curricula. Schools are, perhaps self-evidently, the universal institution of choice for inculcating the next generation with what they need to know and be able to do. However, as emphasized earlier, especially in Chapter 3, a great deal of learning takes place outside of schools as well. Nonetheless, if we want to focus our development efforts on improving learning, then schools are an essential part of the discussion.

The historical and cultural roots of schooling inform contemporary approaches to education. It is commonly thought that the teaching profession came into existence thousands of years ago, no doubt starting with home tutoring by parents or learned scholars in the employ of the wealthy. Most historians give the Chinese credit for creating the first national school system for both administration and the arts in about 1000 BC, mainly designed for, and maintained by, the bourgeois elite.[1] In these schools, one could study poetry, scriptural painting, and Confucian thinking. This education would prepare one for admission into the dynastic imperial administration via its merit-based examination system. As with most forms of traditional education, a great emphasis was put on learning sacred texts and the basic skills of reading and writing.

The links between the Chinese schools that began three millennia ago and the schools of today are stronger than many people realize. Indeed, traditional education (mostly with a religious affiliation) has continued to flourish in many parts of the world, especially in rural and poor contexts where teachers receive little support from national training institutions. Buddhist traditional schools have been maintained in numerous Asian countries, Talmudic Jewish schools have expanded in Israel, evangelical Christian schools are flourishing in the United States, and bush schools still exist in parts of Africa.[2] The most widespread traditional institutions today are Islamic schools called *madrasas*, or Quranic schools—a topic to which we shall return later in this chapter.

Schools as Institutions

Schools are among the most ubiquitous social institutions in the world, attended by millions of children and youth. They are universally thought of as places where children go to learn, whether in rich or poor countries. In these institutions resides the hope not only of governments who provide a vast amount of support, but also of parents and children who look to schooling as the main avenue for social and economic advancement. Schools are valued for a variety of reasons. They are places where highly structured learning takes place under expert guidance in the service of creating a knowledgeable citizenry. For parents, schools provide a safe place to leave their children while they work and (mostly but not always) where their children can learn about morality. And, for development agencies, schools represent the most efficient place where they can assist in governments' efforts to build a skilled and knowledgeable citizenry.

But schools in developing countries also aim to do something on a grander scale, something picked up by Salah even in his small rural Tunisian town—what is sometimes described as a "deep expectation."[3] It is the concept that schooling creates opportunity. Parents from all over the world and in all socioeconomic classes harbor such hopes—that schooling will help their children accomplish more than they did in their own lives.

To achieve such broad goals, most schools today, in the manner of religious schools centuries ago, combine several common features: fixed locations (usually a building); proximity to where the school's children live; teachers who have been trained to varying degrees of competency; and a curriculum typically set by authorized government officials. Of course there are important variations, especially now that digital and off-site resources are becoming available to supplement or sometimes even replace classrooms and schools altogether.[4] Yet, it is important to recognize these common elements, as they remain the focus of a great deal of attention by those who seek to improve schooling around the world.

An example of trying to improve schools based on these factors is described in *Making Schools Work: New Evidence on Accountability Reforms*, a book by three World Bank economists.[5] Using evidence from 22 impact evaluations in 11 developing countries, the authors sought to understand how to improve education by influencing the complex interrelationships between governments, teachers, and students. They view the poor quality of education as part of continued failure of schools to give a "direct voice" to parents and students.[6] As one example, they cite the *Educo*[7] program in El Salvador, where community-elected parent oversight committees provided timely feedback to school leadership, which resulted in better student outcomes. Results from their multi-country dataset showed that the hiring of short-term contract teachers had significant benefits,[8] and that pay-for-performance schemes (such as in India) offered persuasive evidence that incentives for teachers had significant outcomes on educational quality.[9] As with most meta-analyses, these results are highly dependent on the selection of students and programs, and on the moment in time when they were collected.[10]

At an institutional level, it is not surprising that international development planners and researchers have focused on schools as the single best point of leverage. Schools—as a national network of facilities, teachers, and students—provide an invaluable infrastructure and base for many types of interventions. This is true not only for ministers of education, but also for international agencies and organizations who can take advantage of schools as a locus of control and management.[11]

Hidden Costs of Schooling

Sustainable Development Goal #4 aims to ensure that all girls and boys complete free, equitable, and quality primary and secondary education. And in many developing countries, public education is officially "free." In practice, however, schooling can be expensive for a great many families in developing countries, rendering both access and persistence in school a double challenge.[12]

In Rwanda, for example, schooling is mandated as free, but recent research shows that there are significant costs.[13] In order for a child to attend a Rwandan primary or secondary school, basic direct expenses include uniforms, notebooks, and pens, as well as indirect costs for items like shoes and haircuts. In addition, out-of-school tutoring—often required for assuring school advancement—adds substantially to a family's monthly costs.[14] Finally, dues payments to the parent-teacher association (PTA) are nearly obligatory for parents who seek to have their children progress successfully. One 18-year-old Rwandan secondary school student was interviewed about these costs and said:

> Last term I didn't have the amount needed for PTA because I don't have my parents. So when it was time to pay PTA I was sent home. I spent almost two weeks working for the money. Then after getting the 2000 rwf [Rwandan francs] I came back to school. At that time I found out I needed to pay another 200 rwf for my sister who is in Primary 6 in my school. If you don't manage to pay this money the school obliges you to go home. . . . When the school sends you home like three times per week you give up. You say to yourself, "Maybe we were not all created to go to school. Let me stop and maybe God has another plan for me."[15]

Clearly, school costs, even when schooling is supposedly free, can be a substantial burden, and a reason why many children do not continue on in school. To this must be added the opportunity costs of a child who goes to school rather than working to support his or her family. Cross-national studies have compared the percentage of household expenditures on education to keep up with the minimum needs at school. While the percentages vary greatly depending on the income of rich and poor families, it is evident that in countries like Mauritania and Niger, up to 74% of household expenses in poor families are to support schooling—a level that puts education beyond reach for many (see Figure 7.1). This also results in more pressure on adolescent girls to drop out of school and enter the workforce or domestic service in order to support the schooling of their younger siblings.[16]

In addition, school costs and the stress they engender can have a serious impact on the health and social/cognitive development of young learners, as discussed

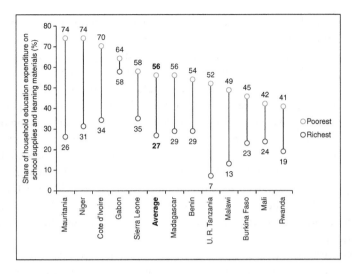

FIGURE 7.1 The Share of Poorer Household Education Expenditure Spent on School Supplies and Learning Materials in Selected African Countries

Source: UNESCO-Pole de Dakar, 2012, adapted from UNESCO (2016b, p. 7)

in Chapter 4. For example, in the Rwanda study, children were very aware of the "pecking order," of the haves and have-nots, in their class. One primary school child reported:

> I was sad when I saw the other children looking smart in their [school] uniforms. I was ashamed [that I didn't have a uniform]. The teacher used to tell the student who didn't have a uniform to stand up [in class]. I was shamed in front of the other students. I told my mother, but she said, "We are poor, I cannot do anything, let us wait, maybe we will get the money."[17]

While growth in school enrollments has continued around the world, it is clear that there are substantial financial burdens for families with limited means. Poor families are increasingly aware of the real costs of "not-so-free" education, and have begun to look for alternatives, like private schooling.

Private Schools

Partly as a response to the growing costs of public schooling, there has been a concomitant growth in private school attendence, even among the poor.[18] This upturn seems mainly due to increased demand among parents for the perceived better-quality education that private schools provide. Thus, the establishment of "low-fee private" (LFP) schools is a spreading phenomenon, with costs not much greater (and sometimes less) than the informal costs of "free" government schools.

During the days of colonialism, private schools existed mainly for the rich, and were often supported by religious missionaries. This continued long after national independence was achieved in many developing countries.[19] More recently, particularly in countries like India and Kenya, LFP schools have sprung up and are sought out by parents seeking enhanced instructional quality and subsequent educational opportunities for their children. Research suggests that even if teachers have fewer formal credentials (such as teaching diplomas), students' outcomes may be higher in private schools (where teacher presence and student discipline is more readily assured) than in public schools, as shown in one recent study in India.[20] Another private-sector initiative, which started in Kenya but has expanded to several other African countries, is a franchise of LFP schools that provides strictly guided curricula and teachers (often just high school graduates without teaching diplomas) who use highly scripted instruction.[21]

Parents appear attracted to LFP schools due to the perception that they are better organized and have less absenteeism among teachers—as exemplified in the following description in India:

> The government schools had virtually no teaching activity. A para-teacher at one school was found to be teaching, while in another school an older child was instructing while the teachers (two were present) sat idly by. In the rest of the government schools there was an air of chaos and neglect, as the teachers simply read the newspaper or chatted with friends. . . . By way of contrast, at the LFP schools there was always an air of seriousness and discipline, with children sitting in orderly rows. . . . It was extremely common to observe children working diligently on their own in their copybooks and then bringing these to the teacher to be checked, while the teachers sat and waited to be approached. . . . There was an overall discipline enforced at the LFP schools that was found to be absent at government schools and it was this and the fact that children learn basic material that parents seized on in their comparisons of the school types.[22]

At present, the evidence on the impact of LFP schools on children's learning in developing countries remains inconclusive. However, when compared with dysfunctional public schools (where teacher absence is high), one can see the appeal of private schools that may be better organized with teachers who are present every day. Even in the most humble settings, such as in rural Andhra Pradesh in India, there has been a near doubling in recent years of children who attend LFP schools.[23] Still, most private schools put little emphasis on robust teacher training, as that would add significantly to the costs of the schools, putting them out of reach for many poor families. As in the West, there is also a concern among policymakers that by taking children out of public schools, the better-off families—though still poor by national standards—are leaving the poorest of the poor in the public classrooms, thereby diminishing the overall quality of the public school.[24]

The rapid expansion in private school enrollments indicates that parents are "voting with their feet" when good (or perceptibly better) schooling choices are made available.[25] Some have argued that the expansion of school privatization is a fact that must be included in poverty reduction strategies.[26] Yet context is also very important. Parents might not be so eager for private schools if there were good government schools nearby. And, when options other than government schools are available, parents in some countries—in the Muslim world in particular—may turn to religious schools for their children's education, as they have over the centuries.

Islamic Schooling: A Case Example

Even though millions of children in dozens of countries attend Islamic schools for either part or all of their education, they have been among the least studied of contemporary educational institutions. In 1979, I embarked with a Moroccan colleague on a five-country comparative study of Islamic schooling in Indonesia, Yemen, Senegal, Morocco, and Egypt.[27] We found that instruction included several common pedagogical characteristics: oral memorization of the Quran; emphasis on correct (that is, accurate and aesthetic) oral rote and group recitation; training in the Arabic script; and strict authoritarian classroom control.[28] In contrast to textbooks used in most modern secular schools, literacy instruction with the Quran as a text provides no opportunity for age-appropriate vocabulary or grammatical structures to be introduced. In addition, the visual illustrations that most secular school primers use to facilitate reading are strictly prohibited for religious reasons in Islamic schools. Hence, learning to read by using the Quran as a primer is a remarkably challenging task for many children (and even more so for the millions of Muslims for whom Arabic is not the mother-tongue).

Islamic schools are not monolithic, however, and vary in some interesting ways across societies. In Morocco, for example, where almost 80% of all children attend Quranic schools for some period of their lives, Islamic schools for older children have largely disappeared, while modernized Quranic preschools have replaced them. In urban Morocco, children are more likely to attend Quranic schools as a form of preschool education (see Figure 7.2). One important reason for an expansion in attendance is the participation of girls, who were once excluded from traditional Moroccan schools. Yet, in other contexts, such as in rural Yemen, only boys and adolescent men attend such schools.

In Senegal, where girls have typically attended Quranic schools, modernization has led to significant changes in pedagogy and curriculum. Rather than emphasizing rote learning of Arabic texts, which are not understood by children who speak only Senegalese languages, many Quranic school teachers employ spoken and written Arabic as a second language.[29] Arabic literacy has the advantage of

FIGURE 7.2   Quranic Preschool in Marrakech, Morocco
Photo by Daniel A. Wagner

being already firmly embedded in the cultural fabric of societies with significant Muslim populations, and hence is a popular language of choice even if it is not (outside the Arabic-speaking world) accepted as a language of public school instruction.[30]

An in-depth portrait of Quranic instruction in Cameroon is informative in this regard. There, children spend nearly all of their time at Quranic school learning verses of the Quran in Arabic, while in the government school they may spend as much as one-third of each school day learning French recitation dialogues. In each context, students memorize a given text with little or no comprehension of the material, as described below.[31]

> In Quranic and public schools in Maroua [Cameroon], Fulbe children are socialized through guided repetition into the use of Arabic and French in the context of activities that are considered fundamental and meaningful by their communities. Across these two educational contexts, the guided-repetition structure is enacted in different ways, for the languages, texts, institutional settings, and identities involved are rooted in socially, culturally, and historically distinct traditions. The highly structured and repetitive nature of language-socialization routines in both settings helps the child develop the linguistic and cultural competencies that are needed to participate in the social worlds

in which Arabic and French are privileged. Thus, despite the fact that most of the speech in the early years of Quranic and public schools is in languages that are not comprehended, children learn to speak, act, and respond to those languages . . . in ways that are locally intelligible.

A number of insights can be drawn from this brief review of Islamic schooling. First, there are some important commonalities between Quranic and secular schools in terms of teacher pedagogy, even if government policymakers often decry the former as archaic and predominantly focused on rote learning.[32] Second, rather than viewing Quranic schools as impediments to development policies of governments or donors, educational planners would do well to consider such religious schools as important resources that could foster better learning outcomes if coupled in reasonable ways with national curricula—both contexts are trying to foster children's learning. While sensitive political questions can arise with respect to religious schooling, especially within today's highly polarized world, it is important to be cognizant of the potential benefits for learning that might exist within Islamic religious schools, especially where public alternatives fall short.[33]

Schools clearly come in numerous varieties, from public to private to religious to new online options. National governments as well as development aid agencies are constantly trying to assess the capabilities of these diverse institutions for learning outcomes, with important consequences for how investments in schooling are made.

Investing in Schools

One way to evaluate the status of school quality is to consider their levels of funding over time. In this regard, it is instructive to see how much spending has been provided by international donors to different levels of schooling—from pre-school through post-secondary—over recent decades (Figure 7.3). As shown, the large gains in international aid over time are in primary schooling (reflecting the emphasis on universal access) and post-secondary schooling (reflecting enrollment growth and high costs).[34]

National government spending on education has also risen in recent years. Most governments currently spend about 20% of their total GNP on public schooling. Only a tiny fraction of GNP is spent on pre-primary education programs (as discussed in Chapter 4).[35] For example, sub-Saharan African governments spend an average of 0.01% of GNP on pre-primary education, while wealthier nations such as Denmark spent about 1% of GNP on such programs.[36] Most government funding for schools in developing countries is spent on primary and secondary education—these are the structured, formal learning contexts described in Chapter 3. This accounts for roughly 75% of national education funding, with the largest remaining portion devoted to post-secondary education and training that has a

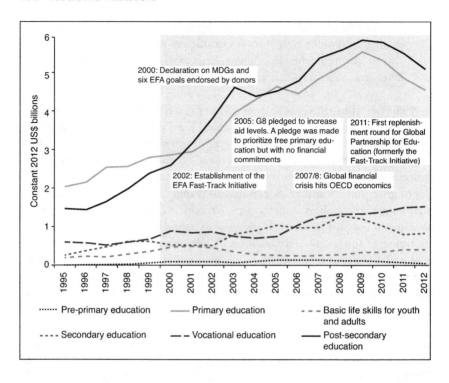

FIGURE 7.3 Aid to EFA Goals by International Donors. Total Aid to Education Commitments, Three-Year Rolling Averages, 1995–2012
Source: UNESCO (2015a, p. 264)

very high cost per capita.[37] In Rwanda in 1999, for example, the government spent nearly 161 times as much on a university student as on a primary school child, but by 2012 the figure had declined to only 12 times as much, due to the Rwandan education reform plan. By contrast, in Peru in 1999, the expenditure per university student was about three times that of a primary school child, and by 2012 the per capita expenditures remained about the same.[38]

In the context of growing school enrollments, class size and student-teacher ratios have also increased significantly, leading to a drop in the measurable quality of classroom learning in many countries. For example, studies have shown that there are on average 59 primary school pupils per classroom teacher in Ethiopia, 60 in Bangladesh, 120 in Malawi, and 145 in Nigeria.[39] These are averages only, with some observers noting that many classes will have as many as 200 or more students per teacher! As illustrated in Figure 7.4, large class sizes are particularly prevalent in the early grades, during what we have noted is a very critical time in a child's cognitive and social development.[40] The negative

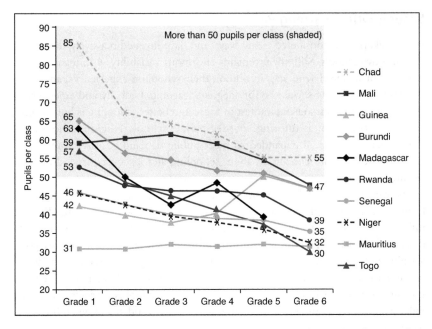

FIGURE 7.4   Average Primary-Level Class Size by Grade (Single-Grade Classes Only)
Source: UNESCO Institute for Statistics (2012, p. 5)

effect of large class size (i.e., with pupil-to-teacher ratios higher than 40:1) on student learning is one of the most significant unintended (though anticipated) consequences of the recent expansion of universal primary schooling in developing countries.[41] Another consequence is the high dropout rates discussed in the previous chapter.[42]

Over the years, research has shown that in wealthier countries, educational funding levels are imperfect predictors of learning achievement.[43] In developing countries, by contrast, a comprehensive meta-analysis was undertaken of nearly 80 studies to determine which investments—school infrastructure characteristics (e.g., class size, total expenditures, and physical characteristics), pedagogical materials (e.g., textbooks, visual aids, and computers), teacher characteristics (e.g., education, training, experience, subject knowledge), and pedagogical practices used by teachers (e.g., teaching methods, homework assignments, student assessment methods)—significantly affected student enrollment and learning.[44] Overall, these results showed that school and teacher characteristics were not especially strong predictors of student learning. Rather, it seemed that teacher attendance (see Chapter 8) and textbook provisions were more directly related to learning achievement. Such analyses highlight the complex and challenging nature of identifying interventions where major school-level investments can make a difference.[45]

Schools Offer Learning Pathways

Policymakers have considered many ways, and have invested massively, to support and improve schools. Still, there remains enormous variability with regard to the numbers of children who stay in school, their schooling experiences, and what the costs of schooling should be for adequate learning. Globally, and especially in developing countries, societal interest in more and better schooling is burgeoning, and alternatives such as tutoring, low-fee private schools, religious schools, and online learning have all expanded to meet public demand. Clearly, parents and governments alike are concerned about schooling and its consequences for their children's learning and future economic and social prosperity.

As institutions, schools have their share of serious problems, from unhygienic facilities and low availability of textbooks to over-crowded classrooms. Beyond infrastructure concerns, how much of schooling is really about learning? As described in this chapter, there are many school-based factors that support good learning outcomes, and others that are stifling. If learning is the best road to development, then schools represent a hugely important pathway (when done well) for learning and personal growth. For Salah in Tunisia, school is a crucial place that will form how he is going to see and engage with the world, if and when he moves to the city.

However, not everyone is enamored of schools as institutions. Former British Prime Minister Winston Churchill—born into a very wealthy family—once famously remarked: "My education was interrupted only by my schooling."[46] While humorous, and overly facile given the likelihood of his many social advantages, Churchill's view is not entirely out of place. A person's education entails much more than access to a classroom. Education, as Churchill correctly saw it, should be fundamentally about learning.

Notes

1. Lee (2000).
2. See Kapitzke (1999) on Jewish schools, Gurugé (1985) on Buddhist schools, and the Vai indigenous literacy in "bush" schools in Liberia (Scribner & Cole, 1981). "Bush" schools are mainly indigenous in character with local customs often undertaken for boys or girls at the time of puberty (see Erny, 1972; Reagan, 2005).
3. Fuller (1991, p. 3). See also the reviews by Boli et al. (1985) and Meyer et al. (1992).
4. See Chapter 9, on the use of new technologies.
5. Bruns et al. (2011).
6. Bruns et al. (2011, p. 12).
7. Educación con Participación de la Comunidad (Education With Community Participation).
8. Particularly in India and Kenya, the authors discuss robust findings at as little as 10% of the cost of civil service teachers.
9. In Muralidharan and Sundararaman (2009), research incorporated 500 state schools in Andhra Pradesh randomly assigned to a pay-for-performance scheme, contract teachers, institutional block grants, and a control group.

10. See more discussion of such meta-analytic studies and randomized control trials (RCTs) in Chapter 11.
11. As noted in Chapter 1, top-down approaches are popular with governments and donor agencies, but that does not imply that effective implementation and successful outcomes are guaranteed.
12. On school fees, see Akaguri (2014) and Kattan and Burnett (2004).
13. Williams et al. (2014). The Rwandan franc (rwf) is valued at about 734 rwf per US dollar, as of 2016.
14. See Chapter 6 on the costs of tutoring.
15. Williams et al. (2014, p. 15). In numerous low-income countries there is an unfortunate tendency among some teachers to refuse to grade or examine students who will not pay them a "tutorial fee."
16. See earlier discussion on gender and education in Chapter 3.
17. Williams et al. (2014, p. 15).
18. For a broad review, see Lewin (2007); also Park et al. (2016).
19. Holmes (2013); many of these were Catholic schools.
20. For a comparison of private and public schooling in South India, see Singh and Sarkar (2015). Similar comments will be readily apparent from those who follow the charter school movement in America, where motivated (contractual) college graduates are brought in to schools as an alternative to experienced and more credentialed expert teachers. For a critique of the private and charter school movement in the United States, see Schneider (2016).
21. See www.bridgeinternationalacademies.com/company/about/. The impact of this program in Kenya is still too new to properly assess (though see some early positive effects reported by Stern and Heyneman, 2013), along with its ability to successfully compete with government schools. For general reviews of private schools see Tooley (2013), Heyneman and Stern (2014), and Mundy and Menashy (2014).
22. Bangay and Latham (2013), cited in Harber (2014), based on Härmä (2010, p. 14). See also Härmä (2009). Fennell (2013) reported similar professionalism and quality in LFP schools in Pakistan.
23. Woodhead et al. (2013, p. 27). The authors conclude: "While private schooling may provide a short-term solution to the educational needs of children in India today, it is unlikely to be the best means of providing education for all children in the longer term in ways that respect equity principles, especially in the absence of strong government regulation including comprehensive public-private partnership arrangements."
24. This conclusion may at first seem counter-intuitive, since class size might be smaller in public school classrooms if more children were to leave to attend private schools. Considerable international research has shown that when more educated families take their children out of public schools, there is far less pressure to improve the schools and hold authorities accountable for performance (e.g., West et al., 2006).
25. Hirschman (1978, p. 96) described privatization as one way that people vote with their feet; that is, if choice is "unequally distributed in modern societies" it inevitably leads to what he termed "ghettoization"—limitations in possibility for those left behind.
26. See Heyneman and Stern (2015).
27. Wagner and Lotfi (1980).
28. Wagner (1989a). While the five-country study is now nearly three decades old, recent work has updated and confirmed the broad trends, especially in North and West Africa; for more recent work, see Boyle (2006), Boyle et al. (2007), Moore (2006), and Williams and Cummings (2015) in Somalia.
29. See the case of the *darra* Quranic schools in Senegal in Barry (2012), Humery (2013), and Toure (2009).
30. See discussion on language of instruction in Chapter 5.

31. Moore (2006, p. 122) reviewed the research on rote learning in her work in Cameroon. Given contemporary prejudice against the term "rote," she opted to call this type of learning "guided repetition."
32. In my own work (Wagner, 1993), I found that rote learning was as prevalent in public schools as it was in the religious schools.
33. The continuing failure of most development agencies (as well as national ministries of education) to consider the importance of this network of traditional Quranic schools is surprising from a practical standpoint in light of the difficulties in achieving universal primary schooling and promoting basic literacy skills. On the other hand, given the political crises in various Muslim societies today, it is understandable that these same agencies hesitate to get more involved. See discussion in Wagner (1999).
34. UNESCO (2015a, p. 264). Note that EFA (Education for All) goals are aligned with the 2015 UN MDGs discussed in Chapter 2.
35. Data on percentage of GNP for different levels of schooling is from UNESCO (2014a).
36. UNESCO (2015a, p. 246); in OECD countries like Denmark, pre-primary spending is up to 1% of government GNP.
37. In 11 African countries, data show that the average government educational expenditures total 46% for primary schooling, 29% for secondary schooling, about 21% for higher education, and about 3.5% for all other NFE (pre-primary, youth, and adult literacy) programs (UNESCO-Pole de Dakar, 2014, p. 135).
38. UNESCO (2015a, p. 258).
39. UNESCO (2009). See also, Ahmed and Arends-Kuenning (2006).
40. As discussed in Chapter 4.
41. Effects of class size remains somewhat inconclusive according to some research, such as Benbow et al. (2007), Hattie (2005), and O'Sullivan (2006). Recent work in the US found little major effect of class size (see Bill & Melinda Gates Foundation, 2010), but this may be due to the limited range of class size differences. The class sizes in developing countries are much larger than in OECD countries. See also Finn and Achilles (1999), Angrist and Lavy (1999), and Smith and Glass (1979). It should be noted that large class sizes do not affect all national educational systems in the same way; Japanese primary school classrooms typically have about 50–60 students on average, and school management and good pedagogy have rarely been a problem (Cummings, 2014).
42. See Chapter 6.
43. OECD (2012).
44. Glewwe et al. (2011). Note that this study was restricted, depending on the comparisons made, to between 40 and 79 research studies, due to the authors' choice to include only a small subset of what they termed "high-quality" studies. For a review of issues related to how studies are chosen to be included in meta-analyses, see Evans and Popova (2015), discussed in Chapter 11. Also see Carnoy et al. (2015) for a three-country comparative study in Africa.
45. Recent findings from the World Bank also reinforce skepticism about school- and classroom-level inputs on student performance (Filmer et al., 2015). The difference in findings in OECD countries compared to developing countries might well be due to the differences in the variance in teacher training, attendance, and other variables between these two large and diverse groups of countries.
46. Churchill (1930/2010).

8

TEACHERS AND PEDAGOGIES

Rachel, Kebe, and Chinelo: Teacher Training in Nigeria[1]

The George International School sits at the end of a side street a few blocks from one of the main boulevards of Kano, a large provincial capital in northern Nigeria. With a population of about 4,500 students, "George" (as everyone calls it) is the largest and oldest private school in the city. It has a strong reputation due to various longstanding relationships with external networks in the UK, and because of these relationships, George regularly receives expert British teacher trainers to work with its own local teachers. The following dialogue stems from a training workshop at the school:

- *Rachel (British Teacher Trainer)*: Here's a question that goes through my mind at some points in our training. Here I am, turning up in Nigeria like some kind of missionary with my bag of tricks. What am I actually doing here? Is that really not an issue for you—being trained by an outsider from Great Britain?
- *Kebe (First Nigerian Teacher)*: Not at all. You have a Ph.D. from a famous university in Britain. If you weren't an expert, I wouldn't be in your workshop.
- *Chinelo (Second Nigerian Teacher)*: I think it's good to be open to new things, and that's the way we see it. We can't be stuck in our old ways. I'm looking for some new techniques that I can adapt for my classes, even if they do come from Britain.
- *Rachel*: You don't have any issues about it at all? You have no worries that I'm just bringing what I learned that was relevant in London, and thinking it would be relevant here in Kano? Doesn't that sound like educational imperialism?
- *Chinelo*: The English language belongs to you, to the British. The science of instruction belongs to you. The textbooks belong to you. Why should we have issues with that?

In previous chapters, teachers were mentioned in a variety of different contexts— they work in preschools, primary schools, secondary schools, religious schools, and non-formal education programs. In this chapter, we consider how teachers develop into agents of change that support children and learning. According to UNESCO, there are more than 30 million primary and secondary school teachers in the world today,[2] and likely around 45 million teachers total if all types are included—making teaching one of the world's largest professions.

Teachers are clearly at the center of the schooling enterprise. They are the enablers who support and instruct students. They are also the recipients of the large-scale systems of financing, curricula, and recruitment. Teachers also build on and utilize their own skills and resources to manage classrooms and promote learning, attitudes, and behaviors on a daily basis.[3] Needless to say, teachers are an essential factor in determining both what and how well children learn.

The opening story about Rachel, Kebe, and Chinelo raises a number of fundamental questions about how teachers learn to teach in developing countries. How does one incorporate Western education methods or comingle them with teaching practices in local settings? Who "owns" the discourse around teaching? How valued is British curriculum expertise? How should we view the variety of teachers and pedagogies available today, as compared with those that existed in earlier times? How much should curricular reforms be developed and/or implemented by local educators versus those from other countries?

In this particular workshop, Kebe and Chinelo seem comfortable with the idea of a foreign expert offering the science of instruction, as determined by a British or Western system of education. At face value, it appears that they were receptive, open, and apparently enthusiastic to learn from Rachel. Yet it leaves us with an uneasy impression, one worth considering in some detail, with respect to several aspects about teachers, their motivations, and the ways innovative teaching methods are disseminated.

To begin, there is no shortage of disparate views on what constitutes good teaching, and even what it means to be a qualified teacher. Teachers would likely say that they are among the most scrutinized (and criticized) professionals in the world. Even so, they are universally considered to be the backbone of all educational systems.

The Role of Teachers in Society

Who becomes a teacher, and how do societies tend to view these individuals? Responses vary remarkably over time and context. In Greek and Roman times, teachers were among the most revered and respected individuals in society. Teachers in primary and secondary schools in France often became the public intellectuals, philosophers, and writers who shaped the culture at large. This has traditionally been true for teachers working within the world's religious faiths as well. Further, if one looks at our most successful education systems—such as those found in Canada, Finland, or South Korea (as determined by outcomes on international learning assessments)—it is not just the high salary levels that have led to above-average teacher quality, but rather the high regard in which teachers are held.[4]

Thus, there are many compelling reasons why young adults decide to become teachers, some of whom go on to spend their entire adult lives in the profession.

A revealing portrait of roughly 400 beginning teachers in Ghana found a number of key reasons why they signed up to teach.[5] Some mentioned the altruistic benefits of helping students learn: "I want to impart knowledge . . . to someone, and to serve as a role model for the young ones to follow." Other Ghanaian teachers spoke of economic security: "In the midst of . . . [rampant] unemployment, my employment [as a teacher] is assured after training."

Pursuing a teaching career also has historically been one of the ways that women have found employment in both industrialized and developing countries. Further, for men and women alike, teaching is a career that is in constant demand and is often transferable if one needs to relocate. As noted, it also offers a degree of social mobility. Teachers may begin in a preschool, move to primary and then secondary schools, and occasionally into a university—each with a higher pay grade. Yet, from this grand tradition—now lost in many of today's nations—the ranks of teachers have expanded exponentially, along with a general decline in their overall training and often socioeconomic status as well.

Teachers as Learners

To become good at teaching, teachers need to know a great deal of information, and stay attuned to changes in both pedagogy and instructional content. Another reason for the historically high regard for teachers (based on surveys in industrialized countries) is due to the rigorous training that they (ideally) undergo.[6] Effective teachers not only need a solid grasp of subject matter knowledge, but also the pedagogical skills to teach what they know and bring out the best in their students.

However, for many teachers, especially those catering to marginalized populations, acquiring such skills is a difficult and complex endeavor, and, for a variety of reasons, some simply never receive the training required to be effective in their jobs. In the United States, the average teacher has already spent nearly 10,000 hours as a student in classrooms, "making teaching the profession with the most intensive and lengthy apprenticeship of any."[7] Yet, in low-income countries, this broadly applicable statistic helps to explain why some teachers—even with little training—believe that they are already competent enough to teach their students. Many see themselves as "experts" simply because they have more education (and official language skills) than their students. Research strongly suggests that to become expert teachers, they need to master key skills, including the ability to: assess student progress; formulate clear learning goals; select instructional strategies; and implement strategies that create learning opportunities.[8] This requires coherent, in-depth and repeated professional training.

However, many teachers in developing countries never receive such training, not even on how to teach their pupils to read, the main gateway to knowledge acquisition.[9] In India, fewer than 9% of primary school teacher candidates passed the Central Teacher Eligibility Test established by the government in 2011, an assessment designed to assure that primary school teachers have mastered the basic

Indian curriculum.[10] Furthermore, many teachers are working in countries that have undergone important socio-demographic and language transformations[11]— such that they may have little or no training that equips them to deal with these changes.[12] For example, shifts in the composition of the student populations result in more ethnically mixed and multilingual classrooms—by language, skill, and age. New technologies—while offering potentially valuable new options for learners—also pose serious training problems for teachers.[13] In Senegal, for example, only 8% of teacher trainees expressed confidence about teaching children to read in local languages.[14] In northern Nigeria, 78% of 1,200 basic education teachers were found to have "limited" knowledge of English, the language of instruction beginning in the upper grades of primary school.[15] In Uganda, teacher training for primary school teachers is comprised of about 260 hours of instructional time devoted to theories and methods of pedagogy, but only 120 hours each to mathematics, language (English), and science. In many cases, there is simply not enough time for teachers to learn necessary subject matter content.[16]

The above issues are exacerbated by the global growth in the number of students in school. Recent surveys suggest that nearly 1.6 million new primary school teachers are now needed (Figure 8.1), a target that has not been possible to meet.

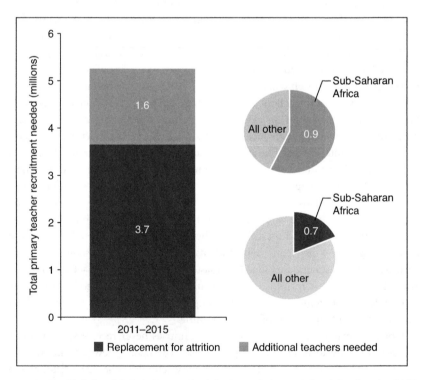

FIGURE 8.1 Global and Sub-Saharan Need for More Primary School Teachers by 2015

Source: UNESCO (2014a, p. 223)

In Mali, for example, only half of all teachers currently meet the qualifications set by the government.[17] In Pakistan, teachers move "up the ranks" with certificates they collect in training classes that are not properly accredited and have minimal relation to the school curricula.[18] The case of Assiatou in Guinea, who sat in one of the back rows of the classroom, sadly typifies the problem of overcrowding and under-resourced instruction at the classroom level.[19]

Of course, many if not most teachers are aware of their own need to learn more, and many would support the increased availability of pre-service and in-service training. In Malawi, 72% of trainees in teacher training colleges said they gained valuable experience by receiving targeted support to assist disadvantaged pupils.[20] Much of this training consists of "expert" teachers (like Rachel in the opening dialogue) who train more junior teachers, in what is known as the "cascade model." Empirical studies of this model have shown that the transfer of skills from one level to the next has been modestly successful at best, for the reasons stated previously, and simply due to the dilution of the information as the cascade proceeds downward.[21] An alternative approach undertaken in Zambia, and based on previous teacher training experiences in Japan, found that a peer-to-peer (teacher-to-teacher) self-training could also improve students' learning outcomes.[22] In this model, primary- or secondary-level teachers share knowledge and skills through collaborative activities, group conversations, and learner-centered teaching methods.

In sum, teachers are not born with the knowledge to teach well—they have a lot to learn. But, oftentimes, they have too few resources, time, or administrative support.[23] As school enrollments have grown and class composition has become more heterogeneous, teachers have found it increasingly difficult to facilitate student learning, provide guided instruction, and simply manage student behavior. Such circumstances can contribute to low morale amongst teachers.[24]

Teacher Motivation

Inadequate training and resources are just some of the challenges that can impact teacher motivation. Some fortunate teachers may work near their homes and can walk to school, but many others may have to travel considerable distances to their classrooms. In the former case, teachers may enjoy close connections with local traditions and ethno-linguistic commonalities, as well as develop a sense of belonging. But for those teachers who have to travel, sometimes to reside in far-off locations, serious problems can emerge. They may be unable to go to school due to inclement weather, or their motivation to go to school that day may be subsumed by something more compelling that needs to be done at home. Also common are situations in which teachers who live in urban settings are assigned to rural districts. For some teachers, such postings may be perceived as particularly onerous, given the lack of usual amenities such as proper sanitation facilities, healthy food, and reliable transportation. It is easy for teachers in these circumstances to feel isolated and unable to do their jobs effectively. Further, being assigned to a school in a distant location might also result in the teacher not speaking the language of the students and families in that community, a hardship that, as discussed previously, requires an additional level of effort and commitment.

Whether teaching in one's own community or not, government agencies have so many teachers to manage that they are often unable to pay their salaries on time or support them properly in terms of providing blackboards, lighting, decent seating, tables, and other basic infrastructure. In other words, some teachers feel poorly treated (and indeed they are), leading to low morale and diminishing motivation.[25] In one recent international survey, less than 33% of lower secondary school teachers believed teaching to be a valued profession in society; the range varied from a low of 5% in France and up to 84% in Malaysia.[26]

Overall, the varied circumstances, contexts, and social perceptions of teaching have a major impact on teacher motivation and ability to facilitate learning. This fact has been recognized by education leaders in many countries, and has led to increased consideration of the kinds of investments needed to assist the teaching profession.

Investing in Teachers

As is evident, adequately trained teachers are essential for children's learning, and both policymakers and parents alike understand this reality.[27] Budget allocations to public educational systems are one way for governments to affirm this perspective. In developing countries, teacher salaries comprise the largest proportion (on average about 82%) of national education budgets, and these percentages have been rising over time. In some countries, such as Liberia, the salaries of teachers comprise nearly 100% of national education expenditures (Figure 8.2).[28]

Yet, despite these growing allocations, teachers in developing countries—who, at one time, were relatively well-paid—have seen their salaries decline relative to other professions, with a related loss in social standing. The dramatic growth of primary schooling stimulated a major recruitment of teachers, many of whom received teaching credentials that were far easier to acquire than other higher education degrees. This "cheapening" of teacher certification has led to decreased quality (skills and experience) within the teaching profession.[29] In an international comparison of secondary mathematics education, only 62% of African children were taught by teachers who were deemed "well-qualified" by their country's own criteria.[30] Furthermore, primary school teachers are often paid less than half the salary of those teaching in secondary schools (Figure 8.3);[31] and the majority of such teachers are women, a fact that puts further downward pressure on both salary and status in developing countries, where women are expected to earn less than men.

Overall, evidence has shown that it is difficult to recruit and maintain competent teachers when the profession as a whole is undervalued. Professional

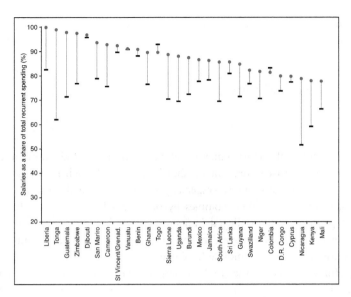

FIGURE 8.2 Salaries as a Share of the Recurrent National Education Budgets, 2012

Note: Gray dots show most recent data; dark bars are 1999 levels.

Source: UNESCO (2015a, p. 250)

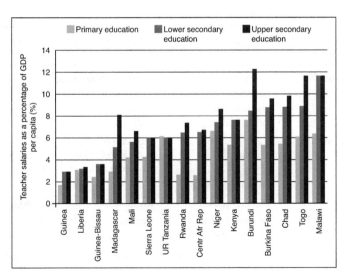

FIGURE 8.3 Teachers' Salaries in Primary, Lower, and Upper Secondary Education by Average GDP Per Capita in Selected Low-Income Countries

Source: UNESCO Institute for Statistics (2011, p. 70)

development is lacking, teachers are less respected, motivation may be missing, gender forces salaries downward, and salaries are held in check by underfunded ministries of education.[32] Further (as we saw in Chapter 7), even the best teachers will be challenged by class sizes that can average well over 50 pupils.[33] There are simply not enough well-trained teachers.[34]

Pedagogies

Modern pedagogical theory emerged along with the introduction of public schools in early 19th-century France, shortly after the French Revolution. Subsequently, the colonial empires—especially the British and the French—spread educational offerings in their colonies by opening school systems. These were designed primarily for privileged indigenous families, with the aim of instilling Western concepts, languages, and histories, as well as providing employment opportunities for upwardly mobile local elites.[35]

A useful summary of the predominant Western pedagogical approaches is provided in Table 8.1. *Behaviorism* most closely resembles traditional models of classic Western education, where memorization, rote learning, strict adherence to teacher directions, and top-down pedagogy are the norm. *Constructivism* (also known as progressive education)—based primarily on the work of Piaget,

TABLE 8.1 Four Major Western Pedagogies

Broad Theoretical School of Thought	Associated Pedagogy	Examples of Pedagogies in Wealthy Countries
Behaviorism	Teacher-centered learning	Whole-class teaching, working together as a collective (Japan, the Pacific Rim)
	"Performance," visible pedagogy	Focus on mastery of skills in a particular sequence
Constructivism	Child-centered learning	Project work; individual activity, experiential, Montessori; Steiner; Pestalozzi in US and Europe
	"Competence" or invisible pedagogy	
Social Constructivism	Teacher-guided	Reciprocal teaching of reading in US
	Learner/student-centered learning	Communicative learning
		Cooperative learning
		Group work element in national strategies, England
Liberationist, Democracy	Critical pedagogies	Critical pedagogies such as "philosophy for children" in England
Critical Theory		Student voice

Source: Adapted from Westbrook et al. (2013, p. 12)

Vygotsky, John Dewey, and Maria Montessori—takes into account the learning level or stage of the individual child's cognitive development. A later version of this approach has been called *social constructivism* or *learner-centered pedagogy*. It views "co-construction" by teacher and student as the best way to learn cooperatively in small groups or in whole-class interactive work.[36] Learner-centered pedagogy, in contrast to lecturing and rote learning, "gives learners, and demands from them, a relatively high level of active control over the contents and processes of learning."[37] Finally, there is *critical pedagogy* (based in part on the work of Paulo Freire[38]), which adheres to the "bottom up" notion that learners (especially marginalized ones) should create their own pedagogy, and should have a voice in what content they learn and how they learn it.[39]

These four pedagogies are not often used in a pure way; that is, teachers typically combine facets of different pedagogies to suit their style and the topic at hand. Also, in spite of a tendency to view the latter three approaches as more modern and acceptable among contemporary scholars, in developing countries even "modern" teachers who have had professional training often adopt the behaviorist approach—what Paulo Freire called the "banking" model that pushes students to remember (or bank) the facts provided by the teacher.

Many teachers naturally gravitate toward pedagogies that will make their own instructional lives easier—sometimes with little attention paid to what students are actually learning. This can lead to rote instruction—perhaps best evidenced in the religious traditions evoked in Chapter 7—that is prominent in developing countries, as many observers have found. In my own research in Morocco, Senegal, and Yemen, teachers in public schools borrowed heavily from the Islamic pedagogical tradition of memorization.[40] Recent work in Ghana showed that teachers reported their continued use of rote pedagogy in classrooms, but ascribed this to colonial trends in education rather than seeing it as an indigenous feature of Ghanaian society.[41]

We have seen that learning is most effective when it is built on prior knowledge, a conclusion that would generally support the use of constructivist or learning-centered approaches.[42] But acceptance of constructivism has come up against a number of challenges, not least of which is in the policy arena in developing countries. Some have pointed out that the promotion of learner-centered pedagogy may run counter to the use of high-stakes examinations that include fixed knowledge from curricula that are mandated by government.[43] Thus, teachers are often under considerable pressure to "teach to the test" so as to meet students' needs (in responding to school examinations) and to protect their own reputations as teachers.

Richard Tabulawa, a Botswana academic, has pointed out that in his country, as well as in Namibia and South Africa, the adoption of learner-centered pedagogy has been mainly undertaken in order to secure development funding, not because of a belief in the pedagogy itself.[44] This contradiction reminds us of Kebe and Chinelo's malleable view of the inherent value of the outside British educator's expertise.[45] But it also creates potential conflicts between what the West sees as central to pedagogical reform, and what local teachers may think with respect to pedagogical practicality.[46] A study of teacher training in Tanzania further explored such global-local tensions.[47] One teacher in the study said of learner-centered pedagogy: "If you are behind and students say 'we are behind in class,' you are in trouble. You are a joker. You are not serious." Overall, Tanzanian teachers' views of knowledge production for pedagogy were found to be importantly influenced by local circumstances. They were "profoundly shaped by the cultural, economic, and social contexts in which they teach," rather than by Western pedagogies simply handed down by their teacher trainers.[48]

The legacy of these colonial educational systems and pedagogies has had mixed results for recipient nations, however one evaluates their purpose or effectiveness. The conversation between Rachel, Kebe, and Chinelo illustrated a subtle debate about the embedded power dynamics that exist when post-colonial pedagogy is imported into distinct cultural contexts.[49]

Appropriate Curricula

National curricula can be seen as a form of educational "social engineering."[50] They determine what a child should know, and thus, by careful retrofitting, what a teacher should teach. Even so, it is difficult to pinpoint exactly how to optimally design a curriculum that appropriately matches the skills of the teacher with the learning levels and knowledge of the student population. This task is particularly difficult in developing countries (and some wealthier countries) when children may come to school with highly varied language skills and knowledge bases.[51] Further, is a curriculum developed by government officials living in the nation's capital city going to be relevant to a rural child? In many circumstances, a one-size-fits-all curricular approach is very unlikely to be suitable for increasingly heterogeneous children.[52]

Naturally, educators have sought to address this issue by adapting their curricula and pedagogy for diverse student populations. One large-scale meta-analysis surveyed more than 1,000 research studies that tried to localize (or indigenize) curricula for particular populations, but was unable to give a clear policy response. The results yielded both positive and negative findings across a variety of interventions that were empirically measurable, such as teacher attitudes and practices, which are summarized in Table 8.2.[53]

The urban-rural "mismatch" described earlier (along with other important differences such as language) often results in what has been termed an "overambitious curriculum," wherein students simply cannot achieve at the government-mandated level.[54] In the case of India, for example, the government adopted Minimum Levels of Learning for grade 5 students across the nation. However, research showed that the average Indian grade 5 student could only understand a fraction of the material in the fifth grade curriculum. Student learning must be

TABLE 8.2 Curricula, Teacher Attitudes, Strategies, and Practices in Developing Countries

Pedagogic Aspect		Positive Examples (Number of Studies)	Negative Examples (Number of Studies)
Attitudes	Training and Pedagogy	Harmonization between culture, training, pedagogy, and classroom contexts makes teachers positive toward new practices (4/2)	Constructions of the teacher as authoritarian prevent understanding of interactive practices (8)
	Students	Positive attitudes toward poor and marginalized students lead to awareness of students' backgrounds, experiences, and abilities (6/1)	Groups of students ignored, especially students with disabilities in large classrooms (6)
Strategies	Paying Attention	Tailoring instruction to specific students, giving tests, homework, constructive feedback, including all students in lesson content and discourse (7/4)	
	Classroom Environment	Lively, warm, and friendly teachers encourage participation. Absence of corporal punishment makes students feel safe (6/2)	
	Student Characteristics	Students' backgrounds, prior knowledge, and local examples drawn upon to make lesson content relevant and meaningful (5/1)	Lesson content overly abstract and irrelevant for students (2)
Practices	Group Work	Verbal interaction in small mixed or ability groups, sharing tasks and resources, monitored by the teacher (15/4)	Permanent rows, little peer interaction, active zone of students at front do best (5)
	Learning Materials	Variety of materials used with textbook, from MP3 (audio players) to stones, integrated with prior knowledge and concept formation (9/5)	Prescriptive and use solely of difficult textbooks, copying from board (7)
	Use of Questions	Open and closed, expanding and probing responses, encouraging student questioning (10/4)	Frequent closed questions, choral responses, one-word answers (7)
	Demonstration	Imaginative, interactive demonstrations and explanations using voice, students, images, based on sound content and pedagogical content knowledge (8/1)	Didactic lecturing, poor content knowledge (13)
	Language	Use of local language gives access to lesson content and encourages verbal interaction (9/3)	Unfamiliar language leads to rote learning and incomprehension (3)
	Lesson Structure	Planned lessons lead to varied sequences of methods and tasks (11/3)	Predictable teaching sequence limits variety of activities (15)

Note: The numbers of studies that reported the pedagogic aspect are shown in parentheses and the number of studies reporting higher student attainment as an outcome are shown following the forward slash.

Source: Westbrook et al. (2013, 38–39)

seen relative to the "curricular pace." When the pace is too steep (i.e., the teacher provides knowledge that is much too difficult, or presents it too quickly) then students are left behind and will learn much less in the grades that follow. With a slower pace that tracks the child's learning level, more and more children can gain knowledge using a given curriculum. A second study, also in India, supported a similar approach that the researchers termed "teaching at the right level"—that is, by grouping students according to their individual learning levels, rather than age or grade level.[55]

When the child does not understand what is transpiring in the classroom, learning is greatly diminished. Yet it is not uncommon to hear teachers say that they are simply "following the curriculum," and it is therefore not their responsibility if students do not learn. To establish an appropriate curriculum requires that teachers build on students' knowledge and skills, and allocate time for effective practice.

Instructional Time on Task

While a focus on the intersection of human resources and needs is important, there are additional factors that determine whether teachers teach effectively and children learn in their classrooms—time is one of these. One of the most troubling research findings in recent years is that many children simply do not have enough *time on task* to learn what is being taught. For instance, an observational study in Kenya found that second grade children were only able to use (put their hands on) printed material for about 3.6 minutes per day on average.[56] Indeed, in many schools, children spend far less time on instructional activities than the curriculum intends. In rural Ethiopia, huge losses in instructional time were due not only to "lost" hours of schooling (such as the fact that government schools were non-operational for about 25% of the days of the school year), but also to teachers being "off task" (i.e., not directly working with the students as mandated by the curriculum) more than half the time.[57] Given such findings, common in many developing countries, it is not surprising that more than 30% of Ethiopian third graders had not learned how to read.[58]

Similarly, a comparative study in Guatemala, Ethiopia, Nepal, and Honduras found that, while schools were officially supposed to be open between 180 and 202 days per year, they in fact only offered classroom instruction for between 56 and 87 days (see Figure 8.4).[59] Reasons for school closings included strikes, teacher illnesses, and teachers' payday. Even when teachers were in classrooms, observational evidence indicated that students were using written materials (including the blackboard) for less than 15% of the available hours (at most 40 minutes per day).[60] Additional findings in Malawi showed that less than half of a child's day in primary school is actually spent on learning tasks with a teacher. That is, of the roughly 640 hours that children were in class, about 300 were spent on direct instruction, while 160 hours were spent with a teacher who was not providing

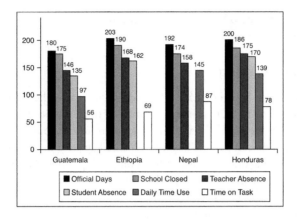

FIGURE 8.4 Equivalent Days of Schooling Available for Teaching and Learning in Four Countries

Source: Moore et al. (2011, p. 253)

instructional support of the curriculum, and nearly 180 hours were spent without any teacher at all.[61] When added to earlier discussions of large class size, limited teacher motivation, and curricular inefficiencies, the simple fact of too few instructional class hours helps provide a sobering picture of why learning achievement is so low.

In rural India, endemic teacher absenteeism impacts negatively on classroom instructional time. One intriguing intervention sought to rectify this by providing students with a digital camera, and tasking them to take a timed and stamped digital photo of their classroom each day. In this way, students and a local NGO were able to monitor the presence or absence of their teachers in real time.[62] Over a period of about 12 months, teacher absenteeism dropped from 42% to about 21% in the schools where photo monitoring was undertaken. The study found that student learning significantly improved as a consequence.[63]

Another way to look at time on task is by considering the types of pedagogical strategies employed by teachers. A study in 32 primary schools in Tanzania utilized a sophisticated method of digitally recording and scoring teacher-student interactions. Researchers discovered that teachers spend most of their instructional time in three main sequential ways: (a) the large majority of time consisted of top-down questions to students as a group; (b) some time was then allowed for student "responses" that were choral and largely rote in nature; and (c) only a small amount of time was allocated for "follow-up" responses by the teacher.[64] In this research, it remains unclear as to whether time and effectiveness trade off against one another—that is, whether more time on traditional pedagogy is balanced with less time on more learner-centered approaches.[65] Even so, this observational approach offers new ways to measure classroom interaction and its consequences.

Teaching for Learning

In this chapter, we have emphasized the centrality of teachers for enhancing learning in schools, and noted the importance of teacher motivation. Substantial evidence has indicated that far too many teachers in developing countries feel unappreciated, undercompensated, and less than adequately trained to teach their students. This, among other factors, leads not only to high rates of teacher absenteeism and attrition, but also to the difficulty of finding sufficient numbers of skilled teachers for classrooms that need them. Investing in teachers as learners, providing pre- and in-service teacher training, as well as assuring that teachers are sufficiently motivated, are among the key ingredients of an effective instructional environment.

Naturally, these trends vary by context and country, but are directly related to the results we have seen earlier about the difficulty in improving children's learning in poor and marginalized communities. Teachers and effective teaching matter a great deal. But to what extent are teachers responsible for children's failure to learn the curriculum? Many argue that teachers are, rather, the symptomatic consequence of educational systems that are underfunded, and pedagogies and curricula that are insufficiently adapted to local contexts. Responses to such questions are matters of public debate in many countries. Placing responsibility is important for understanding appropriate change, but it can safely be said that learning itself should remain the overarching goal.

As Dewey stated nearly a century ago, "[P]rospective teachers come to . . . schools with . . . ideas implicit in their minds. They [also] want to find out how to do things with the maximum prospect of success."[66] Times have not changed in this regard. There is little doubt that if educational systems were more supportive and knowledgeable about what skills and resources are needed to engage and teach poor children, teachers would rise to the challenge. As we move deeper into the 21st century, new opportunities will present themselves to support teachers and learning, such as the use of new technologies, to which we turn in the next chapter.

Notes

1. Adapted from Thompson (2013, p. 48).
2. Bruneforth et al. (2009).
3. For a useful review, see UNESCO (2015b).
4. These, are among the countries where students score highly on international assessments of learning outcomes; see further discussion in Chapter 11. For a national example, see Sahlberg (2011) on Finland.
5. Stephens (2007, pp. 184–186).
6. UNESCO (2005, p. 52). For a broad overview of "teachers as learners," see Feiman-Memser (2012).

7. See Stigler and Miller (in press, p. 3) for an interesting review of teacher expertise.
8. Stigler and Miller (in press, p. 22) developed this expertise approach based on multinational data collection using the TIMMS survey.
9. Gove and Cvelich (2010), as described in Chapter 5 of this volume.
10. Chudgar (2013).
11. See especially Chapter 10.
12. For example, see Hargreaves (1994). Some research has looked at South-South teacher collaboration (Hickling-Hudson, 2004).
13. Darling-Hammond (1996); Hinostroza et al. (2014). See also Chapter 9.
14. UNESCO (2014a).
15. UNESCO (2015b).
16. World Bank (2012b) cited in UNESCO (2015b). For a comparison of teacher professional development in Uganda, Tanzania, and Kenya, see Hardman et al. (2011).
17. UNESCO (2014a, p. 227).
18. Thanks to A. Ghaffar-Kucher for this example from Pakistan (personal communication).
19. See Chapter 5.
20. Mambo (2011), drawn from UNESCO (2015b, p. 8).
21. On the cascade model in South Africa see Dichaba and Mokhele (2012). For a broad review of limitations, see UNESCO (2015b). Also see the discussion of using technology for teacher training in Chapter 9 of this volume.
22. This is the "Lesson Study" model (Jung et al., 2016). Similar results were obtained in a USAID-funded project to train teachers in Morocco around "communities of practice" (Muskin, 2015).
23. Tikly and Barrett (2013).
24. Surprisingly few examples point to effective strategies used to foster students' learning in large-size classrooms, and such examples typically are situated within highly structured, homogenous learning contexts and facilitated by highly trained instructors. For example, Stigler et al. (1982) found that large class sizes in Taiwan and Japan had little impact on the quality of learning. See also Jourdan et al. (2008) and Naylor and Sayed (2014).
25. See Ginsburg (2012) for a critique of development agencies, that tend to ignore teachers' needs and motivations as part of a larger educational enterprise.
26. (OECD, 2014), cited in UNESCO (2015b). These countries participated in OECD's second Teaching and Learning International Survey (TALIS) in 2013.
27. Akiba et al. (2007); Barber and Mourshed (2007); Ginsburg (2012); Heyneman and Loxley (1983); Rivkin et al. (2005). See Jourdan et al. (2008) on the role of teacher training in health education (2005). Nonetheless, in the United States, researchers have found little relationship between teacher training and learning achievement (Hanushek & Rivkin, 2006). Recent evidence from a World Bank comparative study in Uganda, Mozambique, Togo, Nigeria, and Kenya revealed that, even with teachers who were highly trained, only modest gains in learning achievement were found (Filmer et al., 2015).
28. UNESCO (2015a, p. 250); UNESCO (2015b).
29. Chaudhury et al. (2006).
30. Akiba et al. (2007, p. 380). Also, Adedeji and Olaniyan (2011) and Akyeampong et al. (2013). Further, see the work of SACMEQ, in which research showed that many teachers in Africa had fewer skills than they needed in order to effectively teach their own curriculum (UNESCO-IIEP, 2010). In this comparative study of 13 African countries, only three countries had a majority of their reading teachers (grade 6) with substantive professional training.
31. UNESCO Institute for Statistics (2011, p. 70.)
32. Steiner-Khamsi (2015); UNESCO (2014a).

33. See Chapter 7.
34. One way that governments have sought to increase the number of teachers is through direct contracts. In this way, contract teachers—who often lack the training and credentials of regular teachers—are paid on a yearly basis rather than as longstanding governmental employees. In a five-country study in francophone Africa, contract teachers were found to have less commitment to the teaching profession than government teachers, and tended to abandon their work as teachers when some other better-paying opportunity became available (Chudgar, 2015). A broad discussion of this topic may be found in UNESCO (2015a), pp. 200–201.
35. McLaren (2015).
36. See also Schweisfurth (2013a), who states that in this approach: "What is learnt, and how, are shaped by learners' needs, capacities and interests." She also cites Dewey (1938, p. 223) for his focus on the "expression and cultivation of individuality." In an earlier publication, Schweisfurth (2011) found that 72 reviewed projects that employed learner-centered pedagogy revealed few consistent findings.
37. Schweisfurth (2013a, p. 20).
38. Freire (1972/1996).
39. A fifth school of pedagogy is sometimes called *society-centric* and is more narrowly focused than that of a learner-centered classroom. This approach allows for more academic standards to be met, and for a robust emphasis on educating students to be active in their own communities. Thanks to A. Ghaffar-Kucher for this insight (personal communication).
40. See discussion of rote memorization in Chapter 7 and in Wagner (1983c) and Wagner and Lotfi (1983). This research demonstrates not only the pre-colonial origins of rote pedagogy, but also the cognitive basis for the persistence of rote as an attractive strategy for learning (e.g., Mayer, 2002). According to Smail (2017), based on his research in Morocco, teachers at the primary level are committed to modern teaching in rhetoric, but as soon as high-stakes tests are at issue, modern pedagogy is replaced by rote techniques. Moreover, high-stakes testing exists in part as a cultural institution, and also tends to maintain continuity with the French system for the highest performers.
41. Zimmerman (2011, p. 24).
42. See Chapters 4 and 5.
43. Schweisfurth (2013b).
44. Tabulawa (2003).
45. Tabulawa (2009, p. 93) stated further that: "Thus, [learner-centered] pedagogy is viewed in Botswana as a vehicle for developing a preferred kind of society and citizens. It (learner-centered pedagogy) is the nexus between education and the broader political principle of democracy." See also Chisholm and Leyendecker (2008) who see learner-centered pedagogy in sub-Saharan Africa more as a problem of implementation than a criticism of the pedagogy itself.
46. Robin Alexander has argued that effective pedagogy necessarily involves "teacher professional content knowledge, . . . the character and degree of cognitive challenge afforded by teacher-student interaction, and the quality of the information conveyed in teacher-student and student-teacher feedback" Alexander (2015, p. 257).
47. On Tanzania, see Vavrus and Bartlett (2012). Smail (2017) supports this perspective by suggesting that there is no singular local way of viewing learner-centered (modern) pedagogy in Moroccan schools. Rather, modern pedagogy is sometimes mobilized for so-called "modern" subjects (such as English language learning) and is ignored for "traditional" ones (such as Arabic language learning).
48. Vavrus and Bartlett (2012, pp. 651, 634).
49. See Chisholm and Leyendecker (2008) for a useful review of resistance to colonialism in African education.
50. Thanks to J. Muskin for this insight (personal communication).

51. The city of Philadelphia, for example, uses more than 50 languages in its primary schools.
52. Muskin (2015, pp. 100–102). Muskin critiques efforts to achieve scalable solutions through curricular reform by noting that "any single education reform or innovation in effect becomes 10,000 reforms or innovations once delivered into the hands of 10,000 teachers." He speaks of this as a matter of curricular "relevance."
53. Westbrook et al. (2013, p. 28). Even though this meta-analytic study considered more than 1,000 studies, only 62 studies received in-depth reviews (due to methodological limitations in the remaining corpus of studies).
54. This example is based on Pritchett (2013) and Pritchett and Beatty (2015). There are also serious issues related to the measurement and perceptions of curricular pace, as seen in the research of Lefstein and Snell (2013).
55. Banerjee et al. (2016). The importance of local knowledge for teacher training in India has also been studied by Dyer et al. (2004).
56. See Piper and Mugenda (2012, p. 4) for a report on an observational study with second grade children.
57. DeStefano and Elaheebocus (2009, p. 13) also report that "students who reported having missed school the previous week had reading fluency rates of half those of the students who said they had not missed school. . . . By itself, student self-reported attendance explains 35 percent of the variation in a schools average reading fluency." Also, in Ecuador, Araujo et al. (2014) found that by using a video-based method of teacher observations (the Classroom Assessment Scoring System) instructional behaviors were strongly related to learning outcomes. See also Benavot and Gad (2004) for a broad review of instructional time issues in African countries.
58. See Chapter 5 on early grade reading. Alexander (2001) claimed that time on task is overrated as an indicator, but evidence has accumulated in recent years that supports its importance.
59. Moore et al. (2011).
60. Moore et al. (2011, p. 258).
61. Dowd et al. (2014).
62. Duflo et al. (2012). It should be mentioned that these were not regular primary schools, but rather non-formal education centers, which reduces the ability to generalize about the findings. Also teachers were given monetary incentives if they were present in school, and were give a small monetary "fine" if they were absent. The program lasted a little more than two years. Measures of teaching behavior were apparently no different for the treatment and control schools, so that it was likely that more time on task (an increase of about 30% of teacher presence in school) contributed to the learning gains recorded. After one year, in this randomized control trial, the children's test scores in treatment schools were significantly higher than in the control schools. For a broader discussion on incentives to change individual behavior, see Sunstein (2014).
63. In Banerjee et al. (2008) the researchers tried, and failed, to replicate the monitoring approach within a nursing education program in another location in India—so that the longer-term potential of this intervention remains in doubt. As discussed in Chapter 11 of this volume, attempts to generalize from RCTs can be problematic for a variety of reasons.
64. Hardman et al. (2012, p. 828). The three main time allocations, in Hardman, refer to the following: (a) "initiation moves" were those counted as requests for information, teacher questions designed to elicit an answer, cued elicitation when teachers would use a question to check on understanding, teacher check as an affirmative answer from the pupils, teacher directs the class to do something, or pupil question to the teacher; (b) responses were the following moves coded in response to questioning: e.g., boy answer, girl answer, choral response, pupil demonstration, and teacher answer; and (c) refers to the next follow up: whether there was a response, whether

it was affirmed, whether it was praised, whether it was probed, whether it was commented upon, whether the teacher asked another pupil to answer.

65. See Fuller and Clarke (1994), who refer to training as "policy mechanics"—those who try to fix inputs. These are contrasted with "classroom culturalists"—those who worry about disconnections between home and school, or between training in best approaches, and approaches built on tradition. This perspective would seem to apply rather broadly to teachers and learning in many developing countries, and helps to explain the maintenance of traditional pedagogy even when more modern pedagogies are provided in training.

66. Dewey (1929, p. 15).

PART IV

Trends and Challenges

9

NEW TECHNOLOGIES

Problems and Prospects

Vijay: Playing Computer Games in Mumbai

In a large apartment complex on the outskirts of Mumbai, Vijay, a six-year-old boy, lives with his two parents and three-year-old sister. Mumbai is hot and crowded, but having lived in the same place his whole life, Vijay is well-adapted to his circumstances. Every night since he was about two, his mother and father—both secondary school graduates—take turns reading stories to him in Hindi. Vijay's parents are rarely at home together on weekday evenings, as they work extra hours at a local call center, trading off evenings of childcare. Recently, Vijay has started to go to his uncle's apartment two floors down to play computer games in the late afternoons once school is out. When he began last year, his favorite games were the ones that let him chase after monsters. But lately, he has focused more on English language learning apps—games that require him to match the letters and sounds of words, and listen to dialogues of two animated girls planning a party. Afterward, he makes a habit of conversing with his English-speaking uncle for a few minutes. With practice and his parents' moral and financial support, Vijay will likely have a chance to enter a reputable, private English language primary school next fall. Though only beginning his schooling trajectory, Vijay is on his way toward becoming part of a youthful India that is increasingly plugged into the Internet, social media, and downloadable knowledge.

Vijay's situation illustrates an oft-cited observation—that Indian children of relatively modest means can find ways to advance from relative poverty into the globalized middle class with the help of technology. Schools in India—both public and private—are introducing as much technology as possible into the classroom, and encouraging parents (those who can afford it) to use technology to supplement learning in the home. Vijay's parents are aware of this, and are planning to install broadband Internet in their home as soon as they can.

Perhaps nowhere is the use of new information and communication technologies (ICTs) more visible than in the developing world. Vijay is just one of many examples. We might also imagine a Cambodian farmer standing in his rice fields using a mobile phone to call his brother, who is busy ascertaining current prices in the regional farmers' market to determine how much rice they should harvest that day. In rural Ethiopia, illiterate youth use visual images (e.g., a butterfly, ball, or dog) to make and receive mobile phone calls, using an illustrated contact list where each image represents a different person.[1] Or, there is the young mother in Burundi who sends a text message to her local community health worker to say that she thinks she is about to deliver her first child and needs help quickly. New ICTs are of growing importance around the world, and increasingly impact many facets of people's everyday lives and livelihoods.

For more than half a century, educators, policymakers, and the broader public have been excited by the prospect of using technology for educational purposes, and this fascination shows no sign of abating. Radio, television, movies, computers, the Internet, mobile phones, and tablets have, each in their own way, revolutionized how learning and knowledge function in society. What we call "new" technology is constantly changing, and even older technologies (radio, TV, chalkboards, etc.) are still deployed for educational purposes around the world.

In the present discussion, we will consider increased access to educational technology (e.g., the number of children reached by a device or the Internet), and how children's learning (e.g., reading, writing, math, and language skills) and attitudes (e.g., motivation and ambition) may (or may not) be enhanced by ICTs. We ask several broad questions. What is the status of ICT use in developing countries? What, how, and when should ICT devices be utilized to improve learning? In what ways do ICTs improve learning inside and outside of schools? And how should we view the future of ICTs and learning in the years to come?

The Growth of ICTs in Developing Countries

New technologies have begun to change the contexts and practices of learning—often in dramatic ways. Some causes of these changes are obvious. ICTs—including cell phones, smartphones, tablets, and computers, mostly connected to the Internet—have become much cheaper and more powerful with each year that passes. This in turn has led to a massive proliferation of ICT devices across every sector of society. Mobile phones and other connected devices (as evidenced by subscription rates) are outpacing all other forms of communication technology (Figure 9.1).[2] Thus, while school-based learning has traditionally relied on physical tools such as textbooks, chalkboards, and workbooks—as well as teachers—the infrastructure of schooling is rapidly changing.

The increased availability of faster and cheaper mobile devices has had a major impact on learning. Though Vijay currently goes to his uncle's apartment to "play computer," he will have the Internet at home soon, as well as access to smart and Internet-connected mobile devices. He will have access to multimedia, and will likely be able to access Gujarati language materials that will help him stay in touch with his grandparents who are native Gujarati speakers and who do not live in Mumbai. Vijay, if he is able to enter the private school his parents seek for him, will soon be able to get feedback on his progress in school more quickly and reliably,[3] and will likely feel more empowered as a young person connected with others who share his interests. With so many appealing dimensions of ICT proliferation, it is no surprise that spending levels for ICTs have increased rapidly in every region of the world today (Figure 9.2).

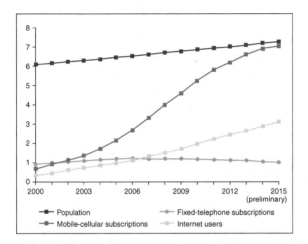

FIGURE 9.1 Estimated Number of Mobile-Cellular Subscriptions, Internet Users, and Fixed–Telephone Subscriptions, 2000–2015 (Billions)

Source: United Nations (2015)

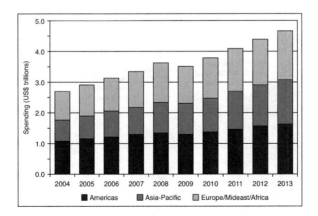

FIGURE 9.2 Growth of ICT Spending by Region, 2004–2013

Source: World Information and Technology Services Alliance (WITSA) (2013, p. 14)

ICTs, Learning, and Education

The reciprocal nature of learning and technology has become more transparent with each succeeding year. ICTs are altering both *what* gets learned, and *how, where* and *when* learning takes place.[4] There is also evidence that search engines (such as Google) are obviating the need to engage in memorization among both school children and adults—another way that ICTs change the way we learn.[5] While most of the research to date on cognitive impacts of ICTs has been collected from within Western countries, similar trends are likely to be seen among children in developing countries where memory skills have traditionally been more valued.[6]

Social media and online message boards are also changing the what/how/where/when of learning, and their growth in recent years has been astronomical (see Figure 9.3). Concomitantly, as many observers have noted, people of all ages are connected more often to their digital devices, spending less time on television, book reading, and other types of learning activities. Whether in rich or poor countries, an increasing percentage of primary and secondary school children, if they have the option, prefer to spend time on a digital device instead of listening to an instructor or reading a textbook.[7] This trend toward augmented connections with the digital world is surely one of the major learning transformations in the world today.

Policymakers have long been captivated by the notion that technology can help the poor (or poor countries) *leapfrog* into the 21st century. This was the idea of Jean-Jacques Servan-Schreiber, a well-known French journalist and politician. In his 1967 book, *Le Défi Américain (The American Challenge)*, Servan-Schreiber spoke of the promise of developing countries to *sauter en avant* (literally, "leap ahead") over Western nations by using new technologies. His book was a global best-seller,

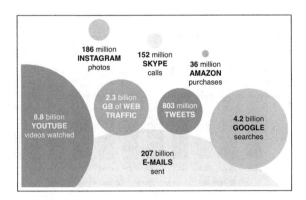

FIGURE 9.3 The Global Daily Use of Social Media

Source: World Bank (2016b, p. 6)

published in 15 languages—and that was decades before the personal computer and the Internet were invented![8]

Leapfrogging remains a popular idea, regularly reiterated by ministers of education, technologists, and many teachers. Today, nearly everyone is looking for a technological "silver bullet" to solve key social and economic problems. A case in point is the World Bank's recent claim that "ICTs can empower the lives of Africans and are driving entrepreneurship, innovation and income growth," while at the same time noting that a significant digital divide continues to separate people by income, age, geography, and gender (see Figure 9.4).[9] In another example, a recent UN report stated: "These days, web 2.0 and mobile technologies are being heralded for their revolutionary potential, not unlike the 1990s when the Internet's potential was only starting to be understood."[10] Such positive views are endemic in the international policy arena. But how much credibility do they really have, with whom and in which contexts?

Since the advent of computers, laptops, and the Internet, two iconic projects— One Laptop Per Child and Hole in the Wall—became among the best-known ICTs for education (ICT4E) projects. *One Laptop Per Child*, developed by researchers at MIT, used brightly colored, user-friendly laptops to appeal to young children, and sold them at a price that was, at the outset, far lower than current market prices.[11] The *Hole in the Wall*, developed in India, designed Internet kiosks that comfortably accommodated the smaller stature of a child.

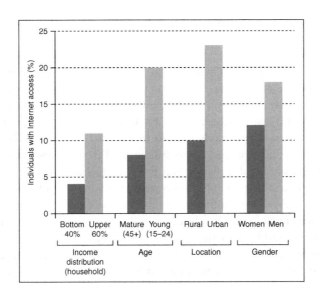

FIGURE 9.4 Within-Country "Digital Divide" in Africa

Source: World Bank (2016b, p. 9)

In the first decade of the 21st century, each project captured worldwide attention, even though there was little or no scientific research that confirmed the learning impact of either initiative.[12] This was an era when the exciting possibility of immense future gains (i.e., leapfrogging) tended to convince both the producers and the recipients of these projects to overlook, for the most part, the need to empirically justify their claims. Alas, many of these optimistic claims turned out to be exaggerated.

Even today there remains a tendency for donors, ministers, non-profits, and private sector technology firms to be uncharacteristically sanguine about the potential impact of technology in developing countries, even in cases where there is little more evidence than photographs of smiling children. In general, there seems to be a consensus that ICTs are (still) the "next big thing."[13] In spite of the view that ICTs are having (and will have) a major impact on education globally, and could help greatly in developing countries, there is a growing chorus of concern.[14] While advocates frequently use words such as *radical*, *revolutionary*, and *game-changing* to describe ICTs, recent empirical reviews and meta-analyses have called into question these overwrought promises.[15] Indeed, a more accurate way of viewing the role of ICTs for education is that some can, when properly deployed, be used to enable and amplify learning.[16] In other words, ICTs offer great potential, but the exaggerations of the recent past must be replaced by thoughtful and empirically grounded approaches in the future.

Part of the problem of measuring the value of ICT4E is that the rapid changes over recent years in the technology itself have made impact evaluation unusually difficult. By the time an evaluation study is completed, the ICT platform (phone, tablet, or software) may have changed so much that the study is no longer relevant.

There are also situations where local leaders may be highly sensitive to the risk of putting expensive computers in locations where theft or damage are realistic threats. In one such case, I was traveling with colleagues to visit an innovative ICT-based education project in rural Ghana. Upon our arrival, the school headmaster promptly took us to a special room where he proudly showed us 50 brand new computers still encased in their unopened original boxes. It was a source of pride for him that they had been kept safe and new for over a year, and that none had been stolen.[17] Seeing the situation from the headmaster's perspective, his decision to protect the computers at the expense of using them made sense. Surely he would be held accountable for a theft, should it occur, and such thefts were endemic in rural Ghana. Presumably, he had not been made aware that such technology has an unforgivingly short shelf-life, and that soon those pristine computers would no longer have operable software.

Of course, shelf-life poses little concern when the traditional infrastructure of schooling consists of blackboards, books, and writing implements. Yet the sad fate of the computers in Ghana was guaranteed by a locked door that would soon reduce their value dramatically. Rapid change in ICT devices and software makes it more and more difficult to assure effective implementation and evaluation.[18] ICT4E only partially resembles other areas of educational reform: a fairly long period of trial and error, followed by slow and incremental changes as the research base develops and well-crafted learning interventions that can be studied. But, unlike teachers and textbooks, the ICTs themselves do not generally retain their value for long.

As noted, the hopes and dreams of an ICT revolution have been present for many years, and were also part of the inception of the first set of UN education goals declared in Senegal in 2000.[19] At the meeting in Dakar, I happened to be part of a roundtable on the possible educational uses in developing countries of the new "information highway" (i.e., a common descriptor of the Internet at the time). One minister of education rose to declare that such developments would take a long time and be too expensive for poor countries—since they were still focused building "ordinary *paved* roads." There was no laughter, and he was right. Even two decades later, many countries are still grappling with providing the Internet to schools. At that time, a few development agencies were early adopters of ICTs; but most were not.[20] Today, there is little doubt that major development investments in ICT4E will grow. Still, a primary question remains: What are the best investments to make? Confusion about which ICT investments to make resides at least in part on the multidimensional nature of decision making in ICT4E.

An ICT4E Conceptual Framework

Perhaps more so than in other areas of education and development, new technologies are not only changing rapidly, but they are subject to the popular imagination of the public and policymakers alike. We (as parents, teachers, agency heads, activists, and students) have a common belief that technology will change our lives, mostly (though not always) in positive ways. But it is not easy to unpack which aspects of ICTs are most important for which purposes. Is it the speed of a device, its memory, its application, its ergonomics, or some other features?

Building on the learning framework in Chapter 3, we suggest an additional conceptual framework to clarify the complex discussions around ICT4E. This framework for ICT4E includes four components: purposes, devices, end users, and contexts. In each ICT4E project, these components are typically found in some fashion or another and combine to produce a *design solution* that is a proffered approach to addressing an educational problem (see Figure 9.5).[21]

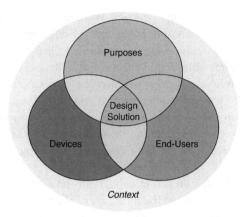

FIGURE 9.5 ICT4E Framework

Source: Wagner (2014b)

Purposes

The purpose of an ICT4E intervention may or may not be explicitly stated by its implementers. Indeed, many projects only allude to the purpose(s), and sometimes ignore the issue entirely, much to the detriment of those who wish to understand their impact and how to build on their approach. Many interventions combine more than a single purpose. For example, the Hole in the Wall initiative, described earlier, sought among other things to show that an ergonomic child-friendly Internet kiosk would help children learn; at the same time, it sought to demonstrate that unstructured learning[22] on the Internet was better than having teachers create Internet-based, directed learning. As it happened, the ergonomics were important in ways the creators of Hole in the Wall never imagined, since this was long before smartphones and tablets created wonderful, easily usable tools for young children. On the other hand, most evidence shows that unstructured learning and simple browsing on the Internet are not very effective.[23]

A few years ago, we undertook a review of mobile learning initiatives in developing countries. From this study, we identified six generic purposes of ICT4E interventions, as described below.[24]

> *Formal learning.* This type of intervention is best characterized as guided or directed learning (mainly in schools, but also in youth and adult NFE programs), corresponding to the two learning quadrants on the top of Figure 3.1a). It incorporates guided inquiry using clearly planned learning objectives in a structured format, which the end user usually experiences through modules or units. Projects that adhere to this purpose typically emphasize the acquisition of new knowledge and skills,

such as vocabulary for reading, or basic arithmetic. For example, Ustad Mobile in Afghanistan is a learning application that runs offline on simple feature phones and provides school-based materials in both Dari and Pashto from the first letter of the alphabet through grade 3 reading and math.[25]

Informal learning. Informal learning covers a range of non-directed (largely self-study) learning activities, such as students using text messages to practice reading or downloading digital materials on mobiles in their local language. Informal learning interventions offer materials or practices that try to engage the learners outside of formal educational settings, such as at home, or even in school but outside of the curriculum (corresponding to the two learning quadrants on the bottom of Figure 3.1a). The Video-Kheti project in India, for example, enables low-literate and novice users to find and watch agriculture-related videos through a text-free, multi-modal interface with speech, graphics, and touch, delivered through tactile smartphones and tablets.[26]

Content provision. Digital content is key to learner comprehension and motivation. Building on findings reviewed in earlier chapters, some ICT interventions try to fill the gap in available print by supplementing with digital materials. However, even today, only limited digital materials are available in local written languages, since more than 75% of the Internet is dominated by only ten primary languages (see Table 9.1). For these reasons,

TABLE 9.1 Languages on the Internet as of 2017 (Users in Millions)

Top 10 Languages	Internet Users	% of Total
English	952	25.2
Chinese	763	20.4
Spanish	294	7.9
Arabic	173	4.6
Portuguese	155	4.1
Indonesian	154	4.1
Japanese	118	3.2
Russian	104	2.8
French	101	2.7
German	84	2.2
Top 10 Languages	2,900	77.5
Other Languages	840	22.5
World Total	3,740	100

Source: http://www.internetworldstats.com/stats7.htm

interventions that provide e-books pre-loaded with local-language stories at varying levels of difficulty are now becoming more commonplace. In one large-scale initiative, over 400,000 Kindle e-books were distributed to students and teachers in sub-Saharan Africa.[27] Still, digital content that is sensitive to local languages is mostly lacking in ICT4E design solutions.

Training. Training interventions contain direct or guided instruction for those who support children's learning—mainly teachers, but also facilitators, school administrators, and parents. The purpose of these interventions is to enhance teachers' pedagogical skills by introducing new curricular content, such as lesson plans that support improved learning. For instance, one initiative in South Sudan used solar-powered digital audio players to provide teaching resources and content in the local languages of Dinka and Bari.[28] The recordings also function as a supplemental literacy tutor for children in school and for children who are not in school but who listen to the recordings in community group meetings.[29]

Data collection and monitoring. Given the increasing importance of accountability in development work, some projects attempt to rapidly assess children's learning gains.[30] Such ICTs aim to provide nearly real-time monitoring of what students do and do not know, and show teachers where to put their instructional efforts so they can remediate the weaknesses they observe. A growing initiative is the Tangerine data collection tablet-based platform, used for keeping tabs on children's early grade reading. It was first used in Kenya and Indonesia, and has now been adopted in multiple countries.[31] These data can also help to empower communities through increased accountability in terms of basic factors such as teacher and student attendance, materials delivery, and spending on school infrastructure.[32] Some projects have "back-end" systems that collect information on how the devices are used, and feed that information back into analyses and planning. These systems may collect a broad range of data from ICT devices, such as the keystrokes used and participation time.[33]

Communication. Some interventions use online communication platforms to exchange and deliver informational content. Though not necessarily centered on curricula, these efforts provide end users with an opportunity to engage in active dialogues with teachers or peers, where skills are practiced informally. Examples include providing real-time updates on market prices via cell phones, or conversational language learning in schools. For example, the Pink Phone Revolution project in Cambodia uses mobile phones to empower women, by allowing them to participate more fully in the marketplace, and to improve their safety and security.[34] By using text messages, women receive current information on agriculture trends, market prices, and relevant disaster preparedness, along with issues of domestic violence.

In sum, the six purposes here provide a topology of how project designers have concentrated their efforts to date. Even so, this list is by no means exhaustive, nor is it guaranteed to persist into the future as the ICT4E field continues to expand and change.

Devices

Devices (and device-based implementations) have been a highly visible feature in the history of technology and education—including radios, televisions, mobile phones, and the Internet. Each of these advances has inspired both consumers and development specialists to imagine what could happen if a particular device were deployed to "solve" a particular social problem.[35] Clearly, devices are necessary, but they are also not sufficient in terms of appropriate and effective design solutions for learning. Indeed, particular devices can sometimes lead in the wrong direction, and use up valuable time and policy energy by going down a path with little in the way of progress.

Let's take another look at the One Laptop Per Child initiative that sought to capitalize on the advantages of relatively low-cost and portable laptops to provide one-to-one computing for children. The MIT-developed laptop was highly attractive, and had features that seemed to portend well for use in developing countries (such as anti-glare screens and peer-to-peer networking). One Laptop Per Child garnered a lot of of media and fiscal attention, and more than one million computers were sold to developing countries from Uruguay to Rwanda. Excitement was in the air. Personally, I can recall a moment at UNESCO in Paris in 2006 when Nicholas Negroponte, an MIT professor and head of the project, demonstrated one of the first One Laptop units at a major international conference. There was near-universal acclaim of those in attendance, with the apparent promise that the laptop would revolutionize education, and would bring the world's knowledge to all children. Though there was reason for optimism at the time, it didn't do either, unfortunately. Multiple evaluation studies found little or no impact on learning. For example, in Peru, where a major investment of more than 850,000 laptops was made, no positive impact was found on students' learning outcomes.[36] While considerable resources have been spent on the One Laptop project, its largely device-based approach has little to show for itself, casting a shadow over many other more worthy efforts.

Of course, not all devices need to be built for education. Some, like the now-ubiquitous mobile phone, can be "re-purposed" for uses by students. Thus, students can use such phones as an avenue to share information on school assignments or to provide peer-to-peer advice on math or reading questions. These projects take advantage of devices that have the greatest penetration (percentage of users) in poor countries, making content available to those who do not have sufficient reading materials in their own local languages.[37] Mobile phones, especially smartphones with multimedia, are already assisting young beginning readers through the use of interactive games, though connectivity remains problematic.[38]

End Users

The third design parameter to consider is the end user. In education, the individual learner (whether in or out of school, whether a teacher or student or manager of the educational system) is the ultimate "end user." Naturally, educational interventions may fail when they are incompatible with the particular interests, languages and cognitive skills of their end users. Conversely, projects are more successful to the degree that they are designed with end user competencies in mind.

With respect to gender, one female-led project used mobile phones in Afghanistan to promote women's literacy.[39] Launched in 2011, this project aimed to teach literacy and empower women and girls—while also providing access to gender-specific information regarding human rights, health, and hygiene—through mobile phone–based learning. Fifty students were selected to participate in the pilot stage: each received a mobile phone, a SIM card, and a notebook. Teachers sent daily text messages to the students who read the incoming message and responded via return text message to demonstrate reading comprehension and writing skills. Women's direct involvement (and care for the interests of end users) was thought to be a key for success.[40]

Contexts

As seen in other educational domains, there is no doubt that social, cultural, and linguistic factors are crucial for effectiveness, even though too few projects provide sufficient contextual details.[41] When the One Laptop Per Child project was originally announced, much was made of its screen—with its matte non-glare surface—that could be used out-of-doors by African students sitting under trees, as it was advertised at the time. What was ignored is that few (if any) African schools would allow the laptops to go out of the classroom. Nor would more privileged students with access to these laptops wish to be seen working under trees when they could work in a school classroom instead! Clearly, project designers must keep contexts in mind as they implement an ICT4E intervention.

Design Solutions

The final and central element of this ICT4E framework is a design solution that follows from a combination of purpose, device, end users, and context.[42] Surprising as it may seem, there are many instances where only one or two parameters—say, the targeted end user and/or the technical parameters of the device employed— are adequately described and detailed, while the remaining parameters are ignored or poorly understood. For example, in one device-centered project, tablets were supplied to poor Ethiopian villages with the idea that, even without English-speaking teachers or textbooks, young primary school children could teach themselves how to read in English.[43] Missing from the design solution was an adequate description of the project's purpose, such as why English was the target language in rural villages where no English was spoken or could be maintained. Clearly, this was a design solution without sufficient forethought, and was destined to fail. When creating appropriate design solutions—whether they start with a device in mind, or a specific set of end users—ICT4E projects face all the usual problems of any development intervention.

ICTs for End User Groups

When new technologies are applied to educational endeavors they can sometimes appear a bit haphazard or even misguided—hence, the ICT4E framework just described. But from an investment perspective—whether by local, national, or international organizations—thinking often revolves around end user (or target population) groups in which they have a particular programmatic interest.

Early Childhood Development

Even though policy interest in early childhood development has grown in recent years, work on the role of ICTs' impact on young children has been limited to mostly OECD countries.[44] Until fairly recently, television, such as the well-known program *Sesame Street*, has received the most attention and was evaluated in terms of teaching the alphabet and other pre-reading skills;[45] more recently in countries like South Africa, it has expanded into teaching HIV/AIDS prevention as well.[46] The positive results of such TV programs appear to be highly dependent on level of exposure and on parental involvement on the one hand, and on ECD instructor training on the other.[47]

With the advent of digital devices (smartphones and tablets, in particular), a variety of new possibilities have opened up in support of young children's exposure to ICTs, as we saw in the opening story of Vijay in Mumbai. These range from games that support early math and reading,[48] to data showing how children learn to read.[49] Some new efforts have been made to develop ways to send text messages to parents in support of parenting skills, similar to those used in the health sector.[50]

Primary Education

ICT investments in primary schools have taken two main forms: (a) improved *access* to ICTs (such as computers and the Internet); and (b) *device-assisted learning* (or direct instruction). For more than a decade, I worked on a project that attempted to address both ICT access and children's reading acquisition in rural, poor, and multilingual populations in Andhra Pradesh (India), and later in Limpopo (South Africa). The project, the *Bridges to the Future Initiative*, provided high-quality learning content in local languages for primary school children in marginalized communities. The main focus was to create mother-tongue literacy content—in multiple languages using multimedia resources—to support children's reading. We also sought to take advantage of the existing ICT infrastructure located in rural schools, which allowed quick expansion and avoided costly purchase of hardware. Both projects were systematically evaluated. In India, the project showed large gains in student motivation, but learning gains were mixed, at least in part due to lack of sufficient time utilization per student.[51] In South Africa, the project had greater resources and improved content in three African languages, as well as English.[52] Children could choose to read in any of the four languages provided, with content organized thematically and woven into a localized story. With this additional attention toward a better design solution, the impact on early reading was very strong.[53]

Also in primary schools, a large meta-analysis of 15 ICT interventions in Latin America found that "guided use" (direct instruction) of technology was key to greater learning impact, rather than just providing devices for informal use.[54] In other words, when students and teachers have an idea of what skills should be learned, with software that is well-defined and with a specified time on task, then the learning impact was significantly improved. Interventions that simply provided access to the Internet or to digital games without guidance had little or no impact on learning.

Overall, the growing compendium of primary school ICT initiatives and research outcomes supports the idea that with a well-crafted design solution that takes into account the needs of the end user, major gains can be made.

Secondary Education

The use of technology in support of secondary education differs from primary education in several key ways. Secondary schools have significant advantages, such as: a longer history of ICT investment; better ICT infrastructure including stable electricity and computer labs (since secondary schools are usually in more urban areas); students who can better understand the international languages that prevail in ICTs and Open Educational Resources;[55] a greater number of teachers who are familiar with ICTs; more opportunities to tailor ICTs by gender;[56] and a closer rapport between students' ICT capabilities and post-schooling employment opportunities that may require them.[57]

It is important to note here that enthusiasm for the growth of ICTs among secondary school (and other) students has been mixed. In wealthy countries, parents, teachers, and policymakers are increasingly concerned that the constant use of (and perhaps "addiction to"[58]) digital devices takes precious time away from more important learning activities (such as reading textbooks, or listening to teachers). These concerns have been growing over time, and reported in the media, as in the well-known article: "Is Google Making Us Stupid?"[59] Data recently collected among secondary school students across more than 40

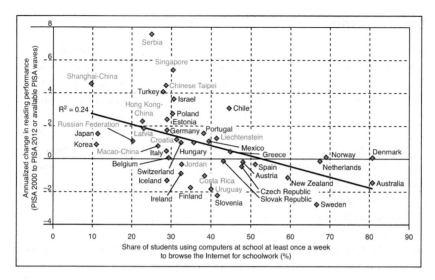

FIGURE 9.6 Trends in Reading Performance and Proportion of 15-Year-Old Students Who Frequently Browse the Internet for Schoolwork at School

Source: OECD (2015, p. 152)

OECD countries supports this same concern, where it was found that a nation's reading achievement *decreased* as a function of the frequency with which high school students spent time browsing the Internet (see Figure 9.6).[60] In other words, evidence is building, at least in some countries, that wholesale adoption of more access and use of ICTs may not be consistently positive for school-based learning achievement.

Some have suggested that technology-based learning will finally leapfrog ahead due to the massive penetration of the Internet. One recent example is the MOOC (massive online open courseware), supported via the Internet. To date, most MOOCs have been geared toward secondary and post-secondary/university students, and their growth has been exponential. While MOOCs have the potential to reach a broader population of learners at scale, their use in developing countries has been challenged in a number of ways.[61] Criticisms are similar to that of other ICT4E projects, and include high dropout rates, limited provision of courseware in languages other than English and other international languages, limited access to broadband Internet connection among local populations, and relatively narrow course offerings in the pre-university domain.[62]

Notwithstanding the above concerns, ICT use in secondary education appears destined to expand as quality improves, teachers become more interested, and workforce demands continue to grow. Whether ICTs can help to radically transform the way that pedagogy is organized for secondary school remains to be seen.

Teacher Education

As discussed in Chapter 8, teachers' education and professional development are essential elements in the quest to improve children's learning. The broad use of ICTs for teacher training has occasionally been reviewed in terms of strengths and weaknesses, human resources, and costs. While there is great potential in this area, the results to date have been lackluster.[63]

However, one recent multi-year intervention in Kenya deserves our attention.[64] The project team distributed three different ICT device configurations (tablets for teacher trainers, tablets for each teacher, and e-readers for students) and also trained a cohort of local primary school teachers. The study consisted of 80 schools, and children's learning gains and cost-effectiveness were measured. By comparing the three types of interventions with control groups (who received no ICT intervention), the researchers found a distinctive learning impact between each of the interventions, but no overall impact relative to the control samples.[65] In terms of cost-effectiveness, however, the most gains per dollar came from the use of tablets by teacher trainers, while the least gains per dollar were those of the e-readers distributed to each individual child.[66] In other words, consideration of the relative cost per unit of learning impact will likely see much more attention in the coming years.[67]

In teacher training, MOOCs may also play a special role, particularly by providing an alternative to the cascade model of teacher training. At its core, the cascade model is based on the transfer of instructional capabilities from expert teachers (or trainers) to less experienced teachers.[68] One way to visualize this method is shown in Figure 9.7 (left side). In this conceptual view, experts (often from OECD countries) are sent to developing countries to train local and regional specialists (as in the Nigerian vignette that opened the previous chapter). One major problem

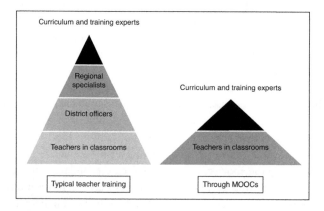

FIGURE 9.7 MOOCs and Teacher Professional Development

Source: Wagner (2014a)

with the typical cascade model is that experts can never fully assure the transfer of their skills to the next level down in the pyramid. Engineers have long described this as the "signal to noise ratio," where the transfer of information loses fidelity from one person to the next. With ICTs, one can "flatten" the pyramid (shown on right side of the figure) by providing the source expertise directly to the recipient teachers—from expert MOOC to classroom teacher. An example of this type of effort can be seen in India, where a program called TESS-India has created a multilingual teacher professional development program through the use of online digital resources.[69]

Current trends also suggest that teachers now have sufficient knowledge about how to use ICTs.[70] This is because teachers today are more likely to have learned their ICT tools before becoming teachers, and their students also are increasingly coming to school with ICT skills learned outside of the classroom. Instead, in the coming years, we can expect that teachers will need to learn how to employ ICTs to improve children's learning that is commensurate with teachers' pedagogical approaches.[71]

Overall, the increased focus on the needs of end user groups in education mirrors that of the private sector. In the private sector, identified groups are targeted for their online interest in particular goods and services—something that is supported with big data collected by marketing firms. In education, a similar process is taking place, in which ICTs are used for different purposes with different end users.[72]

Digital Dilemmas in the Road Ahead

Given today's rapidly changing technological landscape, the digital road ahead will be full of bumps, dips, and (possibly) leaps. ICTs for education represent one area where investment and creative ideas will converge to foster major learning gains. One way to think about the challenges ahead is to address the digital dilemmas that policymakers currently face.

Access Versus Quality

As discussed in earlier chapters, the UN development goals have shifted from access to quality of education.[73] A parallel distinction may be seen in ICT4E. In the early years, say from 2000 to 2010, the idea of expanding access to ICTs (whether through computer labs, or kiosks with the Internet) tended to dominate the discussion. To some extent, there is still momentum for the idea of extending cheap Internet access to people of all social and economic circumstances around the world, including "parachuting" devices or apps into rural villages in poor countries.[74] For the most part, however, research has shown that such access-only projects have a minimal impact on learning outcomes, and that a clear purpose, focused end user targets, and guided use are necessary to make such implementations effective. Investments must be made in the *quality* of learning in ICT4E, with design solutions that maximize the link between ICT devices and the engagement of the user.

Devices Versus Content

We know from our personal experience that new devices are tempting and even seductive. The same allure holds true for development professionals. New technology is glitzy, powerful, fast, exciting, and imaginative. But does it work for the learning goals we seek? That's the big question. Generally, we know that projects with a unique focus on devices are not likely to be successful or sustainable because contextual understanding is often lacking, and current devices will always make way for later devices. Nonetheless, devices that are well-coupled with other components in the ICT4E framework (including connectivity) are more likely to succeed. These solutions will also be highly dependent on what captures an individual's attention.[75] Does this imply that content is more important than the devices themselves? Currently, the answer seems to be "yes"—assuming that the content is designed for specific end user groups and is adapted to cultural context. As ICT4E moves forward, we will likely witness a more complementary blending of devices with appropriate content.

Fixed Costs Versus Total Cost of Ownership

Until a decade ago, ICTs were often thought to be too expensive for development initiatives. Even today, surprisingly little information is available about the actual costs of devices, software, and human resources for implementation of projects. It appears that many ICT4E projects are funded by donors, governments, or private sector agencies (or some combination thereof). This is predominantly a fixed-cost or supply-side approach, and perhaps has been appropriate in the initial stages of ICT4E work. Even the few projects that are integrated into a national curriculum seem to exist primarily because a donor agency has provided support to an education ministry to undertake the project.

To consider the cost implications of ICT4E, it is essential to take into account the total cost of ownership.[76] For example, in one project in South Africa, students used mobile phones provided by a donor, but the costs of texting and social media connection time were a serious impediment.[77] Some have suggested that total costs can be reduced through a *Bring Your Own Device* approach, where learners use their own mobile devices with content loaded from a project implementer.[78] Equipment breakage is another key cost component, though it is sometimes neglected.[79] There are also comparative costs to consider, where variations of ICT inputs can have significantly different costs per unit of learning impact.[80] Overall, cost is a significant barrier that some countries can only overcome with funding from development agencies and/or private sector corporate foundations, but where recurrent costs also need to be taken into account.[81]

Timeframe Pressure Versus Equity

For some policymakers, there is a distinctly time-limited dimension to the implementation of ICT4E projects. Particularly in the private sector, both devices and timeframe tend to push projects into contexts with a device-friendly environment (e.g., with steady electricity), well-trained teachers, and a secure space for equipment. In more challenging contexts, such as in rural areas and in low-income communities, many impediments to effective implementation exist.[82] Improving such contexts takes time, and thus works against an equity orientation. In addition, a "trickle-down" intervention (from, say, urban schools first, then rural schools) is possible in principle, but timing is such that the rural effort may simply not happen. Therefore, a *pro-poor* or pro-equity approach in ICT4E is needed—placing the emphasis and focus directly on the bottom of the pyramid.[83]

Public Sector Versus Private Sector

ICT4E is unusual in the public education sector, since it is necessarily joined with the private sector's ability to provide ICT devices (including Internet access). In other words, without the private sector, ICT4E initiatives would happen far less often and would be far less worthwhile (never mind less exciting). Further, when the public sector has, at times, sought to compete with the private sector, the private sector typically produced cheaper and better products before the initiative could achieve scale. Examples abound, especially when claims for cheap development tools are promoted as game-changers, but often cannot deliver on promises.[84]

The private sector marketplace overwhelmingly drives personal usage, such that the window of usability of purpose-built devices is rather short-lived (about two to three years on average). ICT4E programs that are built upon robust and well-populated devices (such as mobile phones, or tablets, or LCD projectors) are more likely to succeed long enough to establish a program of learning that merits the investment. A blend of public sector goals with private sector device capabilities is the best path forward.

In-Depth Versus Scaling Up Approaches

One of the main attractions of ICTs in education is their potential scalability. As with apps and Internet-driven commerce (e.g., the Uber app), marketing to large populations—that is, scaling up with a single tool—is potentially very cost-effective. With the right design solution, the ability to scale up in ICT4E reduces the per-person cost (and growth in the return on investment) in direct proportion to the size of the denominator—as with the rise of MOOCs today. There are also in-depth (linguistically focused) approaches to ICT4E, as in the Bridges to the Future Initiative in India (described earlier). Some of these may not be scalable in the near term, but may allow for an expanded understanding of what might work in the future and provide models for best practice. Most ICT4E projects today are not very scalable, as they are typically in the pilot or project-based phase of work. Nonetheless, being able to go to scale (locally, nationally, or internationally) in well-defined ways is ultimately what will drive the expansion of ICTs for learning and education at a per-person cost that will decline significantly in future years.[85]

Big Data Versus Small Data

The advent of social media, the growth of personal digital devices, and the ability of providers to capture individual use on a large scale has led to the advent of big data—that is, the collection of massive amounts of information from large numbers of end users. At present, the education field is only just beginning to pay attention to big data, while in the health and economic sectors big data has already become, well, very big! Take, for example, recent attempts to measure poverty in developing countries. In Rwanda, mobile phone ownership was used to infer poverty status. Previously, to collect such poverty statistics, a national household survey was undertaken at a cost of more than US $1 million, and it required 12 to 18 months to complete. By contrast, a comparable big data analysis of mobile phone usage cost only US $12,000 and took four weeks—a massive savings in time and money.[86] In another study, mobile phones were used to collect the numbers and types of stories of interest to student readers in seven diverse countries, from Ethiopia to Pakistan.[87] With the increasing use of social media and connected devices, there is sure to be a major input of big data into ICT4E, which will allow for a far better understanding of how design solutions are used at scale.[88] Yet, as big data use is growing, there is increasing concern that its wholesale adoption may mask small data that in turn help explain outcomes in particular contexts.[89]

In sum, new technologies are exciting and enticing in many ways. Those who are old enough may remember, perhaps with some nostalgia, the onset of emails, floppy disks, "high-speed" modems, mobile phones, USB sticks, and so on. With cutting-edge devices and applications being produced at an unceasing pace, it is perilous to predict what innovative technologies may be available in the coming years. Nonetheless, there are a number of key design ideas (based on the notion of purposes described earlier) in the ICT4E framework that will likely be important over the next decade or so (Box 9.1). Each would help build a solid base for supporting and implementing ICT-based learning in the service of learning equity.

New Opps for New Apps

There will undoubtedly be new opportunities ("opps") for new ICT4E applications ("apps") in the coming years. ICTs inherently promote an expanding vision of what it means to be a skilled and informed citizen in a world that is both continuously transformed by information and social media as well as buffeted by the headwinds of global change.

BOX 9.1   IDEAS FOR INNOVATION IN ICT4E

a. Where an installed base of computers (or devices) already exists, provide local content to support reading instruction in multiple languages (including mother-tongue) in primary schools.

b. Implement and assess the comparative learning impact of differing ICT inputs in multiple sites in various countries.

c. Carry out qualitative/ethnographic studies of the use of mobiles in the home and out of school, to ascertain the ability of educational institutions to use these devices to support learning.

d. Select one of the most disadvantaged populations in a developing country (e.g., poor rural girls who are out of school) and create a design solution specifically for them—with adequate resources to recalibrate and overcome obstacles.

e. Undertake a device inventory among the one or more marginalized populations in one or more developing countries, perhaps using graphical information systems (GIS) technology.

f. Undertake in-depth studies of the constraints of local capacity on success.

g. Collect and use educational "big data." With the increase in digitally collected learning outcomes, ministries of education can begin to detect local and regional systemic problems in instruction, closer to real-time decision making.

h. Enable teachers to receive digital support information that is relevant to their instruction, and in real time. This might include: instructional materials, advice from mentors, knowledge about individual student's learning progress, language support tools (in multilingual classrooms), or daily messaging to parents and siblings.

Source: Wagner (2014b)

At the tender age of six, these social changes already play an important role in Vijay's life in Mumbai. For Vijays of all ages and contexts, ICTs will soon be able to offer innovative educational tools that help meet the United Nations development goals for 2030. Whether in poor parts of Mumbai or elsewhere around the world, the power of technology offers an unprecedented opportunity, but it also contains the seeds for increased disparities between the rich and the poor. It is essential that the spotlight stay oriented toward learning among the poor to prevent ever-widening economic and opportunity gaps that continue to grow as a result of the pressures of globalization and environmental changes.

Notes

1. Robinson-Pant (2016, p. 104).
2. With technology restrictions recently ending in Myanmar, mobile operators are competing to make it the first smartphone-only country in the world. Currently, less

than 10% of cell phone users own smartphones. See: www.ictworks.org/2014/08/20/myanmar-will-be-the-first-smartphone-only-country/.

3. Increases in reliability stem in part from the fact that fewer hands touch the data that is collected for analysis. See further discussion later in this chapter.

4. On the relationship between cognitive skills and the use of ICTs, see Terras and Ramsey (2012); on how and when, see for example Toyama (2015) and Traxler (2009, 2010).

5. See Carr (2008) and Sparrow et al. (2011).

6. See Chapters 5 and 7.

7. Tolani-Brown et al. (2009). Others have found that students' continuous interaction with web-based literacy activities is having a significant impact on reading skills, such as reduced ability of students to stay focused on reading extended text (Leu et al., 2009). A recent book by Baron (2016) discusses the "fate of reading" in the age of the Internet and social media, and the growing interest of children to read "on screen." Such findings are rapidly evolving, and more research is needed across contexts and countries.

8. Servan-Schreiber (1967).

9. World Bank (2012a, p. 5); on the digital divide, see World Bank (2016b, p. 9). Even in the United States there are growing concerns about disparities and digital divides, as in a similar *New York Times* report: www.nytimes.com/2016/02/23/technology/fcc-internet-access-school.html. For a critical review, see Unwin (2009).

10. UNDP (2013b, p. 1).

11. One Laptop per Child (2013). The initial "sticker price" was to be US $100, but that low price was never achieved, and as discussed later in this chapter, the cost of the laptop is only a fraction of the total cost of ownership and implementation.

12. Sugata Mitra (2003) established the Hole in the Wall initiative while based at the National Institute for Information Technology (NIIT) in India. With respect to Hole in the Wall (HIWEL, 2013), Internet access was seen as the primary goal, and little effort was made to create more than informal and user-friendly kiosks. Empirical research on this initiative is surprisingly limited, but see Mitra (2003), DeBoer (2009), and Arora (2010).

13. For some generally positive perspectives, among many, see Kozma (2011), Guardian (2013), UNESCO (2013a), and Winthrop and Smith (2012). See Wagner and Kozma (2005) for an earlier review on technology and literacy.

14. For examples of mistakes that have been made, see Trucano's (2010) enlightening blog on *worst practices* in ICTs for education: "Dump hardware in schools, hope for magic to happen . . . ; Think about educational content only after you have rolled out your hardware; . . . Make a big bet on an unproven technology; . . . Don't think about (or acknowledge) total cost of ownership."

15. Some of these critical reviews include: Barrera-Osorio and Linden (2009), Clarke et al. (2013), Cuban (2003), Dodson et al. (2012), McEwan (2015), Warschauer (2004), and Wagner (2005). See also Trucano (2012).

16. See Clarke et al. (2013) on ICT4D as an enabler; and Toyama (2015) on the idea of ICTs as amplifiers of impact. A similar perspective was taken by the World Bank (2016b) in their call for "analog complements" to digital inputs, based on non-digital foundations in developing countries; and see Heeks (2014) on potential for ICTs and the UN development goals.

17. For more on this research effort, see Wagner et al. (2004).

18. Multi-year impact evaluations are particularly at risk when ICTs are undergoing rapid change.

19. The EFA (Education for All) goals were declared in Dakar, Senegal, in 2000. In the same year, a UN ICT Taskforce was created, but it is now defunct; see a historical description at: www.itu.int/wsis/basic/faqs_answer.asp?lang=en&faq_id=88. For the 2030 UN SDGs, see: https://sustainabledevelopment.un.org/TFM.

20. For example, see the work of IDRC-Canada, Elder et al. (2014), and the World Bank's Infodev (www.infodev.org).

21. This framework was developed in Wagner (2014b). Other frameworks exist as well, such as: the FRAME model of Koole (Koole and Ally, 2006; Koole et al., 2010), which shares the notion of convergence, but is less focused on design solutions, and a set of "first principles" for ICT4E (see Gaible et al., 2011). Also Pachler et al. (2010) provide a useful discussion of the cultural features that must be considered in effective designs. UNICEF also has provided a framework at: http://unicefstories.org/2013/08/06/child-friendly-technology-framework/.
22. This was termed "minimally invasive education" by Mitra (2003).
23. See later discussion of Arias-Ortiz and Cristia (2014).
24. In this report, 44 projects in developing countries were analyzed (Wagner, 2014b).
25. See Ustad Mobile (Paiwastoon, 2013). Also, the Bridges to the Future Initiative in South Africa (Castillo, 2017) promotes reading acquisition through supplementary instruction using mobile tablets, as well as instruction supported by desktop computers. An early evaluation of this computer-based approach was undertaken in India (Wagner et al., 2010). In Niger, Aker et al. (2011) used mobiles to teach beginning reading and math to adults.
26. Cuendet et al. (2013). In a second example, the BBC Janala (Walsh & Shaheen, 2013) project, in Bangladesh, aims to teach English language listening and reading skills using a combination of interactive audio and mobile technology along with print and other ICT-based materials. Three-minute audio English lessons and quizzes are accessible through text messages using cell phones.
27. See the Worldreader project (UNESCO, 2014b). Another project, Sesame Workshop's *M Is for Mobile* initiative (Stewart, 2013), has begun to consider the potential of existing mobile technologies to reach educators and families that may have limited access to traditional media channels in India.
28. Across Radio (Pioneers Australia, 2012).
29. EDC has a long history of work with interactive radio instruction (for example, in Zanzibar; EDC, 2011) and more recently with English language acquisition in Colombia and the Dominican Republic (EDC, 2014). In Mali, EDC (2011) used Internet-enabled mobile phones to offer primary teachers access to resources and suggested lesson plans for French literacy instruction.
30. See Wagner (2011a) and further discussion in Chapter 11.
31. On Tangerine, see Pouezevara and Strigel (2011).
32. Uganda and Peru have both implemented this type of monitoring through the UNICEF EduTrac program (UNICEF, 2016). Thanks to N. Castillo (personal communication) for this suggestion.
33. For example, e-EGRA (EDC, 2011–12), piloted in Mali and the Philippines.
34. Mendoza and Vergel de Dios (2012); Yardley (2011). Similarly, the Yoza Project (2009–2013) in South Africa incorporated the use of mobile phones to communicate learning content and m-novels (short digital novellas) to create social media communities that foster literacy.
35. Several donors were able to anticipate earlier than many national authorities about the lack of effectiveness of initiatives like One Laptop per Child and Hole in the Wall (Trucano, 2012).
36. Cristia et al. (2012); also Beuermann et al. (2015) and Nugroho & Lonsdale. (2010). Poor results were found in Uruguay; see Ferrando et al. (2011) on the first study, and later research by de Melo et al. (2013). A One Laptop Per Child study in China, using a randomized experiment in some Beijing schools, found significant improvement in student computer skills after a six-month intervention program, but no impact on basic skills learning; Mo et al. (2012). See also Fajebe et al. (2013) on a program that used these laptops for teacher education in Rwanda.
37. See, for example, the work of Jukes et al. (2016), on the role of text messaging in reducing primary school dropout, and the work of Alcoholado et al. (2012), on the use of multiple mice. See also UNESCO (2014b).

38. In developing countries, some early examples are from Ho et al. (2009) and Medhi et al. (2007). See also Unwin (2014). Thanks to T. Unwin (personal communication) for his observations on connectivity.
39. Undertaken by the Afghan Institute of Learning, and reported in Wagner (2014b, p. 127).
40. Wagner (2014b, 2016). See also Dodson et al. (2013). Other interventions that have targeted specific ethno-linguistic groups by providing reading content in locally appropriate languages (or multilingual content) have found significant gains in student motivation for learning, such as *1001 Stories* (Wagner, 2014b, p. 21).
41. For examples on cultural and qualitative issues in the ICT domain, see Hauser (2013) and Rangaswamy and Cutrell (2012).
42. For a similar conceptualization, see Design-Based Research Collective (2003).
43. Talbot (2012). It seems that this example was not followed up by empirical research evidence; it simply disappeared.
44. See, for example, Bolstad (2004), Kalas (2010), and Kalas (2012).
45. For a recent overview, see Hinostroza et al. (2014). See ACER (2010) for work with Australian indigenous children. For international impact, see Cole (2009).
46. Schierhout (2005).
47. Hinostroza et al. (2014); Baydar et al. (2008). In Paraguay, Bolivia, Honduras, Indonesia, Tanzania, and Malawi, work using interactive radio instruction seems to have had an overall positive impact on the effectiveness of training ECD specialists. See Naslund-Hadley et al. (2012) and Ho and Thukral (2009).
48. See Flannery et al. (2013), Gómez et al. (2013), and Shuler (2012).
49. Pouezevara and Strigel (2011).
50. D'Sa et al. (2014) conducted applied research on behalf of Save the Children that used text messages to remind fathers how they should parent their children on a weekly basis in Bangladesh.
51. Wagner et al. (2010).
52. The African languages are Sepedi, Xitsonga, and Venda. For a sample of the multimedia software, see http://literacy.org/media. The Bridges to the Future Initiative, in South Africa (BFI-SA) was implemented by the Molteno Institute for Language and Literacy, based in Johannesburg, South Africa. Together, the International Literacy Institute (University of Pennsylvania) and Molteno were co-recipients of the 2014 UNESCO Confucius Prize for the work on the BFI-SA.
53. Wagner and Castillo (2016); Castillo (2017). The results of an experimental study in South Africa conducted with children assessed in grade 1, and then followed into grade 2, showed a significant gain (about 0.37 Cohen's *d* score) to their reading scores when compared with a control group that did not have the multimedia content. However, when seen across projects among primary school children in developing countries where design solutions have often been inadequate, meta-analyses have generally shown only occasional positive gains (Tamim et al., 2011). Several other studies in primary schools in developing countries include: Barrera-Osorio and Linden (2009) in Colombia; Carrillo et al. (2010) in Ecuador; Kam (2013) and Pawar et al. (2006) in India; and Zurita and Nussbaum (2004) in Chile. In relatively wealthy OECD countries, with more infrastructure in place, results have been more consistently positive (OECD, 2012); in the United States, see Campuzano et al. (2009).
54. See Arias-Ortiz and Cristia (2014). Note that one of the 15 studies analyzed included children in secondary school.
55. Open Educational Resources (OER). OERs refer to teaching and learning materials mainly in digital form that reside in the public domain. In an interesting review by Butcher and Associates (2014), Butcher (p. 8) raises a legitimate concern about OERs as currently used, namely that "new models are now predominantly old educational 'wine' in new skins: that we are primarily harnessing the innovation of OER only

to reproduce content-heavy, top-down models of education that were developed hundreds of years ago . . . , models in which the student is still primarily a passive 'consumer' . . . whose main task is to complete standardized assessment tasks in order to receive accreditation. These educational models—still so dominant in most countries around the world—no longer meet the needs of society . . . for the complex, information-driven world in which they find themselves."

56. In a review of non-formal education initiatives for adolescent girls in more than a dozen developing countries, it was found that ICTs can provide a new way to challenge "unequal power relations and increasing participation of marginalized girls" using community development centers (UNICEF, 2012, p. 5).

57. National case studies in Bangladesh (Khan et al., 2012) and Nigeria (Adomi & Kpangban, 2010) are among the many that support these points. A review of the use of ICT4E in United States secondary schools may be found in Leask and Pachler (2013). See also Raftree (2013) on the use of mobiles in workforce development in developing countries; and Levy and Murnane (2007) on this issue in industrialized countries.

58. Graham and Nikolova (2012).

59. Carr (2008).

60. OECD (2015, p. 152). It should be noted that these data show a relationship via correlation only, so that we really do not know what variable or variables led to the decline in reading.

61. Wagner (2014a); Castillo et al. (2015). See the University of Pennsylvania MOOCs4D website at www.moocs4d.org; as well as: Bartholet (2013) and Liyanagunawardena et al. (2014).

62. Kizilcec et al. (2017) found, in an interesting recent study, that one of the reasons for high dropout rates in disadvantaged communities was what was termed the "social identity threat" among users in developing countries. With MOOC users mainly based in India, Pakistan, and Egypt, an intervention that sought to help users feel more of a sense of "belonging" or comfortable (with less challenge to their identity) within the broader cohort of users worldwide resulted in significantly lower dropout rates.

63. Gaible and Burns (2005). See Unwin (2005) for a policy review largely on Africa. An earlier comprehensive review, mainly on the United Kingdom, was undertaken by Cox et al. (2003). A later review on ICT and teacher training in the United States was done by Lawless and Pellegrino (2007). For a multilateral and global perspective, see UNESCO (2008).

64. See Piper and Kwayumba (2014) in the PRIMR intervention study (also discussed in Chapter 5). Note also that data collection was done via a tablet-based assessment system (Pouezevara & Strigel, 2011; Strigel & Pouezevara, 2012).

65. Piper et al. (2016).

66. Another way of looking at these results is that each of the three interventions is better than no intervention. Thus, spending less (on teachers with tablets) cannot be equated with better learning overall, just more "bang for the buck." This argument is similar to a report that argued that more funding does not necessarily bring better learning outcomes in OECD countries (Mourshed et al., 2010). It should also be emphasized that substantial resources were invested on educational innovations with both the curriculum and teacher training before the ICT-based intervention in Kenya, a key factor that is often missing in quickly deployed ICT projects in many countries.

67. Other studies on ICTs and teacher training are accumulating. For example, in Australia (Pegrum et al., 2013) and on mobile phones in Malaysia (Ismail et al., 2013). See also the example in Chapter 8 of using digital cameras to track teacher instruction time in schools in India.

68. On the cascade model, see earlier discussion in Chapter 8.

69. See www.tess-india.edu.in/about-tess-india. TESS-India is led by the Open University UK and Save the Children India, funded by UK Aid.

70. This change in trends suggests that some well-known ICT teacher training programs, such as Intel's Teach to the Future program, and World Links (reviewed in Gaible & Burns, 2005), will be unlikely to receive significant investments in the coming years.

71. One project that is sensitive to global climate change is being undertaken in the Brazilian Amazon. The Inter-American Development Bank has invested in virtual schooling where there is limited teacher capacity or presence. Master teachers record lessons in a regional media center, and this is then broadcast live to various rural areas. The master teacher can call on learners and ask questions about the lesson content in real time while a classroom technician helps with the technology. See www.gse.harvard.edu/news/ed/14/09/radical-idea-rainforest.

72. Left out of this discussion is that of special needs students, mainly due to a lack of substantive investments in developing countries. Yet it is clear that the special needs population is at least as big in poor countries as it is in wealthier countries. According to Samant et al. (2013), well over half the population in low-income countries have one or more of the following: visual and hearing impairments, as well as other injuries/diseases that impact the way children learn and grow. One notable project involved the teaching of children with disabilities in Bangkok and Addis Ababa; see Schiemer and Proyer (2013).

73. See Chapter 3.

74. See earlier discussion of the Kindles to Ethiopia project, in Talbot (2012).

75. Wu (2016) describes the continuing fight for human attention (literally the eyeballs) as a way of selling content via social media and the Internet.

76. Total cost of ownership (TCO) refers to all the costs: hardware, maintenance, training, electricity, and so forth.

77. Yoza Project (2009–2013).

78. For a discussion of TCO in developing countries, see Moretti (2011); for a similar discussion of the "total burden of assessments" in developing countries, see Wagner et al. (2011a) and Wolff (2007). Few projects have tried Bring Your Own Device approaches, but see one such effort in Hong Kong (Wong, 2014).

79. In some ICT4E projects, up to 40% of devices broke during use and needed to be replaced during the one-school-year trial (Wagner, 2014b).

80. See earlier discussion of Kenya's PRIMR intervention (Piper & Kwayumba, 2014).

81. Private sector corporate foundations may include firms like Microsoft and Intel, or increasingly mobile phone operators.

82. See also discussion of implementation science in Chapter 11.

83. Wagner (2001); Wagner et al. (2004); Wagner (2009). See Chapter 12.

84. As noted earlier, MIT sought to produce "cheap" laptops in the One Laptop per Child initiative. Also the "simputer" in India, announced in 2002, and which disappeared a few years later after much media attention, is one of many that comes to mind. See: http://en.wikipedia.org/wiki/Simputer.

85. UNICEF (2016) completed a report on ICT and going to scale, downloadable at: www.educationinnovations.org/sites/default/files/Journeys to Scale—Full Report.pdf

86. Blumenstock et al. (2015); Hilbert (2016).

87. The project was undertaken by Worldreader in association with UNESCO in Ethiopia, Ghana, India, Kenya, Nigeria, Zimbabwe, and Pakistan. See UNESCO (2014b).

88. The UN has also joined the big data movement as part of the SDG process; see: http://unstats.un.org/unsd/trade/events/2015/abudhabi/presentations/day3/02/2b%20A-Using%20Big%20Data%20for%20the%20Sustainable%20Development%20Goals%2010222015.pdf

89. See Kizilcec et al. (2017) for research that shows how individual and social differences can account for persistence on MOOCs in developing countries.

10

GLOBALIZATION AND THE ENVIRONMENT

Matheus: Environmental Change and Migration in Brazil

Eighteen-year-old Matheus and his family recently moved to Rio de Janeiro from Paricatuba, a village on the outskirts of Manaus in central Brazil. Paricatuba is situated along the many tributaries of the huge Amazon River basin. With giant logs regularly transported downriver from the tropical rain forest, the village and its surroundings have suffered from mass deforestation. Among the many consequences of this largely destructive and illegal industry are environmental changes due to the loss of high-level tree canopy, as well as the departure of wildlife in the river and forest that have lost their natural habitats. This destabilization has made the small-scale farming and fishing industries that maintained the livelihood of Matheus's family more and more precarious. After years of delay and uncertainty, his father finally took a job in a shoe-making factory in Rio de Janeiro, allowing the family—father, mother, and four siblings—to migrate to this huge city of over six million inhabitants. They joined Matheus's two uncles who had moved there some years earlier. Matheus's younger brothers and his sister now find themselves in public schools that are overcrowded, and their rural life skills (such as picking fruit, cutting wood, and fishing) have little value in the large metropolis. Matheus himself finished eighth grade in Manaus, and did passably well, but never found steady employment. On weekends he would earn some cash by helping deliver vegetables from a neighbor's farm to the market. In Rio, however, he is still looking for a job.

———————

The past few decades have been marked by a number of "mega-trends" that have had an outsized impact on international development. One of these is globalization—the economic and cultural processes by which the world is rapidly being integrated. Globalization has dramatically accelerated the flow of goods, services, people, and knowledge around the world. It has fundamentally reordered the economic playing field. The mega-trend of cross-border migration—both voluntary and forced—has reshaped communities through cultural assimilation (and friction), as has rural-to-urban migration and the rise of vast urban landscapes. Further demographic mega-trends in population growth and composition (from lowered aging populations in the West, to massive increases in youth populations in Africa and the global South) are creating challenges for education institutions designed originally to serve a very different polity.

Against this backdrop, the environmental limits of an economic growth agenda for development are becoming clearer—starkly illustrated by the looming threat of climate change. We see this clearly in the case of Matheus and his family who now find themselves in Rio, a city with its own immense problems. Understanding the impact of these global mega-trends on human development and learning is essential if we are to adapt and prosper—both as societies and as individuals.

Globalization

Modern globalization has its roots in colonial exploration, one of the early forms of international development. In those times, globalization took the form of discovery and trade. Whether we think of Marco Polo and the Silk Road to China, or Cortes in the Americas, discovery soon led to trade, commerce, and the exchange of new science and technology—with outcomes that were both positive and negative.[1] Over the centuries that followed, globalization continued apace, and connected all parts of the planet in countless ways.

The last several decades have been marked, however, by a dramatic acceleration in the breadth and depth of globalization's impact on societies and individuals around the world. Technology has, as noted in the previous chapter, played a huge role, particularly through the Internet and the increasing use of social media. In his 2005 bestselling book *The World Is Flat*, journalist Thomas Friedman described the kinds of changes that he accurately predicted would result from the rise of globalization.[2] Part of his argument was that globalization would flatten, or reduce, many differences in the world—differences that had been maintained for many years by the distances of time and space between cultures. Friedman foresaw that cultural differences and insularity would fade, leading to a world where competition would necessarily expand and intensify between nations. He also posited that economic markets would help drive competition between the skills and knowledge of workers, thereby expanding global productivity and increased global trade. Friedman was prescient.[3]

But how do current trends in globalization impact, or derive from, what and how we learn? At one level, globalization has resulted in large-scale advances in science, technology, information flow, transportation, and commerce. That is to say, much of what we call "modernization" today is a consequence of people learning new things, and learning how to apply those things in their own contexts. Take medicine, for example. Though its origins have been attributed to many parts of the world (China, the Middle East, and Europe—just to name three), modern medicine is now a community composed of knowledge brokers who publish online in multiple worldwide journals.

The study of education is likewise a global enterprise, and as with all global enterprises, must be understood and adapted for cultural relevance. Since globalization is now a fundamental reality, we must investigate what people need to learn in order to participate and benefit from it. How can global opportunities for learning be expanded? Consider the growth of English as an international language. In earlier chapters, we discussed the rise of English as a dominant language in schools in many countries. Through a recursive set of economic circumstances and geopolitically driven realities, the English language has come to predominate in universities and in science more generally. This has benefitted certain countries and hindered others. Yet, as people have sought professional advancement in the global arena, they have had to learn English or apply the English they know to their chosen field. As a result, a rapidly growing class of English-speaking and well-trained professional workers has been created.

One consequence is the major growth in "off-shore" English-speaking employment undertaken in countries like India and Bangladesh, where back-office and highly skilled—but relatively low-wage—labor can be deployed in support of international commerce. The rise of English as an international language has naturally facilitated the globalization of the marketplace of labor as well as that of ideas. This is one example illustrates that what and how people learn is increasingly transferrable from one country to another, particularly for industries that can tailor their jobs to this expanding international workforce.

In sum, the skills, knowledge, attitudes, and values of globalized workers have given rise to a new form of social and economic mobility. Learning is key to this process. But the process clearly does not impact everyone equally. There will be the haves and have-nots when it comes to the possession of relevant skills for this new global economic landscape. Globalization has undoubtedly helped many who were born poor, but there are limits as well.

Population Growth and Urbanization

Over the last quarter-century, the world's population has increased by about 50%—from 5 billion people to nearly 7.5 billion people, with most of this growth happening in developing countries. The rate of change across age groups has been dramatic, particularly in terms of younger demographics. As shown in Figure 10.1, developing countries have a discernible "youth bubble" that is creating serious problems for both education and economic planners. The pressure of this bubble, when linked to the school dropout problem discussed earlier, makes increased unemployment much more likely. In some parts of the world, there are just too many young people trying to enter the workforce for the number of jobs available, making employment opportunities difficult or impossible to find even for those with school credentials.[4]

Increased urbanization is a related phenomenon. As shown in Figure 10.2, about 30% of the world's population lived in urban areas in 1950, while this number jumped to about 54% by 2014. Today, nearly 90% of the remaining rural populations in the world live in Africa or Asia, and about one in eight urbanites lives in

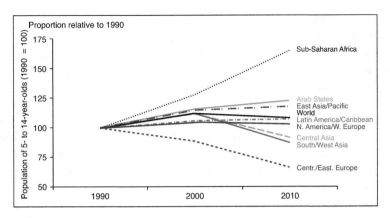

FIGURE 10.1 Population of 5- to 14-Year-Olds, by Region, 1990, 2000, and 2013

Source: UNESCO (2015a, p. 22)

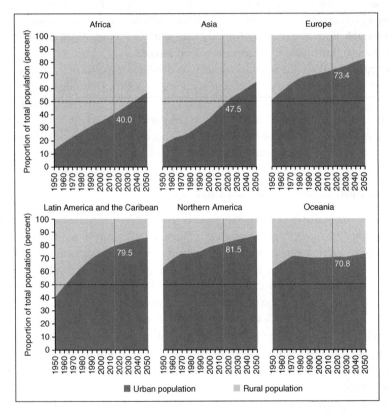

FIGURE 10.2 Urban and Rural Population as Proportion of Total Population, by Major Regions, 1950–2050

Source: United Nations (2014, p. 8)

one of 28 enormous megacities, each home to more than 10 million inhabitants.[5] These large population transfers have multiple causes, but most seem related to the perception that well-being and earning potential are better in the city (with the converse in rural areas). Whether these perceptions are accurate depends in large part on the characteristics of the particular urban setting, such as employment opportunities, availability of health services, and sanitation. One additional factor is access to better schools.

As noted earlier, urban schools tend to have better infrastructure (including textbooks and technology) as well as better-trained teachers, when compared with rural schools. Thus, demographic changes will lead to more children having access to urban schools, classroom size will continue to expand, and pressures on teachers will grow concomitantly—thereby reducing, for many children, the quality of their education.[6] Urban parents, in turn, face multiple difficulties in supporting their children's learning, especially if they are not citizens or permanent residents. They may have trouble finding schools for their children to attend and will have their own learning-related challenges—both in terms of finding employment, and in adopting new culturally (and linguistically) appropriate behaviors.

Migration and Civil Conflict

A major consequence of globalization and demographic change is human migration. In the period from 1990 to 2010, the number of international immigrants increased by nearly 60 million people worldwide, with over 200 million people living outside their country of origin by 2010 (see Figure 10.3).[7] The rate of internal migration, or movement of people within

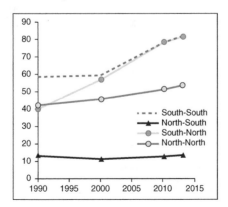

FIGURE 10.3   Numbers (in Millions) of International Migrants by Origin and Destination, 1990–2013

Source: United Nations, Department of Economic and Social Affairs (2013, p. 2)

countries, is about the same as the external international migration rate, with both showing significant increases in the global South over recent decades.[8] The broad trends of migration are not only massive and growing, but are also highly related to political instability, civil conflicts, natural disasters, and climate change.[9]

In such instances, families who migrate often face major threats to their safety. They also confront the challenge of adapting to new environments that will likely expose them to different languages, cultures, and education systems—with major implications for the learning contexts of their daily lives. In schools, student migrants must cope with differences in social behavior and language of instruction, and then will have to demonstrate skills and levels of achievement that may vary in important ways from their village, region, or nation of origin—as in Matheus's case.[10] In Turkey, internal migration from Eastern to Western regions, primarily from rural areas to urban centers, con-tributes to educational disadvantage. Rural migrants in Turkish cities tend to settle in squatter areas that reinforce a legacy of inequality and low school performance.[11]

Involuntary migrants (or forcibly displaced persons)—those who are pushed out due to civil conflict—face even more dire circumstances. In 2015, the United Nations reported that nearly 60 million people were forcibly displaced world-wide in the previous 15 years, approximately half of whom were children under the age of 18 (see Figure 10.4). In addition, natural disasters, environmental and climate change, and economic crises add millions to those who are subject to

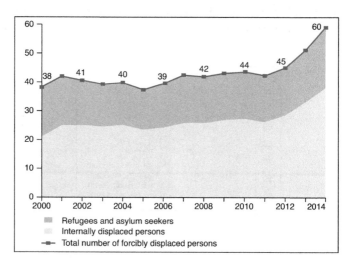

FIGURE 10.4 Number of Forcibly Displaced Persons in Conflict Zones, 2000–2014 (in Millions)

Source: United Nations (2015a, p. 23)

broken educational systems. Current estimates are that 200 million children live in conflict-afflicted contexts.[12]

Over the years, international agencies have tried to find concrete educational solutions to the challenges of internal and external migration. Some have placed increased attention on early childhood programs, supporting what are called "child-friendly spaces." The main function of such programs is to provide a physically and psychologically safe environment and routine where children can play, use visualization and role-playing to reduce anxieties, and can interact in normal ways with peers and adults. In Uganda, for example, childcare workers are trained explicitly in such techniques, and are able to increase children's sense of safety as well as pro-social behaviors.[13]

Some agencies have provided temporary buildings and school-feeding programs. In support, prepackaged education kits such as "schools in a box" have been provided for needy primary-school-aged children.[14] The main objective of these efforts has been to restart schools as quickly as possible, and to provide a degree of normalcy by reestablishing access to schooling. Not surprisingly, learning achievement for children from poor households or marginalized groups is negatively affected by civil conflict. In Guatemala, the education gap between indigenous people in conflict-affected areas and the rest of the indigenous population increased from 0.4 years to 1.7 years during nearly four decades of civil war.[15]

Internal and external migration flows are not just a consequence of civil conflict, however; they are also one of its probable causes. Some conflicts derive from grievances between proximate social and cultural groups that have gone unresolved for years, decades, or even centuries. Others are driven at least in part by globalization and population growth, as well as climate change, such as the increase in droughts in Africa and Asia.[16] Still other disturbances may result from social media, where activist groups are able to mobilize resentments and animosity that can lead to acts of violence. The Arab Spring events, beginning in 2010, represent a contemporary example of this phenomenon in multiple countries.

As with other mega-trends, migration and civil conflicts can lead to the disruption of the stability needed for educational institutions to thrive.[17] For children living in such circumstances, learning does not cease, but rather the contexts and practices of learning, as described in Chapter 3, inevitably shift. Sometimes children live as refugees in settlement camps or they may be on the unfortunate road to exile. Their educational future has been aptly and sadly described as caught "between the global promise of universal human rights, the definition of citizenship rights within nation-states, and the [impossible] realization of these sets of rights in everyday practices."[18] Unfortunately, refugee children are often caught somewhere between their culture of origin and the cultures in which they find themselves through sometimes multiple perilous migrations.

The Environmental Imperative

In an era in which environmental sustainability is now taking precedence, much of what we do in our everyday lives has to be rethought—sooner than later. Given this new and profound reality, it is clear that economic progress can no longer be understood as "more is better," due to the finite nature of the Earth's resources. We must be fully conscious of the terrible risks associated with climate change, as pressures grow and threaten the available resources on this planet. The balancing act—between ecological constraint and economic development—will not be easy. Nation building—indeed, much of human well-being—has depended until now on the extraction of resources. Depletion and consumption of these resources at the current rate is no longer possible without paying a heavy if not irreversible price.

Resource scarcity and climate change will inevitably exacerbate many of the challenges tied to global trends impacting human development around the world. This is surely why the United Nations added the word *sustainable* to the 2030 Sustainable Development Goals. Present-day consumerist habits will not fade quickly, however, nor will more sustainable habits be adopted across the world to equal degrees or on the same timeline. For these reasons, the SDGs will be critical for both policy and action in the coming decades, especially by focusing attention on living within our planetary means.

As Steven Pinker, a cognitive scientist, remarked, "[T]he goal of education is to make up for the shortcomings in our instinctive ways of thinking about the physical and social world."[19] Pinker thought that the human mind is not well-programmed to perceive the "invisible" risks of nature given our stone-age brains. The complex and probabilistic trends in climate change run counter to ingrained ways of thinking about our everyday lives, even if most of the world is more or less aware of catastrophic fluctuations that are currently taking place.[20] Only in recent years have we become able to call climate change a global crisis.[21]

Yet, more than two decades ago, Robert Kaplan, a writer and journalist, in a highly publicized and farsighted article in the *Atlantic Monthly*, claimed that environmental constraints would likely bring "disease, overpopulation, unprovoked crime, scarcity of resources, refugee migrations, the accumulating erosion of nation-states and international borders, and the empowerment of private armies, security firms, and international drug cartels."[22] Reflecting on recent Ebola pandemics, massive out-migrations, civil conflicts, and rising income inequality enables us to see how close the world has conformed to Kaplan's predictions, particularly in poor and unstable regions. Kaplan suggested that the positivistic road to development—as proffered by development agencies until fairly recently—might take some very nasty turns.

Even earlier, more than a century ago, climate scientists began warning us about the problems associated with a changing climate, with ever more greenhouse gases (especially CO_2) being emitted into the atmosphere, rising temperatures in the oceans, and dramatic changes in weather patterns.[23] During this same time, concern grew about the depletion of forests that absorb CO_2, and the melting of glacial ice at the North and South poles. In addition, there is growing worry about the reduction in biodiversity (both flora and fauna) through which hope of better adaptation to such global environmental changes must reside. Fewer species of fish, insects, and diversity of land resources will necessarily limit the ability of Earth's complex ecosystems to adapt to climate change challenges.[24] In sum, it is clear that the world's ecological "footprint" is no longer sustainable (Figure 10.5) and will leave many societies highly vulnerable in the not too distant future.

Vulnerability is multifaceted, with diverse causes and consequences. There are populations that reside in high-risk geographical and ecological zones—including those at low sea levels, those in tropical climates that are becoming ever warmer, and those that are undergoing major environmental destruction (as in Matheus's family in the Amazon). The risks for such vulnerable populations are well-documented—they make up just 5% of the world's population, but are estimated to possess 22% of the world's land on which 80% of the planet's biodiversity is located.[25] Some ecosystems are especially vulnerable to shifts in climate, such as those that exist in small island states, on coasts, at high altitudes, or in Arctic regions—areas where even minor climactic shifts may threaten indigenous livelihoods of hunting, fishing, and farming. Others may be affected by long-term decisions to expand industrial agriculture production, or

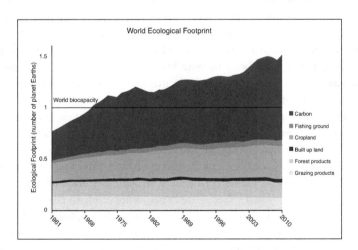

FIGURE 10.5 The World Ecological Footprint Attempts to Account for Demands (1961–2010) on the Biosphere (e.g., Carbon Emissions), Food Sources, Consumer Goods, and the Amount of Land Needed for Cities and Roads

Source: www.footprintnetwork.org/

global businesses that force people off of their ancestral lands, leading to more migration.[26]

Adapting to environmental change seems so daunting that many countries have made only marginal planning for such eventualities—that is, learning what to expect and what to do. Even so, there are some informative initiatives currently underway. In Latin America (Ecuador and Bolivia, in particular), the idea of *buen vivir* (living well) has become part of the vision of indigenous peoples' response to such environmental threats—learning about the binding relationship between humans, nature, and the universe. This perspective, now part of school curricula, sees nature as a living being that is "indissoluble, interdependent, balanced and in a complementary relationship with the universe and with humans." In this way, "harmony" within communities is based on a system of respect for all its members as "transmitters of traditional knowledge."[27] Using schools and curricula as a way to foster innovative approaches to environmental adaptation is a critical step in the right direction.

Building on this approach, scientists are now beginning to consider the serious role that a knowledgeable—environmentally literate—citizenry will play in managing climate change and environmental sustainability. One widely cited *Science* report found that the international community should change its priorities, moving to "fund more educators rather than just engineers" as a key to environmental sustainability.[28] Based on data from 167 countries from 1970 to 2010, the study found that higher levels of education (especially that of women in child-bearing ages) led to significantly decreased levels of disaster-related fatalities (including from climate change).[29] Findings supported the hypothesis that education leads to an augmented "adaptive capacity" in both pre-disaster phase (e.g., stockpiling emergency supplies, living in low-risk areas, or undertaking disaster preparedness measures), as well as in post-disaster aftermath phase (e.g., coping better with both income loss and the psychological impacts of natural disasters). Simply put, more education seems to reduce environmental vulnerability, and can save lives.

Reciprocally, environmental change and climate disasters are known to directly impact education provision and learning achievement. As shown in Figure 10.6, the poor in low-income countries already have substantially lower secondary school completion rates due to climate change disasters. And there will no doubt be a plethora of negative consequences for learning when the full consequences of environmental and climate change are better understood. To take one example, experts estimate that by 2050, 27 million people in Bangladesh will be at risk from sea level rise. Increased flooding will likely increase internal migration from rural areas to the massively crowded capital, Dhaka. With a school system already afflicted by national disasters—such as Cyclone Sidr in 2007, when 849 schools were destroyed, affecting the schooling of 140,000 students—adding environmental disasters to the mix makes this country one of the most susceptible to educational degradation.[30]

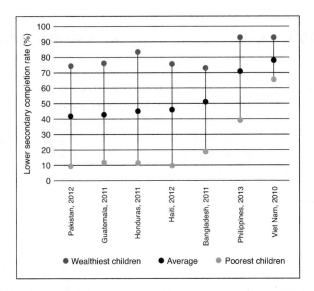

FIGURE 10.6 Impact of Climate Change Disasters on Secondary School Completion in Seven Countries

Source: UNESCO (2016a, p. 34)

Growth Is Not the Answer

How can the world adequately respond to climate and environmental threats to sustainability; how should developing countries respond to increasing globalization, migration, and demographic changes; and what role can learning play to address the challenges from such emerging global mega-trends? What people know, how they think, and the ways they act will be central to effective development solutions.

Promoting a growth agenda for international development is clearly not sustainable—and never has been. Large-scale changes due to globalization and environmental degradation began long ago, and increasingly threaten millions of people in many parts of the world, especially the poor who, under current circumstances, have many fewer options than those with greater means. There is cause for hope, fortunately, as evidenced by initiatives ranging from heightened environmental awareness in the public and private sectors, and technological advances, as well as from collective regional, national, and international policies such as the 2015 UN climate agreement in Paris. Effective actions stemming from these initiatives will, in turn, depend on an increasingly knowledgeable, open-minded, and aware global citizenry.

In sum, a global citizenry that is continuously learning is essential. And learning will need to be coupled with progressive political choices to accommodate migrants like Matheus who have the most to lose and whose human rights must

BOX 10.1 LEARNING, ADAPTATION, AND SUSTAINABLE DEVELOPMENT

"Adaptation" is becoming a euphemism for social injustice on a global scale. While the citizens of the rich world are protected from harm, the poor, the vulnerable and the hungry are exposed to the harsh reality of climate change in their everyday lives. Put bluntly, the world's poor are being harmed through a problem that is not of their making. The footprint of the Malawian farmer or the Haitian slum dweller barely registers in the Earth's atmosphere.

Source: Tutu (2010, p. xvi)

be acknowledged and respected. The world's inhabitants will increasingly need to learn how to adapt to unprecedented global stresses. Those who have impacted the Earth the least should be given the opportunity to learn what they need to know to control and protect their own lives, individually and collectively—as movingly stated by Nobel Prize winner Desmond Tutu (see Box 10.1).

Our tools for measuring global change, whether in climate or learning, have improved. And they will become, as discussed in the next chapter, an essential way for maintaining accountability. As we all know, the planetary ground has literally changed under our collective feet. Over the next decade and beyond, the 2030 UN goals will require heightened effort and vigilance to address the demands of a sustainable future.

Notes

1. Wallerstein (2000, p. 250), cited in Breidlid (2013) stated that "the processes that are usually meant when we speak of globalization . . . have existed for some 500 years." For more on globalization, see: Albrow and King (1990, p. 8), for example, who defined globalization as "all those processes by which the peoples of the world are incorporated into a single world society." Also see Dollar and Kraay (2002), Ezcurra and Rodríguez-Pose (2013), Stiglitz (2002, 2012), Stromquist and Monkman (2014), and Wade (2004). In economics, Goldin and Katz (2009) have termed this the "race between education and technology." In their view, increases in the educational attainment of United States workers were typical through the post–World War II decades when high school graduates later became college graduates. Today—with the slowdown in education at various levels—Americans are not keeping up with industry's needs for more technologically skilled workers. Globalization can be seen therefore as a positive force for trade and commerce, or as a negative force leading to more extensive domination by wealthy countries and international corporations. See alternatives described by Haines et al. (2012, p. 2195).
2. Friedman (2005).
3. See also Friedman (2016) for an update on these issues.

4. This surplus of (over)credentialing was long ago called the "diploma disease" by Dore (1976).
5. United Nations (2014).
6. See Chapter 7.
7. Department of Economic and Social Affairs, United Nations, official statistics, http://esa.un.org/migration/p2k0data.asp.
8. UNDP (2009); International Organization for Migration (2010); Skeldon (2012).
9. Pachauri/UNDP (2014, p. 52) states: "There is high confidence that sustained warming greater than some threshold would lead to the near-complete loss of the Greenland ice sheet over a millennium or more, causing a global mean sea level rise of up to 7 metres. . . . [T]he coastal population could grow from 1.2 billion people in 1990 to 1.8–5.2 billion people by the 2080s, depending on assumptions about migration. With increases in global population, the number of people vulnerable to sea level rise will also likely increase."
10. Yoshikawa and Kalil (2011); Suárez-Orozco et al. (2009).
11. UNESCO (2010, p. 71).
12. Pigozzi et al. (2014).
13. Pigozzi et al. (2014). See also: Buchert (2013) and International Network for Education in Emergencies (INEE).
14. Penson and Tomlinson (2007).
15. Boothby and Melvin (2007), cited in Pigozzi et al. (2014). For more on indigenous approaches, see Cunningham (2010) and Gudynas (2011).
16. Von Uexkull et al. (2016).
17. Chaffin (2010) and Pigozzi et al. (2014).
18. Dryden-Peterson (2016, p. 473). How the world has dealt with refugee children has varied significantly since the mid-20th century. After World War II, new UN institutions such as UNESCO and especially the UN High Commissioner on Refugees (UNHCR) took responsibility for the education of refugees, particularly focusing on post-secondary studies. However, in 1985 UNHCR shifted their focus to supporting longstanding settlements with direct aid for getting young children into schools, often organized within the settlements themselves. In recent years the UNHCR has focused increasingly on how to integrate children into national school systems where the settlements are located. See Dryden-Peterson (2016) for a broad overview.
19. Cited in Williams (2011), from Pinker (2007, p. 439).
20. Wagner (2017) described some of the cognitive constraints on thinking about climate change. In the United States, counterintuitive evidence has shown that education is sometimes associated with climate denial (Kahan et al., 2012; Lee et al., 2015). Clearly, there are social-psychological factors of importance, as described by Zaval and Cornwell (2016). A further discussion of cognitive and social dimensions of climate decision making is provided by Gardiner (2006), who reviewed how difficult it is for one generation of citizens to make environmental cutbacks in order to serve the next generation. One anecdote, in terms of challenges of the environment to everyday thinking, has been termed the "$200 hamburger." As cited in Ricciardi (2010, p. 309), in a review of Patel (2009), who cited Dunne (1994): "[T]he true cost of a McDonald's hamburger should be US $200 if one includes the full spectrum of implied costs associated with its carbon footprint, water use, soil degradation, and the hidden health costs for treating diet related diabetes and heart disease from its consumption."
21. Sachs (2015, p. 394) writes: "There has never been a global economic problem as complicated as climate change. It is simply the toughest public policy problem that humanity has ever faced. [I]t is an absolutely *global crisis*. Climate change affects every part of the planet, and there is no escaping from its severity and threat. Humanity in the modern period has faced some pretty terrible threats, including nuclear annihilation along with mass pandemic diseases. Climate change ranks right up there on

the scale of risks, especially for future generations." See also Hansen et al. (2015, p. 20119): "We conclude that multi-meter sea-level rise would become practically unavoidable. Social disruption and economic consequences of such large sea-level rise could be devastating. It is not difficult to imagine that conflicts arising from forced migrations and economic collapse might make the planet ungovernable, threatening the fabric of civilization."

22. Kaplan (1994, p. 3).
23. Arrhenius (1896), a Nobel Prize–winning chemist, first wrote about carbon dioxide concentrations as having a deleterious effect on the atmosphere. See also a useful summary on climate change and development in Sachs (2015).
24. In Howard (2013), Richard Louv states: "The word 'sustainability' is problematic, because to most people it means stasis, survival, and energy efficiency. We have to do those things, but that only goes so far in igniting the imagination. Increasingly, [we need to talk] about a 'nature-rich society,' a different way to look at the future that is not just about survival, but about something much better." Also see a discussion on nature and sustainability in the context of social change in McMichael (2011, pp. 9–11).
25. See UNDP (2011, pp. 54–56).
26. One interesting effort is the Sandwatch Initiative that brings communities into direct contact with the ecological changes that affect their lives. Sandwatch is a network of NGOs, schools, and youth groups working together in the Caribbean, Europe, Africa, Asia, and South America to monitor and enhance beach environments Anderson (2010, p. 10). See Sandwatch: www.sandwatch.ca. See also Kagawa and Selby (2012, p. 209) on disaster risk reduction, who write: "Disaster risk increases when an exposed, vulnerable and ill-prepared population or community encounters a hazard event."
27. UNESCO (2016a, p. 27), adapted from Cunningham (2010) and Gudynas (2011). For a review of how national curricula are approaching environmental sustainability, see Opertti and Brylinski (2016).
28. Lutz et al. (2014, p. 1061).
29. Lutz et al. (2014, p. 1062). See also Wals et al. (2014) and Wals and Lenglet (2016, p. 60).
30. Reported in UNESCO (2016a, p. 33). The 2017 back-to-back hurricanes Harvey and Irma disrupted schooling for millions of children in the Caribbean and the United States.

11
MEASUREMENT OF LEARNING

Teboho and Mpho: Measuring Learning in Limpopo

Teboho, age 13, is in second grade at Shayandime Primary School. He's one of the oldest children in his class, having entered school late at age nine, and having repeated both grades 1 and 2. The school's buildings are fashioned out of adobe walls and zinc roofing, and situated in a small rural village in Limpopo Province in the far northern part of South Africa. Just a few dozen miles from the Zimbabwe border, the area is dotted with traditional houses called *rondavels*, an adapted version of the southern Africa-style hut. Baboons roam the school grounds freely and are known to slip through the spaces between the red-mud blocks and corrugated roofing and vandalize the classrooms at night in search of food. Despite the occasional broken window, the school is not without resources. It is one of a number of schools in the region that has received donations of early-model desktop computers, though many of them are now inoperable. In the classroom, Teboho spends most of his time copying sentences from the chalkboard in Venda, the language he and his classmates speak, and occasionally in English. Teboho cannot adequately read in either language and there are few in-class activities that support creativity and critical thinking skills. His teachers don't pay much attention to Teboho, and they assume he will fail to pass into upper primary school.

About four hours away by car, in Limpopo's provincial urban capital, Polokwane, seven-year-old Mpho attends Central Elementary School. Mpho entered Central at age six, and has kept up with his work so that he is now in second grade as well, though he is nearly six years younger than Teboho. With brick paths around its perimeter, Central boasts a state-of-the-art computer lab and a smartboard with a projector—rivaling the equipment available at the local university. There are no broken windows and no baboons. The teachers use structured lesson plans, and the parents are an integral part of the school culture. Given Central's appealing environment, provincial officials proudly exhibit it to visiting national and international education planners. Mpho looks forward to class each day, and is motivated to learn and to be connected to South Africa's future.

His teachers think highly of him, and give him good grades. All expect that he will move smoothly from primary to secondary school, and perhaps even to university.[1]

In this chapter, we focus on how the measurement of learning is understood and undertaken, and the implications, limitations, and potential of utilizing findings on the quality of learning. Among the main questions addressed are: What makes data credible? In what ways does sampling impact measurement? How should we compare learning outcomes? And, how should implementation science lead to improved development policy and practice? The overall intention is to understand how better measurement can help to support effective learning outcomes in developing countries. While there are numerous technical issues to be addressed, it is clear that a data-driven reality—based on improved measurement tools—has arrived, and bodes well for the future of learning and learning equity.

Statistics on learning and educational achievement are collected by many agencies that monitor variables such as reading levels, cognitive scores, and grade repetition. Much of these data are imperfectly collected, often due to a lack of resources and insufficiently trained testers and teachers.[2] As a consequence, results for school decision makers, and for teachers as well, may be only weakly supported. Still, as the English mathematician Karl Pearson once said: "If you haven't measured something, you really don't know very much about it."[3] As we have seen throughout this volume, learning can only be adequately understood if there are commonly accepted methods for measuring it—the central thrust of this chapter.

Comparisons of rural and urban contexts—such as those in Limpopo Province—often show sharply diverging social and infrastructural characteristics, like the opening descriptions of Teboho and Mpho's educational circumstances. Results tend to confirm that they represent, essentially, two different worlds of education. The South Africa Annual National Assessment (SAANA) that is administered at the end of each school year measures progress in student achievement in grades 1 through 6.[4] The rural Shayandime Primary School, evaluated by this measure, belongs to the lowest quintile of the country's poverty index, due in part to high illiteracy rates among parents, insufficient training for teachers, and poor school infrastructure.[5] By contrast, Central Elementary School ranks in the middle (third) quintile with normally distributed student scores, though these are somewhat below the national urban norms for the Mathematics and Home Language reading competencies for grade 3. Most parents of children who attend Central have completed some secondary school education and beyond, the teachers are well-trained, and the school infrastructure rivals that of public schools in large cities like Johannesburg.

The contrast in the SAANA test performance between these two schools raises important questions: Why does Shayandime have only a handful of high achievers, while the rest of its students—like Teboho—cluster around the lower end of the achievement continuum? And, within urban Central Elementary, why are the scores more normally distributed even if below the national average? A research response likely points to the crucial role that social and family influences have on predicting learning outcomes of children like Teboho and Mpho. In these instances, social background information about the individual students was not collected, but research has shown that a combination of such factors likely affects who feels or is entitled to sit closer to the front in large classrooms and/or is motivated for learning. Understanding and measuring how well children learn can be daunting, making it essential to know how to disaggregate sample populations with different social characteristics.[6]

Research and Credibility

Economists have a significant influence on research and policymaking in international development (see Chapter 1), especially within large international agencies such as the World Bank. When James Wolfensohn became President of the World Bank, he reportedly asked how many attendees at a large in-house World Bank meeting on education were trained as education specialists or as economists. The story goes that nearly all of those who raised their hands were economists. By contrast, when reviewing research published in education journals, the large majority of authors are those trained in the disciplines of psychology, anthropology, sociology, and linguistics—not in economics. In other words, there is a sizeable gap between those who produce most educational research and those in major agencies who make international education policy decisions.

In international education, development experts may have very different purposes for the approaches they take, depending on both the funding and presumed consumers of their findings. For example, an academic researcher might wish to publish findings that build on earlier theories of international development. Or a development agency might ask a researcher to focus on whether a particular intervention was considered successful two years after implementation. Since researchers usually have a particular disciplinary training and employ different methodologies, the data gathered may look quite different depending on who gathered it. Broadly speaking, there are four main approaches that guide research in international development.

- *Knowledge-driven research.*[7] Knowledge-driven research is best characterized by what scientific journals seek to publish—new findings that build upon a prior knowledge base of particular topics. This largely academic approach is common across the social sciences. Usually the foundation of doctoral dissertations, wherein a student researcher follows in the footsteps of her/his mentor, such studies serve to critique or elaborate on a particular theory, hypothesis, or finding. Directly utilizing the research in order to improve real-world impact (such as through development work) is often not the objective.[8]

- *Policy-driven research.* Policy-driven research typically involves investigating the nature, causes, and impact of alternative public policies, with particular emphasis on determining the policies that will most likely achieve given goals. As discussed in earlier chapters, the UN Sustainable Development Goals include specific targets in education such as "ensure . . . equitable and quality primary and secondary education."[9] Researchers often contribute to such policy efforts by helping to operationally define terms like "equitable" and "quality." Often, the research community has already played a role by incorporating or promoting research related to particular policy interests. There may be instances, of course, in which proposed policies reflect unrealistic or premature aspirations, rather than pragmatic roadmaps to achieving the goals.[10]

- *Decision-driven research.* As part of policymaking, applied interventions may be funded in order to discover "what works"—i.e., an impact evaluation study. For example, researchers might evaluate a preschool intervention program to examine the degree to which it was implemented properly (e.g., Were there enough classrooms available? Were enough teachers and children present?), and if learning outcomes related to the instructional inputs provided (e.g., were the teachers well-trained?), as compared to programs without the intervention.[11] In other words, did the project achieve the goals set forth, and which variables influenced specific outcomes?[12]

- *Context-driven research.* Context-driven research is culture-specific, often undertaken by ethnographers or cultural anthropologists using participant observation techniques. Research findings are recognized as subjective, and tend to emphasize the special characteristics of particular contexts and small community-level populations. Here, the purpose is largely to understand the unique relationships within contexts and groups rather than the common elements that might occur across contexts. For example, as described in Chapter 5, the number of books in the home and parental attitudes to children's reading acquisition may be highly impactful in Rwanda (where books at home are scarce), but much less impactful in the United States (where books at home are much more common).

Whichever approach is selected, research that can be directly used for policymaking depends primarily on its credibility. This means that well-trained specialists must achieve broad agreement on the merits and relevance of a particular set of findings, even if they might disagree with the interpretation of such findings.

In point of fact, there are numerous ways to think about credibility, going beyond the particular statistical or methodological approaches or tools available to researchers. Indeed, many assumptions about credibility are made before statistical tests are even employed. Is an assessment credible if the enumerator (tester) does not speak the child's language? Is an assessment credible if some children have taken many such tests before, while for others this is the first time? The answers to these types of questions depend on contextual information that is sometimes overlooked.

Let us take, for example, a recent World Bank publication on the role of cognition and behavior in development work.[13] Among other things, the report found that significant interpretation biases existed in how World Bank development professionals estimated their local partners' perspectives on optimism versus pessimism in developing countries. More specifically, World Bank staff conducted interviews in three locations (Jakarta, Nairobi, and Lima), and were asked to predict how poor people in these cities rated their "helplessness in dealing with life's problems." Nearly 50% of the World Bank professionals predicted that "most poor people" in Jakarta would agree with the following statement: "I feel helpless in dealing with the problems of life," but, in reality, only 8% of the poor people sampled agreed with that statement (see Figure 11.1). We all have biases, of course. But when development experts have inaccurate perceptions, planning can be far off the mark. Such an example—coming from well-trained observers within a major

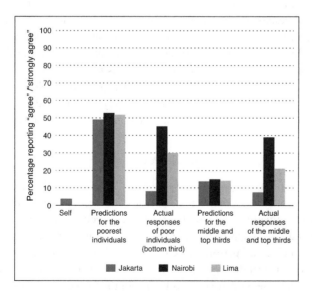

FIGURE 11.1 Helplessness in Dealing With Life's Problems; survey question: "I feel helpless in dealing with the problems of life."

Source: World Bank (2015b, p. 188)

organization—serves as a collective reminder that credibility must be anchored in deep cultural understanding.

Validity and Reliability

In the scientific arena, the two most oft-cited dimensions of credibility are *validity* and *reliability*. The validity of any measurement tool can be understood in multiple ways. Internal validity is determined by the degree to which findings can be linked to the conceptual rationale for the intervention, by minimizing systematic error or bias. How does this work for research in international development? Using Mpho's situation and assessing reading levels with the EGRA tool,[14] we might ask: Do questions on a multiple-choice assessment actually relate to (a) his ability to read, (b) his ability to recall what he read earlier, or (c) what he can glean from contextual knowledge in the test? External validity refers to the degree of generalizability by context and by population, since a test that might be valid in London may have little validity in Polokwane. Further, a reading assessment used effectively for one group of mother-tongue speakers may be inappropriate for children who are second language speakers of that same language. The prime concern with regard to validity is that if data is aggregated without sufficient regard to local context, they may misrepresent learning outcomes.

Reliability, by contrast, is usually measured in two quantitative ways. In a broad sense, it refers to the likelihood that a set of findings is "reproducible" if all the conditions of the study are kept constant or nearly so. For example, the degree to which Mpho's results on a reading assessment is highly correlated with outcomes when he takes the same (or equivalent) test a second time constitutes high reliability.[15] A second common way to measure reliability is to look at the internal consistency of the assessment items: Do the items in each part of an assessment have a strong association with one another?[16] If Mpho does well on decoding of text in his mother-tongue, and also scores relatively well on reading comprehension items in the assessment, this indicates high inter-item reliability.

Emic and Etic: The Impossible Dialectic

The above quantitative approaches to credibility have been challenged by qualitative researchers who focus on context-specific ethnographic observations.[17] There has always been a natural and essential tension between context-specific (or *emic*) and universalistic (*etic*) approaches to measurement. Take, for example, the definition of an "intelligent" person. An emic approach would consciously focus on local words or cultural descriptors of intelligence as perceived, say, in Kampala as contrasted with those used in New York City. In the former, intelligence might be defined as something akin to thoughtful wisdom; in the latter, it might be defined as the ability to multitask. Etic approaches are those that would define "intelligence" as a universal concept, measuring individuals across cultures along a single continuum. For example, in both Kampala and New York City, testing individuals on how many random numbers can be recalled in a row—assuming that this task is more or less equivalent to both groups—would be an etic task.[18] Others have noted that trying to simultaneously target the local and the generalizable is irreconcilable from a statistical perspective.[19] While impossible in theory (strictly speaking),[20] we must in practice pay attention to both emic and etic perspectives in cross-national measurement work.[21]

Research Designs

A wide variety of research studies has been described in this book, but most—when dealing with human development and learning—have come in three broad research designs. Each has strengths and limitations that are important to bear in mind.

Cross-Sectional Studies

As described earlier, human development specialists put a great premium on studying children across the life span, from birth onward.[22] The vast majority of studies on how children develop and learn over time has been cross-sectional—the assessment of different children at different ages. For example, we reviewed reading research that compared reading fluency of children at ages four, six, and eight years or in different grade levels. This cross-sectional approach has some key advantages: the data can be gathered quickly (within weeks or months), allows for greater reliability of data collection, and provides the opportunity to try new intervention approaches for policy inputs much more quickly. A key limitation in cross-sectional studies is that different children are part of the cross-age samples, such that differences across ages may be confounded with other differences that might exist across the population samples themselves. In developing countries, this latter problem may be exacerbated by rapid socio-demographic changes within communities due to changing economics and migration.

Longitudinal Studies

Longitudinal studies are those that track the same children across time. For example, in Chapter 4, longitudinal research considered the return on investment of learning interventions for young children who were assessed again in adulthood. The influence of this work has been dramatic in terms of policy consequences that have fed directly into the new SDG on early learning. Such a design avoids the problem (in cross-sectional work) of having different children at each different age, and it also enables more robust statistical techniques.[23]

In the mid-1980s, I had the opportunity to lead one of the first longitudinal studies of learning and reading in Morocco.[24] Its main purpose was to study the role of culturally specific factors on how children learn to read at home and in school, in poor urban and rural contexts. The study tracked students from preschool through grade 8, utilizing detailed measures of reading acquisition designed specifically for early reading in Arabic.[25] The Moroccan population sample enabled a comparison of learning trajectories by age, as well as gender, type of preschool experience (none, modern, or Quranic), maternal language (Arabic or Amazigh), and a range of other factors such as sibling and parental literacy and household material wealth. The research helped pave the way for localized reading assessments (see later discussion) and the design of household literacy surveys.[26] It also expanded the understanding of first and second language reading acquisition, and the role of religious education in supporting modern schooling.

Longitudinal studies can also assist in helping design specific learning measurement tools. Research has found, for example, that the learning trajectories of children's reading skills follow different patterns and durations, with some components being more constrained in scope and time of mastery than others.[27] For example, the alphabetic principle is acquired quickly when compared to vocabulary and comprehension skills.[28] Learning the names and sounds associated with letters in any alphabet is a relatively small universe of knowledge when compared to learning new vocabulary words throughout one's life.[29] Phonemic awareness includes a larger knowledge base, but most children in wealthier countries learn the essential features of phonemic rhyming, segmenting, and blending in the primary grades. A longitudinal study of such skills is the only way we can truly understand the relationship between the acquisition of different reading component skills.[30]

Overall, longitudinal designs can offer unique insights into understanding human development and learning. Their increased use in developing countries seems essential if we wish to be able to make claims about how specific inputs produce long-term consequences.

Randomized Controlled Trials

Researchers have used numerous approaches to resolve issues of credibility by improving methodological rigor. Among the most prominent is the use of randomized controlled trials (RCTs)—often considered the gold standard of scientific methodology.[31] An RCT seeks to establish a credible link between a specific intervention and a hypothesized set of outcomes. The randomization of populations into sample treatment groups provides evidence that is predicated on the notion that other factors beyond the parameters of the study have not significantly influenced the observed outcomes. In the field of medicine, researchers produce this kind of controlled experimental environment by randomly assigning one group to receive a particular treatment or intervention (e.g., a pain relief pill) while another group receives a placebo (e.g., a sugar pill). With all other conditions being held constant, researchers can confidently make causal claims (of pain reduction) that are based on comparisons of the two groups. Earlier, we described the use of electronic devices (iPads or tablets) for teacher training in Kenya, pointing out that one (randomly selected) group of teachers was provided with tablets while a second "control" group was not, allowing for a clear comparison of the impact of technology.[32]

While producing a truly controlled experiment within the context of social sciences requires complex and multiple components, the practice of randomly assigning groups to receive an intervention has become increasingly popular.[33] The trend toward using RCT designs has grown in part due to the pressures of policymakers and finance ministers who seek to be more certain that public funding supports interventions that will bring expected results. Even so, there are limitations inherent in social experimental designs. For example, RCTs can limit the kinds of questions that can be addressed; meta-analyses of RCTs (a collection of similar studies) may not agree with one another; and more generally, RCTs sometimes fail to take into account the role of context and the limits of generalization.[34] As the use of RCTs has expanded in recent years, such work has begun to improve in important ways. In one recent study on learning in Kenyan schools, researchers reported that the original RCT design and measurement tools used required important context-driven changes that were based on preliminary findings.[35]

In the end, each research design has its pluses and minuses. Even so, implementation failures—or disputes over credible methodological claims—are all part of the necessary steps toward understanding what might work better and add to the cumulative science of development.[36] This requires that researchers and policymakers become informed about and build on previous research findings, a time-consuming but essential task. It is useful to think back on how issues of credibility affect the ways that researchers from different social sciences view the development process. Psychologists tend to work toward universal findings that build upon experimental designs (similar to RCTs), while anthropologists seek to make certain that their findings are valid in terms of local context and cultures. Each research design adds value.[37]

Learning Assessments

The methodologies through which learning is measured have played an integral part in the expansion of education since the beginning of public schooling. At the dawn of the 20th century, Alfred Binet—a founder of French psychology and standardized intelligence tests, as well as an early mentor of Jean Piaget—was asked by the French government to develop an assessment instrument that could help predict which students would be most likely to "learn well" and therefore succeed in public schools.[38] This attempt to predict school achievement was a watershed moment in the use of learning assessments for making educational policy. Over the next century, educators and policymakers across the world have endeavored to make decisions about education, curricula, teaching, and schooling based on such assessments (most often embedded in school examinations). Some assessments focused primarily on individual advancement in school, while others were oriented toward shaping national educational policy.

The use of learning assessments has clearly become a driver for policymakers to more closely monitor and invest in education. As such, the practice of national learning assessments has doubled or tripled in most regions over the past 25 years. (Figure 11.2).[39] Furthermore, the participation of developing countries in international assessments has also risen dramatically (Figure 11.3).[40] This rise in the use of

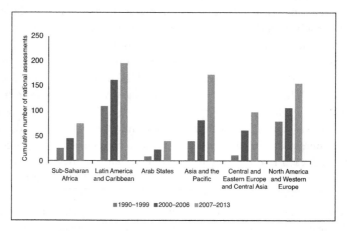

FIGURE 11.2 Cumulative Number of National Learning Assessments, by Region, 1990–1999, 2000–2006 and 2007–2013.

Source: Benavot, A., & Köseleci, N. (2015), p. 5)

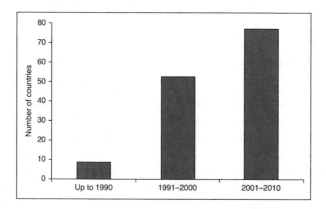

FIGURE 11.3 Developing Countries in Large-Scale Educational Assessments

Source: Lockheed (2010, p. 513)

assessments, and educational systems that depend on them, poses new opportunities and challenges for developing countries.[41] The opportunity exists, for example, to make better evidence-based judgments both within and across countries.[42] The challenges can also be substantial, since all assessments include real costs in time and resources, and interpretations of results can be controversial.[43]

Smaller, Quicker, Cheaper Assessments

Assessments have a variety of purposes, and can take myriad forms.[44] There are small, sample-based assessments that I have termed "smaller, quicker, cheaper" (SQC)—such as the EGRA, discussed in Chapter 5. By being *smaller* (and localized), such assessments can include as consumers not only top experts, but also administrators and teachers, and possibly employers, communities, and parents—whatever makes the most sense for the purposes of the study. These assessments can also take advantage of their modest size by more deeply exploring the multiple (and often context-dependent) factors that affect learning outcomes, such as language of instruction, language of assessment, and opportunity to learn. That is, moreover, what the EGRA and similar assessments often seek to achieve. Overall, the smaller-size advantage also means that the requirements can be better tailored to the human capacity limitations within many low-income countries.

The *quicker* aspect of SQC assessments means that they are designed to be created, implemented, and analyzed as speedily as possible. To achieve this speed, such assessments forego strict international comparability, and emphasize early detection, so as to implement new policies that can be judged on their near term impact.[45] High frequency of assessment becomes a key way to assure goal-related results. Furthermore, with quicker assessments, it becomes possible to provide results in nearly real time—within a matter of weeks or months if need be—and most likely in time for the policymaker who authorized the study to see its outcomes, a not insignificant factor! Needless to say, assessments that can be conducted in real time can have enormous payoff as well for teachers, schools, and students, whose lives could be affected positively by the results (as discussed in citizen-led assessments below).

Third, SQC assessments are generally *cheaper*. There is an old saying: "If you think knowledge is expensive, try ignorance." If the educational policies one is trying to apply are failing, then the cost of such failures should be compared to the cost of determining how to rectify inadequate policies. Surprisingly, the costs of relatively expensive versus cheaper assessments have only infrequently been the focus of policy attention. However, on a cost-per-person basis there is some similarity between large-scale educational assessments (LSEAs) and SQC assessments because of the economies of scale in the former. Yet the total costs of LSEAs can be quite considerable when taking into account the number of countries who participate, the amount of high-level professional expertise required, and the technical requirements of data collection and analyses.[46] Naturally, there are trade-offs in using cheaper assessments, such as having to limit sample sizes, the length of tests created, and the number of trained personnel who can be employed. Most efficiencies are more easily achieved in SQC assessments because the degree of comparability is limited, and the focus can be on a limited set of local or national policy goals. SQC assessments, especially in an era when frequency and timeliness are becoming more important, will likely result in a cheaper way of doing the business of assessment.

When considering the type of assessment that would be most useful, it is important to consider their distinctive features. In addition to SQC and LSEAs, there are household-based educational surveys and national examinations—each with different goals and outcomes. These constitute a "continuum" of learning assessments as shown in Figure 11.4.[47] To the left side of the continuum are SQC assessments that are, as noted earlier, more informal (i.e., less likely to be linked to a school curriculum); are lower cost (i.e., on total cost basis);[48] take less time to administer (i.e., smaller samples mean less testing); and usually have "low stakes" (i.e., the student's advancement in school is not tied to the test outcome).[49] To the right side of the continuum, these same four dimensions tend toward the opposite direction (i.e., formal, higher cost, more time, higher stakes).

Assessments on the left side tend to be of most value in providing a localized understanding of learning, so that schools and teachers may find ways of

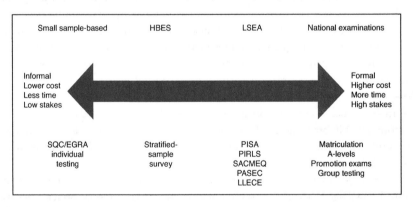

FIGURE 11.4 Assessment Continuum—Ranging From SQC Hybrid Assessments to LSEA and National Examinations

Acronyms: Household-based educational surveys (HBES); Large-scale educational assessments (LSEA); Smaller, quicker, cheaper (SQC); Early grade reading assessment (EGRA); Program for International Student Assessment (PISA); Progress in International Reading Literacy Study (PIRLS); Southern and Eastern Africa Consortium for Monitoring Educational Quality (SACMEQ); Programme d'Analyse des Systèmes Eductifs des Pays de la CONFEMEN (PASEC); and Latin American Laboratory for Assessment of the Quality of Education (LLECE).

Source: Wagner (2011a, p. 45), after Kanjee (2009)

intervening to improve student outcomes. Assessments on the right side are largely used by policymakers at the national or international level, and allow for comparisons by country or region.

Citizen-Led Assessments

Over the past decade or so, a variation of SQC assessments has appeared, called *citizen-led assessments*. Begun by Pratham, a large national NGO in India, the *Annual Status of Education Report* (ASER) uses simple tests of reading and math to provide a quick and relatively inexpensive way of determining the quality of schooling in villages across every state in India. Initially, the ASER report was met with substantial resistance from the Indian government, in part because the results pointed to a high degree of teacher absenteeism and student failure, and also because the data were collected by community volunteers rather than as part of the formal government apparatus with trained data collection agents.

In the ensuing years, the ASER report was not only accepted by Indian governmental agencies, but it also influenced similar assessments in other countries such as Mali, Kenya, Tanzania, and Uganda.[50] It is worth taking a moment to emphasize that such citizen-led assessments can bring substantial political and social pressure in a way that most research studies have not been able to do heretofore. This type of assessment is typically led by a national team that designs the survey, analyzes the data, and disseminates the findings. The Mali assessment, for example, provides exceptionally quick feedback by having NGO volunteers convene community-level meetings where they gather local authorities (e.g., village heads) to share information about the survey just conducted.[51] The localization and practical value of assessments at the ground level can build strong community interest and support well beyond what internationally run studies can typically provide.

A citizen-led assessment usually includes multiple stakeholders who must be taken into account. Thus, it is critical to understand the theory of change embodied in its approach (Figure 11.5).[52] Low scores can help stoke the demand for more and better services (e.g., fewer teacher absences, better-trained teachers, more textbooks), while higher scores can reassure parents of the adequacy of instruction for their children. For the most part, learning outcomes reported in the ASER have not improved according to current research, but the hope is that such feedback will lead to better results in the future.[53] Unfortunately, even with these attempts to provide further information to parents, findings from surveys in Uganda, Tanzania, and Kenya indicate that the relationship between students' learning and parental satisfaction is minimal. In Tanzania, for example, 80% of parents think that government schools are addressing their children's needs "fairly well" or "very well," yet only 30% of children in grade 4 could pass a grade 2 literacy and

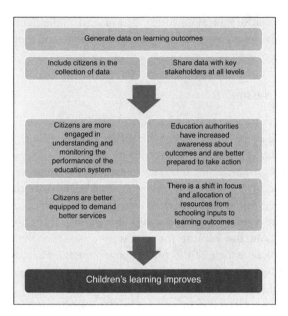

FIGURE 11.5   Citizen–Led Assessments: Theory of Change

Source: Results for Development Institute (2015, p. 12)

numeracy assessment.[54] In other words, most parents seemed to think their children were doing fine in school, even when they were not.

Speed and Accuracy

In 1954, Paul Fitts, an experimental psychologist, famously wrote about certain limitations in human cognition—namely the cognitive "trade-off" between speed and accuracy.[55] The more we aim for speed in responding to some event, the less accurate we are in describing it, and vice versa. Later known as Fitts' Law, this concept was applied in many ways, including how cockpit controls in jet aircraft are built so that they utilize simplified displays for speed of processing of visual information while assuring greater accuracy.

In learning assessments, there is a parallel kind of trade-off to speed and accuracy. Large international assessments have a complex structure, must be vetted across multiple teams of specialists, and are typically carried out on a three-year, five-year, or even ten-year cycle of repetition. These aspects lead to increased accuracy,[56] but they take time. However, if the goal is for a tighter relationship between findings and policies that can be implemented during the annual school cycle or within the mandate set by a minister of education, then greater timeliness of assessments is required. Achieving quicker turnaround time, as in the Mali example cited earlier, generally necessitates the use of localized instruments that can report out quickly, and a smaller sample size (and lower cost) that allows for greater frequency of repetition. In other words, SQC assessments may be less accurate, but provide information when it can be most practically used.

Recall from the previous chapter how technology-based data collection using mobile devices can increase both the reliability of data collection (reducing enumerator errors and obliging that all boxes be filled in) and the speed by which data can be sent to a processing center. In international assessments, it is not unusual for it to take years, not months, to receive a full report from a UN or other international agency.[57] With ICT-based assessments, and smaller measurement instruments, valuable time can be saved. This shortening of the timeline of data collection has implications for improving the speed of feedback both for the individual learner as well as for communities and policymakers.

The above examples underscore the importance of measurement as a way to evaluate policies and hold policymakers accountable, as well as provide feedback to local communities. There is much to be done to achieve this kind of data-driven accountability that promotes learning. Feedback must be more timely, especially in the many countries where national educational authorities still rely upon data gathered at the end of a school year—too late to make a significant difference in children's learning. This is one reason that formative assessments, done during the school year, as in the SQC localized models, are becoming more popular.[58] Fitts' Law remains a useful way to think about assessment options: when accuracy over time is required (e.g., building the scientific knowledge base), then longitudinal and in-depth studies are attractive; however, when data are needed more quickly and for active policy impact, then SQC approaches should be given priority.

Sampling

As discussed in Chapter 3, it is widely accepted that humans learn by "sampling" their environment, beginning by using their built-in senses from the moment of birth. Obviously, no infant, child, or adult can possibly take in the totality of information available in the environment. We learn to discriminate what we see, hear, touch, smell, and taste. This sampling of what's going on around us is multi-determined, and directly impacts how and what we learn.[59] Parents are part of this sampling too. Consciously and unconsciously, family members and others prepare young children to adapt, learn, and survive by exposing them to the range of situations that become the foundation of their lives. Thus, children become prepared to handle life's challenges through these exposures and experiences.

Learning specialists must similarly "sample" the population in order to reliably estimate outcomes. Those participating in assessments should be representative of the population (or sub-population) of a country, and outcomes should be valid across multiple countries in a comparative framework. To accomplish this complex task, researchers must choose: (a) a range of *skills* to be assessed (the skills sample), (b) a *population* to be included (the population sample), and (c) a set of *contextual variables* (sample of intervening variables or correlates). It is important to understand these three types of samples, as each poses empirical and statistical challenges to understanding learning outcomes.

Skills Samples

Humans learn best when they take samples of their informational environment—whether in schools, via word of mouth, or, increasingly, via Internet search engines. This relatively simple observation is relevant since one of the most vexing problems researchers encounter when evaluating learning is how to generalize from one sampling of human skills to another. Thus, sampling a finite set of skills (e.g., reading, math, memory), and knowing about the contextual situations in which the skills are practiced, are key elements of learning assessments. But as described throughout this book, the selection of skills can be quite different from early childhood through adulthood, can vary by context, and can involve both cognitive and social skills.

Population Samples

In Chapter 1, it was noted that only a small fraction of the world's social science research is conducted with poor populations in developing countries. Instead, most social science research has concentrated on what some have called the "WEIRD" (Western, educated, industrialized, rich, and democratic) populations living primarily in wealthy countries, or in the privileged strata of non-Western ones.[60] It seems clear that social science researchers should explicitly address questions of representation and external validity, but often they do not. These critiques may also apply to international development specialists, since much of the available research on learning is limited by scientific datasets drawn from population samples living mainly in middle- to high-income countries. Fortunately, this trend is now beginning to change.[61]

When it comes to international large-scale assessments, poor populations may be excluded from, or underrepresented, in samples that are supposed to be nationally representative.[62] This often happens for one or both of the following reasons: expediency (i.e., it may require too much time or too many resources to fully represent each socio-demographic strata) and national politics (i.e., marginalized groups may not be considered important enough for policymakers and/or they may not be citizens). Thus, it is not unusual for national assessments to oversample the easier-to-reach urban areas, rather than rural areas. Furthermore, in some developing countries, the difficulty of (literally) tracking down nomadic children or studying children in fragile and conflict-ridden situations can make it difficult and expensive for education authorities to study such children.[63] A UNESCO report describes how marginalization can threaten educational attainment, as these children face many challenges, such as "inequalities, stigmatization, and discrimination linked to wealth, gender, ethnicity, language, location, and disability."[64] The degree to which groups are, or are not, included in population samples has serious implications when norms are developed for learning outcomes. Within developing countries (and in most wealthy countries, for that matter), it is not unusual (unfortunately) for majority populations to treat certain minority groups as inferior or as people who "cannot learn."[65]

Contextual Variables

A key aspect of any learning assessment is its ability to pinpoint which contextual variables explain why there is a relationship between the population studied and the skill outcomes. These contextual variables include socioeconomic factors (e.g., family income, access to health care), learning supports (e.g., maternal literacy, teacher training credentials), and learning processes (e.g., time on task, class size). The potential universe of such contextual factors is quite large, as described in earlier chapters. Assessment planners face serious challenges in deciding which correlates to include given the limits on overall respondent time.[66]

In sum, to measure learning, researchers must make at least three key decisions: (1) select the skills to be assessed; (2) determine the type of population sampling methodology to apply (e.g., individual, group, or computer-based testing); (3) and choose contextual and demographic variables (e.g., child's age, year in school, gender, socioeconomic status). Each option is tied to a set of assumptions and compromises, and each will influence the validity, reliability, and practical feasibility of the chosen assessment approach.[67] Further, assessments must be designed so that they can respond to dynamic changes over time, including changes due to globalization, as discussed in the previous chapter. In a real sense, learning assessments are estimates of what a person might know, but are certainly not, and never can be, comprehensive.

Thus, there is no perfect assessment or perfect test. Rather, there are only samplings of individual skills in specific contexts. These may or may not be good estimates or models of behavior. As George Box, a noted British statistician, wrote, "[A]ll models are wrong, but some are useful." In this sense, learning assessments may be more or less *useful*, but can never fully represent the knowledge or skills of any individual.[68]

Finally, we must consider who undertakes and employs the sampling methods. Whether policymakers, psychometricians, school district leaders, or local teachers, they all come to the task of sampling skills, populations, and contexts with their own experiences and points of view. Choices about which skills to sample, among which populations, and in which contexts and languages, add potential bias to an already complex set of more traditional sampling issues such as sample size, clustering, and stratification.[69] In order to address such biases, a range of methods—including tailored sampling and subsample designs, matching samples, oversampling marginalized populations, and mixed methods designs—may be needed.[70]

Comparability

The "social" in social science makes explicit the notion that we are talking about groups of people that can be *compared* with one another. One implication is that these groups have something in common with each other (for example, gender, nationality, or language) that constitutes a reference group. Thus, when development specialists wish to compare boys with girls, or Pakistan with India, or French speakers with Wolof speakers in Senegal, the assumption is that each of these groups is similar in some ways and not in others.

Comparability is also central to global education databases, such as the large-scale data collection carried out by the UNESCO Institute for Statistics (UIS), the World Bank, and OECD. Comparability can be understood in a number of distinct ways. First, international or regional assessments can use comparable statistics to make statements concerning which countries (or regions) are "ahead" or "behind" others. Sometimes called *league tables*, this approach to understanding learning outcomes can be useful in persuading national or international leaders that they should either feel satisfied with their educational system (when test scores are high relative to others) or disappointed (when scores are relatively low). This seems to have most merit when the choices to be made apply to proximal situations, rather than distal ones. For example, consider a Latin American country that has adopted a particular bilingual education program that appears to work well in primary school. If the education minister in a neighboring country believes that the case is similar enough to his or her own national situation, then it makes good sense to compare the scores on, for example, primary school reading tests. A more distal comparison—finding that a certain kind of bilingual education program in Canada seems to be effective—might be less persuasive to a Latin American policymaker.[71]

The majority of large-scale educational assessments utilize standardized tests in a particular domain, such as reading, math, or science. With a few notable exceptions (e.g., PISA[72]), these assessments generally serve to evaluate the degree to which the student has actually learned the curriculum (as demonstrated by the assessment) compared to what is presumed to have been taught. Such assessments are usually administered to large groups in writing (and more recently via computer) within school settings. In contrast, SQC assessments (e.g., EGRA) are usually administered individually.[73] Results from the data collected across these two types of assessment methodologies add additional unknowns into the question of comparability.

The Bottom of the Pyramid

The "bottom of the pyramid" (discussed in Chapter 1) consists of one to two billion children and adults who are part of vulnerable and marginal populations.[74] The representativeness of a sample population, as noted earlier, is fundamental for all learning assessments, and relates to the earlier discussion of how to understand cultural differences.[75] Nonetheless, it is often the case that many poor children are systematically excluded from measurement in LSEAs that typically utilize samples of children enrolled in school, and exclude out-of-school children.[76] In addition, LSEAs may exclude those who have not sufficiently mastered the language of the assessment, and those who are dyslexic or have other mental or physical handicaps. A recent review illustrates this point, showing that LSEAs are strongly biased toward sampling children in the high-income category for grades 8–10 (see Figure 11.6).

SQC and citizen-led assessments, with their emphasis on testing in mother-tongue and the propensity to sample inclusively, are more likely to broadly accommodate children in low-income populations.[77] As shown in Figure 11.7, sampling *all* children of a certain age (not just those in a particular grade) can result in very large differences in learning outcomes in countries like Pakistan and Tanzania, leading to major divergences in policy development. Clearly, many children in these two countries have repeated one or more grade levels—in other words, they are already falling behind and have much lower reading scores. This

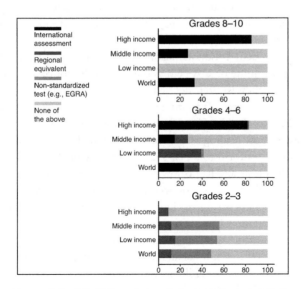

FIGURE 11.6 Share of the World Population Ages 6–15 Included in Sampling Frame of Various International Assessments

Source: Sandefur (2016, p. 2)

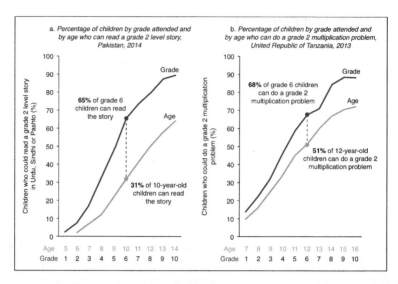

FIGURE 11.7 Differences in Reading and Mathematics Outcomes When All Children Versus Only School-Going Children are Reported in Assessments in Pakistan and Tanzania

Source: UNESCO GEM Report team analysis using Pakistan ASER and United Republic of Tanzania Uwezo data. Adapted from UNESCO (2016a, p. 197).

is precisely the situation of Teboho and Mpho, as we saw in the opening story in South Africa. Teboho, studying in a rural school, is already five years older than his classmates, and will likely drop out soon, while Mpho will continue his upward trajectory.

As noted earlier, EGRA uses oral reading fluency (calculated as the number of correct words per minute or CWPM) as the main indicator of a child's ability to read.[78] Reading fluency is often defined as an average of about 50–60 CWPM in low-income countries.[79] Two studies using EGRA can help to clarify how Teboho's and Mpho's worlds of learning intersect with problems of measurement. The first relates to how reading assessments are designed with the assumption that student scores will conform to a bell-shaped curve, with about half the students scoring above the mean, and half below the mean. In very poor learning contexts, however, this normal curve may not occur.[80] In a review of cross-national reading studies, for example, normative reading outcomes were found to vary dramatically by country. Figure 11.8a shows the distribution of reading fluency in an Asian country indicating near-normal distribution, while Figure 11.8b shows a strong skew to the left in a sub-Saharan African country. In the African country, there were many zero scores—children who simply could not read a single word, a situation very much like that of Teboho (and Azra's daughter in Chapter 6).[81]

Such "non-normal" statistical distributions are not unusual at the bottom of the pyramid. The consequences are twofold. First, from a scientific perspective, the

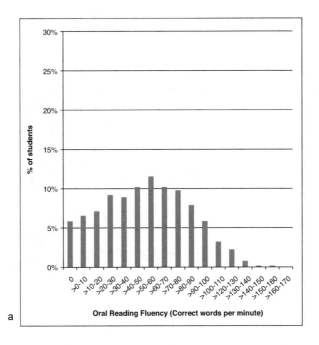

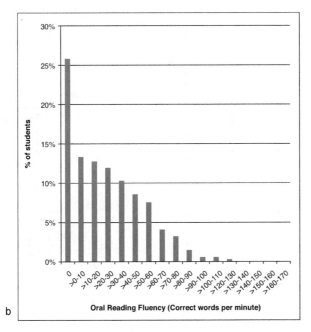

FIGURES 11.8a & 11.8b Distribution of EGRA Oral Reading Fluency in: (a) an Asian Country; and (b) in a Sub-Saharan African Country

Source: Dubeck and Gove (2015, pp. 319–320)

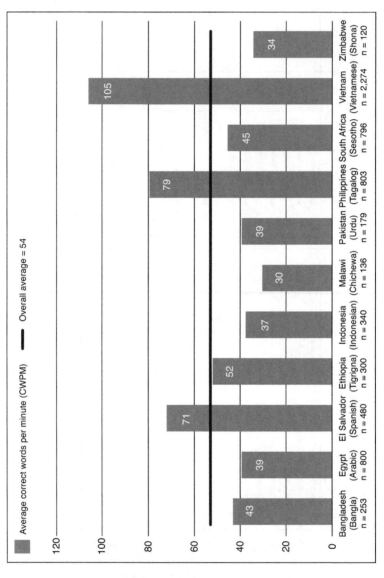

FIGURE 11.9 Average Fluency Among Grade 3 Children With Reading Comprehension by Country

Note: The Y axis is the number of correct words per minute (CWPM) in reading fluency, using EGRA assessments.

Source: Dowd et al. (2016, p. 75)

data show that the African country sample had a modal score of zero, meaning that the plurality of the group could not read a single word; however, the Asian sample appears more in line with the Western normative bell-shaped distribution where the modal score is about 50–60 CWPM.[82] Second, from a practical perspective, these data raise questions about the need for better indicators at the lower end of the curve—probably by including emergent literacy measures such as oral language skills and letter knowledge.[83] Better methodological tools are also needed that can disaggregate learning outcomes both between and within countries in contexts of high poverty.[84]

Another way to study learning achievement is through the measurement of reading comprehension, comparing this with children's reading fluency rates. This, too, can be problematic across divergent populations, where fluency for adequate comprehension was found to vary from 30 to 105 in CWPM across 11 countries (see Figure 11.9).[85] This result demonstrates that children from diverse backgrounds—such as Teboho and Mpho in their respective schools—may need to be instructed differently, rather than being held to a single reading fluency benchmark. And it is particularly important since there is an inherent possibility that the push for reading at faster fluency speeds can lead to a decrement in reading comprehension.[86]

This discussion reprises the question of an assessment's purpose. If the purpose is to compare a school's or nation's learning achievement with another, then group comparison is required, even with its many challenges.[87] Alternatively, if the purpose is to better understand how those at the bottom of the pyramid learn, then localized measures will likely be more useful.

Gathering Evidence: Three Principles

From birth onward, our senses discriminate what to attend to and what to ignore. The same is true with evidence, as was aptly described a half-century ago by Thomas Kuhn in his description of "paradigm shifts" in science—we are often highly selective in the evidence we use.[88] While there are many ways that personal and scientific evidence can be gathered, three principles are relevant to the discussion of how to gather evidence in international development.

If You Cannot Measure It, You Cannot Manage It[89]

This principle is widely cited in many fields, and it is becoming increasingly central to how development institutions and professionals think about their work. Measurement is crucial, even if not everyone agrees on what and how to measure. In this volume, we have supported the view that credible research evidence depends on measurement, and should be an essential component for all substantive development efforts. As implied here, yardsticks do not come in a "one size fits all" approach, but rather must be appropriate for the diverse populations and contexts being measured. So, yes to measurement, but we must also pay very careful attention to cultural specifics. Development specialists need to be conscious of the imperative to measure as well as the trade-offs between different types of measurement approaches.

If All You Have Is a Hammer, Everything Looks Like a Nail[90]

Psychologists have long known about "functional fixedness"—the notion that habits of thinking can create blockages that prevent creative and flexible thinking.[91] With this example about a hammer, we find the same general point: even if a hammer is effective for a particular nail—such as the Internet (hammer) for exploring new types of fertilizers (nail)—this does not imply that the Internet will be equally effective for learning to read (a very different nail). Thus, the approach suggested here favors using evidence that is locally gathered. In other words, we should not simply apply results from one location to another while assuming that the consequences will be the same. This is particularly the case when the cultural context varies in important ways. Both hammers and nails vary greatly and finding the right mix is one of the most important development challenges. Over time, development professionals and agencies have sought the proverbial *magic bullet* in order to scale up a generalizable solution of some kind (such as discussed in technology apps in Chapter 9). In other words, they seek to increase the benefit-cost ratio.[92] While such solutions are tempting (indeed seductive), they contain serious constraints on, and liabilities for, development success.

Looking Only Where There's Light[93]

First, the story: A policeman sees a man searching for something under a streetlight and asks what the man has lost. He says he lost his keys and they both look under the streetlight together. After a few minutes the policeman asks if he is sure he lost them here, and the man replies that no, he lost them in the park. The policeman asks why he is searching under the streetlight and the man replies, "This is where the light is." About two or three decades ago, the world community thought that most of the world's development problems could be solved if every child had access to school, or if every parent were literate. We now know that each of the United Nations development goals is fraught with difficult challenges—both of definition and appropriateness of policy and practice. Individuals and international professionals and agencies typically look for solutions that are convenient, within their competencies, and where there is a proverbial "streetlight." Looking for your keys in other places (that is, where the lighting is very limited) poses major development challenges since detailed knowledge of local cultural contexts is not easily obtained, but it is what skilled development specialists must do if they are to reach those most in need.

Accountability

Accountability derives from the Latin *computare* (to calculate). Today, in the world of research, the term usually refers to the ways (through measurement) we hold policymakers *accountable* for the decisions they make. This chapter is, broadly speaking, about the ways that development agencies and other stakeholders are or can be held to account.

In most countries, educational specialists and statisticians are the principal guardians of educational data that policymakers use—from learning assessments to graduation rates. This guardianship of knowledge—leading at times to a lack of transparency—stems mostly from the complexities of collecting large datasets, as well as generating and interpreting statistics and empirical results. With respect to learning assessments, reticent policymakers might understandably worry about publicizing achievement differences between children of varying social backgrounds (such as by ethnolinguistic groups, gender, private and public schools, and so forth). Findings that highlight differences between groups can lead to sensitive and politically uncomfortable policy debates. These situations cannot be avoided, and probably should not be. At the same time, they can also be distracting and politically motivated in ways that do not promote the kind of careful evaluation that is desirable when so much is at stake. Still, data transparency is the key to accountability and policy change. Having access to research findings is a way to empower people and policymakers alike.[94]

In wealthy countries, too, when parents and community groups become aware of cross-national assessment results, they can start to enact social and political change by advocating for resources, expertise, small class sizes, and other desirable components of quality schools. Government ministers, in turn, can seek increased funding—and this can happen when results are either poorer or better than expected. In short, greater transparency can lead to enhanced involvement on the part of all stakeholders.

Overall, accountability with regard to learning outcomes, and in education more generally, is becoming increasingly valued across the globe—and by an ever-wider array of stakeholders. This trend toward better measurement and resulting accountability requires careful thought and planning. Multiple stakeholders at all levels will need to find ways to collaborate on both the inputs to educational research and measurement, and the outputs and interpretations that shape decision making. There will be tensions and disagreements about goals and consequences, but the overall trend is toward better information to inform better policies.

Implementation Science

When Jim Yong Kim became President of the World Bank in 2012, he announced plans to construct a new science of delivery—or *implementation science*—that would span the work of that institution. Developed initially within the health profession, the concept of implementation science derives from the fact that the best development ideas often fail as a result of poor implementation, rather than mistaken ideas.[95] In health, for example, a common problem might be how to deliver an important vaccine that has to be kept in a "cold chain," such that it does not lose its effectiveness upon delivery.[96] Similarly, in education, personal computers may be purchased and distributed to create state-of-the-art computer labs in poor schools. However, if maintenance is not provided or electricity ceases to function or teachers are not trained, then implementation becomes a major stumbling block. If we were to imagine the percentage of good ideas that fail due to poor implementation (including lack of sustainable funding), it would be very high.

One of the most difficult implementation questions concerning learning assessments and surveys is how much data, and of which kind, to collect. The idea that one can collect "just enough" data—much easier said than done—is sometimes called "evidence-centered design."[97] Each of the international, regional and localized assessments described earlier utilizes measurement tools and surveys that are most often undertaken at the school level, with techniques that allow for the assessment of reading fluency and comprehension. As noted, comparing implementations of seemingly similar assessments can also be problematic due to the widely varying contexts in which such activities take place.[98]

In sum, many of the best methods for implementing sound designs and incorporating innovative tools for learning measurement require skills and training that can be highly technical in nature. And they need to be applied on the ground by individuals who have an in-depth understanding of local conditions, local languages, and local attitudes. Combining these sets of skills under a single or even several craniums has always be one of the major challenges in social science research.

Measurement for Learning

At the outset, we saw that Teboho and Mpho differed notably in their personal and educational life progress, although each resides within the same poor province in South Africa. Each child is in second grade, but Teboho has not learned well, has repeated grades, and will likely be unable to attend secondary school. For Mpho, things will be quite different—he has, it seems, a bright future ahead. The gap between Teboho and Mpho will likely be maintained for their whole lives, much as Oscar Lewis maintained in his theory of culture and poverty.[99]

Some critics of learning assessments maintain that such testing represents the "tail wagging the dog." They argue that assessments have too great an influence over how and what children learn. One example is the tendency to push (through assessments) for faster reading fluency that may be counterproductive for children's reading comprehension. Another is the case of trying to assure international comparability in assessments while marginalized groups get left further behind. Even with such limitations, good measurement tools and methods as well as a thorough analysis of the collected data represent the only way that learning and education will be improved over the long haul. There's an old saying: "if you torture the data long enough, it will confess!"[100] Such confessions are what we are aiming for.

We have seen numerous examples of how securing better ways to measure learning outcomes—for individuals, teachers, communities, and policymakers—can help make a positive difference. Many challenges remain, but important progress is being made—such as with SQC and citizen-led localized assessments, RCTs, longitudinal studies, and practices of implementation science. Important findings in these and related areas will help advance development work and reduce learning inequality well into the future.

Notes

1. Adapted from Wagner and Castillo (2014).
2. See Jerven (2013). "[N]umbers [on African development] are poor. This is not just a matter of technical accuracy. The arbitrariness of the quantification process produces observations with very large errors and levels of uncertainty. . . . International development actors are making judgments based on erroneous statistics. Governments are not able to make informed decisions because existing data are too weak or the data they need do not exist" (p. xi). This is not only in Africa, since "some problem surrounds the collection and compilation of official statistics in all countries" (p. 1).
3. Cited in Upgren (2008, p. 7).
4. Data cited in this case example are from the South Africa Department of Basic Education (2013).
5. South African schools are categorized according to a poverty index based on the relative wealth or poverty of the community, and are grouped into quintiles. When the SAANA was administered there, only a small fraction of the children in grade 3 scored above the national norm, while the large majority scored in the bottom 10%, creating a bimodal distribution.
6. Many researchers have studied the impact of social stratification on school results (e.g., Buchmann & Hannum, 2001; Benedict & Hoag, 2011; Korinek & Punpuing, 2012; Lu & Treiman, 2011).
7. The original distinction between knowledge-driven and decision-driven research is derived from Masters (1984).
8. One personal anecdote might be permissible here. I served a few years ago on a dissertation faculty jury in France that was based on multiple years of doctoral student research on educational practices in a rural village in West Africa. Most of the comments by the other (French) faculty focused on the theoretical and conceptual implications of the student's findings. When my turn came, I asked the student what she would say to the country's Minister of Education about any possible practical or policy implications of what was an excellent in-depth piece of social science research. The student exclaimed that her professors wouldn't have allowed her to be "practical" as a matter of academic principle—that might endanger the "neutrality" of her research. Her response followed very much on the knowledge-driven approach favored by many scholars.
9. See specific UN SDG education targets in Chapter 2.
10. A case in point, described in Chapter 5, was USAID's multi-year All Children Reading project that sought to help 100 million children read in the early grades. Considerable research was funded in order to try to meet that goal, though developing the research and practice approach depended greatly on the financial resources committed up front.
11. Savedoff et al. (2006, p. 12) states: "Generating knowledge about whether a program achieved its basic aims requires impact evaluation, which analyzes and documents the

extent to which changes in the well-being of the target population can be attributed to a particular program or policy. Such evaluation tries to answer the question: 'What difference did this program make?' Impact evaluation asks about the difference between what happened with the program and what would have happened without it."

12. Increasingly, such evaluation studies are employing randomized controlled trials, discussed later in this chapter.

13. World Bank (2015b, p. 188).

14. See Chapter 5 on EGRA, the early grade reading assessment. See Cozby (2012) for a useful review on research methodology, and Hambleton and Kanjee (1995) on validity across cultures.

15. This has been difficult to achieve across the social sciences in general; recent reports from the field of psychology have found reproducibility to be much lower than expected (Van Bavel et al., 2016) and highly dependent on contextual variation.

16. This is inter-item reliability, measured by Cronbach's *alpha* statistic. See also: http://en.wikipedia.org/wiki/Cronbach's_alpha. Of course, reliability implies little about the validity of the instrument; that is, a high alpha statistic does not indicate whether or not a test is relevant to educational outcomes.

17. Bartlett and Garcia (2011); Blackledge and Creese (2010).

18. See Wagner (2004). Some researchers also see this as one way to think of the boundary between the disciplines of anthropology (emic) versus psychology (etic). See Gielen (2016) for a useful discussion of emic versus etic, and the inevitable overlap between these two concepts; and for an earlier discussion, see Harris (1976).

19. Also, see the work of Weisberg (2014, p. 15) on *willful ignorance*, which he defines as the "inescapable fact that probabilities are not geared directly to individuals. An assessment of probability can of course be *applied* to any particular individual, that is a matter of judgment. By choosing a statistically based probability, you effectively regard this individual as a random member of the population upon which the statistics were derived. In other words, you *ignore* any distinguishing features of the individual or his circumstances that might modify the probability."

20. The well-known essay of Leszek Kolakowski on impossibility refers to "How to Be a Conservative-Liberal-Socialist." See: http://people.virginia.edu/~smd5r/Kolak01.htm. Thanks to L. Crouch for this illustration.

21. Some draw attention to how culture is embedded with "value-laden ways of doing things that make some sense as they occur together" (Rogoff & Angelillo, 2002, p. 216). Thus, cultures (and nations) should not (in this view) be used simply as "data points" on a chart, as has been done by various UN and regional agencies as well as those testing theories across cultures. In psychology, this approach (cultures as data points) may be seen in the sub-discipline of *cross-cultural psychology*; here, a researcher might test a concept in culture A and then in culture B, and claim that all differences amount to the "differences" between cultures A and B. In fact, there may be many similarities and differences other than in the test items (and in the items themselves). Long ago, Cole and Scribner (1974) described some of the advantages and disadvantages in trying to compare data from one culture to another. When nations are used as data points, how should we interpret the imbalance between large countries (such as China) and small ones (such as Costa Rica)? Rather, it is essential to determine which identifiable cultural factors and populations need to be sampled in order to determine particular outcome results.

22. See Chapter 2, on the work of Bronfenbrenner.

23. Bowles (2014).

24. See Wagner (1993).

25. Two overlapping cohorts were used.

26. See Wagner and Srivastava (1989) for one of the first household literacy surveys, undertaken in Zimbabwe.

27. Paris (2005). Constrained skills are also limited in variance, since the upper limit is fixed and is attained relatively quickly in middle and upper income contexts.
28. This relative speed is likely to be the case in both wealthy and poor contexts. Nonetheless, the learning of the alphabetic principle (and the alphabet) may be much slower in poor contexts in developing countries, as numerous EGRA studies have shown (RTI, 2009).
29. Scarborough (1998) reviewed 61 beginning literacy studies (largely in the United States) and found that the strongest individual difference predictor of reading ability in first through third grade was letter name identification in kindergarten, across all 24 research samples measuring this variable. However, by first grade, letter name knowledge was no longer the strongest predictor of later reading ability, and was most often eclipsed by phonological processing skills, such as letter sound knowledge and phoneme synthesis and analysis tasks.
30. This is also one reason why studies of first and second language acquisition require longitudinal studies.
31. The RCT methodology was apparently first used in medical research in the late 18th century and RCTs continue to be the preferred methodology in medical research today. RCTs became popular in the social sciences and education with the work of Stigler (1992); for an overview, see Boruch and Rui (2008).
32. See Piper and Kwayumba (2014), described in Chapter 10. This RCT assumed, as in the aspirin example, that everything else was held constant between the two experimental and control groups—an assumption often challenged in the context of social interventions as discussed below. See also Burde (2012).
33. Among others, Kremer and Holla (2009), Banerjee and Duflo (2011), Bruns et al. (2011), and McEwan (2015) have provided support for the use of RCTs in international development work. A broad review on the use of RCTs for understanding education impact in developing countries was undertaken by Ganimian and Murnane (2016).
34. For each of these three critiques, see (respectively): Pritchett (2009) on question limitations; Evans and Popova (2015) on meta-analyses; and Castillo and Wagner (2014) on limitations of generalization. Also, for a useful general critique, see Ravallion (2012, p. 106) who wrote: "Even under ideal conditions, an RCT only delivers an estimate of the mean impact on those treated in the experimental population, and we learn little or nothing about the distribution of impacts from a standard RCT. . . . Also, the question of why the intervention did or did not have impact in that population remains most often open." As L. Crouch (personal communication) suggests "Unlike in medical experiments where there is at least the attempt to use *double-blinding* (that is, neither the recipients nor the treatment providers know who is in the treatment group) or even *triple-blinding* (where even the analysts do not know who is in the treatment group), in social science this is essentially impossible. Contamination from the treatment to the control group, especially if the treatment appears to be working, is also much harder if there is no blinding." Finally, the well-known mathematician, John W. Tukey, recognized that an over-reliance on statistical hypothesis testing "often conceals underlying or hidden variables in an analysis, particularly relevant while examining the inequalities in education. Rather, additional methods of triangulation or support (e.g., by employing exploratory data analysis) . . . are needed to provide qualitative description based on contextualization" (cited in Jacob & Holsinger, 2008, p. 6).
35. Kipsang and Piper (2017). This adaptive RCT in Kenya is relatively unusual. The large majority of RCT-based studies rarely have the time and resources to adapt and elaborate on earlier assumptions.
36. Karlan and Appel (2016).
37. At the other end of the spectrum, researchers who support purely local solutions sometimes fail to understand the possibility of generalization and scalability upon which policymakers are dependent. See Easterly (2014) and his critique of "experts," and a rejoinder on the substantial need for development expertise (Wagner, 2015b).

38. Nicolas et al. (2013) provides a useful history of Binet's work on intelligence testing and schooling in France as a basis for future school assessments.
39. Benavot and Köseleci (2015). This domain has become its own small industry, as exemplified by the Educational Testing Service (ETS), OECD/PISA assessments, the International Association for the Evaluation of Educational Achievement (IEA), and others. See also early report by Benavot and Tanner. (2007).
40. Lockheed (2010).
41. Kamens and McNeely (2010); Meyer and Benavot (2013).
42. Chromy (2002); Greaney and Kellaghan (2008).
43. Broadly speaking, the costs include: (1) opportunity costs (what could be accomplished if a particular assessment was not done); (2) human resources (including training of highly skilled staff); and (3) actual budget costs ("total cost of assessments").
44. For a broader review, see Wagner (2011a); earlier work along these lines may be found in Wagner (1990; 2003).
45. See Wagner (2010b; 2011a). SQC literacy assessments can be traced to Wagner and Srivastava (1989) and subsequent work in Wagner (1993), and Wagner et al. (1999).
46. On comparative costs of assessments, see Wagner et al. (2011).
47. This continuum also implies that not every assessment aligns exactly in a particular spot in a linear fashion; that is, some assessements may appear to the left or right of the arrowheads in some components but not on each.
48. In addition to Wagner et al. (2011) there is also a recent study on the costs of using citizen-led assessments, similarly with lower relative costs (Results for Development Institute, 2015, p. 22).
49. For students, high or low stakes are, however, a matter of individual perception. While it is often assumed that formal assessments and examinations are "high stakes," it is not necessarily the case that smaller-scale assessments are universally perceived by students as "low stakes." See Carnoy et al. (2003) for a broad discussion.
50. Results for Development Institute (2015). In a technical review of these citizen-led assessments, the authors found them to be generally reliable and valid for their purpose of providing a snapshot of reading and math levels based on individualized assessments, mainly in local languages.
51. Results for Development Institute (2015, pp. 13, 21).
52. A theory of change generally refers to the way that project implementers define long-term goals, and then maps backward to identify needed precursors or preconditions that foster the achievement of the goals. For another version of using outcome data to support a theory of change, see Vogel (2012).
53. Results for Development Institute (2015).
54. Pritchett et al. (2013, p. 22), from Uwezo (2011).
55. Fitts (1954).
56. What statisticians sometimes call granularity or density of the data.
57. Wagner (2011a).
58. Assessments are usually either *formative* (to determine during the learning process how to modify or shape learning before the end of the intervention period, such as having the instructor change her pedagogy) or *summative* (to measure what has been learned at the end during specified instructional inputs; e.g., end-of-year exam). Each of these assessment approaches is highly dependent on sampling and comparability.
59. Kahneman (2011).
60. See Arnett (2008), as well as Heinrich et al. (2010).
61. Wagner (2014c; 2015e).
62. Engel and Feuer (2014); Wagner (2010b).
63. See also Chapter 5 on out-of-school children.
64. UNESCO (2010, p. 5).
65. See Pigozzi et al. (2014) for a critique of such labeling.

66. Thanks to I. Gal (personal communication) for his thoughts on this issue.
67. Braun and Kanjee (2006); Wagner (2010b, 2011a).
68. Thanks to L. Crouch for the reference to Box (1976). See also the discussion of William Labov's contrast between linguistic "competence" versus "performance" in Cole and Bruner (1971), which made a very similar point about actual competence always being underestimated by observable performance.
69. See earlier discussion in this chapter about cognitive biases (World Bank, 2015b).
70. On sampling methods, see Lohr (2009). Those engaged in international LSEAs are not unaware of the complexities of population sampling. One way that they attempt to control for large socioeconomic variation within and across populations is through the surveys that measure individual income levels or family assets. A useful discussion can be found in Cresswell et al. (2015), wherein the OECD's PISA for Development design is discussed. Sampling constraints on international and comparative assessments are discussed in Meyer and Benavot (2013).
71. However, proximity is not always the most pertinent feature. For example, in the United States and Japan, rivalries between educational outcomes and economic systems have been a matter of serious discussion and debate over many years (Stevenson & Stigler, 1982). In a more recent example, senior officials in Botswana were interested in knowing how Singapore came to score first in mathematics on several LSEAs (Gilmore, 2005; see also Sjoberg, 2007). On the overall politics of comparability, see Steiner-Khamsi (2010).
72. OECD's PISA assessments cover a number of key knowledge domains such as literacy, lifelong learning, and mathematics, but they are not linked to any particular national curriculum. OECD states this clearly: "Rather than examine mastery of specific school curricula, PISA looks at students' ability to apply knowledge and skills in key subject areas and to analyze, reason, and communicate effectively as they examine, interpret and solve problems." See: www.oecd.org/pisa/aboutpisa/pisafaq.htm.
73. For example, EGRA is primarily based on a number of reading fluency skills developed originally for diagnostic purposes in beginning reading; see Chapter 5.
74. See Wagner et al. (in press), *Learning at the bottom of the pyramid.*
75. For further description of sampling within major LSEAs, see Wagner (2011a, pp. 37–50).
76. A recent study of the TIMSS found that immigrant girls were dramatically underrepresented in their international survey. See: www.iea.nl/sites/default/files/publications/Electronic_versions/IEA_Policy_Brief_12_November2016.pdf.
77. On high- versus low-income sampling, see Sandefur (2016).
78. See in Chapter 5 on the EGRA.
79. By comparison, CWPM is about 100–120 with comprehension in OECD countries by about grade 2–3.
80. Dudley-Marling and Gurn (2010); Gurn (2010).
81. Dubeck and Gove (2015). The Asian or African countries in this study were not identified by the authors.
82. Western fluency rates are more typically around 100–120 CWPM in grades 2–3.
83. See Chapter 4 discussion on ECD and reading; for example, the work of Dowd and Pisani (2013).
84. In another example, if mothers in a research study are shown to have variations in their literacy skills, then conclusions based on "maternal literacy" will need to be more nuanced than previous bivariate (literate vs. illiterate) categorizations. See earlier discussion of the work of LeVine et al. (2012) in Chapter 6.
85. Dowd et al. (2016). Adequate reading comprehension meant the level of reading fluency corresponding to achieving 80% of comprehension questions answered correctly.
86. As pointed out in Chapter 5, it can be detrimental for children to feel that they must read quickly, especially in situations when children do not understand what they are reading, such as in a second language (L2). The empirical support for "reading too

fast"—or rather, decoding too fast—is only circumstantial at present, but there are good reasons to worry about it given the limitations on teacher training (as discussed in Chapter 8). Piper and Zuilkowski (2016) point out that timed EGRA assessments (as compared to untimed ones) do not seem to lead to lower fluency scores, and thus can lead to lower cost of assessment (i.e., more children tested/day). Even so, teachers who emphasize speed over accuracy (cf. Fitts' Law) could lead to lower reading comprehension; further research is needed on this question. Other concerns about EGRA have been voiced by Hoffman (2012) and Pritchett and Beatty (2015).

87. Researchers who undertake international LSEAs are aware of limitations of the national rankings. For example, Mullis et al. (2016, p. 68), in the TIMSS 2015 study, state that: "League tables draw an inordinate amount of attention to national means, but educational authorities would be remiss if they also did not monitor how well low and high achievers are doing."

88. Kuhn (1962).

89. Attributed to Peter Drucker, a major management figure. No citation is available.

90. Attributed to Maslow (1966, p. 15) who wrote: "I suppose it is tempting, if the only tool you have is a hammer, to treat everything as if it were a nail."

91. Duncker (1945), a gestalt psychologist, did the original experiments which found that using a set of specific tools to solve a problem could prevent human subjects from thinking more creatively about the use of the same tools on different problems. This finding has been replicated in many contexts and cultures.

92. The notion of a "magic bullet" can be directly linked to the earlier medical model that uses RCTs to determine if a single type of pill or treatment can cure a disease. We have argued here that education and social science methodologies pose numerous challenges to a single-solution approach to multifactorial situations.

93. Freedman (2010), attributed to Kaplan (1964).

94. Cerdan-Infantes and Filmer (2015).

95. See a definition of "implementation science" in health at: www.fic.nih.gov/research-topics/pages/implementationscience.aspx.

96. A cold chain refers to the need for some medicines (e.g., vaccines) to be kept at a particular cool temperature in order for the drug's effectiveness to be maintained.

97. Braun and Kanjee (2006). This has also been termed the "right-sizing" of data collection.

98. See also McCall (2009).

99. See Chapter 1.

100. Attributed to the British economist Ronald Coase (circa 1977).

12

LEARNING EQUITY

A New Agenda for Development

Balandur: Village Inequality in Northern India

The village of Balandur in Northern India exemplifies the complex local dynamics that often impact the overall effectiveness of development projects.[1] Within Balandur, different groups of villagers, defined by caste or gender, face radically different opportunities for economic and social mobility. Disadvantage in one dimension is reinforced by disadvantage in others, and they combine to perpetuate stark inequalities over generations. Unsurprisingly, disparities in education are wide, but have declined over the years due to a few successful government interventions. In the late 1950s, about 20% of men and only 1% of women were literate. But by 2011, 81% of men were literate, along with 41% of women.[2] Education has increasing value in Balandur, as the villagers have learned that it enhances the likelihood of finding a more modern job outside the village. However, most villagers still believe that educating girls is less important than boys, since adult women are expected to be immersed in child rearing and domestic work. In addition, many upper-caste villagers believe that education is not important or even suitable for the lower castes. The Balandur village assembly (*panchayat*) is a governing body that reflects the villagers' inclination to enforce these more traditional views and power structures. In 1984, the panchayat decreed that at least one woman must serve as a member, but in reality the designated woman was rarely consulted and seldom attended any meetings. All decisions are still made by a village leader who comes from one of the privileged, upper-caste groups. Between the late 1950s and early 2000s, numerous government-funded programs were introduced to the village: a public works road-building program, free public schooling, and basic health care. However, many of the projects failed to get off the ground and only programs that enjoyed strong backing from the politically advantaged members of the village were allowed to thrive, once again reinforcing existing inequalities.

Bumper stickers, wall posters, and other artifacts from popular culture have made the phrase "Think Globally, Act Locally" commonplace today,[3] and it is still applied to a wide range of problems, including those in the field of education.[4]

In villages like Balandur, we recognize that local intra-group relationships often determine who "gets ahead." This type of social hierarchy clearly privileges certain groups and individuals more than others. Despite government efforts and the fact that much has changed in Balandur over the decades, traditional views can still determine "who deserves what" in the village.

In this chapter, the bumper sticker phrase is particularly apt. We have been examining the impact of global changes on learning and education, while at the same time emphasizing the importance of gathering local information, respecting local perceptions, and creating localized learning assessments. From the Balandur example, we need to ask: How do we reduce inequality in learning outcomes not only across societies but also within them?[5] In other words, how can greater learning equity be achieved?

The Search for a Global Learning Metric

The fourth goal of the UN SDGs includes text that is designed to ensure that all girls and boys complete *equitable* and *quality* primary and secondary education leading to *relevant* and *effective* learning outcomes.[6] While certainly a noble endeavor on the surface, the aspirations reflected in the key words—equitable, quality, relevant, and effective—raise important questions about how such goals can be implemented and measured. Let's reconsider the story of Teboho and Mpho in South Africa that opened the previous chapter. How can their education be made equitable if each has a very different learning trajectory? How should the quality of their learning be measured? How useful is it to compare Teboho and Mpho on a single global scale that is relevant and effective across the world, so that policymakers in South Africa know that they are meeting international goals? Irrespective of UN goals, how much emphasis should there be on helping each of these two boys and other children in Limpopo achieve their learning potential?

Recall the work of Alfred Binet who was asked how best to determine which French children would benefit most from learning in school.[7] Since that time, education policymakers have been searching unsuccessfully for a universally functional measure of learning—that is, a global metric by which the learning of all children might be measured. Building on recent decades of research—mainly through comprehensive work on large-scale educational assessments—policymakers in many countries have continued to push for this type of global learning metric.[8] This search is reinforced as well by the UN SDGs which mandate that governments report on national progress toward global education targets.[9] However, it is equally evident that children like Teboho and Mpho—with diverse skills and needs, as well as very different personal stories—are unlikely to benefit directly or in the same way from the existence of such global targets. When important national and international education policy debates happen, Teboho and Mpho are rarely the focus of attention.[10]

In addition, a global learning metric (composed of a cluster of skills assessments such as in reading and mathematics) assumes a normative approach to learning, usually by comparing the mean and standard deviation of national scores. However, for a variety of reasons mentioned in the previous chapter, the poorest and most marginalized populations may not be represented in those norms.[11] Indeed, most international attention and resources have been concentrated on raising *average* scores rather than directly helping children to learn better. Donald T. Campbell, one of the leading thinkers in measurement methods, once warned of overly focusing on a single metric rather than the underlying processes the metric was supposed to measure. Termed "Campbell's Law," it stated that: "The more any quantitative social indicator is used for social decision-making, the more subject it will be to corruption pressures and the more apt it will be to distort and corrupt the social processes it is intended to monitor."[12] A global learning metric poses just such an obstacle for achieving learning equity.

Fortunately, there are two ways out of this conundrum that are both possible and useful. The first involves trying to *close the gap* in the learning disparities between those at the bottom and those at the top of the scale. The second involves attempting to *raise the floor*—rather than just the average score—of learning outcomes of the poor and marginalized.[13]

Closing the Gap

In the post–World War II era, as noted earlier, there was a propensity to measure poverty in terms of GNP per capita.[14] One major area of interest based on this approach was to create better ways to measure how poverty impacts social mobility. In an influential book published in 1972, entitled *Inequality*, the sociologist Christopher Jencks sought to investigate social and economic differences within the United States along with ideas for reducing disparities between groups.[15] Jencks's work and that of others led to large-scale efforts to develop new ways to uncover factors, such as income disparities, related to social inequality.

Income Gini Index

One important approach to the study of social inequality had its origins much earlier in the work of the Italian statistician, Corrado Gini.[16] As it was eventually called, the Gini Coefficient (also expressed as a normalized Gini Index) measures the statistical disparities within a population sample.[17] The *Income Gini Index* has been most commonly used to measure income (or wealth) inequality in a national population. The Gini Index ranges from zero to one, where higher values indicate greater inequality. A zero Income Gini Index score would mean the society is egalitarian in terms of income.

In the village of Balandur discussed at the beginning of this chapter, disparities were maintained over decades. Similar to Bourdieu's notion of "cultural capital," research shows a close relationship between inequality in income, social class, and education, and this relationship tends to be maintained by traditional values over multiple generations.[18] This is where the Gini Index can help provide a relatively simple way to clarify disparities among larger populations. The Income Gini Index does not require strict comparability of the metrics of income—for example, income in the United Kingdom can be measured in pounds sterling, while India it can be measured in rupees.

Recent national analyses show that the Income Gini Index ranges from about 0.26 in Norway, 0.34 in India, 0.45 in the United States to 0.52 in Brazil and 0.63 in South Africa—with the latter among the most economically unequal countries today.[19] There are, quite obviously, major differences in income inequality within and across national populations. Overall, the Income Gini Index has become widely used as one of the primary ways for describing economic inequity.

Education Gini Index

Researchers have also studied education inequality—what has been termed the *Education Gini Index*. In a World Bank paper in 2001, a Gini Coefficient was calculated as a way to compare educational attainment (i.e., average years of schooling achieved) across countries and over time.[20] Subsequent work, as in Figure 12.1, showed that the Education Gini Index has decreased slowly over the past

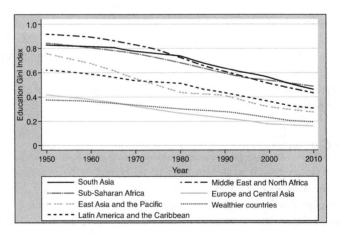

FIGURE 12.1 Education Gini Index by Region: 1950–2010

Note: The curves represent the years of schooling that have accumulated in the population by region, over six decades of data gathering.

Source: Wail et al. (2011, p. 23)

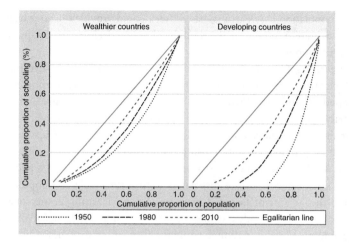

FIGURE 12.2 Education Gini Coefficient (Lorenz Curve), Economically Wealthier Countries and Developing Countries: 1950, 1980, 2010, and 2009

Note: The curves represent the years of schooling that have accumulated in the population, over three decades of data gathering.

Source: Wail et al. (2011, p. 24)

half-century, with the least equitable regions making the most (even if modest) improvements over time. As of 2010, developing countries were still substantially less equitable than wealthier countries (Figure 12.2).[21]

Unfortunately, with the Education Gini Index, we do not know what a school year means in Pakistan as compared to a school year in Ecuador or Canada—each country likely has different demands for the number of required days of schooling as well as different amounts of teacher absences.[22] What matters most about the education index is the disparity of school access within a particular population of school-aged children who may or may not be enrolled in school.

Learning Gini Index

Building upon these two previous Gini Indices, let's consider the formulation of a *Learning Gini Index*. This new Index could support international development researchers and practitioners in three key ways. First, a Learning Gini Index would enable a better understanding of learning gaps over time between various segments of a country's population.[23] Second, such an Index would provide a way to compare Indices across different metrics of learning, since only learners within a specified population would be measured on the same scale. Third, a Learning Gini Index would build on previous income and education Indices in a coherent way. For example, policymakers and economists regularly make use of the Income Gini Index as a easy-to-comprehend metric for understanding economic equity within a national population.[24] A learning-based Index could provide the same clarity and simplicity that are needed to make thoughtful policy decisions regarding resource allocation in support of learning equity.

The Learning Gini Index could function at several levels: national (e.g., South Africa), provinicial (e.g., Limpopo Province), or subnational (e.g., speakers of Sepedi in Limpopo Province). The Index could employ any usable learning metric that has been normed on a particular population.[25] For example, the Learning Gini Index could be used in separate South African provinces (i.e., could be province-specific), using the EGRA instrument in different languages, as well as SACMEQ instrument in other provinces.[26] In principle, it would be possible to calculate disparities within these selected populations to determine the impact of targeted interventions on learning equity over time. Thus, a Learning Gini Index would be a way to sidestep some of the nettlesome problems of cross-national comparability or equivalency (discussed in the previous chapter), by delivering a consistent measure of disparities within well-defined populations rather than differences in normative averages across diverse populations.[27]

With a Learning Gini Index, the gap between the top performers and those at the bottom could be studied and potentially narrowed. Data from certain international assessments already support the hypothesis that greater learning equity can lead to higher national-level learning outcomes.[28] These findings suggest that it is often the bottom quintile(s) of learning performance that disproportionately bring national averages down. It is also possible to find a virtuous cycle between learning equity and income equity. The results from the 2014 PIAAC found a strong relationship between countries with a lower Income Gini Index (i.e., low income inequality) and those with better math skills (see Figure 12.3).[29]

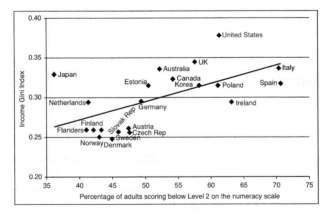

FIGURE 12.3 Relationship Between the Percentage of Adults With Low Proficiency in Numeracy and the Income Gini Index

Source: Van Damme (2014, p. 5)

While causation is impossible to determine without a direct intervention, we can hypothesize that a narrowing of skill levels within national populations might help reduce income inequality as well.

Some years ago, Alan Krueger, then-Chair of President Obama's Council of Economic Advisers, proposed using the Income Gini Index to ascertain economic mobility in OECD countries.[30] Follow-up research using PISA results found that a high national Income Gini Index (high inequality) was strongly correlated with intergenerational transmission of learning (see Figure 12.4).[31] Rich people not only use their wealth to support better education for their children (as expected), but as the Index grows larger, families with the same levels of wealth seem to pass even more advantage to their children's learning. This finding is reminiscent of the "Matthew effect" discussed earlier—namely that those who get a head start in learning tend to stay ahead over time.[32]

We can view these correlational findings in two different ways. On the one hand, when viewed from the goal of narrowing societal differences, the learning gap appears to widen with increasing income inequality.[33] On the other, it is possible to see that if the link between parental wealth and learning outcomes can be reduced—that is, by improving learning outcomes irrespective of parents' wealth—and a narrowing of income inequality could result.[34]

The recent history of South Africa tends to support this latter, more optimistic perspective. With its very high income inequality during the *apartheid* era, public expenditure for White pupils was almost five times that of Black pupils. However, a large redistribution of funding between 1991 and 2004 led to a much more equitable pattern of educational spending, continuing through today. While there remain major disparities in family wealth, the differences in learning outcomes have declined over the years, particularly in historically disadvantaged regions—in other words, closing the funding gap among the poor is related to more equitable learning outcomes.[35] And, while Teboho's and Mpho's educational differences reveal that problems with school management and poorly trained teachers still exist, the learning gap seems to be narrowing in South Africa.

The South Africa example and others like it substantiate the potential of a Learning Gini Index. As noted in previous chapters, most developing countries have large within-country learning disparities. Added to this are the serious difficulties of comparability of national norms with other countries. Thus, a Learning Gini Index—with its more transparent and culturally sensitive way of analyzing and comparing groups—can assist in understanding and improving learning equity across and within societies.

Raising the Floor

In many countries today, the strong focus of public policy is on the "middle class"—whether this refers to income, years of schooling, or learning. This makes good sense, since the majority population in most countries (and its largest voting

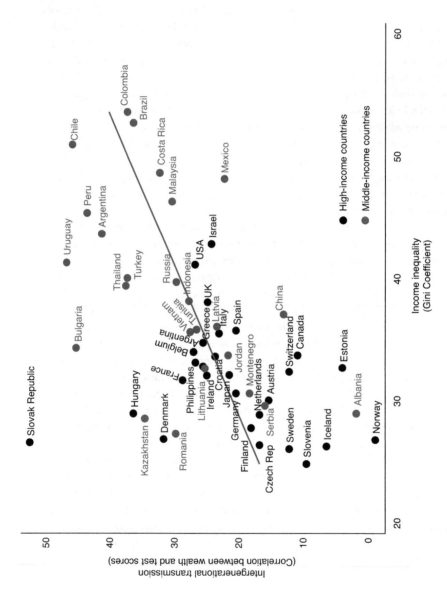

FIGURE 12.4 Relationship Between Income Inequality and the Rich-Poor Learning Gap (Using PISA Assessment Results)

Source: Sandefur (2015)

bloc) is comprised of "average" people who are, politically and statistically, in the middle group of any population. Even so, this focus on the middle comes with social and economic costs. When it comes to large-scale investments in developing countries, international and national budget support for the very poor has been surprisingly limited. National ministries of education have generally been preoccupied with trying to meet the considerable demands of the expansion of school access and the teacher corps over recent decades.[36] The situation is similar for international donors.[37]

A minister of education might rightly ask the following question: Can the needs of the poor be better addressed by raising outcomes for the middle of the population—thereby "lifting all boats" as the saying goes—or by directly addressing the needs of the very poor? If the latter (as argued here), then why not address their learning needs by directly *raising the floor*?[38] Too little attention has been paid to this straightforward question in developing countries.

Let's take the case of reading proficiency, a key goal in national and international educational policy. In Figure 12.5, three groups of countries are compared, each with the average of three countries' reading scores by level attained—thereby producing a set of normal curves.[39] In the context of the UN goals, the

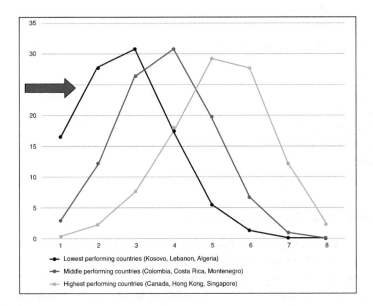

FIGURE 12.5 Performance of Three Groups of Countries at Various PISA Proficiency Levels. (The y-axis shows the percentage of students at each of eight proficiency levels of PISA 2015 in reading)

Note: The arrow indicates the shift from lowest-performing countries toward middle- and highest-performing countries.

Source: Crouch (in press)

"lowest-performing" countries (on the left side) would seek to become "middle-performing" or "higher-performing" countries (further to the right side). From these data, it appears that the most important gains can be made through a reduction of scores at the lower end of the normal curve. In other words, if Algeria (in the lowest-performing curve) is interested in reaching levels of performance comparable to Colombia (in the middle-performing group), it could make this transition most easily by helping its lowest-performing learners become middle-range learners. By contrast, Algeria would not be able to achieve as much success by trying to move its better-than-average learners to the top, since there is less room to grow. Similar results were found in an international mathematics study that compared gains (and losses) between 2011 and 2015—those countries with improved national scores showed the largest gains within the most underperforming parts of the sample populations.[40]

Thus, instead of trying to raise the mean scores of learning outcomes, policymakers might make greater gains overall by raising the floor (the lowest scores or quintiles). In addition to the practicality of this approach, there would be substantial social and moral value in the way nations treat their most disadvantaged populations. With the advent of the SDGs and increased attention to learning levels, much more attention needs to be paid directly to lowest-performing learners—those at the bottom of the pyramid.

To summarize, there are two practical routes that could help promote a stronger pro-equity learning agenda. The first is to reduce disparities through the application of a Learning Gini Index that focuses attention on the narrowing of learning gaps. The second is to build competencies more directly, and more generally, by raising the floor for those most in need. These two approaches are complementary: by raising the floor, the gaps are reduced, and by narrowing the gaps, the floor will likely be raised. In terms of development work, however, the Learning Gini Index and raising-the-floor approaches will likely lead to new and different types of learning measurement tools, as well as much needed pro-poor interventions in support of learning equity.[41]

Toward a Learning Equity Agenda

Over the past half-century we have developed a greater awareness of the pressing need to reduce poverty throughout the world, and have witnessed an overall increase in aid for international development. To date, most development efforts have attempted to improve countries' economic levels, a widely accepted proxy for the human condition. It is sometimes said: If only poor people could have more income, better roads, and specialized medical care, then their lives would be "better."

In practice, we know that economic opportunity is just one input into overall human prosperity and well-being. As some countries and individuals have become far wealthier than ever before, the limits of narrow economic growth policies to enhance human development have become ever more apparent—especially in the context of climate change, technological advancement, and civil conflict. In addition, we know that countries (and people) do not develop in a linear way, but are part of cumulative and fluctuating processes induced and propelled by social and global pressures.

Learning, we have argued, is the core driver and consistent thread underpinning human development. From the day we are born—from early childhood through adulthood—learning is the universal and ever-present phenomenon that drives and shapes each person's life. Yet, learning, though explicitly recognized as part of the UN SDGs, occupies a small fraction of the current international development architecture. As discussed, there are multiple reasons for this relative neglect. Economic theory still drives development in the public's mind, and in the programs of most development agencies. As we have seen, policymakers typically find it easier to measure years of schooling than to assess the quality of learning—clearly we should do both. Also, learning takes time to achieve—and is highly subject to cultural variation—making it difficult for both the public and policymakers to keep in mind. And finally, researchers and development specialists are needed to design technically sound ways to measure learning as well as to foster new approaches such as the Learning Gini Index.

Yes, learning is a complex phenomenon. Still, with the findings and tools described in this book, improvements in learning equity are now within our grasp. Five key perspectives, each drawn from the preceding chapters, are essential for undertaking a learning equity agenda.

1. *Learning happens across the life span—in and out of school.* As we know from human development research and from the learning framework reviewed earlier, learning is a lifetime endeavor and happens across every imaginable context. While we tend to situate it as something that occurs mainly for children in schools, it is much broader and deeper than that. In Morocco, Naima's skills were not learned in school, but rather through informal and unstructured processes.[42] She was enterprising, of course, but she was afforded opportunities to assume responsibility for commercial and public exchanges that gave her essential knowledge and skills. Though she would likely score poorly on an international assessment, Naima and her entire family benefit from what she learned informally, as millions of children and adults do in their villages, towns, and cities around the world. Our task is to construct educational inputs in ways that maximize what people learn over the life span—in schools, but also in homes and other informal learning and work environments.

2. *Learning is local.* It is sometimes said: "all politics are local." The same is true for learning. Some agencies and experts have called for global benchmarks that assist in the statistical mission of comparing progress across regions and countries, a natural goal for high-level policy deliberations. But we have seen that the

push for a single global metric is largely irrelevant for the most disadvantaged. Rather, we need to recognize the continuing importance of local adaptation for individuals in specific contexts. Local schools and teachers are critical components of social and institutional attempts to support human learning. While government-funded schools are often required to work at scale, they should be supported in efforts to accommodate diversity within countries and regions. Both formal and informal learning opportunities must be supported, and these often require very different types of inputs and organization. Promoting local, scalable, and collaborative approaches is an essential cornerstone for improved learning for everyday life as well as social and economic mobility.

3. *New technologies need hope, not hype.* New technologies have the potential to transform how we learn—in fact, they're already doing so. Six-year-old Vijay demonstrated this through his skillful handling of his uncle's computer.[43] Such commonplace and improvisational browsing on the Internet and game playing will help children like Vijay develop skills and confidence. Yet successful technological transformations will likely stem from carefully designed efforts that amplify skills that children are expected to learn because of purposeful design. Our job is to separate practical and empirically supported interventions from the "hype" around new technologies. Though the past is littered with unfocused efforts and inadequate outcomes, we have gained a lot from these endeavors. Evidence shows that by using the power of technology to tailor instruction to individual and cultural needs we can strengthen effective learning in school and out.

4. *Effective measurement is essential.* Empirical evidence is the currency of any successful development project. Yet experts frequently do not have enough reliable data to be assured that their various projects will work over time, across contexts, and have the potential for generalization. Recall the adage mentioned earlier: "If you cannot measure it, you cannot manage it."[44] Localized measurement—that is, quicker and cheaper—is particularly important for addressing the learning problems of the poor and marginalized. In the case of Teboho and Mpho in South Africa, nuanced measurement tools will be essential for understanding how to assist each boy in his unique circumstance. Not all assessments are created equal, and they often serve quite different purposes. For example, large-scale international assessments have been shown to be highly reliable and empirically robust, but they may be of little use to a minister of education struggling with inadequate learning in populations at the bottom of the pyramid. Longitudinal research helps to discern longer-term impact and returns on investment. Understanding which measures and research designs are useful for particular interventions will be fundamental in order to enhance learning equity.

5. *Learning promotes sustainable development.* Our rapidly changing world is upsetting decades and even centuries of consistent economic growth. With globalization, climate change, and migration (just to name a few mega-trends

discussed), we find that our common expectations—and our planet's survival—are no longer guaranteed. Matheus's family settled for many generations in the Amazon fluvial heartland; now they must adapt to life in Rio, a dramatic change in their family's history as they respond to the new pressures facing them.[45] Take their situation and multiply it by tens of millions and one can begin to envision the scope of the global problems that lie ahead. With changes in the environment and geopolitical uncertainties, we must face new realities and risks. The United Nations and its member countries were right to place the word "sustainable" at the front end of its 2030 set of international development goals.

Learning as Development

The broad imperative to improve what and how we learn is one of the great challenges of the 21st century. The stakes are high and substantial investments in education—through the kind of learning equity agenda proposed here—will need to be made. Human and fiscal resources will have to be committed and used wisely, and policymakers, government officials, researchers, and communities will need to work together to push this agenda forward collectively and collaboratively. This will not be easy, but it is possible.

We know that learning—our most renewable resource—is the foundation of human development in all societies—from Balandur to Bamako to Boston. Unfortunately, not every child, youth or adult is able to access and receive what they need to learn for the challenges ahead. Those at the bottom, with the most to lose, must be given opportunities already given to others, to learn what they need to know to engage in the world meaningfully and productively. *Learning as development* is an approach whose time has come.

Notes

1. Adapted from World Bank (2006), based on Drèze et al. (1998), with data updates and village name altered for the purpose of anonymity.
2. Based on current government estimates that are largely derived from school enrollments. Actual rates of literacy may be lower, as noted in Chapter 6.
3. This aphorism was first used in the early 20th century by the Scottish biologist Patrick Geddes, a town planner famous for building towns from a regional perspective that factored in the surrounding environment. In Geddes's (1915) view, city planners should carefully build communities according to the parameters of each localized ecology, while also understanding the broader environmental implications of their project.
4. Grauer (1989).
5. The World Bank (2006) brought the word *equity* into the title of its key *World Development Reports*. It is important to consider for a moment the definitions of *equality* and *equity*—terms that are sometimes confused with one another. In this discussion, we define them in the domain of international development as follows: equality is being equal in terms of quantity, rank, status, or value (e.g. two groups

of students have the same average number of years of schooling). Equity refers to the social justice ramifications of any outcome in relation to the fairness, justness, and impartiality of its distribution in any social group (e.g., within one group of students, some may have many more years of schooling than others), as described in Jacob and Holsinger (2008, p. 4). In other words, equity may be defined as the equal treatment of equals, as well as the unequal treatment of unequals, when socially justified. For example, equity may require unequal treatment, such as the poor or handicapped receiving more funding in order to better achieve equality, or what in the United States is called "affirmative action." (Thanks to L. Crouch for his insights). Equity has a second useful definition as well: the value of a material wealth (such as home ownership). Equity, therefore, is not only one's relative place in the possession of material wealth, but also the kind of total accumulation of wealth. In health, for example, the availability of HIV/AIDS retroviral medicines can be equitably distributed across a country, but one can also build equity in health by virtue of consistently maintaining a healthy lifestyle.

6. For a review of SDGs, and the education targets, see Chapter 2.
7. Some of Binet's work (see also Chapter 11) led to the development of intelligence tests, which are themselves a form of global metric, and one that has not escaped some of the considerable criticism of cultural bias (e.g., Neisser et al., 1996).
8. See Chapter 11. Also, the work of the OECD using the PISA; and in developing countries with the *PISA for Development*, see Cresswell et al. (2015) and Willms and Tramonte (2014).
9. One of the major SDG-related efforts toward global metrics was conducted by the Learning Metrics Task Force (Brookings, 2011); UNESCO Institute for Statistics and Brookings Institution, 2013); Robinson (2011); and the Global Alliance to Monitor Learning, at: http://uis.openplus.ca/gaml/. More recently, there is the report of the International Commission on Financing Global Education Opportunity (2016). In November 2016, there was an international conference on this topic; see: https://education.asu.edu/globalmetrics.
10. International agencies are not unaware of such limitations. One relevant document (UNESCO Institute for Statistics, 2014, p. 2) reported that "the objective is to develop empirically derived learning metrics in mathematics and reading that will support national governments to effectively measure and monitor learning outcomes for policy purposes."
11. One might reasonably ask if norms can be developed for marginalized populations. The answer is yes, but the requisite work requires time, funding, and political will. The point here is that governments and international agencies have generally been focused on the middle and top end of the metrics spectrum, rather than at the bottom of the pyramid.
12. Campbell (1979, p. 85). Cited in Stigler and Miller (in press).
13. Barber and Fullan (2005) described both approaches in the US context; see Wagner and Kaul (2006) in the Middle East and North Africa. See also Mourshed et al. (2010) in a broad international review. Around the same time, similar perspectives appeared in the health field; see Heymann (2006) and Heymann and Earle (2009).
14. See Chapter 1.
15. Jencks (1972).
16. Gini (1909).
17. Statistically speaking, the Gini Index is the area occupied under a Lorenz curve (see Figure 12.2), and this is "dimensionless." This means that it can be essentially used to measure the degree of dispersion (or disparity) of a metric in any normally distributed population.
18. See Bourdieu and "cultural capital," discussed in Chapter 1.
19. See http://data.worldbank.org/indicator/SI.POV.GINI?end=2014&start=2008.

20. Thomas et al. (2001). A later World Bank report by Ferreira and Gignoux (2014) built on the Thomas paper with later data from PISA. See also Harttgen et al. (2010) in a review of economic disparities on educational attainment across 37 countries.

21. Figures 12.1 and 12.2 are based on Wail et al. (2011); "wealthier" countries consist of 24 selected OECD countries, as described in their analysis. An in-depth study in India (Agrawal, 2014), undertaken with a large sample in rural and urban areas, confirmed these same trends. Over the period 1993–2009, the Education Gini Index showed that, while illiteracy was more than 50% in 1993, less than 32% of the population remained illiterate in 2009, a decline of about 1% per annum. In India, most of the change over three decades was found in the urban areas where school attendance was expanding, rather than in rural areas.

22. In other words, the Gini Education Index does not take into account the quality of the schooling received—that is, learning outcomes—which may vary widely. Also, see earlier discussion of the actual days of effective classroom learning, as described in Chapter 8.

23. Progress on this with TIMSS data (Mullis et al., 2016) was mentioned earlier, in terms of deciles of population scores; see also Thomas et al. (2001).

24. Thanks to R. Boruch for his insights on the Gini Index.

25. By "usable" we mean a metric that has been gathered and utilized previously on a well-defined population, and that exhibits the expected statistical properties of a normal curve with sufficient variation (and granularity) that allows for comparisons within the sample population, as discussed in Chapter 11.

26. See previous chapter for discussion of EGRA and SACMEQ.

27. There are potential technical issues with the notion of comparing different scales (such as PISA and EGRA), since their compositions and distributions are quite different. Adjustments would need to be made so that dispersion varies in a normative way within population samples, as has been utilized in many international assessments.

28. See Freeman et al. (2010) for research on the TIMSS assessment. Only a limited number of low-income countries are included in the TIMSS assessments (see Chapter 11).

29. This finding reported by Van Damme (in press) is based on PIAAC (Programme for the International Assessment of Adult Competencies) data in 23 OECD countries.

30. Krueger (2012) called this the "Great Gatsby Curve." The name of the curve refers to the lead character (Jay Gatsby) in F. Scott Fitzgerald's novel *The Great Gatsby*, who rises from being a low-level bootlegger to becoming a wealthy Long Island socialite—hence a person of social mobility.

31. Sandefur (2015). Based on the 2014 PISA international assessments in 52 OECD countries. Correlations were 0.71 for reading and 0.75 for math.

32. See Chapter 5.

33. Sandefur (2015) interpreted these findings as an indication that living in a poor family was more of a determinant of learning outcomes than living in a poor country.

34. A limitation is that the PISA data are from middle- and high-income countries, as discussed in Chapter 11. Clearly, more data are needed from low-income countries, something that can be achieved either through more inclusive LSEAs, or through regional or national assessments.

35. Crouch et al. (2008).

36. See Chapters 3 and 7.

37. Donor support has not been sufficiently focused on the most disadvantaged (on raising the floor) for a variety of reasons. In Chapter 4, it was shown that higher education has been receiving massively more donor aid than early childhood programs. Recent data (UNESCO, 2015a, p. 265) indicate that donor aid for developing countries comprised US $7.6 billion annually for higher and secondary education combined,

compared to US $5.6 billion for primary education (including ECD and NFE programs), even though the latter constituency has more than double the population participation and includes those most in need. UNESCO (2015a, p. 267) affirmed this financial reality: "[T]he countries most in need of aid for basic services—low income countries and fragile states—should not be left behind and, indeed, should be prioritized. However, the share of basic education aid disbursements going to low-income countries actually declined from 40% to 34% over the decade."

38. For example, Stern (2016).
39. Crouch (in press). The figure shows a small set of selected countries out of 72 that were in the PISA 2015 international assessment of reading. PISA currently represents a small fraction of low-income countries.
40. Mullis et al. (2016, p. 64), Trends in International Mathematics and Science Study (TIMSS), studied children at grades 4 and 8 in 57 countries. The greatest gains were in the bottom 10% of the national population sample in eighth grade mathematics in the countries studied.
41. A current limitation of the Gini and raise-the-floor empirical analyses is that the LSEAs (upon which the present analyses were based) included only a small number of developing countries. Rose (2015) points out the limitations of such LSEAs in terms of fostering equity.
42. See Chapter 3 for the story about Naima.
43. See Chapter 9 for the story about Vijay.
44. See Chapter 11 for the story about Teboho and Mpho.
45. See Chapter10 for the story about Matheus.

EPILOGUE

The Challenges Ahead

Assiatou's Second Chance

It's three years later, and Assiatou, now 11 years'old, is still in school in her village in Guinea. Her instructor, Monsieur Mamadou, was able to participate in a government-sponsored training program that helped him design a better curriculum for his students. Now, instead of being largely ignored, Assiatou finds herself called upon regularly, even though she's still sitting in the back rows of the classroom. Textbooks are given to each student, and Monsieur Mamadou, as well as other teachers in the school, use new and progressive materials recently provided by a revitalized ministry of education. Children in the school now learn to read in first and second languages at a pace that better fits their individual skill levels. A palpable sense of community spirit has been built among students, teachers, and even parents since they all participated in discussions about the proposed changes in the school. Assiatou has learned to read, and by doing so is not only able to complete her homework each day, but also regularly helps her mother decipher medicine prescriptions from the local health clinic, ensuring her safety and continued well-being.

Assiatou was afforded a "second chance."[1] The Guinean Ministry of Education—with support from external development agencies in collaboration with school administrators, teachers, and parents—was able to transform the school's curriculum and significantly improve its overall functioning. While Monsieur Mamadou is not an expert in the pedagogical innovations that were implemented, he has learned valuable techniques and ideas, and is more highly motivated to apply them with his students.

This change in Assiatou's life was not happenstance. It is only through increased understanding and conviction on the part of many stakeholders that such improvements became possible. While research of the sort covered in this book gives credence to the innovations implemented in Assiatou's school (and elsewhere), it is the courage, commitment, and resources of individual communities, professionals, and policymakers willing to take informed risks that allows real change to happen on the ground. Though stagnation remains in many places, it's vital that we remember that improvement is possible.

Geography Is Not (Necessarily) Destiny

In June 1812, Napoleon, the Emperor of France, led a large force of nearly 680,000 soldiers to invade Russia, thinking it key to winning the war. It is believed that at the time he asserted the well-known phrase, "Geography is destiny."[2] Napoleon, it turns out, was right about this strategy, but wrong about who would benefit from it. His invasion failed in part due to an unexpectedly harsh winter, but also because the Russian army had its own geographical strategy, and lured the French army so deeply into the countryside that their supply lines could be cut off.

In the domain of education and international development, policymakers sometimes act as if geography is destiny, and with a hubris similar to Napoleon's. Development specialists, too, propose strategies based on imperfect understandings of the people that they seek to help—this is inevitable. Like the French on the Russian steppes approaching Moscow long ago, development workers may fail to fully account for circumstance and context, or they may simply do a poor job of implementation. The notion that research and data will necessarily predict the likelihood of success in education is as risky as Napoleon's invasion. Yes, we need all the research we can get, but the work of international development is necessarily iterative.

In this book, learning has been shown to be highly malleable, and predominantly determined by human agency—more so than by geography or textbooks or class size. We have seen numerous examples of how development interventions—implemented by individuals, teachers, communities, and policymakers—can help make positive changes across a wide range of contexts and cultures. Consider again the discussion of the Learning Gini Index in the previous chapter. The notion that we can reduce the disparity in learning between the haves and have-nots within countries—that is, advancing learning equity—is one way that we can sidestep some of the complexities of comparing one society's values, attitudes, and assessment outcomes with another's. The point is that our goal should not necessarily be to compare learning *between* nations, but rather focus on narrowing gaps between people *within* nations, and *within* communities. Where a child is born or grows up should not dictate her or his destiny.

If we look at the long path of development work—from its dark history in pre-colonial and colonial times to the more scientific and (mainly) more nuanced approaches that we see today—there has been much progress. This does not mean that the field is without controversy and debate. Serious criticism may be levied at claims and counter-claims about learning, education, and development. Examples of inadequate implementation and misguided beliefs are well-known both to specialists and to the public. Though it's evident that many have struggled to find answers and failed, these so-called failures contribute to our cumulative knowledge and understanding of how to improve the lives of people around the world.

The Challenges Ahead

Faced with today's unprecedented geopolitical and environmental pressures, international development requires a reorientation. The primacy of economics in the field—while unlocking tremendous potential in some cases—only narrows the decision-making framework of many development and government agencies. We must move toward an agenda that puts human development closer to the center of global ambitions, and prioritizes learning as the thread that binds each phase of a human life into a coherent whole. Making this shift will require a formidable increase in collaboration across disciplines, sectors, and geographies, and a true reframing of the vision and objectives of development efforts around the world.

It won't be easy. But enough of the pieces are there, shaped by the efforts and ideas of many who aspired to make a difference. This book is an attempt to assemble those pieces across contexts and cultures as a basis for future work to be done. We are never done learning.

Notes

1. This builds on the story of Assiatou in Chapter 5.
2. The phrase "geography is destiny" is attributed to Napoleon, but also is claimed by others. See Kaplan (2017).

REFERENCES

Abadzi, H. (2009). Instructional time loss in developing countries: Concepts, measurement, and implications. *The World Bank Research Observer, 24*(2), 267–290.

Abadzi, H. (2014). How to improve schooling outcomes in low-income countries? The challenges and hopes of cognitive neuroscience. *Peabody Journal of Education, 89*(1), 58–69.

Aboud, F. E. (2006). Evaluation of an early childhood preschool program in rural Bangladesh. *Early Childhood Research Quarterly, 21*(1), 46–60.

Abu-Rabia, S., & Siegel, L. S. (2002). Reading, syntactic, orthographic, and working memory skills of bilingual Arabic-English speaking Canadian children. *Journal of Psycholinguistic Research, 31*, 661–678.

ACER. (2010). *Using television to improve learning opportunities for Indigenous children.* Canberra: Australian Council for Educational Research.

Adams, A. V. (2008). *Skills development in the informal sector in sub-Saharan Africa.* Washington, DC: The World Bank.

Adams, M. H. (1990). *Beginning to read: Thinking and learning about print.* Cambridge, MA: MIT Press.

Adedeji, S. O., & Olaniyan, O. (2011). *Improving the conditions of teachers and teaching in rural schools across African countries.* UNESCO: International Institute for Capacity Building in Africa.

Adelman, J. (2013). *Worldly philosopher: The odyssey of Albert O. Hirschman.* Princeton, NJ: Princeton University Press.

Aderinoye, R. A., Ojokheta, K. O., & Olojede, A. A. (2007). Integrating mobile learning into nomadic education programme in Nigeria: Issues and perspectives. *The International Review of Research in Open and Distributed Learning, 8*(2), 1–16.

Adler, A. (2016). *Teaching well-being increases academic performance: Evidence from Bhutan, Mexico, and Peru.* Ph.D. dissertation. Philadelphia: University of Pennsylvania.

Adler, A., & Seligman, M. E. P. (2016). Using wellbeing for public policy: Theory, measurement, and recommendations. *International Journal of Wellbeing, 6*(1), 1–35.

Adomi, E. E., & Kpangban, E. (2010). Application of ICTs in Nigerian secondary schools. *Library Philosophy and Practice (e-journal).* http://digitalcommons.unl.edu/cgi/viewcontent.cgi?article=1353&context=libphilprac

Agrawal, T. (2014). Educational inequality in rural and urban India. *International Journal of Educational Development, 34*, 11–19.

Ahmed, A., & Arends-Kuenning, M. (2006). Do crowded classrooms crowd out learning? Evidence from the food for education program in Bangladesh. *World Development, 34*(4), 665–684.

Aikman, S. (1999). Schooling and development: Eroding Amazon women's knowledge and diversity. In Heward, C. & Bunwaree, S. (Eds.), *Gender, education, and development*. New York: Zed Books. Pps. 65–82.

Aikman, S., & Unterhalter, E. (Eds.). (2005). *Beyond access: Transforming policy and practice for gender equality in education*. London: Oxfam.

Ainsworth, M. D. S. (1977). Attachment theory and its utility in cross-cultural research. In Leiderman, P. H., Tulkin, S. R., & Rosenfeld, A. H. (Eds.), *Culture and infancy*. New York: Academic Press. Pps. 49–68.

Akaguri, L. (2014). Fee-free public or low-fee private basic education in rural Ghana: How does the cost influence the choice of the poor? *Compare: A Journal of Comparative and International Education, 44*(2), 140–161.

Aker, J. C., Ksoll, C., & Lybbert, T. (2012). Can mobile phones improve learning? Evidence from a field experiment in Niger. *American Economics Journal: Applied Economics, 4*(4), 94–120.

Akiba, M., LeTendre, G. K., & Scribner, J. P. (2007). Teacher quality, opportunity gap, and national achievement in 46 countries. *Educational Researcher, 36*(7), 369–387.

Akyeampong, K., Lussier, K., Pryor, J., & Westbrook, J. (2013). Improving teaching and learning of basic maths and reading in Africa: Does teacher preparation count? *International Journal of Educational Development, 33*, 272–282.

Albaugh, E. A. (2013). *States of languages and languages of states: Natural and unnatural language spread in West Africa*. American Political Science Association Conference, Chicago.

Albaugh, E. A. (2014). *State-building and multilingual education in Africa*. New York: Cambridge University Press.

Albrow, M., & King, E. (Eds.). (1990). *Globalization, knowledge and society*. London: Sage.

Alcoholado, C., Nussbaum, M., Tagle, A., Gomez, F., Denardin, F., Susaeta, H., Villalta, M., & Toyama, K. (2012). One mouse per child: Interpersonal computer for individual arithmetic practice. *Journal of Computer Assisted Learning, 28*(4), 295–309.

Alexander, R. J. (2001). *Culture and pedagogy: International comparisons in primary education*. London: Blackwell.

Alexander, R. J. (2015). Teaching and learning for all? The quality imperative revisited. *International Journal of Educational Development, 40*, 250–258.

Alidou, H., Boly, A., Brock-Utne, B., Diallo, Y. S., Heugh, K., & Wolff, H. E. (2006). *Optimising learning and education in Africa: The language factor*. Paris: ADEA, GTZ, Commonwealth Secretariat.

Alkire, S., Foster, J., Seth, S., Roche, J. M., & Santos, M. E. (2015). *Multidimensional poverty measurement and analysis*. New York: Oxford University Press.

Allais, S. (2012). Will skills save us? Rethinking the relationships between vocational education, skills development policies, and social policy in South Africa. *International Journal of Educational Development, 32*(5), 632–642.

All Children Reading. (2011). *Project website*. http://allchildrenreading.org

Anderson, A. (2010). *Combating climate change through quality education*. Policy Brief. Washington, DC: Brookings Global Economy and Development.

Anderson, C. A., & Bowman, M. J. (1965). *Education and economic development*. London: Frank Cass.

Anderson-Levitt, K. (Ed.). (2003). *Local meanings, global schooling: Anthropology and world culture theory*. New York: Palgrave-Macmillan.

Angrist, J. D., & Lavy, D. (1999). Using Maimonides' rule to estimate the effect of class size on scholastic achievement. *Quarterly Journal of Economics, 114*, 533–575.

Araujo, M. C., Carneiro, P., Cruz-Aguayo, Y., & Schady, N. (2014). A helping hand? Teacher quality and learning outcomes in Kindergarten. Unpublished Report. Washington: Inter-American Development Bank.

Arias-Ortiz, E., & Cristia, J. (2014). *The IDB and technology in education: How to promote effective programs?* Washington, DC: Inter-American Development Bank.

Arnett, J. (2008). The neglected 95%: Why American psychology needs to become less American. *American Psychologist, 63*(7), 602–614.

Arnove, R., & Torres, C. (Eds.). (1999). *Comparative education: The dialectic between the global and the local.* Lanham, Md.: Rowman & Littlefield.

Arora, P. (2010). Hope-in-the-wall? A digital promise for free learning. *British Journal of Educational Technology, 41*, 689–702.

Arora, R. K., & Goyal, R. (1995). *Indian public administration: Institutions and issues.* New Delhi: New Age International.

Arrhenius, S. (1896). On the influence of carbonic acid in the air upon the temperature of the ground. *The London, Edinburgh, and Dublin Philosophical Magazine and Journal of Science, 41*(251), 237–276.

Asadullah, M. N., & Chaudhury, N. (2015). The dissonance between schooling and learning: Evidence from rural Bangladesh. *Comparative Education Review, 59*(3), 447–472.

Asadullah, M. N., & Rahman, S. (2009). Farm productivity and efficiency in rural Bangladesh: The role of education revisited. *Applied Economics, 41*(1), 17–33.

Asfaw, A., & Admassie, A. (2004). The role of education on the adoption of chemical fertiliser under different socioeconomic environments in Ethiopia. *American Journal of Agricultural Economics, 30*(3), 215–228.

August, D., & Shanahan, T. (Eds.). (2006). *Developing literacy in second language learners: Report of the national reading panel on language minority and youth.* Mahwah, NJ: Lawrence Erlbaum Associates.

Azariadis, C., & Drazen, A. (1990). Threshold externalities in economic development. *The Quarterly Journal of Economics, 105*(2), 501–526.

Azariadis, C., & Stachurski, J. (2005). Poverty traps. In Aghion, P., & Durlauf, S. N. (Eds.), *Handbook of economic growth.* New York: Elsevier. Pps. 295–384.

Babson, A. (2010). *The place of English in expanding repertoires of linguistic code, identification and aspiration among recent high school graduates in Limpopo Province, South Africa.* Ph.D. dissertation. Ann Arbor: University of Michigan.

Ball, J. (2010). *Enhancing learning of children from diverse language backgrounds: Mother tongue-based bilingual or multilingual education in the early years.* Paris: UNESCO.

Ball, J., Paris, S. G., & Govinda, R. (2014). Literacy and numeracy skills among children in developing countries. In Wagner, D. A. (Ed.), *Learning and education in developing countries: Research and policy for the post-2015 UN development goals.* New York: Palgrave Macmillan. Pps. 26–41.

Banerjee, A., Banerji, R., Berry, J., Duflo, E., Kannan, H., Mukherji, S., Shotland, M., & Walton, M. (2016). *From proof of concept to scalable policies: Challenges and solutions, with an application.* No. w22931. National Bureau of Economic Research.

Banerjee, A. V., Benabou, R., & Mookherjee, D. (Eds.). (2006). *Understanding poverty.* London: Oxford University Press.

Banerjee, A. V., & Duflo, E. (2011). *Poor economics: A radical rethinking of the way to fight poverty.* New York: Public Affairs.

Banerjee, A. V., Duflo, E., & Glennerster, R. (2008). Putting a band aid on a corpse: Incentives for nurses in the Indian public health care system. *Journal of the European Economic Association, 6*(2–3), 487–500.

Bangay, C., & Latham, M. (2013). Are we asking the right questions? Moving beyond the state vs non-state providers debate: Reflections and a case study from India. *International Journal of Educational Development, 33*(3), 244–252.

Barber, M., & Fullan, M. (2005). Tri-level development: It's the system. *Education Week, 24*(25), 32–35.

Barber, M., & Mourshed, M. (2007). *How the world's best-performing school systems come out on top.* London: McKinsey & Company.

Baron, N. S. (2016). *Words onscreen.* New York: Oxford University Press.

Baroody, A. J., & Dowker, A. (Eds.). (2003). *The development of arithmetic concepts and skills: Recent research and theory.* Mahwah, NJ: Lawrence Erlbaum Associates.

Barrera-Osorio, F., & Linden, L. L. (2009). *The use and misuse of computers in education: Evidence from a randomized experiment in Colombia.* World Bank Policy Research Working Paper Series, No. 4836.

Bartholet, J. (2013). Hype and hope. *Scientific American, 309*(2), 53–61.

Bartlett, K., Stephenson, P., & Cadain, L. (2013). Parents and communities: The key to understanding "faith-based" early childhood services and programs. In Britto, P. R., Engle, P. E., & Super, C. (Eds.), *Handbook of early childhood development research and its impact on global policy.* New York, NY: Oxford University Press. Pps. 290–307.

Bartlett, L., Dowd, A. J., & Jonason, C. (2015). Problematizing early grade reading: Should the post-2015 agenda treasure what is measured? *International Journal of Educational Development, 40,* 308–314.

Bartlett, L., & Garcia, O. (2011). *Additive schooling in subtractive times: Bilingual education and Dominican immigrant youth in the Heights.* Nashville: Vanderbilt University Press.

Bassi, M., Busso, M., Urzua, S., & Vargas, J. (2012). *Disconnected: Skills, education, and employment in Latin America.* Washington, DC: Interamerican Development Bank.

Bateson, G. (1972/2000). *Steps to an ecology of mind: Collected essays in anthropology, psychiatry, evolution, and epistemology.* Chicago: University of Chicago Press.

Baydar, N., Kagitcibasi, Ç., Kuntay, A., & Goksen, F. (2008). Effects of an educational television program on preschoolers: Variability in benefits. *Journal of Applied Developmental Psychology, 29*(5), 349–360.

Beaudry, P., Green, D. A., & Sand, B. M. (2016). The great reversal in the demand for skill and cognitive tasks. *Journal of Labor Economics, 34*(S1), S199–S247.

Becker, G. S. (1964). *Human capital.* National Bureau of Economic Research No. 80. New York: Columbia University Press.

Behrman, J. R., Calderon, M. C., Preston, S. H., Hoddinott, J., Martorell, R., & Stein, A. D. (2009a). Nutritional supplementation in girls influences the growth of their children: Prospective study in Guatemala. *The American Journal of Clinical Nutrition, 90*(5), 1372–1379.

Behrman, J. R., Parker, S., & Todd, P. (2009b). Schooling impacts of conditional cash transfers on young children: Evidence from Mexico. *Economic Development and Cultural Change, 57,* 439–477.

Behrman, J. R., Sengupta, P., & Todd, P. (2005). Progressing through PROGRESA: An impact assessment of a school subsidy experiment in rural Mexico. *Economic Development and Cultural Change, 54,* 237–275.

Bekman, S., & Aksu-Koc, A. (2009). *Perspectives on human development, family, and culture.* New York: Cambridge University Press.

Belsky, J., & Pluess, M. (2013). Beyond risk, resilience, and dysregulation: Phenotypic plasticity and human development. *Development and Psychopathology, 25,* 1243–1261.

Beltrán, A. C., & Seinfeld, J. N. (2010). *La heterogeneidad del impacto de la educación inicial sobre el rendimiento escolar en el Perú.* Lima: CIUP.

Benavot, A. (2008). The organization of school knowledge: Official curricula in global perspective. In Resnik, J. (Ed.), *The production of educational knowledge in the global era.* Rotterdam: Sense Publishers. Pps. 55–92.

Benavot, A., & Gad, L. (2004). Actual instructional time in African primary schools: Factors that reduce school quality in developing countries. *Prospects, 34,* 291–310.

Benavot, A., & Köseleci, N. (2015). *Seeking quality in education: The growth of national learning assessments, 1990–2013.* Paper commissioned for the EFA Global Monitoring Report 2015. Paris: UNESCO.

Benavot, A., & Tanner, E. (2007). *The growth of national learning assessments in the world, 1995–2006.* Background Paper Prepared for EFA Global Monitoring Report 2008. Paris: UNESCO.

Benbow, J., Mizrachi, A., Oliver, D., & Said-Moshiro, L. (2007). *Large class sizes in the developing countries: What do we know and what can we do?* Educational Quality Improvement Program, Classroom, Communities, Schools and USAID. Washington, DC: American Institutes for Research.

Benedict, M., & Hoag, J. (2011). Seating location in large lectures: Are seating preferences or location related to course performance? *Journal of Economic Education, 35*(3), 215–239.

Benedict, R. (1934/1989). *Patterns of culture.* New York: Houghton Mifflin.

Benedict, R. (1938). Continuities and discontinuities in cultural conditioning. *Psychiatry, 1*(2), 161–167.

Bennell, P. (1999). *Learning to change: Skills development among the economically vulnerable and socially excluded in developing countries.* Employment and Training Paper 43. Geneva: International Labor Organization.

Bennett, J. A. H., & Berry, J. (1987). The future of Cree syllabic literacy in Northern Canada. In Wagner, D. A. (Ed.), *The future of literacy in a changing world* (revised ed.). Cresskill, NJ: Hampton. Pps. 271–290.

Benson, C. J. (2004). *The importance of L1-based schooling for educational quality.* Commissioned Study for EFA Global Monitoring Report 2005. Paris: UNESCO.

Benson, C. J., & Wong, K. M. (2015). Development discourse on language of instruction and literacy: Sound policy and Ubuntu or lip service? *Reconsidering Development, 4*(1), 1–16.

Bernard van Leer Foundation. (2016). *Early childhood matters: Advances in early childhood development.* Report No. 125. https://bernardvanleer.org/app/uploads/2016/06/Early-Childhood-Matters-2016.pdf. Accessed November 23, 2016.

Bernhardt, E. (2005). Progress and procrastination in second language reading. *Annual Review of Applied Linguistics, 25,* 133–150.

Berry, C., Barnett, E., & Hinton, R. (2015). What does learning for all mean for DFID's global education work? *International Journal of Educational Development, 40,* 323–329.

Berry, J. W. (2009). Living together in culturally-plural societies: Understanding and managing acculturation and multiculturalism. In Bekman, S. & Aksu-Koc, A. (Eds.), *Perspectives on human development, family, and culture.* London: Cambridge University Press. Pps. 227–238.

Beuermann, D. W., Cristia, J., Cueto, S., Malamud, O., & Cruz-Aguayo, Y. (2015). One Laptop Per Child at home: Short-term impacts from a randomized experiment in Peru. *American Economic Journal: Applied Economics, 7*(2), 53–80.

Bever, T. G. (1982). *Regressions in mental development: Basic phenomena and theories.* Mahwah, NJ: Lawrence Erlbaum Associates.

Bialystok, E., Luk, G., & Kwan, E. (2005). Bilingualism, biliteracy, and learning to read: Interactions among languages and writing systems. *Scientiic Studies of Reading, 9*(1), 43–61.

Bill & Melinda Gates Foundation. (2010). *Empowering effective teachers: Readiness for reform.* Issue Brief. Redmond, WA: Bill & Melinda Gates Foundation.

Birdwhistell, R. (1960). Review of Oscar Lewis's five families: *Mexican case studies in the culture* of poverty. New York: Basic Books. *American Anthropologist, 62,* 534–535.

Blachman, B. A., Schatschneider, C., Fletcher, J. M., Murray, M. S., Munger, K. A., & Vaughn, M. G. (2014). Intensive reading remediation in grade 2 or 3: Are there effects a decade later? *Journal of Educational Psychology, 106*(1), 46.

Blackledge, A., & Creese, A. (2010). *Multilingualism: A critical perspective.* London: Continuum.

Bloom, B. S., Engelhart, M. D., Furst, E. J., Hill, W. H., & Krathwohl, D. R. (1956). *Taxonomy of educational objectives: The classification of educational goals, Handbook I: Cognitive domain.* New York: Longmans, Green.

Blumenstock, J., Cadamuro, G., & On, R. (2015). Predicting poverty and wealth from mobile phone metadata. *Science, 350*(6264), 1073–1076.

Boli, J., Ramirez, F. O., & Meyer, J. W. (1985). Explaining the origins and expansion of mass education. *Comparative Education Review, 29*(2), 145–170.

Bolstad, R. (2004). *The role and potential of ICT in early childhood education: A review of New Zealand and international literature.* New Zealand Council for Educational Research. www.educationcounts.govt.nz/publications/ict/4983

Boothby, N., & Melvin, C. (2007). *Towards best practice in school-based psychosocial programming: A survey of current approaches.* Program on Forced Migration and Health, Mailman School of Public Health. New York: Columbia University.

Bornstein, M. H. (2010). *Handbook of cultural developmental science.* New York: Taylor & Francis.

Bornstein, M. H., & Putnick, D. L. (2012). Cognitive and socioemotional caregiving in developing countries. *Child Development, 83*(1), 46–61.

Boruch, R., & Rui, J. (2008). From randomized controlled trials to evidence grading schemes: Current state of evidence-based practice in social sciences. *Journal of Evidence-Based Medicine, 1,* 41–49.

Boukous, A., & Institut Royal de la Culture Amazighe (Rabat). (2012). *Revitalizing the Amazigh language: Stakes, challenges, and strategies.* Rabat: Institut Royal de la Culture Amazighe.

Bourdieu, P. (1977). *Outline of a theory of practice.* London: Cambridge University Press.

Bourdieu, P. (1986). The forms of capital. In Richardson, J. (Ed.), *Handbook of theory and research for the sociology of education.* New York: Greenwood Press. Pps. 241–258.

Boutieri, C. (2016). *Learning in Morocco: Language politics and the abandoned educational dream.* Bloomington: Indiana University Press.

Bowers, J. S. (2016). Psychology, not educational neuroscience, is the way forward for improving educational outcomes for all children: Reply to Gabrieli (2016) and Howard-Jones et al. (2016). *Psychological Review, 123*(5), 628–635.

Bowlby, J. (1969). *Attachment, vol. 1 of attachment and loss.* New York: Basic Books.

Bowles, R. P. (2014). Review of advances in longitudinal methods in the social and behavioral sciences, edited by Jeffrey R. Harring and Gregory R. Hancock. *Structural Equation Modeling: A Multidisciplinary Journal, 21*(4), 651–652.

Bowles, S., & Gintis, H. (1976). *Schooling in capitalist America* (Vol. 57). New York: Basic Books.

Box, G. E. P. (1976). Science and statistics. *Journal of the American Statistical Association, 71,* 791–799.

Boyle, H. N. (2006). Memorization and learning in Islamic schools. *Comparative Education Review, 50*(3), 478–495.

Boyle, H. N., Seebaway, S. Z., Lansah, I., & Boukamhi, A. (2007). *Islamic education sector study—Ghana*. Washington, DC: USAID.

Bransford, J. D., Brown, A. L., & Cocking, R. R. (Eds.). (2000). *How people learn: Brain, mind, experience, and school*. Washington: National Academy Press.

Braslavsky, C. (Eds.). (2006). *Textbooks and quality learning for all: Some lessons learned from international experiences* (Vol. 355). Geneva: Unesco-IBE.

Braun, H., & Kanjee, A. (2006). Using assessment to improve education in developing nations. In Cohen, J. E., Bloom, D. E., & Malin, M. (Eds.), *Improving education through assessment, innovation, and evaluation*. Cambridge, MA: American Academy of Arts and Sciences. Pps. 1–46.

Bray, M., & Lykins, C. (2012). *Shadow education: Private supplementary tutoring and its implications for policy makers in Asia*. Manila: Asian Development Bank.

Brazelton, T., & Greenspan, S. (2001). *Irreducible needs of children: What every child must have to grow learn and flourish*. Jackson, TN: DaCapo Press.

Breidlid, A. (2013). *Education, indigenous knowledges, and development in the global South: Contesting knowledges for a sustainable future* (Vol. 82). New York: Routledge.

Britto, P. R. (2015). *Presentation at UN World Education Forum*. Incheon, Korea. Unpublished. New York: UNICEF.

Britto, P. R., Oketch, M., & Weisner, T. S. (2014). Non-formal education and learning. In Wagner, D. A. (Ed.), *Learning and education in developing countries: Research and policy for the post-2015 UN development goals*. New York: Palgrave Macmillan. Pps. 74–90.

Britto, P. R., Ulkuer, N., Hodges, W. P., & McCarthy, M. F. (2013). Global policy landscape and early child development. In Britto, P. R., Engle, P. L., & Super, C. M. (Eds.), *Handbook of early childhood development research and its impact on global policy*. London: Oxford University Press. Pps. 65–81.

Brock-Utne, B. (2012). Language and inequality: Global challenges to education. *Compare: A Journal of Comparative and International Education, 42*(5), 773–793.

Bronfenbrenner, U. (1977). Toward an experimental ecology of human development. *American Psychologist, 32*(7), 513.

Bronfenbrenner, U. (1994). Ecological models of human development. In Husen, T., & Postlethwaite, T. N. *International Encyclopedia of Education* (Vol. 3, 2nd ed.). Oxford: Elsevier.

Brookings. (2011). *A global compact on learning: Taking action on education in developing countries*. Washington: Brookings.

Brown, J. S., Collins, A., & Duguid, P. (1989). Situated cognition and the culture of learning. *Educational Researcher, 18*, 32–42.

Bruneforth, M., Gagnon, A., Wallet, P., & UNESCO Institute for Statistics. (2009). *Projecting the Global Demand for Teachers: Meeting the Goal of Universal Primary Education by 2015, Technical Paper 3*. Montreal: UNESCO Institute for Statistics.

Bruner, J. S., & Greenfield, P. M. (1966). (Eds.) *Studies in Cognitive Growth*. New York: Wiley.

Bruns, B., Filmer, D., & Patrinos, H. A. (2011). *Making schools work: New evidence on accountability reforms*. Washington: World Bank.

Buchert, L. (2013). Introduction—understanding education, fragility and conflict. *Prospects, 43*(1), 5–15.

Buchmann, C., & Hannum, E. (2001). Education and stratification in developing countries: A review of theories and research. *Annual Review of Sociology, 27*, 77–102.

Burde, D. (2012). Assessing impact and bridging methodological divides: Randomized trials in countries affected by conflict. *Comparative Education Review, 56*(3), 448–473.

Butcher, N. & Associates. (2014). *Harnessing OER to drive systemic educational change in secondary schooling.* Report to the William and Flora Hewlett Foundation. https://docs. google.com/file/d/0B5FQbmPL4C6TRDlBaFo3QnRjcUk/edit?pli=1

Camfield, L. (2015). 'Character matters': How do measures of non-cognitive skills shape understandings of social mobility in the global North and South? *Social Anthropology, 23*(1), 68–79.

Campbell, D. T. (1979). Assessing the impact of planned social change. *Evaluation and Program Planning, 2*(1), 67–90.

Campbell-Hyde, B. (nd). *Breaking ground: Environmental and social issues of the three gorges dam in China.* www1.american.edu/ted/ICE/china-dam-impact.html

Campuzano, L., Dynarski, M., Agodini, R., Rall, K., & Pendelton, A. (2009). *Effectiveness of reading and mathematics software products: Findings from two student cohorts* (p. 111). Washington, DC: U.S. Department of Education, Institute of Education Sciences, National Center for Education Evaluation and Regional Assistance.

Canagarajah, S. (Ed.). (2005). *Reclaiming the local in language policy and practice.* Mahwah, NJ: Lawrence Erlbaum Associates.

Care, E., Anderson, K., & Kim, H. (2016). *Visualizing the breadth of skills movement across education systems.* Washington, DC: Brookings.

Carneiro, P., & Heckman, J. J. (2003). *Human capital policy.* Working Paper 9495. Cambridge, MA: NBER.

Carnoy, M. (1974). *Education as cultural imperialism* (p. 236). New York: Longman.

Carnoy, M. (1999). *Globalization and education reform: What planners need to know.* Paris: UNESCO.

Carnoy, M., Elmore, R., & Siskin, L. (Eds.). (2003). *The new accountability: High schools and high-stakes testing.* New York: Routledge.

Carnoy, M., Ngware, M., & Oketch, M. (2015). The role of classroom resources and national educational context in student learning gains: Comparing Botswana, Kenya, and South Africa. *Comparative Education Review, 59*(2), 199–233.

Carr, N. (2008). Is Google making us stupid? What the Internet is doing to our brains. *Atlantic Monthly,* July/August, 1–8.

Carr-Hill, R. (2012). Finding and then counting out-of-school children. *Compare: A Journal of Comparative and International Education, 42*(2), 187–212.

Carr-Hill, R. (2013). Missing millions and measuring development progress. *World Development, 46,* 30–44.

Castillo, N. M. (2017). *Technology for improving early reading performance in multi-lingual settings: Evidence from rural South Africa.* Ph.D. dissertation. Philadelphia: University of Pennsylvania.

Castillo, N. M., Lee, J., Zahra, F. T., & Wagner, D. A. (2015). MOOCS for development: Trends, challenges, and opportunities. *Information Technologies and International Development, 11*(2), 35–42.

Castillo, N. M., & Wagner, D. A. (2014). Gold standard? The use of randomized controlled trials for international educational policy. *Comparative Education Review, 58*(1), 166–173.

Cerdan-Infantes, P., & Filmer, D. (2015). *Information, knowledge and behavior: Evaluating alternative methods of delivering school information to parents.* World Bank Policy Research Working Paper, No. 7233, 1–37. Washington, DC: World Bank.

Chaffin, J. (2010). *Education and opportunity: Post-primary and income growth.* New York: Inter-Agency Network for Education in Emergencies.

Chall, J. S. (1983). *Stages of reading development.* New York: McGraw-Hill.

Chang, H. J. (2002). *Kicking away the ladder: Development strategy in historical perspective.* New York: Anthem Press.

Chaudhury, N., Hammer, J., Kremer, M., Muralidharan, K., & Rogers, F. H. (2006). Missing in action: Teacher and health worker absence in developing countries. *Journal of Economic Perspectives, 20*(1), 91–116.

Chi, M. T., Glaser, R., & Farr, M. J. (2014). *The nature of expertise.* New York: Psychology Press.

Chick, J. K. (2002). Constructing a multi-cultural national identity: South African classrooms as sites of struggle between competing discourses. *Journal of Multilingual and Multicultural Development, 23*(6), 462–478.

Chisholm, L., & Leyendecker, R. (2008). Curriculum reform in post-1990s sub-Saharan Africa. *International Journal of Educational Development, 28*(2), 195–205.

Chromy, J. R. (2002). Sampling issues in design, conduct, and interpretation of international comparative studies of school achievement. In Porter, A. C. & Gamoran, A. (Eds.), *Methodological advances in cross-national surveys of educational achievement.* Washington: National Academies Press. Pps. 80–114.

Chudgar, A. (2013). Teacher labor force and teacher education in India: An analysis of a recent policy change and its potential implications. *International Perspectives on Education and Society, 19*, 55–76.

Chudgar, A. (2015). Association between contract teachers and student learning in five francophone African countries. *Comparative Education Review, 59*(2), 261–288.

Churchill, W. (1930/2010). *My early life: 1874–1904.* New York: Simon and Schuster.

Ciampa, P. J., Vaz, L. M., Blevins, M., Sidat, M., Rothman, R. L., Vermund, S. H., & Vergara, A. E. (2012). The association among literacy, numeracy, HIV knowledge and health-seeking behavior: A population-based survey of women in rural Mozambique. *Plos One, 7,* 1–8.

Clarke, A. M., & Clarke, A. D. B. (2000). *Early experience and the life path.* London: Jessica Kingsley Publishers.

Clarke, S., Wylie, G., & Zomer, H. (2013). ICT 4 the MDGs? A perspective on ICTs' role in addressing urban poverty in the context of the millennium development goals. *Information Technologies and International Development, 9*(4), 55–70.

Clayton, T. (1998). Beyond mystification: Reconnecting world-system theory for comparative education. *Comparative Education Review, 42*(4), 479–496.

Cocking, R. R. (1994). Ecologically valid frameworks of development: Accounting for continuities and discontinuities across contexts. In Greenfield, P. M. & Cocking, R. R. (Eds.), *Cross-cultural roots of minority child development.* New York: Psychology Press. Pps. 393–409.

Cohen, J., & Easterly, W. (Eds.). (2010). *What works in development? Thinking big and thinking small.* Washington, DC: Brookings Institution Press.

Colclough, C. (2012). Education, poverty and development—mapping their interconnections. *Comparative Education, 48*(2), 135–148.

Cole, C. F. (2009). What difference does it make?: Insights from research on the impact of international co-productions of Sesame Street. *NHK Broadcasting Studies, 7,* 157–177.

Cole, M., & Bruner, J. S. (1971). Cultural differences and inferences about psychological processes. *American psychologist, 26*(10), 867.

Cole, M. (1998). *Cultural psychology: A once and future discipline.* Cambridge, MA: Harvard University Press.

Cole, M., Gay, J., Glick, J., & Sharp, D. (1971). *The cultural context of learning and thinking.* New York: Basic Books.

Cole, M., & Scribner, S. (1974). *Culture and thought.* New York: Wiley.

Collier, G. (1994). *Social origins of mental ability.* New York: John Wiley & Sons Inc.

Collier, P. (2007). *The bottom billion: Why the poorest countries are failing and what can be done about it.* London: Oxford University Press.

Commeyras, M., & Inyega, H. N. (2007). An integrative review of teaching reading in Kenyan primary schools. *Reading Research Quarterly, 42,* 258–281.

Coombs, P. H. (1968). *The world educational crisis: A systems analysis* (Vol. 30). New York: Oxford University Press.

Coombs, P. H. (1985). *The world crisis in education: The view from the eighties* (Pps. 136–170). New York: Oxford University Press.

Cortina, R. (Ed.). (2014). *The education of indigenous citizens in Latin America.* Clevedon, UK: Multilingual Matters.

Costantini, D. (2008). *La "mission" civilisatrice.* Paris: La Découverte.

Cox, M., Webb, M., Abbott, C., Blakeley, B., Beauchamp, T., & Rhodes, V. (2003). ICT and pedagogy: A review of the research literature. In Cox, M. & Abbott, C. (Eds.), *ICT in schools research and evaluation.* London: Department for Education and Skills. Pps. 1–58.

Coyne, C. (2013). *Doing bad by doing good: Why humanitarian action fails.* Stanford: Stanford University Press.

Cozby, C. (2012). *Methods in behavioral research.* Boston: McGraw-Hill.

Cresswell, J., Schwantner, U., & Waters, C. (2015). *A review of international large-scale assessments in education: Assessing component skills and collecting contextual data: PISA for development.* Paris: OECD.

Cristia, J. P., Ibarrarán, P., Cueto, S., Santiago, A., & Severín, E. (2012). *Technology and child development: Evidence from the One Laptop Per Child program.* IDB Working Paper IDB-WP-304. Washington: Inter-American Development Bank.

Crosson, A. C., & Lesaux, N. K. (2010). Revisiting assumptions about the relationship of fluent reading to comprehension: Spanish-speakers' text-reading fluency in English. *Reading and Writing, 23*(5), 475–494.

Crosson, A. C., Lesaux, N. K., & Martiniello, M. (2008). Factors that influence comprehension of connectives among language minority children from Spanish-speaking backgrounds. *Applied Psycholinguistics, 29*(4), 603–625.

Crouch, L. (2015). *Stumbling at the first step: Crisis at the foundation in developing country education.* Unpublished Technical Report. Washington, DC: RTI.

Crouch, L. (in press). Making the pyramid less pyramidal? In Wagner, D. A., Boruch, R. F., & Wolf, S. (Eds.). *Learning at the bottom of the pyramid.* Paris: UNESCO-IIEP.

Crouch, L., Gustafsson, M., & Lavado, P. (2008). Measuring educational inequality in South Africa and Perú. In Holsinger, D. B. & Jacob, W. J. (Eds.), *Inequality in education.* Netherlands: Springer. Pps. 461–484.

Cuban, L. (2003). *Oversold and underused: Computers in the classroom.* Cambridge, MA: Harvard University Press.

Cuendet, S., Medhi, I., Bali, K., & Cutrell, E. (2013). *VideoKheti: Making video content accessible to low-literate and novice users.* Paper presented at CHI 2013, Paris, April 27–May 2, 2013. http://research.microsoft.com/pubs/183489/Cuendet-CHI2013-VideoKheti-Final.pdf

Cummings, W. K. (2014). *Education and equality in Japan.* Princeton: Princeton University Press.

Cummins, J. (2000). *Language, power, and pedagogy: Bilingual children in the crossfire* (Vol. 23). Clevedon, England: Multilingual Matters.

Cummins, J., Swain, M., Nakajima, K., Handscombe, J., Green, D., & Tran, C. (1984). Linguistic interdependence among Japanese and Vietnamese immigrant students. In Rivera, C. (Ed.), *Communicative competence approaches to language proficiency assessment: Research and application*. Clevedon, England: Multilingual Matters. Pps. 60–81.

Cunningham, M. (2010). Laman laka: Our indigenous path to self-determined development. In Tauli-Corpuz, V., Enkiwe-Abayao, L., & de Chavez, R. (Eds.), *Towards an alternative development paradigm: Indigenous peoples' self-determined development*. Baguio City, Philippines: Tebtebba Foundation. Pps. 89–116.

Dachyshyn, D., & Kirova, A. (2008). Understanding childhoods in-between: Sudanese refugee children's transition from home to preschool. *Research in Comparative and International Education, 3*(3), 281–294.

Danaher, K. (Ed.). (1994). *50 years is enough: The case against the World Bank and the International Monetary Fund*. Boston: South End Press.

Darling-Hammond, L. (1996). The quiet revolution: Rethinking teacher development. *Educational Leadership, 53*(6), 4–10.

Dasen, P. R. (1984). The cross-cultural study of intelligence: Piaget and the Baoule. *International Journal of Psychology, 19*(1–4), 407–434.

Daswani, C. J. (2001). *Language education in multilingual India*. Delhi: UNESCO.

DeBoer, J. (2009). The relationship between environmental factors and usage behaviors at 'Hole-in-the-wall' computers. *International Journal of Educational Development, 29*, 91–98.

de Corte, E. (2010). Historical developments in the understanding of learning. In Dumont, H., Istance, D., & Benavides, F. (Eds.), *The nature of learning: Using research to inspire practice*. Paris: Organization for Economic Cooperation and Development. Pps. 35–67.

Delors, J. (1996). *Learning: The treasure within*. Report of the Commission on Education for the 21st Century. Paris: UNESCO.

de Melo, G., Machado, A., Miranda, A., & Viera, M. (2013). *Profundizando en los efectos del Plan Ceibal*. Mexico City: CIDE.

Design-Based Research Collective. (2003). Design-based research: An emerging paradigm for educational inquiry. *Educational Researcher, 32*(1), 5–8.

DeStefano, J., & Elaheebocus, N. (2009). *School effectiveness in Woliso, Ethiopia: Measuring opportunity to learn and early grade reading fluency*. Washington: Academy for Educational Development.

DeWalt, D. A., Berkman, N. D., Sheridan, S., Lohr, K. N., & Pignone, M. P. (2004). Literacy and health outcomes. *Journal of General Internal Medicine, 19*(12), 1228–1239.

Dewey, J. (1929). *The sources of a science of education*. New York: Horace Liveright.

Dewey, J. (1938). *Logic: The theory of inquiry*. New York: Henry Holt.

Dichaba, M. M., & Mokhele, M. L. (2012). Does the cascade model work for teacher training? Analysis of teachers' experiences. *International Journal of Educational Sciences, 4*(3), 249–254.

Dichter, T. W. (2003). *Despite good intentions: Why development assistance to the Third World has failed*. Amherst: University of Massachusetts Press.

Dickenson, D. K., McCabe, A., Clark-Chiarelli, N., & Wolf, A. (2004). Cross-language transfer of phonological awareness in low-income Spanish and English bilingual preschool children. *Applied Psycholinguistics, 25*, 323–347.

Diener, E., & Seligman, M. E. (2004). Beyond money toward an economy of well-being. *Psychological Science in the Public Interest, 5*(1), 1–31.

Diener, E., Tay, L., & Oishi, S. (2013). Rising income and the subjective well-being of nations. *Journal of Personality and Social Psychology, 104*(2), 267.

Dobbs, R., Madgavkar, A., Barton, D., Labaye, E., Manyika, J., & Roxburgh, C. (2012). *The world at work: Jobs, pay, and skills for 3.5 billion people.* Washington: McKinsey Global Institute.

Dodson, L., Sterling, S. R., & Bennett, J. R. (2012). Considering failure: Eight years of *ITID* research. *Information Technology and International Development, 9*(2), ICTD2012 Special Issue, 19–34.

Dodson, L. L., Sterling, S., & Bennett, J. K. (2013, December). Minding the gaps: Cultural, technical and gender-based barriers to mobile use in oral-language Berber communities in Morocco. In *Proceedings of the Sixth International Conference on Information and Communication Technologies and Development: Full Papers-Volume 1.* Cape Town, South Africa: Association for Computing Machinery. Pps. 79–88.

Dollar, D., Kleineberg, T., & Kraay, A. (2016). Growth still is good for the poor. *European Economic Review, 81,* 68–85.

Dollar, D., & Kraay, A. (2002). Spreading the wealth. *Foreign Affairs,* January/February, 120–133.

Dore, R. (1976). *The diploma disease: Education, qualification and development.* London: Allyn and Unwin.

Dowd, A. J. (2011). An NGO perspective on assessment choice: From practice to research to practice. *Compare: A Journal of Comparative and International Education, 40*(3), 541–545.

Dowd, A. J. (2012). *Essential enablers of quality needed in ISLAs: The home literacy environment and the opportunity to learn.* Westport, CN: Draft Manuscript, Save the Children.

Dowd, A. J., Friedlander, E., & Guajardo, J. (2014). Opportunity to Learn (OTL): A framework for supporting learning? In Varghese, N. V. (Ed.), *From schooling to learning.* Paris: UNESCO-IIEP. Pps. 95–107.

Dowd, A. J., Friedlander, E., Jonason, C., Leer, J., Sorensen, L. Z., Guajardo, J., D'Sa, N., Pava, C., & Pisani, L. (2017). Life-wide learning for early reading development in twelve African and Asian sites. In McCardle, P., Mora, A., & Gove, A. (Eds.), *Progress toward a literate world: Early reading interventions in low-income countries.* New Directions for Child and Adolescent Development, (155), 31–49

Dowd, A. J., & Pisani, L. (2013). Two wheels are better than one: The importance of capturing the home literacy environment in large scale assessments of reading. *Research in Comparative and International Education, 8*(3), 359–372.

Dowd, A. J., Pisani, L., & Borisova, I. (2016). Evaluating early learning from age 3 to grade 3. In UNESCO Institute for Statistics (Ed.), *Understanding what works in oral reading assessments.* Montreal: UNESCO-UIS. Pps. 66–80.

Downing, J. (Ed.). (1966). *The first international reading symposium: Oxford 1964: Papers on reading readiness, approaches to reading, reading failure and developments in teaching reading.* London: Cassell.

Downing, J. (1973). *Comparative reading: Cross-national studies of behavior and processes in reading and writing.* New York: Macmillan.

Drèze, J., Lanjouw, P., & Sharma, N. (1998). Economic development in Palanpur, 1957–93. In Lanjouw, P. & Stern, N. (Eds.), *Economic development in Palanpur over five decades.* New York: Clarendon Press. Pps. 114–239.

Droop, M., & Verhoeven, L. (1998). Background knowledge, linguistic complexity, and second-language reading comprehension. *Journal of Literacy Research, 30,* 253–271.

Dryden-Peterson, S. (2016). Refugee education: The crossroads of globalization. *Educational Researcher, 45*(9), 473–482.

D'Sa, N., Borisova, I., & Nahis, M. I. (2014). *Enhancing early child development by engaging fathers: Evaluation of a father support and education program in rural Bangladesh.* Paper presented at CIES Annual Meetings, Montreal, March.

D'Souza, D. (1995). *The end of racism: Principles for a multicultural society.* New York: Free Press.

Dubeck, M. M., & Gove, A. (2015). The early grade reading assessment (EGRA): Its theoretical foundation, purpose, and limitations. *International Journal of Educational Development, 40,* 315–322.

Dubow, S. (1995). *Scientific racism in modern South Africa.* London: Cambridge University Press.

Duckworth, A. (2016). *Grit: Passion, perseverance and the science of success.* New York: Random House.

Duckworth, A. L., Peterson, C., Matthews, M. D., & Kelly, D. R. (2007). Grit: Perseverance and passion for long-term goals. *Journal of Personality and Social Psychology, 92*(6), 1087.

Dudley-Marling, C., & Gurn, A. (Eds.). (2010). *The myth of the normal curve.* New York: Peter Lang.

Dudley-Marling, C., & Lucas, K. (2009). Pathologizing the language and culture of poor children. *Language Arts, 86*(5), 362–370.

Duff, D., Tomblin, J. B., & Catts, H. (2015). The influence of reading on vocabulary growth: A case for a Matthew effect. *Journal of Speech, Language, and Hearing Research, 58*(3), 853–864.

Duflo, E., Hanna, R., & Ryan, S. P. (2012). Incentives work: Getting teachers to come to school. *The American Economic Review, 102*(4), 1241–1278.

Duflo, E., Kremer, M., & Robinson, J. (2008). How high are rates of return to fertilizer? Evidence from field experiments in Kenya. *The American Economic Review, 98,* 482–488.

Duncan, R. G., & Rivet, A. E. (2013). Science learning progressions. *Science, 339*(6118), 396–397.

Duncker, K. (1945). On problem solving. *Psychological Monographs, 58*(5) (Whole No. 270), 1–113.

Dunne, N. (1994). Why a hamburger should cost 200 dollars—the call for markets to reflect ecological factors. *Financial Times,* 12 January.

Durgunoglu, A. Y., & Oney, B. (2002). Phonological awareness in literacy acquisition: It's not only for children. *Scientific Studies of Reading, 6*(3), 245–266.

Dutcher, N. (2004). *Expanding educational opportunity in linguistically diverse societies.* Washington, DC: Center for Applied Linguistics.

Dyer, C., Choksi, A., Awasty, V., Iyer, U., Moyade, R., & Nigam, N. (2004). Knowledge for teacher development in India: The importance of local knowledge for in-service education. *International Journal of Educational Development, 24,* 39–52.

Dynamic Measurement Group. (2008). *DIBELS 6th edition technical adequacy information.* Tech. Rep. No. 6. Eugene, OR. http://dibels.org/pubs.html

Easterly, W. (2006). *The white man's burden: Why the West's efforts to aid the rest have done so much ill and so little good.* New York: Penguin.

Easterly, W. (2014). *The tyranny of experts.* New York: Penguin.

Easterly, W. (2016). The war on terror vs. the war on poverty. *New York Review of Books, 63*(18), 64–65.

Easton, P. (2014). *Sustaining literacy in Africa: Developing a literate environment.* Paris: UNESCO.

Ebbinghaus, H. (1913). *Memory: A contribution to experimental psychology* (No. 3). Ann Arbor, MI: University Microfilms.

EDC [Educational Development Center]. (2011–12). *eEGRA: Usable reading results—Right now!* http://eegra.edc.org/

EDC [Educational Development Center]. (2014). http://englishforlatinamerica.org/research/

EDC [Education Development Center]. (2011). *PHARE project*. http://idd.edc.org/projects/mali-usaidphare-program-program-harmonisé-dappui-au-renforcement-de-leducation

Eisenstadt, S. N. (2000). Multiple modernities. *Daedalus, 129*(1), 1–29.

Elder, L., Emdon, H., Fuchs, R., & Petrazzini, B. (Eds.). (2014). *Connecting ICTs to development: The IDRC experience*. Ottawa: Anthem/IDRC.

Elley, W. E. (2000). The potential of book floods for raising literacy levels. *International Review of Education, 46*(3), 233–255.

Engel, L. C., & Feuer, M. J. (2014). Five myths about international large-scale assessments. *Quality Assurance in Education, 22*, 18–21.

Engle, P. L., & Black, M. M. (2008). The effect of poverty on child development and educational outcomes. *Annals of the New York Academy of Sciences, 1136*(1), 243–256.

Engle, P. L., Black, M. M., Behrman, J. R., de Mello, M. C., Gertler, P. J., Kapiriri, L. M., & International Child Development Steering Group. (2007). Child development in developing countries 3: Strategies to avoid the loss of developmental potential in more than 200 million children in the developing world. *The Lancet, 369*, 229–242.

Eriksson, K. (2014). Does the language of instruction in primary school affect later labour market outcomes? Evidence from South Africa. *Economic History of Developing Regions, 29*(2), 311–335.

Erny, P. (1972). *L'enfant et son milieu en Afrique noire, essai sur l'education traditionnelle*. Paris: Payot.

Escobar, A. (1991). Anthropology and the development encounter: The making and marketing of development anthropology. *American Ethnologist, 18*(4), 658–682.

Evans, D. K., & Popova, A. (2015). *What really works to improve learning in developing countries? An analysis of divergent findings in systematic reviews*. Policy Research Working Paper 7203. Washington: World Bank.

Ezcurra, R., & Rodríguez-Pose, A. (2013). Does economic globalization affect regional inequality? A cross-country analysis. *World Development, 52*, 92–103.

Fagerlind, I., & Saha, L. J. (1983). *Education and national development: A comparative perspective*. New York: Pergamon.

Fajebe, A. A., Best, M. L., & Smyth, T. N. (2013). Is the one laptop per child enough? Viewpoints from classroom teachers in Rwanda. *Information Technologies and International Development, 9*(3), 29.

Feiman-Memser, S. (2012). *Teachers as learners*. Cambridge, MA: Harvard Education Press.

Feldman, D. H. (1994). *Beyond universals in cognitive development*. Norwood, NJ: Ablex Publishing.

Fennell, S. (2013, May). Low-fee private schools in Pakistan: A blessing or a bane: Low-fee private schooling: Aggravating equity or mitigating disadvantage. In Srivastava, P. (Ed.), *Low-fee Private Schooling: Aggravating equity or mitigating disadvantage?* Oxford: Symposium Books Ltd. Pps. 65–80.

Ferguson, J. (1990). *The anti-politics machine: 'Development', depoliticization and bureaucratic power in Lesotho*. New York: Cambridge University Press.

Fernald, A., Marchman, V. A., & Weisleder, A. (2013). SES differences in language processing skill and vocabulary are evident at 18 months. *Developmental Science, 16*(2), 234–248.

Ferrando, M., Machado, A., Perazzo, I., Vernengo, A., & Haretche, C. (2011). Aprendiendo con las XO: El impacto del Plan Ceibal en el aprendizaje *Serie Documentos de Trabajo*. Mexico City: Instituto de Economía, Facultad de Ciencias Económicas y de Adminstración, Unversiad de la República.

Ferreira, F. H., & Gignoux, J. (2014). The measurement of educational inequality: Achievement and opportunity. *The World Bank Economic Review, 28*(2), 210–246.

Ferreiro, E., & Teberosky, A. (1982). *Literacy before schooling.* London: Heinemann.

Filmer, D., Molina, E., & Stacy, B. (2015). *What goes on inside the classroom in Africa? Assessing the relationship between what teachers know, what happened in the classroom, and student performance.* Draft Technical Report. Washington: World Bank. https://aefpweb. org/sites/default/files/webform/aefp40/Filmer%20Molina%20Stacy%20(2015)%20 What%20Goes%20on%20Inside%20Classroom%20Africa.pdf

Finn, J., & Achilles, C. (1999). Tennessee's class size study: Findings, implications, misconceptions. *Educational Evaluation and Policy Analysis, 21*(2), 97–109.

Fitts, P. M. (1954). The information capacity of the human motor system in controlling the amplitude of movement. *Journal of Experimental Psychology, 47,* 381–391.

Flannery, L. P., Silverman, B., Kazakoff, E. R., Bers, M. U., Bontá, P., & Resnick, M. (2013, June). *Designing ScratchJr: Support for early childhood learning through computer programming.* Proceedings of the 12th International Conference on Interaction Design and Children. New York: Association of Computing Machinery. Pps. 1–10.

Foehr, U. G. (2006). *Media multitasking among American youth: Prevalence, predictors and pairings.* New York: Kaiser Family Foundation.

Forget-Dubois, N., Dionne, G., Lemelin, J.-P., Perusse, D., Tremblay, R. E., & Boivin, M. (2009). Early child language mediates the relation between home environment and school readiness. *Child Development, 80,* 736–749.

Fowler, A. (2013). *Striking a balance: A guide to enhancing the effectiveness of non-governmental organisations in international development.* London: Routledge.

Freedman, D. H. (2010). *Wrong: Why experts keep failing us.* New York: Little, Brown and Company.

Freeman, R. B., Machin, S., & Viarengo, M. (2010). *Variation in educational outcomes and policies across countries and of schools within countries.* NBER Working Paper Series No. 16293. Washington, DC: NBER.

Freire, P. (1972/1996). *Pedagogy of the oppressed.* London: Penguin.

Freire, P., & Macedo, D. (2005). *Literacy: Reading the word and the world.* London: Routledge.

Friedlander, E. (2015). *Towards learning for all: Understanding the literacy ecology in rural Rwanda.* Ph.D. dissertation. Palo Alto: Stanford.

Friedlander, E., & Goldenberg, C. (2016). *Literacy boost in Rwanda: Impact evaluation of a two year randomized control trial.* Palo Alto: Stanford.

Friedman, T. L. (2005). *The world is flat: A brief history of the twenty-first century.* New York: Farrar, Straus and Giroux.

Friedman, T. L. (2016). *Thank You for being late: An optimist's guide to thriving in the age of accelerations.* New York: Farrar, Straus and Giroux.

Friis-Hansen, E., & Duveskog, D. (2012). The empowerment route to well-being: An analysis of farmer field schools in East Africa. *World Development, 40*(2), 414–427.

Fuller, B. (1991). *Growing-up modern: The western state builds third-world schools.* New York: Routledge.

Fuller, B., & Clarke, P. (1994). Raising school effects while ignoring culture? Local conditions and the influence of classroom tools, rules, and pedagogy. *Review of Educational Research, 64*(1), 119–157.

Gabrieli, J. D. E. (2009). Dyslexia: A new synergy between education and cognitive neuroscience. *Science, 325,* 280–283.

Gaible, E., Bloome, T., Schwartz, A., Hoppes Poché, J., & Vota, W. (2011). *First principles: Designing effective education programs using Information and Communication Technology (ICT)—A compendium.* Washington, DC: USAID.

Gaible, E., & Burns, M. (2005). *Using technology to train teachers.* Washington, DC: infoDev.

Gakidou, E., Cowling, K., Lozano, R., & Murray, C. J. (2010). Increased educational attainment and its effect on child mortality in 175 countries between 1970 and 2009: A systematic analysis. *The Lancet, 376*(9745), 959–974.

Galton, F. (1869). *Hereditary genius.* London: Macmillan.

Ganimian, A. J., & Murnane, R. J. (2016). Improving education in developing countries: Lessons from rigorous impact evaluations. *Review of Educational Research, 85,* 1–37.

Garcia, O., & Wei, L. (2014). *Translanguaging: Language, bilingualism and education.* London: Palgrave Pivot.

Gardiner, S. M. (2006). A perfect moral storm: Climate change, intergenerational ethics and the problem of moral corruption. *Environmental Values, 15,* 397–413.

Gardner, D. P. (1983). *A nation at risk.* Washington, DC: The National Commission on Excellence in Education, US Department of Education.

Geddes, P. (1915). *Cities in evolution.* London: Williams.

Geertz, C. (1973). *The interpretation of cultures.* New York: Basic Books.

Gelman, R., & Gallistel, C. R. (1978). *The child's understanding of number.* Cambridge, MA: Harvard University Press.

Gertler, P. J., Heckman, J., Pinto, R., Zanolini, A., Vermeersch, C., Walker, S., Chang, S. M., & Grantham-McGregor, S. (2014). Labor market returns to an early childhood stimulation intervention in Jamaica. *Science, 344*(6187), 998–1001.

Gertler, P. J., Patrinos, H. A., & Rubio-Codina, M. (2012). Empowering parents to improve education: Evidence from rural Mexico. *Journal of Development Economics, 99*(1), 68–79.

Gielen, U. P. (2016). The cross-cultural study of human development. In Gielen, U. P. & Roopnarine, J. (Eds.), *Childhood and adolescence: Cross-cultural perspectives and applications* (2nd ed.). New York: Praeger. Pps. 3–45.

Gilman, N., & Ticktin, M. (2014). From antipolitics to post-neoliberalism: A conversation with James Ferguson. *Humanity, 5*(2), 247–259.

Gilmore, A. (2005). *The impact of PIRLS (2001) and TIMSS (2003) in low- and middle-income countries: An evaluation of the value of world bank support for international surveys of reading literacy (PIRLS) and mathematics and science (TIMSS).* New Zealand: IEA.

Gini, C. (1909/1997). Concentration and dependency ratios (in Italian). *Reprinted in English translation in Rivista di Politica Economica, 87,* 769–789.

Ginsburg, H. P., Klein, A., & Starkey, P. (1998). The development of children's mathematical thinking: Connecting research with practice. In Sigel, I. & Renninger, A. (Eds.), *Handbook of child psychology: Child psychology and practice* (5th ed., Vol. 4). New York: John Wiley & Sons. Pps. 401–476.

Ginsburg, M. (2012). Teachers as learners. In Klees, S. J., Samoff, J., & Stromquist, N. P. (Eds.), *The World Bank and education: Critiques and alternatives.* Boston: Sense Publishers. Pps. 83–93.

Gleitman, L. R., Newport, E. L., & Gleitman, H. (1984). The current status of the motherese hypothesis. *Journal of Child Language, 11*(1), 43–79.

Glewwe, P., Hanushek, E., Humpage, S., & Ravina, R. (2011). *School resources and educational outcomes in developing countries: A review of the literature from 1990 to 2010.* NBER Working Papers No. 17554. Cambridge, MA: National Bureau for Economic Research.

Glewwe, P., Kremer, M., & Moulin, S. (2007). *Many children left behind? Textbooks and test scores in Kenya.* NBER Working Paper 13300. Cambridge, MA: National Bureau of Economic Research.

Goldin, C. D., & Katz, L. F. (2009). *The race between education and technology.* Cambridge, MA: Harvard University Press.

Golinkoff, R. M., Can, D. D., Soderstrom, M., & Hirsh-Pasek, K. (2015). (Baby) talk to me: The social context of infant-directed speech and its effects on early language acquisition. *Current Directions in Psychological Science, 24*(5), 339–344.

Gómez, F., Nussbaum, M., Weitz, J. F., Lopez, X., Mena, J., & Torres, A. (2013). Co-located single display collaborative learning for early childhood education. *International Journal of Computer-Supported Collaborative Learning, 8*(2), 225–244.

Goody, J., & Watt, I. (1968). The consequences of literacy. In Goody, J. (Ed.), *Literacy in traditional societies.* Cambridge: Cambridge University Press. Pps. 27–68.

Gove, A., & Cvelich, P. (2011). *Early reading: Igniting education for all.* Report by Early Grade Learning Community of Practice (Revised Edition). Washington: RTI.

Gove, A., & Wetterberg, A. (2011). *The early grade reading assessment: Applications and interventions to improve basic literacy.* Research Triangle Park: RTI.

Graham, C., & Nikolova, M. (2012). *Does access to information technology make people Happier? Insights from well-being surveys from around the world.* Washington, DC: Brookings Working Paper 53.

Grantham-McGregor, S., Bun Cheung, Y., Cueto, S., Glewwe, P., Richer, L., Strupp, B., & The International Child Development Steering Group. (2007). Developmental potential in the first five years for children in developing countries. *The Lancet, 369*(9555), 60–70.

Grauer, S. R. (1989). *Think globally, act locally: A Delphi study of educational leadership through the development of international resources in the local community.* San Diego: University of San Diego Press.

Gray, W. S. (1956). *The teaching of reading and writing: An international survey.* Paris: UNESCO.

Greaney, V., & Kellaghan, T. (2008). *Assessing national achievement levels in education: National assessment of educational achievement* (Vol. 1). Washington: World Bank.

Greaney, V., Khandker, S. R., & Alam, M. (1999). *Bangladesh: Assessing basic learning skills.* Washington: World Bank.

Greenberg, D., Ehri, L. C., & Perin, D. (2002). Do adult literacy students make the same word-reading and spelling errors as children matched for word-reading age? *Scientific Studies of Reading, 6,* 221–243.

Greenfield, P. M., & Bruner, J. S. (1966). Culture and cognitive growth. *International Journal of Psychology, 1*(2), 89–107.

Greenfield, P. M., & Cocking, R. R. (2014). *Cross-cultural roots of minority child development.* New York: Psychology Press.

Gross National Happiness Centre [GNH Centre]. (2013). *Quote from King of Bhutan.* www.facebook.com/GNHCentre/posts/462230373841877

Groves, L., & Hinton, R. (Eds.). (2013). *Inclusive aid: Changing power and relationships in international development.* London: Routledge.

Guarcello, L., Lyon, S., Rosati, F., & Valdivia, C. A. (2007). *Children's work non-market activities and child labour measurement: A discussion based on household survey data.* UCW Working Paper. Geneva: International Labor Organization.

Guardian, The. (2013). Technology for good: Innovative use of technology by charities. www.techsoup.org/technology-for-good-report

Gudynas, E. (2011). Buen vivir: Today's tomorrow. *Development, 54*(4), 441–447.

Gurn, A. (2010). Conclusion: Re/visioning the ideological imagination in (special) education. In Dudley-Marling, C. & Gurn, A. (Eds.), *The myth of the normal curve*. New York: Peter Lang. Pps. 241–256.

Gurugé, A. (1985). Buddhist education. In Husen, T. & Postlethwaite, T. N. (Eds.), *International encyclopedia of education: Research and studies*. New York: Pergamon Press.

Haines, A., Alleyne, G., Kickbusch, I., & Dora, C. (2012). From the Earth Summit to Rio+ 20: Integration of health and sustainable development. *The Lancet, 379*(9832), 2189–2197.

Hall, G. S. (1891). The contents of children's minds on entering school. *The Pedagogical Seminary, 1*(2), 139–173.

Hambleton, R. K., & Kanjee, A. (1995). Increasing the validity of cross-cultural assessments: Use of improved methods for test adaptation. *European Journal of Psychological Assessment, 11*(3), 147–157.

Hanlon, J., Barrientos, A., & Hulme, D. (2010). *Just give money to the poor: The development revolution from the global South*. Sterling, VA: Kumarian Press.

Hansen, J., Sato, M., Hearty, P., Ruedy, R., Kelley, M., Masson-Delmotte, V., Russell, G., Tselioudis, G., Cao, J., Rignot, E., Velicogna, I., Kandiano, E., von Schuckmann, K., Kharecha, P., Legrande, A. N., Bauer, M. & Lo, K. (2015). Ice melt, sea level rise and superstorms: Evidence that 2 C global warming is highly dangerous. *Atmospheric, Chemistry, and Physics Discussion, 23*, 20059–20179.

Hanushek, E. A. (1995). Interpreting recent research on schooling in developing countries. *The World Bank Research Observer, 10*(2), 227–246.

Hanushek, E. A., & Rivkin, S. G. (2006). Teacher quality. *Handbook of the Economics of Education, 2*, 1051–1078.

Hanushek, E. A., & Woessmann, L. (2007). *Education quality and economic growth*. Washington: World Bank.

Hanushek, E. A., & Woessmann, L. (2012). Do better schools lead to more growth? Cognitive skills, economic outcomes, and causation. *Journal of Economic Growth, 17*(4), 267–321.

Hanushek, E. A., & Woessmann, L. (2015). *Universal basic skills: What countries stand to gain*. Paris: OECD.

Harber, C. (2004). *Schooling as violence: How schools harm pupils and societies*. London: Routledge.

Harber, C. (2014). *Education and international development: Theory, practice, and issues by Clive Harber*. Oxford: Symposium Books.

Hardman, F., Abd-Kadir, J., & Tibuhinda, A. (2012). Reforming teacher education in Tanzania. *International Journal of Educational Development, 32*, 826–834.

Hardman, F., Ackers, J., Abrishamian, N., & O'Sullivan, M. (2011). Developing a systemic approach to teacher education in sub-Saharan Africa: Emerging lessons from Kenya, Tanzania and Uganda. *Compare: A Journal of Comparative and International Education, 41*(5), 669–683.

Hargreaves, A. (1994). *Changing teachers, changing times: Teachers' work and culture in the postmodern age*. New York: Teachers College Press.

Härmä, J. (2009). Can choice promote education for all? Evidence from growth in private primary schooling in India. *Compare: A Journal of Comparative and International Education, 39*(2), 151–165.

Härmä, J. (2010). School choice for the poor? The limits of marketisation of primary education in rural India. *CREATE Research Monograph, Pathways to Access series 23*. Brighton, UK: University of Sussex.

Harris, M. (1976). History and significance of the emic/etic distinction. *Annual Review of Anthropology, 5*, 329–350.

Hart, B., & Risley, T. R. (2003). The early catastrophe: The 30 million word gap by age 3. *American Educator, 27*(1), 4–9.

Harttgen, K., Klasen, S., & Misselhorn, M. (2010). Pro-poor progress in education in developing countries? *Review of Economics and Institutions, 1*(1), 1–48.

Hattie, J. (2005). The paradox of reducing class size and improving learning outcomes. *International Journal of Educational Research, 43*(6), 387–425.

Hauser, L. (2013). Qualitative research in distance education: An analysis of journal literature 2005–2012. *American Journal of Distance Education, 27*, 155–164.

Heath, S. B. (1983). *Ways with words: Language, life, and work in communities and classrooms.* New York: Cambridge University Press.

Heckman, J. J. (2006). Skill formation and the economics of investing in disadvantaged children. *Science, 312*(5782), 1900–1902.

Heckman, J. J. (2011). The economics of inequality: The value of early childhood education. *American Educator*, Spring, *35*, 31–47.

Heckman, J. J., & Kautz, T. (2012). Hard evidence on soft skills. *Labour Economics, 19*(4), 451–464.

Heeks, R. (2014). *ICT4D 2016: New priorities for ICT4D, policy practice and WSIS in a post-2015 world.* Development Informatics: Working Paper Series No. 59. Manchester, UK: University of Manchester.

Heinrich, J., Heine, S., & Norenzayan, A. (2010). The weirdest people in the world? *Behavioral Brain Science, 33*(2–3), 85–135.

Helliwell, J. F., Layard, R., & Sachs, J. (2015). *World happiness report: Compendium of the UNDP human development report.* New York: UNDP.

Hélot, C., & Laoire, M. (2011). *Language policy for the multilingual classroom: Pedagogy of the possible.* Bristol: Multilingual Matters.

Henderson, A. T., & Berla, N. (1994). *A new generation of evidence: The family is critical to student achievement.* Washington: National Committee for Citizens in Education.

Hess, R. D., & Holloway, S. D. (1984). Family and school as educational institutions. *Review of Child Development Research, 7*, 179–222.

Heugh, K. (2006). Cost implications of the provision of mother tongue and strong bilingual models of education in Africa. In Alidou, H., Boly, A., Brock-Utne, B., Diallo, Y., Heugh, K., & Wolff, H. (Eds.), *Optimizing learning and education in Africa: The language factor—a stock-taking research on mother tongue and bilingual education in Sub-Saharan Africa.* Paris: IIEP/ADEA. Pps. 138–156.

Heugh, K. (2015). Epistemologies in multilingual education: Translanguaging and genre—companions in conversation with policy and practice. *Language and Education, 29*(3), 280–285.

Heward, C., & Bunwaree, S. (Eds.). (1999). *Gender, education, and development.* New York: Zed Books.

Heymann, J. (2006). *Forgotten families: Ending the growing crises confronting children and working parenting in the global economy.* Oxford, UK: Oxford University Press.

Heymann, J., & Earle, A. (2009). *Raising the global floor: Dismantling the myth that we can't afford good working conditions for everyone.* Stanford: Stanford University Press.

Heyneman, S. P., & Loxley, W. (1983). The effect of primary-school quality on academic achievement across twenty-nine high- and low-income countries. *American Journal of Sociology, 88*(6), 1162–1194.

Heyneman, S. P., & Stern, J. M. (2014). Low cost private schools for the poor: What public policy is appropriate? *International Journal of Educational Development, 35,* 3–15.

Heyneman, S. P., & Stern, J. M. (2015). Development and education. In Dixon, P., Humble, S., & Counihan, C. (Eds.), *Handbook of international development and education.* Cheltenham, UK: Edward Elgar Publishing. Pps. 20–46.

Hickling-Hudson, A. (2004). South—South collaboration: Cuban teachers in Jamaica and Namibia. *Comparative Education, 40*(2), 289–311.

Hilbert, M. (2016). Big data for development: A review of promises and challenges. *Development Policy Review, 34*(1), 135–174.

Hinostroza, J. E., Isaacs, S., & Bougroum, M. (2014). Information and communications technologies for improving students' learning opportunities and outcomes in developing countries. In Wagner, D. A. (Ed.), *Learning and education in developing countries: Research and policy for the post-2015 UN development goals.* New York: Palgrave Macmillan. Pps. 42–57.

Hirschman, A. O. (1958). *The strategy of development.* New Haven, CT: Yale University Press.

Hirschman, A. O. (1978). Exit, voice, and the state. *World Politics, 31,* 90–107.

Hirschman, A. O. (1981). *Essays in trespassing: Economics to politics and beyond.* New York: Cambridge University Press.

Hirsh-Pasek, K., & Golinkoff, R. M. (2012). How babies talk. In Odom, S., Pungello, E., & Gardner-Neblett, N. (Eds.), *Re-visioning the beginning: Developmental and health science contributions to infant/toddler programs for children and families living in poverty.* New York: Guilford Press. Pps. 77–101.

HIWEL [Hole in the Wall Education Limited]. (2013). *Project website.* www.hole-in-the-wall.com

Ho, J., & Thukral, H. (2009). *Tuned in to student success: Assessing the impact of interactive radio instruction for the hardest-to-reach.* Washington, DC: Education Development Center, Inc.

Ho, M. R., Smyth, T. N., Kam, M., & Dearden, A. (2009). Human-computer interaction for development: The past, present, and future. *Information Technologies and International Development, 5*(4), 1.

Hoffman, J. V. (2012). Why EGRA—a clone of DIBELS—will fail to improve literacy in Africa. *Research in the Teaching of English, 46*(4), 340–357.

Holmes, B. (2013). *Educational policy and the mission schools: Case studies from the British empire.* New York: Routledge.

Hornberger, N. (2003). *Continua of biliteracy: An ecological framework for educational policy, research, and practice in multilingual settings.* Bristol: Multilingual Matters.

Hornberger, N., & Vaish, V. (2009). Multilingual language policy and school linguistic practice: Globalization and English-language teaching in India, Singapore and South Africa. *Compare: A Journal of Comparative and International Education, 39*(3), 305–320.

Howard, B. C. (2013). Connecting with nature boosts creativity and health: Interview with Richard Louv. *National Geographic Magazine,* June 30. See: http://news.nationalgeographic.com/news/2013/06/130628-richard-louv-nature-deficit-disorder-health-environment/

Howie, S., & Hughes, C. (2000). South Africa. In Robitaille, D., Beaton, A., & Plomb, T. (Eds.), *The impact of TIMSS on the teaching and learning of mathematics and science.* Vancouver: Pacific Educational Press. Pps. 139–145.

Humery, M.-E. (2013). *L'écriture du pulaar (peul) entre l'arabe et le français, dans la vallée du fleuve Sénégal.* Theses de doctorat. Paris: Centre Anthropologie de l'Écriture (EHESS).

Huntington, S. P. (1996). *The clash of civilizations and the remaking of world order.* New York: Simon and Schuster.

Inkeles, A., & Smith, D. H. (1974). *Becoming modern: Individual change in six developing countries.* Cambridge, MA: Harvard University Press.

International Commission on Financing Global Education Opportunity. (2016). *The learning generation: Investing in education for a changing world.* New York: ICFGEO.

International Labour Organization (ILO). (1989). *Indigenous and Tribal peoples convention, C169, 27 June 1989, C169.* www.ilo.org/dyn/normlex/en/f?p=NORMLEXPUB:1 2100:0::NO::P12100_INSTRUMENT_ID:312314

International Network for Education in Emergencies (INEE). (2016). *Minimum standards for education: Preparedness, response, recovery.* www.ineesite.org/en/minimum-standards

International Organization for Migration. (2010). *World migration report 2010: The future of migration—Building capacities for change.* http://publications.iom.int/bookstore/index. php?main_page=product_info&cPath=37&products_id=665

Ismail, I., Bokare, S. F., Azizan, S. N., & Azman, N. (2013). Teaching via mobile phone: A case study on Malaysian teachers' technology acceptance and readiness. *The Journal of Educators Online, 10*(1), 1–38.

Jacob, W. J., & Holsinger, D. B. (2008). Inequality in education: A critical analysis. In Holsinger, D. B. & Jacob, W. J. (Eds.), *Inequality in education.* Netherlands: Springer. Pps. 1–33.

Jahoda, G. (1973). Psychology and the developing countries: Do they need each other? *International Social Science Journal, 25,* 461–474.

Jamison, D. T., & Lau, L. J. (1982). *Farmer education and farm efficiency.* Baltimore, MD: Johns Hopkins University Press.

Jamison, D. T., & Moock, P. R. (1984). Farmer education and farm efficiency in Nepal: The role of schooling, extension services, and cognitive skills. *World Development, 12,* 67–86.

Jencks, C. (1972). *Inequality: A reassessment of the effect of family and schooling in America.* New York: Basic Books.

Jerven, M. (2013). *Poor numbers: How we are misled by African development statistics and what to do about it.* Ithaca: Cornell University.

Johansson, E. (1987). Literacy campaigns in Sweden. In Arnove, R. F. & Graff, H. J. (Eds.), *National literacy campaigns.* New York: Plenum. Pps. 65–98.

Johnson, J. R., & Welsh, E. (2000). Comprehension of 'because' and 'so': The role of prior event representation. *First Language, 20,* 291–304.

Jourdan, D., Samdal, O., Diagne, F., & Carvalho, G. (2008). The future of health promotion in schools goes through the strengthening of teacher training at a global level. *Global Health Promotion, 15*(3), 36–38.

Jukes, M. C. H., Turner, E. L., Dubeck, M. M., Halliday, K. E., Inyega, H. N., Wolf, S., Zuilkowski, S. S., & Brooker, S. J. (2016). Improving literacy instruction in Kenya through teacher professional development and text messages support: A cluster randomized trial. *Journal of Research on Educational Effectiveness, 10*(3), 449–481.

Jung, H., Kwauk, C., Nuran, A., Robinson, J. P., Schouten, M., & Tanjeb, S. I. (2016). *Lesson study: Scaling up peer-to-peer learning for teachers in Zambia.* Washington, DC: Brookings.

Kagan, J., Moss, H. A., & Sigel, I. E. (1963). Psychological significance of styles of conceptualization. *Monographs of the Society for Research in Child Development, 28*(4), 73–112.

Kagawa, F., & Selby, D. (2012). Ready for the storm: Education for disaster risk reduction and climate change adaptation and mitigation. *Journal of Education for Sustainable Development, 6*(2), 207–217.

Kagitcibasi, C. (1996). *Family and human development across cultures: A view from the other side*. Mahwah, NJ: Lawrence Erlbaum Associates.

Kahan, D. M., Peters, E., Wittlin, M., Slovic, P., Ouellette, L. L., Braman, D., & Mandel, G. (2012). The polarizing impact of science literacy and numeracy on perceived climate change risks. *Nature Climate Change, 2*(10), 732–735.

Kahneman, D. (2011). *Thinking, fast and slow*. New York: Macmillan.

Kalas, I. (2010). *Recognizing the potential of ICT in early childhood education: Analytica survey*. UNESCO Institute for Information Technologies in Education. Moscow: IITE. http://iite.unesco.org/pics/publications/en/files/3214673.pdf

Kalas, I. (2012). *ICTs in early childhood care and education: A policy brief*. UNESCO Institute for Information Technologies in Education. Moscow: IITE. http://iite.unesco.org/pics/publications/en/files/3214720.pdf

Kam, M. (2013). Mobile learning games for low-income children in India: Lessons from 2004–2009. In Berge, Z. & Muilenburg, L. (Eds.), *Handbook of mobile learning*. New York: Routledge. Pps. 617–628.

Kamens, D. H. (2015). A maturing global testing regime meets the world economy: Test scores and economic growth, 1960–2012. *Comparative Education Review, 59*(3), 420–446.

Kamens, D. H., & McNeely, C. L. (2010). Globalization and the growth of international educational testing and national assessment. *Comparative Education Review, 54*(1), 5–25.

Kamil, M. L., Mosenthal, P. B., Pearson, P. D., & Barr, R. (Eds.). (2000). *Handbook of reading research: Volume III*. Mahwah, NJ: Lawrence Erlbaum Associates.

Kanbur, R., & Sumner, A. (2011). Poor countries or poor people? Development assistance and the new geography of global poverty. *Journal of International Development, 24*(6), 686–695.

Kanjee, A. (2009). *Assessment Overview*. Presentation at Conference on Developing a Vision for Assessment Systems. READ Technical Group. Washington, DC: World Bank.

Kapil, R. L. (1966). On the conflict potential of inherited boundaries in Africa. *World Politics, 18*(4), 656–673.

Kapitzke, C. (1999). Literacy and religion: The word, the holy word, and the world. In Wagner, D. A., Venezky, R. L., & Street, B. V. (Eds.). *Literacy: An international handbook*. Boulder, CO: Westview Press. Pps. 113–118.

Kaplan, A. (1964). *The conduct of inquiry: Methodology for behavioral science*. New York: Transaction Publishers.

Kaplan, R. D. (1994). The coming anarchy: How scarcity, crime, overpopulation, tribalism, and disease are rapidly destroying the social fabric of our planet. *Atlantic Monthly*, 44–76.

Kaplan, R. D. (2017). *Earning the Rockies: How geography shapes America's role in the world*. New York: Random House.

Karlan, D., & Appel, J. (2016). *Failing in the field: What we can learn when field research goes wrong*. Princeton: Princeton University Press.

Karoly, L. A., Kilburn, M. R., & Cannon, J. S. (2005). *Proven benefits of early childhood interventions*. Santa Monica, CA: Rand Corporation.

Kattan, R. B., & Burnett, N. (2004). *User fees in primary education*. Washington, DC: World Bank.

Kellaghan, T., Greaney, V., & Murray, S. (2009). *Using the results of a national assessment of educational achievement* (Vol. 5). World Bank Publications.

Keller, G. (2005). The education gospel: The economic power of schooling (review of M. Lazerson and N. Grubb). *The Review of Higher Education, 29*(1), 132–134.

Kenny, C. (2011). *Getting Better: Why global development is succeeding—and how we can improve the world even more*. New York: Basic Books.

Kerfoot, C., & Simon-Vandenbergen, A. M. (2014). Language in epistemic access: Mobilising multilingualism and literacy development for more equitable education in South Africa. *Language and Education, 29*(3), 1–9.

Khan, M. H. S., Hasan, M., & Clement, C. K. (2012). Barriers to the introduction of ICT into education in developing countries: The example of Bangladesh. *International Journal of Instruction, 5*(2), 61–80.

King, K. (2011). Skills and education for all from Jomtien (1990) to the GMR of 2012: A policy history. *International Journal of Training Research, 9*, 16–34.

Kipling, R. (1929). The white man's burden: The United States and the Philippine Islands, 1889. In *Rudyard Kipling's Verse: Definitive Edition*. Garden City, NY: Doubleday. Pps. 323–324.

Kipsang, R. B., & Piper, B. (2017). *Theory based evaluation in Kenya: Using research to inform national scale implementation*. Unpublished presentation at the Meetings of the Comparative and International Educaton Society, Atlanta, GA.

Kizilcec, R. F., Saltarelli, A. J., Reich, J., & Cohen, G. L. (2017). Closing global achievement gaps in MOOCs. *Science, 355*(6322), 251–252.

Klees, S. J. (2010). Aid, development, and education. *Current Issues in Comparative Education, 13*, 7–28.

Klees, S. J. (2016). Human capital and rates of return: Brilliant ideas or ideological dead ends?. *Comparative Education Review, 60*(4), 644–672.

Klees, S. J. (2017). Financing Education and All the Other SDGs: Global Taxation is Needed! *NORRAG News*. http://www.norrag.org/financing-education-and-all-the-other-sdgs-global-taxation-is-needed/

Knight, K. W. (2016). Public awareness and perception of climate change: A quantitative cross-national study. *Environmental Sociology, 2*(1), 101–113.

Koda, K. (2007). Cross-linguistic constraints on second-language reading development. In K. Koda (Ed.), *Reading and language learning*. Malden, MA: Blackwell Publishing. Pps. 1–34.

Koda, K., & Reddy, P. (2008). Cross-linguistic transfer in second language reading. *Language Teacher, 41*(4), 497–508.

Komatsu, H., & Rappleye, J. (2017). A new global policy regime founded on invalid statistics? Hanushek, Woessmann, PISA, and economic growth. *Comparative Education, 53*(2), 1–26.

Koole, M., & Ally, M. (2006). *Framework for the rational analysis of mobile education (FRAME). A model for evaluating mobile learning devices*. Thesis. Athabasca University, Athabasca.

Koole, M., McQuilkin, J. L., & Ally, M. (2010). Mobile learning in distance education: Utility or futility? *Journal of Distance Education, 24*, 59–82.

Koretz, D. (2008). *Measuring up: What educational testing really tells us*. Cambridge, MA: Harvard University Press.

Korinek, K., & Punpuing, S. (2012). The effect of household and community on school attrition: An analysis of Thai youth. *Comparative Education Review, 56*(3), 474–510.

Kozma, R. (2011). *Transforming education: The power of ICT policies*. Paris: UNESCO. Pps. 1–34.

Kraay, A., & McKenzie, D. (2014). Do poverty traps exist? Assessing the evidence. *The Journal of Economic Perspectives, 28*(3), 127–148.

Kremer, M., Brannen, C., & Glennerster, R. (2013). The challenge of education and learning in the developing world. *Science, 340*(6130), 297–300.

Kremer, M., & Holla, A. (2009). Improving education in the developing world: What have we learned from randomized evaluations? *Annual Review of Economics, 1*, 513–542.

Kroeber, A. L., & Kluckhohn, C. (1952). *Culture: A critical review of concepts and definitions*. Papers 47. Boston: Peabody Museum of Archaeology and Ethnology, Harvard University.

Krueger, A. (2012). *The rise and consequences of inequality*. Presentation made to the Center for American Progress, January 12.

Kubler-Ross, E. (1969). *On death and dying*. New York, NY: Macmillan.

Kuecken, M., & Valfort, M. A. (2013). When do textbooks matter for achievement? Evidence from African primary schools. *Economics Letters, 119*(3), 311–315.

Kuhl, P. K. (2010). Early language learning and literacy: Neuroscience implications for education. *Mind, Brain, and Education, 5*, 128–142.

Kuhn, T. S. (1962). *The structure of scientific revolutions* (1st ed.). Chicago: University of Chicago Press.

Ladipo, O., Murray, T. S., & Greaney, V. (2009). *Using the results of a national assessment of educational achievement* (Vol. 5). Washington: World Bank.

Ladson-Billings, G. (1995). Toward a theory of culturally relevant pedagogy. *American Educational Research Journal, 32*(3), 465–491.

Lake, A. (2011). Early childhood development—global action is overdue. *The Lancet, 378*(9799), 1277–1278.

Lareau, A. (2011). *Unequal childhoods: Class, race, and family life*. Berkeley: University of California Press.

Larsen, A. F., & Lilleør, H. B. (2014). Beyond the field: The impact of farmer field schools on food security and poverty alleviation. *World Development, 64*, 843–859.

Lave, J., & Wenger, E. (1991). *Situated learning: Legitimate peripheral participation*. Cambridge: Cambridge University Press.

Lawless, K. A., & Pellegrino, J. W. (2007). Professional development in integrating technology into teaching and learning: Knowns, unknowns, and ways to pursue better questions and answers. *Review of Educational Research, 77*(4), 575–614.

Lee, T. H. (2000). *Education in traditional China: A history* (Vol. 13). Netherlands: Brill.

Lee, T. M., Markowitz, E. M., Howe, P. D., Ko, C. Y., & Leiserowitz, A. A. (2015). Predictors of public climate change awareness and risk perception around the world. *Nature Climate Change, 5*(11), 1014–1020.

Lefstein, A., & Snell, J. (2013). Beyond a unitary conception of pedagogic pace: Quantitative measurement and ethnographic experience. *British Educational Research Journal, 39*(1), 73–106.

Leiderman, P. H., Tulkin, S. R., & Rosenfeld, A. H. (Eds.). (1977). *Culture and infancy: Variations in the human experience*. New York: Academic Press.

Lerner, D. (1958). *The passing of traditional society*. Glencoe, IL: The Free Press.

Lesaux, N. K., & Geva, E. (2006). Synthesis: Development of literacy in language minority students. In August, D. & Shanahan, T. (Eds.), *Developing literacy in second language learners: Report of the national reading panel on language minority and youth* (Chapter 3). Mahwah, NJ: Lawrence Erlbaum Associates. Pps. 53–74.

Lesaux, N. K., Pearson, M. R., & Siegel, L. S. (2006). The effects of timed and untimed testing conditions on the reading comprehension performance of adults with reading disabilities. *Reading and Writing, 19*(1), 21–48.

Lesgold, A. M., & Welch-Ross, M. (Eds.). (2012). *Improving adult literacy instruction: Options for practice and research*. Washington, DC: National Academies Press.

Leu, D. J., O'Byrne, W. I., Zawilinski, L., McVerry, J. G., & Everett-Cacopardo, H. (2009). Expanding the new literacies conversation. *Educational Researcher, 38*(4), 264–269.

Levin, H. M. (2014). More than just test scores. *Prospects: Quarterly Review of Comparative Education, 42*(3), 1–18.

LeVine, R. A. (1977). Child rearing as cultural adaptation. In Leiderman, P. H., Tulkin, S. R., & Rosenfeld, A. H. (Eds.). *Culture and infancy.* New York: Academic Press. Pps. 15–27.

LeVine, R. A. (2004). Challenging expert knowledge: Findings from an African study of infant care and development. In Gielen, U. P. & Roopnarine, J. (Eds.), *Childhood and adolescence: Cross-cultural perspectives and applications.* Westport, CT: Praeger. Pps. 149–165.

LeVine, R. A., Dixon, S., LeVine, S., Richman, A., Keefer, C., Leiderman, P. H., & Brazelton, T. B. (1994). *Child care and culture: Lessons from Africa.* New York: Cambridge University Press.

LeVine, R. A., LeVine, S., Schnell-Anzola, B., Rowe, M. L., & Dexter, E. (2012). *Literacy and mothering: How women's schooling changes the lives of the world's children.* New York: Oxford University Press.

Levy, F., & Murnane, R. J. (2007). How computerized work and globalization shape human skill demands. In Suarez-Orozco, M. M. (Ed.), *Learning in the global era: International perspectives on globalization and education.* Berkeley: University of California Press. Pps. 158–174.

Lewin, K. M. (2007). *The limits to growth of non-government private schooling in sub-Saharan Africa.* Research Monograph No. 5. Sussex: CREATE.

Lewis, M., & Lockheed, M. (2007). Social exclusion: The emerging challenge in girls' education. In Lewis, M. & Lockheed, M. (Eds.), *Exclusion, gender and education: Case studies from the developing world.* Pps. 1–27.

Lewis, O. (1959). *Five families: Mexican case studies in the culture of poverty.* New York: Basic Books.

Lewis, O. (1998). The culture of poverty. *Society, 35*(2), 7–9.

Li, J., Johnson, S. E., Han, W. J., Andrews, S., Kendall, G., Strazdins, L., & Dockery, A. (2014). Parents' nonstandard work schedules and child well-being: A critical review of the literature. *The Journal of Primary Prevention, 35*(1), 53-73.

Liyanagunawardena, T., Williams, S., & Adams, A. (2014). The impact and reach of MOOCs: A developing countries' perspective. *eLearning Papers,* Special edition, 38–46.

Lockheed, M. E. (2010). Policies, performance and panaceas: The role of international large-scale assessments in developing countries. *Compare: A Journal of Comparative and International Education, 42*(3), 509–545.

Lohr, S. (2009). *Sampling: Design and analysis.* New York: Nelson Education.

Loomba, A. (2015). *Colonialism/postcolonialism.* New York: Routledge.

Lu, Y., & Treiman, D. J. (2011). Migration, remittances and educational stratification among Blacks in Apartheid and Post-Apartheid South Africa. *Social Forces, 89*(4), 1119–1143.

Luria, A. R. (1976). *Cognitive development: Its cultural and social foundations.* Cambridge, MA: Harvard University Press.

Luria, A. R. (1987). *The mind of a mnemonist: A little book about a vast memory.* Cambridge, MA: Harvard University Press.

Lutz, W., Muttarak, R., & Striessnig, E. (2014). Universal education is key to enhanced climate adaptation. *Science, 346*(6213), 1061–1062.

Lyubomirsky, S., Sheldon, K. M., & Schkade, D. (2005). Pursuing happiness: The architecture of sustainable change. *Review of General Psychology, 9*(2), 111.

Maamouri, M. (1998). *Language education and human development: Arabic diglossia and its impact on the quality of education in the Arab region.* Philadelphia: Penn Linguistic Data Consortium.

Mambo, M. N. (2011). *Report on achievements under the DAPP/UNICEF partnership: Pre-service training of female teachers.* Blantyre, Malawi: Development Aid from People to People.

Mangione, P., & Speth, T. (1998). The transition to elementary school: A framework for creating early childhood continuity through home, school, and community partnerships. *Elementary School Journal, 98*(4), 381–397.

Mani, A., Mullainathan, S., Shafir, E., & Zhao, J. (2013). Poverty impedes cognitive function. *Science, 341*(6149), 976–980.

Manyika, J., Chui, M., Miremadi, M., Bughin, J., George, K., Willmott, P., & Dewhurst, M. (2017). *A future that works: Automation, employment, and productivity.* Washington, DC: McKinsey.

Maren, M. (2009). *The road to hell: The ravaging effects of foreign aid and international charity.* New York: Simon and Schuster.

Martinez, S., Naudeau, S., & Pereira, V. (2012). *The promise of preschool in Africa: A randomized impact evaluation of early childhood development in rural Mozambique.* Washington, DC: World Bank Group & Save the Children.

Marx, K. (1887). *Capital: A critique of political economy.* www.marxists.org/archive/marx/works/1867-c1/

Marzano, R. (2001). *Designing a new taxonomy of educational objectives: Experts in assessment.* Thousand Oaks, CA: Sage.

Maslow, A. (1943). A theory of human motivation. *Psychological Review, 50*(4), 370–396.

Masters, J. C. (1984). Psychology, research, and social policy. *American Psychologist, 39*, 851–862.

Mayer, R. E. (2002). Rote versus meaningful learning. *Theory Into Practice, 41*(4), 226–232.

Mazrui, A. A. (1975). The African university as a multinational corporation: Problems of penetration and dependency. *Harvard Educational Review, 45*(2), 191–210.

McCall, R. B. (2009). Evidence-based programming in the context of practice and policy. *SRCD Social Policy Report, 23*(3), 3–20.

McClelland, D. (1961). *The achieving society.* Princeton, NJ: Van Nostrand.

McCoy, D. C., Peet, E. D., Ezzati, M., Danaei, G., Black, M. M., Sudfeld, C. R., Fawzi, W., & Fink, G. (2016). Early childhood developmental status in low- and middle-income countries: National, regional, and global prevalence estimates using predictive modeling. *PLoS Medicine, 13*(6), e1002034.

McEwan, P. J. (2015). Improving learning in primary schools of developing countries: A meta-analysis of randomized experiments. *Review of Educational Research, 85*, 353–394.

McGrath, S. (2012). Vocational education and training for development: A policy in need of a theory? *International Journal of Educational Development, 32*(5), 623–631.

McLaren, P. (2015). *Pedagogy of insurrection: From resurrection to revolution.* New York: Peter Lang.

McMichael, P. (2011). *Development and social change: A global perspective* (5th ed.). New York: Sage Publications.

McNamara, R. S. (1973). *Address to Board of Governors.* Nairobi, Kenya: World Bank Group, September 24, 1973.

Mead, M. (1928). *Coming of age in Samoa: A psychological study of primitive youth for western civilization.* New York: Blue Ribbon Books.

Mead, M. (1964). *Continuities in cultural evolution.* New York: Transaction Publishers.

Medhi, I., Sagar, A., & Toyama, K. (2007). Text-free user interfaces for illiterate and semiliterate users. *Information Technologies and International Development, 4*(1), 37–50.

Mehler, J., Pallier, C., & Christophe, A. (1998). Language and cognition. *Advances in Psychological Science, 1*, 381–398.

Mendoza, D., & Vergel de Dios, B. (2012). *The Pink phone revolution in Cambodia: A case study*. Phnom Penh: OXFAM.

Merton, R. K. (1968). The Matthew effect in science. *Science, 159*(3810), 56–63.

Meyer, H. D., & Benavot, A. (Eds.). (2013). *PISA, power and policy: The emergence of global educational governance*. Oxford: Symposium Books.

Meyer, J. W., Ramirez, F. O., & Soysal, Y. N. (1992). World expansion of mass education, 1870–1980. *Sociology of Education, 65*, 128–149.

Michaelowa, K. (2001). Primary education quality in francophone Sub-Saharan Africa: Determinants of learning achievement and efficiency considerations. *World Development, 29*(10), 1699–1716.

Milanovic, B. (2016). *Global inequality: A new approach for the age of globalization*. Cambridge: Harvard University Press.

Miller, K. F., Smith, C. M., Zhu, J., & Zhang, H. (1995). Preschool origins of cross-national differences in mathematical competence: The role of number naming systems. *Psychological Science, 6*, 56–60.

Mitra, S. (2003). Minimally invasive education: A progress report on the 'hole-in-the-wall' experiments. *British Journal of Educational Technology, 34*(3), 367–371.

Mo, D., Swinnen, J., Zhang, L., Yi, H., Qu, Q., Boswell, M., & Rozelle, S. (2012). *Can One Laptop Per Child reduce the digital divide and educational gap? Evidence from a randomized experiment in migrant schools in Beijing*. Working Paper 233. Rural Education Action Project. Palo Alto: Stanford.

Mochizuki, Y., & Bryan, A. (2015). Climate change education in the context of education for sustainable development: Rationale and principles. *Journal of Education for Sustainable Development, 9*(1), 4–26.

Moll, L. C. (Ed.). (1990). *Vygotsky and education: Instructional implications and applications of sociohistorical psychology*. New York: Cambridge University Press.

Moll, L. C., Amanti, C., Neff, D., & Gonzalez, N. (1992). Funds of knowledge for teaching: Using a qualitative approach to connect homes and classrooms. *Theory Into Practice, 31*(2), 132–141.

Moore, A.-M. S., DeStefano, J., & Adelman, E. (2011). Time misspent, opportunities lost: Use of time in school and learning. In Jacob, W. J., John, N., & Hawkins, J. N. (Eds.), *Policy debates in comparative, international, and development education*. New York: Palgrave. Pps. 247–264.

Moore, L. C. (2006). Learning by heart in Qur'anic and public schools in northern Cameroon. *Social Analysis, 50*(3), 109–126.

Mosse, D. (2013). The anthropology of international development. *Annual Review of Anthropology, 42*, 227–246.

Mourshed, M., Chijioke, C., & Barber, M. (2010). *How the world's most improved school systems keep getting better*. New York: McKinsey.

Moyo, D. (2009). *Dead aid: Why aid is not working and how there is a better way for Africa*. New York: Farrar, Straus and Giroux.

Mufanechiya, A., & Mufanechiya, T. (2011). Using mother tongue as a medium of instruction in the teaching of mathematics in the Zimbabwean junior primary schools: Desirable or feasible? *Journal of Asian Scientific Research, 1*(4), 194.

Mullainathan, S., & Shafir, E. (2013). *Scarcity: Why having too little means so much*. New York: Henry Holt.

Mullis, I. V., Martin, M. O., & Loveless, T. (2016). *20 years of TIMSS: International trends in mathematics and science achievement, curriculum, and instruction*. International Association for the Evaluation of Educational Achievement. Boston: Boston College.

Mundy, K., & Menashy, F. (2014). The World Bank and private provision of schooling: A look through the lens of sociological theories of organizational hypocrisy. *Comparative Education Review, 58*(3), 401–427.

Muralidharan, K., & Sundararaman, V. (2009). *Teacher performance pay: Experimental evidence from India.* National Bureau of Economic Research Working Paper 15323, Cambridge, MA: NBER.

Murdock, G. P. (1959). *Africa: Its peoples and their culture history.* New York: McGraw-Hill.

Muskin, J. A. (1997). Becoming an independent entrepreneur in the informal sector of northern Côte d'Ivoire: What role can primary schooling play? *International Journal of Educational Development, 17*(3), 265–283.

Muskin, J. A. (2012). Educating youth for entrepreneurship in work & life: Experience of a junior secondary school project in Morocco. *Journal of International Cooperation in Education, 15,* 107–127.

Muskin, J. A. (2015). From good ideas to good practice: Putting teachers at the center of education improvement, where they belong. *Educational Assessment, Evaluation and Accountability, 27*(1), 93–102.

Mustard, J. F., & Young, M. E. (2007). Measuring child development to leverage ECD policy and investment. Young, M. E. & Richardson, L. M. (Eds.), *Early Child Development From Measurement to Action: A Priority for Growth and Equity.* Washington, DC: World Bank Publications. Pps. 253–292.

Muthwii, M. (2004). Language of instruction: A qualitative analysis of the perception of parents, pupils, and teachers among the Kalenjin in Kenya. *Language, Culture, and Curriculum, 17,* 15–32.

Myers, R. G. (1995). *The twelve who survive: Strengthening programs of early childhood development in the Third World.* Ypsilanti: High/Scope Press.

Nag, S., Chiat, S., Torgerson, C., & Snowling, M. J. (2014). *Literacy, foundation learning and assessment in developing countries.* London: DFID.

Naslund-Hadley, E., Martínez, E., Loera, A., & Hernández-Agramonte, J. M. (2012). *Leading the way to math and science success: Challenges and triumphs in Paraguay.* Washington, DC: IDB. http://publications.iadb.org/bitstream/handle/11319/668/Leading%20the%20Way%20to%20Math%20and%20Science%20Success:%20Challenges%20and%20Triumphs%20in%20Paraguay.pdf?sequence=1

National Reading Panel. (2000). *Teaching children to read: An evidence-based assessment of the scientific research literature on reading and its implications for reading instruction: Reports of the subgroups.* Bethesda, MD: NICHD.

Naylor, R., & Sayed, Y. (2014). *Teacher quality: Evidence review.* Canberra: Office of Development effectiveness, Commonwealth of Australia.

Neisser, U. (1967/2014). *Cognitive psychology.* Washington, DC: Psychology Press.

Neisser, U., Boodoo, G., Bouchard, T. J., Jr., Boykin, A. W., Brody, N., Ceci, S. J., Halpern, D. R., Loehlin, J. C., Perloff, R., Sternberg, R. J., & Urbina, S. (1996). Intelligence: Knowns and unknowns. *American Psychologist, 51*(2), 77.

Neuman, M. J., Kimberly Josephson, K., & Chua, P. G. (2015). *Early childhood care and education (ECCE) personnel in low- and middle-income countries: A review of the literature.* Paris: UNESCO.

Nicolas, S., Andrieu, B., Croizet, J.-C., Sanitioso, R. B., & Burman, J. T. (2013). Sick? Or slow? On the origins of intelligence as a psychological object. *Intelligence, 41*(5), 699–711.

Nores, M., & Barnett, S. (2010). Benefits of early childhood interventions across the world: (Under)investing in the very young. *Economics of Education Review, 29,* 271–282.

Norton, B., & Toohey, K. (2011). Identity, language learning, and social change. *Language Teaching*, *44*(4), 412–446.

Nove, A., Hulton, L., Martin-Hilber, A., & Matthews, Z. (2014). Establishing a baseline to measure change in political will and the use of data for decision-making in maternal and newborn health in six African countries. *International Journal of Gynecology & Obstetrics*, *127*(1), 102–107.

Nsamenang, B. (2011). The importance of mixed age groups in Cameroon. In Kernan, M. & Singer, E. (Eds.), *Peer relationships in early childhood education and care*. New York: Taylor & Francis. Pps. 61–73.

Nsamenang, B., & Tchombe, T. M. S. (Eds.). (2011). *Handbook on Africa educational theories and practices*. Paris: Harmatton.

Nugroho, D., & Lonsdale, M. (2010). *Evaluation of OLPC programs globally: A literature review* (Version 4). Canberra: ACER.

Nussbaum, M. C. (2011). *Creating capabilities*. Cambridge, MA: Harvard University Press.

OECD. (2012). *Equity and quality in education: Supporting disadvantaged schools and students*. Paris: OECD Publishing.

OECD. (2013). *Skilled for life? Key findings from the survey of adult skills*. Paris: OECD.

OECD. (2014). *TALIS 2013 results: An international perspective on teaching and learning*. Paris: OECD.

OECD. (2015). *Students, computers and learning: Making the connection*. Paris: OECD.

OECD/Statistics Canada. (1995). *Literacy, Economy and Society*. Paris: OECD.

Ogbu, J. (1978). *Minority education and caste* (Vol. 581). New York: Academic Press.

Oketch, M. (2007). To vocationalise or not to vocationalise? Perspectives on current trends and issues in technical and vocational education and training (TVET) in Africa. *International Journal of Educational Development*, *27*(2), 220–234.

OLPC [One Laptop Per Child]. (2013). *Project website*. http://one.laptop.org/

Oney, B., & Durgunoglu, A. Y. (1997). Beginning to read in Turkish: A phonologically transparent orthography. *Applied Psycholinguistics*, *18*, 1–15.

Opertti, R., & Brylinski, E. (2016). *Global monitoring of target 4.7: Themes in national curriculum frameworks*. GEM Background Paper. Paris: UNESCO-IBE.

Osborne, A. B. (1996). Practice into theory into practice: Culturally relevant pedagogy for students we have marginalized and normalized. *Anthropology and Education Quarterly*, *27*(3), 285–314.

O'Sullivan, M. C. (2006). Teaching large classes: The international evidence and a discussion of some good practice in Ugandan primary schools. *International Journal of Educational Development*, *26*(1), 24–37.

Pachler, N., Cook, J., & Bachmair, B. (2010). Appropriation of mobile cultural resources for learning. *International Journal of Mobile and Blended Learning*, *2*, 1–21.

Paiwastoon. (2013). *Project website*. http://svr1.paiwastoon.net/mliteracy/

Palmer, R. (2007). *Skills development, the enabling environment and informal micro-enterprise in Ghana*. Ph.D. dissertation. Edinburgh: University of Edinburgh.

Paris, S. G. (2005). Reinterpreting the development of reading skills. *Reading Research Quarterly*, *40*, 184–202.

Paris, S. G., & Paris, A. H. (2006). The influence of developmental skill trajectories on assessments of children's early reading. In Damon, W., Lerner, R., Renninger, K. A. & Siegel, I. E. (Eds.), *Handbook of child psychology: Vol. 4. Child psychology in practice* (6th ed.). Hoboken, NJ: John Wiley & Sons. Pps. 48–74.

Park, H., Buchmann, C., Choi, J., & Merry, J. J. (2016). Learning beyond the school walls: Trends and implications. *Annual Review of Sociology*, *42*, 231–252.

Partant, F. (1982). *La fin de developpement: Naissance d'une alternative*. Paris: Maspero.

Patrinos, H. A., & Velez, E. (2009). Costs and beniets of bilingual education in Guatemala: A partial analysis. *International Journal of Educational Development, 29*, 594–598.

Pawar, U. S., Pal, J., & Toyama, K. (2006). Multiple mice for computers in education in developing countries. *Proceedings of the Information and Communication Technologies and Development*, Pps. 64-71.

Paxson, C., & Schady, N. (2005). Child health and economic crisis in Peru. *The World Bank Economic Review, 19*(2), 203–223.

Paxson, C., & Schady, N. (2007). Cognitive development among young children in Ecuador: The roles of wealth, health, and parenting. *Journal of Human Resources, 42*(1), 49–84.

Pegrum, M., Howitt, C., & Striepe, M. (2013). Learning to take the tablet: How preservice teachers use iPads to facilitate their learning. *Australasian Journal of Educational Technology, 29*(4), 464–479.

Pellegrino, J. W., & Hilton, M. L. (Eds.). (2012). *Education for life and work: Developing transferable knowledge and skills in the 21st century*. Washington: Division of Behavioral and Social Sciences and Education, National Academy of Sciences.

Penson, J., & Tomlinson, K. (2007). *Rapid response: Programming for education needs in emergencies*. Paris: CfBT Education Trust and IIEP-UNESCO.

Peyton, J. K. (2015). Language of instruction: Research findings and program and instructional implications. *Reconsidering Development, 4*(1), 16–34.

Pflepsen, A. (2015). *Planning for language use in education: Best practices and practical steps to improve learning outcomes*. Washington, DC: USAID Africa Bureau.

Pfost, M., Hattie, J., Dorflor, T., & Artelt, C. (2014). Individual differences in reading development: A review of 25 years of empirical research on Matthew effects in reading. *Review of Educational Research, 84*(2), 203–244.

Phillips, D., & Schweisfurth, M. (2014). *Comparative and international education: An introduction to theory, method, and practice*. London: A&C Black.

Pigozzi, M. J., Carrol, B., Hayden, J., & Ndaruhutse, S. (2014). Fragile and conflict-affected situations. In Wagner, D. A. (Ed.), *Learning and education in developing countries: Research and policy for the post-2015 UN development goals*. New York: Palgrave Macmillan. Pps. 58–73.

Piketty, T., & Goldhammer, A. (2014). *Capital in the twenty-first century*. Cambridge: Belknap Press.

Pinker, S. (2007). *The stuff of thought: Language as a window into human nature*. London: Viking.

Pintrich, P. R. (1994). Continuities and discontinuities: Future directions for research in educational psychology. *Educational Psychologist, 29*(3), 137–148.

Pioneers Australia. (2012). *South Sudan: Across radio*. www.pioneers.org.au/Projects/OARF/ACROSS-Radio-SOUTH-SUDAN.aspx

Piper, B., & Korda, M. (2011). *EGRA Plus: Liberia*. Program Evaluation Report. RTI International.

Piper, B., & Kwayumba, D. (2014). *The Primary Math and Reading Initiative (PRIMR), Kisumu Information and Communication Technology (ICT) Intervention: Endline report*. Washington, DC: RTI.

Piper, B., & Mugenda, A. (2012). *The primary math and reading (PRIMR) initiative: Baseline report*. Technical Report. Research Triangle Park. NC: RTI International.

Piper, B., & Miksic, E. (2011). Mother tongue and reading: Using early grade reading assessments to investigate language-of-instruction policy in East Africa. In *The early grade reading assessment: Applications and interventions to improve basic literacy*. Research Triangle Park, NC: RTI Press. Pps. 139–182.

Piper, B., & Zuilkowski, S. S. (2016). The role of timing in assessing oral reading fluency and comprehension in Kenya. *Language Testing, 33*(1), 75–98.

Piper, B., Zuilkowski, S. S., & Mugenda, A. (2014). Improving reading outcomes in Kenya: First-year effects of the PRIMR initiative. *International Journal of Educational Development, 37*, 11–21.

Piper, B., Zuilkowski, S. S., & Ongele, S. (2016). Implementing mother tongue instruction in the real world: Results from a medium-scale randomized controlled trial in Kenya. *Comparative Education Review, 60*(4), 776–807.

Platas, L. M., Ketterlin-Geller, L. R., & Sitabkhan, Y. (2016). Using an assessment of early mathematical knowledge and skills to inform policy and practice: Examples from the early grade mathematics assessment. *International Journal of Education in Mathematics, Science and Technology, 4*(3), 163–173.

Pollitt, E. (1990). *Malnutrition and infection in the classroom.* Paris: UNESCO.

Postiglione, G. A. (2013). *China's national minority education: Culture, schooling, and development.* London: Routledge.

Pouezevara, S., & Strigel, C. (2011). Using information and communication technologies to support EGRA. In Gove, A. & Wetterberg, A. (Eds.), *The early grade reading assessment: Applications and interventions to improve basic literacy.* Durham, NC.: Research Triangle Institute. Pps. 183–226.

Prahalad, C. K. (2006). *The fortune at the bottom of the pyramid: Eradicating poverty through profits.* Upper Saddle River, NJ: Wharton School Publishing.

Pritchett, L. (2009). The policy irrelevance of the economics of education: Is normative as positive just useless, or worse? In Cohen, J. & Easterly, B. (Eds.), *What works in development: Thinking big and thinking small.* Washington, DC: The Brookings Institution. Pps. 130–164.

Pritchett, L. (2013). *The rebirth of education: Schooling ain't learning.* Washington, DC: Center for Global Development.

Pritchett, L., Banerji, R., & Kenny, C. (2013). *Schooling is not education! Using assessment to change the politics of non-learning.* Washington, DC: Center for Global Development.

Pritchett, L., & Beatty, A. (2012). The negative consequences of overambitious curricula in developing countries. *Center for Global Development Working Paper* 12-035. Pps. 1–53.

Pritchett, L., & Beatty, A. (2015). Slow down, you're going too fast: Matching curricula to student skill levels. *International Journal of Educational Development, 40*, 276–288.

Pritchett, L., & Summers, L. H. (1996). Wealthier is healthier. *Journal of Human Resources, 31*, 841–868.

Proctor, H. (2013). Kurt Koffka and the expedition to Central Asia. *PsyAnima, Dubna Psychological Journal, 6*(3), 43–52.

Psacharopoulos, G. (1985). Returns to education: A further international update and implications. *Journal of Human Resources, 20*(4), 583–564.

Psacharopoulos, G., & Patrinos, H. A. (2004). Returns to investment in education: A further update. *Education Economics, 12*(2), 111–134.

Puchner, L. (2001). Researching women's literacy in Mali: A case study of dialogue among researchers, practitioners, and policy makers. *Comparative Education Review, 45*(2), 242–256.

Putnam, R. D. (2015). *Our kids: The American dream in crisis.* New York: Simon and Schuster.

Radelet, S. (2016). Prosperity rising: The success of global development-and how to keep it going. *Foreign Affairs, 95*, 85–95.

Raftree, L. (2013). *Landscape review: Mobiles for youth workforce development.* Washington, DC: USAID.

Rahnema, M. (1990). Participatory action research: The 'last temptation of saint' development. *Alternatives: Global, Local, Political, 15*(2), 199–226.

Rajan, K., Kennedy, J., & King, L. (2013). Is wealthier always healthier in poor countries? The health implications of income, inequality, poverty, and literacy in India. *Social Science & Medicine, 88,* 98–107.

Rakoff, J. (2016). Neuroscience and the Law: Don't Rush In. *The New York Review of Books.* www.nybooks.com/articles/2016/05/12/neuroscience-and-the-law-dont-rush-in/

Ramalingam, B. (2013). *Aid on the edge of chaos: Rethinking international cooperation in a complex world.* London: Oxford University Press.

Rangaswamy, N., & Cutrell, E. (2012). Anthropology, development and ICTs: Slums, youth and the mobile Internet in urban India. *Infromation Technology and International Development, 9*(2), 51–63.

Ravallion, M. (2012). Fighting poverty one experiment at a time: A review of Abhijit Banerjee and Esther Duflo's Poor economics: A radical rethinking of the way to fight global poverty. *Journal of Economic Literature, 50*(1), 103–114.

Reagan, T. (2005). *Non-Western educational traditions: Indigenous approaches to education thought and practice* (3rd ed.). Mahwah, NJ: LEA.

Reddy, P. P., & Koda, K. (2013). Orthographic constraints on phonological awareness in biliteracy development. *Writing Systems Research, 5*(1), 110–130.

Reed, N. A. (2001). *The caste war of Yucatan.* Palo Alto: Stanford University Press.

Reimers, M., & Klasen, S. (2013). Revisiting the role of education for agricultural productivity. *American Journal of Agricultural Economics, 95*(1), 131–152.

Research Triangle Institute (RTI). (2009). *Early grade reading assessment toolkit.* Washington, DC: RTI International.

Research Triangle Institute (RTI). (2015). *Early learning assessments: A retrospective.* Paris: UNESCO Background paper for EFA Global Monitoring Report 2015.

Results for Development Institute. (2015). *Bringing learning to light: The role of citizen-led assessments in shifting the education agenda.* Policy Report. Washington, DC: R4D. http://r4d.org/knowledge-center/bringing-learning-light-role-citizen-led-assessments-shifting-education-agenda-0

Ricciardi, J. (2011). Review of Raj Patel, the value of nothing: How to reshape market society and redefine democracy. London: Portobello Books. *Journal of Asian and African Studies, 46*(3), 307–313.

Richter, L. M., Daelmans, B., Lombardi, J., Heymann, J., Boo, F. L., Behrman, J. R., Lu, C., Lucas, J. E., Perez-Escamilla, R., Dua, T., Bhutta, Z. A., Stenberg, K, Gertler, P., & Darmstadt, G. L. (2016). Investing in the foundation of sustainable development: Pathways to scale up for early childhood development. *The Lancet, 389*(10064), 103–118.

Rindermann, H., & Baumeister, A. E. (2015). Parents' SES vs. parental educational behavior and children's development: A reanalysis of the Hart and Risley study. *Learning and Individual Differences, 37,* 133–138.

Rist, G. (2008). *The history of development: From Western origins to global faith.* London: Zed Books.

Rivkin, S., Hanushek, E., & Kain, J. (2005). Teachers, schools and academic achievement. *Econometrica, 73*(2), 417–458.

Robertson, S. L., & Dale, R. (2015). Towards a 'critical cultural political economy' account of the globalising of education. *Globalisation, Societies and Education, 13*(1), 149–170.

Robinson, J. P. (2011). *A global compact on learning: Taking action on education in developing countries.* Center for Universal Education at Brookings. Washington, DC: Brookings Institution.

Robinson-Pant, A. (2016). *Learning knowledge and skills for agriculture to improve rural livelihoods*. Paris: UNESCO.

Rodney, W. (1972). *How Europe underdeveloped Africa*. Washington, DC: Howard University Press.

Rogoff, B., & Angelillo, C. (2002). Investigating the coordinated functioning of multifaceted cultural practices in human development. *Human Development, 45*, 211–225.

Rogoff, B., & Lave, J. (Eds.). (1984). *Everyday cognition: Its development in social context*. Cambridge, MA: Harvard University Press.

Rose, P. (2015). Three lessons for educational quality in post-2015 goals and targets: Clarity, measurability and equity. *International Journal of Educational Development, 40*, 289–296.

Rosenblatt, D. (2004). An anthropology made safe for culture: Patterns of practice and the politics of difference in Ruth Benedict. *American Anthropologist, 106*(3), 459–472.

Rostow, W. W. (1960). *The stages of economic growth: A non-communist manifesto*. New York: Cambridge University Press.

RTI/USAID. (2012). *Student performance in reading and mathematics, pedagogic practice, and school management in Doukkala Abda, Morocco*. Washington: USAID/RTI.

Rubens, A., & Crouch, L. (2009). *Early Grade Mathematics Assessment (EGMA): A conceptual framework based on mathematics skills development in children*. EdData II Technical Report. Washington: USAID.

Rutter, M., & O'Connor, T. G. (2004). Are there biological programming effects for psychological development? Findings from a study of Romanian adoptees. *Developmental Psychology, 40*, 81–94.

Sachs, J. D. (2005). *The end of poverty: Economic possibilities for our time*. New York: Penguin.

Sachs, J. D. (2015). *The age of sustainable development*. New York: Columbia University Press.

Sahlberg, P. (2011). *Finnish lessons: What can the world learn from educational change in Finland?* New York: Teachers College Press.

Samant, D., Matter, R., & Harniss, M. (2013). Realizing the potential of accessible ICTs in developing countries. *Disability and Rehabilitation: Assistive Technology, 8*(1), 11–20.

Samoff, J., & Carroll, B. (2004). Comments on the promise of partnership and continuities of dependence. *African Studies Review, 47*(1), 201–207.

Sandefur, J. (2015). Great gatsby revisited: How inequality explains learning outcomes around the world. *Blog Post*. www.cgdev.org/blog/great-gatsby-curve-younger-and-poorer-how-inequality-explains-learning-outcomes-around-world

Sandefur, J. (2016). *The case for global standardized testing*. Washington, DC: Center for Global Development.

Savedoff, W. D., Levine, R., & Birdsall, N. (2006). *When will we ever learn? Improving lives through impact evaluation*. Washington, DC: Center for Global Development.

Saxe, G. B., & de Kirby, K. (2014). Cultural context of cognitive development. *Wiley Interdisciplinary Reviews: Cognitive Science, 5*(4), 447–461.

Sayre, R. K., Devercelli, A. E., Neuman, M., & Wodon, Q. (2015). *Investing in early childhood development: Review of the World Bank's recent experience*. Washington, DC: World Bank.

Scarborough, H. S. (1998). Early identification of children at risk for reading disabilities: Phonological awareness and some other promising predictors. In Shapiro, B. K., Accardo, P. J., & Capute, A. J. (Eds.), *Specific reading disability: A view of the spectrum*. Timonium, MD: York Press. Pps. 79–119.

Schiemer, M., & Proyer, M. (2013). Teaching children with disabilities: ICTs in Bangkok and Addis Ababa. *Multicultural Education & Technology Journal, 7*(2/3), 99–112.

Schierhout, G. (2005). *Impact assessment of a new programming component on HIV and AIDS*. Johannesburg: Takalani Sesame Project, South African Broadcasting Corporation

Ltd, Department of Education of South Africa and Sesame Workshop supported by USAID and Sanlam.

Schliemann, A. D., Araujo, C., Cassundé, M. A., Macedo, S., & Nicéas, L. (1998). Use of multiplicative commutativity by school children and street sellers. *Journal for Research in Mathematics Education, 29*(4), 422–435.

Schneider, M. K. (2016). *School choice: The end of public education?* New York: Teachers College Press.

Schneider, M. K., & Stern, E. (2010). The cognitive perspective on learning: Ten cornerstone findings. In Organisation for Economic Co-Operation and Development (OECD) (Ed.), *The nature of learning: Using research to inspire practice*. Paris: OECD. Pps. 69–90.

Schultz, T. (1961). Investment in human capital. *American Economic Review, 51*, 1–17.

Schweisfurth, M. (2011). Learner-centred education in developing country contexts: From solution to problem? *International Journal of Educational Development, 31*(5), 425–432.

Schweisfurth, M. (2013a). *Learner-centred education in international perspective: Whose pedagogy for whose development?* London: Routledge.

Schweisfurth, M. (2013b). Learner-centred education in international perspective. *Journal of International and Comparative Education, 2*(1), 1–8.

Scribner, S., & Cole, M. (1981). *The psychology of literacy*. Cambridge: Harvard University Press.

Segall, M., Campbell, D. T., & Herskovits, M. J. (1966). *The influence of culture on visual perception*. Indianapolis, IN: Bobbs-Merrill.

Seligman, M. E. P. (2011). *Flourish*. New York, NY: Simon & Schuster.

Seligman, M. E. P., & Csikszentmihalyi, M. (2000). Positive psychology: An introduction. *American Psychologist, 55*, 5–14.

Seligson, M. A. (1998). The dual gaps: An updated overview of theory and research. In Seligson, M. A., Passé-Smith, J. T., & Seligson, M. A. (Eds.), *Development and underdevelopment: The political economy of global inequality*. Boulder, CO: Lynne Rienner Publishers. Pps. 3–8.

Sen, A. (1979/2010). Equality of what? In MacMurrin, S. M. (Eds.), *The Tanner lectures on human values* (Vol. 4, 2nd ed.). Cambridge: Cambridge University Press. Pps. 195–220. http://tannerlectures.utah.edu/_documents/a-to-z/s/sen80.pdf

Sen, A. (1999). *Development as freedom*. New York: Anchor books.

Servan-Schreiber, J. J. (1967). *Le défi Americain*. Paris: Denoel.

Seymour, P. H., Aro, M., & Erskine, J. M. (2003). Foundation literacy acquisition in European orthographies. *British Journal of psychology, 94*(2), 143–174.

Shonkoff, J. P. (2010). Building a new biodevelopmental framework to guide the future of early childhood policy. *Child Development, 81*(1), 357–367.

Shuler, C. (2012). *iLearn II: An analysis of the education category of apple's app store*. New York: Joan Ganz Cooney Center at Sesame Workshop.

Silva, E. (2007). *On the clock: Rethinking the way schools use time*. Washington, DC: Education Sector.

Simon, H. A. (1979). Rational decision making in business organizations. *American Economic Review, 69*, 493–513.

Singh, R., & Sarkar, S. (2015). Does teaching quality matter? Students learning outcome related to teaching quality in public and private primary schools in India. *International Journal of Educational Development, 41*, 153–163.

Sitabkhan, Y. (2015). '¡Chalinas a 20 Pesos!': Children's economic ideas developed through selling. *Mind, Culture, and Activity, 22*(3), 269–279.

Sjoberg, S. (2007). PISA and 'real life challenges': Mission impossible? In Hopmann, S. T., Brinek, G., & Retzl, M. (Eds.), *PISA according to PISA: Does PISA keep what it promises?* Vienna: LIT Verlag. http://folk.uio.no/sveinsj/Sjoberg-PISA-book-2007.pdf

Skeldon, R. (2012). Migration transitions revisited: Their continued relevance for the development of migration theory. *Population, Space and Place, 18*(2), 154–166.

Smail, G. (2017). Politicized pedagogy in Morocco: A comparative case of teachers of English and Arabic. *International Journal of Educational Development, 53*, 151–162.

Small, M. L., Harding, D. J., & Lamont, M. (2010). Reconsidering culture and poverty. *The Annals of the American Academy of Political and Social Science, 629*(1), 6–27.

Smith, M. L., & Glass, G. V. (1979). *Relationship of class size to classroom processes, teacher satisfaction and pupil affect: A meta-analysis.* San Francisco: Far West Laboratory for Educational Research and Development.

Smits, J., Huisman, J., & Kruijff, K. (2008). *Home language and education in the developing world.* Background paper prepared for the Education for All Global Monitoring Report 2009, Overcoming Inequality: Why governance matters. Paris: UNESCO.

Snow, C. E., Burns, M. S., & Griffin, P. (1998). *Preventing reading difficulties in young children.* Washington: National Academy Press.

Snow, C. E., & Kang, J. Y. (2006). Becoming bilingual, biliterate, and bicultural. In Renninger, K. A., Sigel, I. E., Damon, W., & Lerner, R. M. (Eds.), *Handbook of child psychology: Vol. 4. Child psychology in practice* (6th ed.). New York: Wiley. Pps. 75–102.

South Africa Department of Basic Education (SADBE), South Africa. (2013). *Report on the annual national assessment of 2013: Grades 1 to 6 & 9.* Pretoria: DBE. www.education.gov.za/LinkClick.aspx?fileticket=Aiw7HW8ccic%3D&tabid=36

Sparrow, B., Liu, J., & Wegner, D. M. (2011). Google effects on memory: Cognitive consequences of having information at our fingertips. *Science, 333*(6043), 776–778.

Sperber, J. (2013). *Karl Marx: A nineteenth-century life.* New York: Norton.

Spratt, J. E. (1988). *Passing and failing in Moroccan primary schools: Institutional and individual dimensions of grade repetition in a selective school system.* Ph.D dissertation. Philadelphia: University of Pennsylvania.

Stanovich, K. E. (1986). Matthew effects in reading: Some consequences of individual differences in the acquisition of literacy. *Reading Research Quarterly, 21*, 360–407.

Steiner-Khamsi, G. (2010). The politics and economics of comparison. *Comparative Education Review, 54*(3), 323–342.

Steiner-Khamsi, G. (2015). Teachers and teacher education policies. In McCowan, T. & Unterhalter, E. (Eds.), *Education and international development: An introduction.* New York: Bloomsbury Publishing. Pps. 149–168.

Stephens, D. (2007). *Culture in education and development principles, practice and policy: Bristol papers in education.* London: Symposium Books.

Stern, A. (2016). *Raising the floor: How a universal basic income can renew our economy and rebuild the American dream.* New York: Public Affairs.

Stern, J. M., & Heyneman, S. P. (2013). Low-fee private schooling: The case of Kenya. In Srivastava, P. (Ed.), *Low-fee private schooling: Aggravating equity or mitigating disadvantage?* London: Symposium Books. Pps. 105–128.

Sternberg, R. J., Grigorenko, E. L., & Kidd, K. K. (2005). Intelligence, race, and genetics. *American Psychologist, 60*(1), 46.

Stevenson, H. W. (1972). *Children's learning.* New York: Appleton-Century-Crofts.

Stevenson, H. W., & Stigler, J. W. (1982). *The learning gap: Why our schools are failing and what we can learn from Japanese and Chinese education.* New York: Summit.

Stewart, A. (2013). *"M" is for mobile: Sesame Workshop's mobile initiatives in India.* Presentation at Connected Living Asia Summit mEducation, Shanghai, 25 June. www.gsma.com/connectedliving/wp-content/uploads/2013/03/MAE-Connected-Living-Summit_Sesame.pdf

Sticht, T. G., Beeler, M. J., & McDonald, B. A. (1992). *The intergenerational transfer of cognitive skills, Vol. 1: Programs, policy, and research issues; Vol. 2: Theory and research in cognitive science.* Norwood, NJ: Ablex Publishing.

Stigler, J. W., Lee, S. Y., Lucker, G. W., & Stevenson, H. W. (1982). Curriculum and achievement in mathematics: A study of elementary school children in Japan, Taiwan, and the United States. *Journal of Educational Psychology, 74*, 315–322.

Stigler, J. W., & Miller, K. F. (in press). Expertise and expert performance in teaching. In Anders Ericsson, K. (Ed.), *Cambridge handbook of expertise and expert performance* (2nd ed.). New York: Cambridge University Press.

Stigler, S. M. (1992). A historical view of statistical concepts in psychology and educational research. *American Journal of Education, 101*(1), 60–70.

Stiglitz, J. E. (2002). *Globalization and its discontents.* New York: W. W. Norton.

Stiglitz, J. E. (2012). Macroeconomic fluctuations, inequality, and human development. *Journal of Human Development and Capabilities, 13*(1), 31–58.

Stiglitz, J. E., Sen, A., & Fitoussi, J. P. (2009). *The measurement of economic performance and social progress revisited: Reflections and Overview.* SciencesPo: Paris. Pps. 1–63. See: https://hal-sciencespo.archives-ouvertes.fr/file/index/docid/1069384/filename/wp2009-33.pdf

Strauss, S. (1981). Cognitive development in school and out. *Cognition, 10*(1), 295–300.

Strauss, S., & Stavy, R. (1982). *U-shaped behavioral growth.* New York: Academic Press.

Street, B. V. (1984). *Literacy in theory and practice.* Cambridge, UK: Cambridge University Press.

Street, B. V. (1999). The meanings of literacy. In Wagner, D. A., Venezky, R. L., & Street, B. V. (Eds.), *Literacy: An international handbook.* Boulder, CO: Westview Press. Pps. 34–40.

Street, B. V. (2001). *Literacy and development: Ethnographic perspectives.* London: Routledge.

Strickland, D. S., & Barnett, S. (2003). Literacy interventions for preschool children considered at risk: Implications for curriculum, professional development, and parent involvement. In: Fairbanks, C., Worthy, J., Maloch, B., Hoffman, J. V., & Schallert, D. (Eds.), *52nd yearbook of the National Reading Conference.* Oak Creek, WI: National Reading Conference Inc. Pps. 104–116.

Strigel, C., & Pouezevara, S. (2012). *Mobile learning and numeracy: Filling gaps and expanding opportunities for early grade learning.* Working Document. Durham, NC, USA: Research Triangle Institute.

Stromquist, N. P. (2016). Using regression analysis to predict countries' economic growth: Illusion and fact in education policy. *Real-World Economics Review, 76*, 65–74.

Stromquist, N. P., & Monkman, K. (2014). Defining globalization and assessing its implications for knowledge and education. In Stromquist, N. P. & Monkman, K. (Eds.), *Globalization and education: Integration and contestation across cultures.* New York: Roland and Littlefield. Pps. 1–19.

Suárez-Orozco, C., Rhodes, J., & Milburn, M. (2009). Unraveling the immigrant paradox: Academic engagement and disengagement among recently arrived immigrant youth. *Youth and Society, 41*(2), 151–185.

Sulzby, E., & Teale, W. (1991). Emergent literacy. In Barr, R., Kamil, M. L., Mosenthal, R. B., & Pearson, P. D. (Eds.), *Handbook of reading research* (Vol. 2). New York: Longman. Pps. 273–285.

Sumner, A. (2012). Where will the world's poor live? An update on global poverty and the new bottom billion. *Center for Global Development, Working Paper 305*, 1–33.

Sumner, A., & Mallett, R. (2012). *The future of foreign aid: Development cooperation and the new geography of global poverty.* London: Palgrave Macmillan.

Sunstein, C. R. (2014). *Why nudge? The politics of libertarian paternalism.* New Haven, CT: Yale University Press.

Super, C. M., & Harkness, S. (1986). The developmental Niche: A conceptualization at the interface of child and culture. *International Journal of Behavioral Development, 9*(4), 545–569.

Suspitsyna, T. (2010). Accountability in American education as a rhetoric and a technology of governmentality. *Journal of Education Policy, 25*(5), 567–586.

Swidler, A. (1986). Culture in action: Symbols and strategies. *American Sociological Review, 51*(2), 273–286.

Tabulawa, R. (2003). International aid agencies, learner-centred pedagogy and political democratisation: A critique. *Comparative Education, 39*(1), 7–26.

Tabulawa, R. T. (2009). Education reform in Botswana: Reflections on policy contradictions and paradoxes. *Comparative Education, 45*(1), 87-107.

Talbot, D. (2012). Given tablets but no teachers, Ethiopian children teach themselves. *MIT Technology Review,* September 8. See: http://www.technologyreview.com/news/506466/given-tablets-but-no-teachers-ethiopian-children-teach-themselves/

Tamim, R. M., Bernard, R. M., Borokhovski, E., Abrami, P. C., & Schmid, R. F. (2011). What forty years of research says about the impact of technology on learning: A second-order meta-analysis and validation study. *Review of Educational Research, 81*(1), 4–28.

Tanner, J. C., Candland, T., & Odden, W. S. (2015). *Later impacts of early childhood interventions: A systematic review.* IEG Working Paper 2015/3. Washington: Independent Evaluation Group, World Bank Group. Pps. 1–203.

Taylor, S., & Coetzee, M. (2013). *Estimating the impact of language instruction in South African primary schools: A fixed effects approach (No. 21/13).* Stellenbosch Economic Working Papers. Stellenbosch, South Africa: Stellenbosch University.

Tepperman, J. (2016). *The fix: How nations survive and thrive in a world in decline.* New York: Duggan.

Terras, M. M., & Ramsey, J. (2012). The five central psychological challenges facing effective mobile learning. *British Journal of Educational Technology, 43*, 820–832.

Thomas, V., Wang, Y., & Fan, X. (2001). *Measuring education inequality-Gini coefficients of education.* No. WPS2525. Washington, DC: The World Bank.

Thompson, P. (2013). Learner-centred education and 'cultural translation'. *International Journal of Educational Development, 33*, 48–58.

Tikly, L., & Barrett, A. M. (2011). Social justice, capabilities and the quality of education in low income countries. *International Journal of Educational Development, 31*(1), 3–14.

Tikly, L., & Barrett, A. M. (2013). *Education quality and social justice in the global South: Challenges for policy, practice and research.* New York: Routledge.

Tolani-Brown, N., McCormac, M., & Zimmermann, R. (2009). An analysis of the research and impact of ICT in education in developing country contexts. *Journal of Education for International Development, 4*(2), 1–12.

Tooley, J. (2013). Challenging educational injustice: 'Grassroots' privatisation in South Asia and sub-Saharan Africa. *Oxford Review of Education, 39*(4), 446–463.

Topping, K. (2005). Trends in peer learning. *Educational Psychology: An International Journal of Experimental Educational Psychology, 25*, 631–645.

Tough, P. (2012). *How children succeed: Grit, curiosity, and the hidden power of character.* New York: Houghton Mifflin Harcourt.

Toure, C. (2009). *Evaluation d'etape de l'experimentation du trilinguisme et de la formation professionnelle dans des daaras des regions de Dakar, Thies, Diourbel et Kaolack.* Dakar: UNICEF/Ministere de l'Education de Senegal.

Toyama, K. (2015). *Geek heresy: Rescuing social change from the cult of technology.* New York: PublicAffairs.

Traxler, J. (2009). Learning in a mobile age. *International Journal of Mobile and Blended Learning, 1*, 1–12.

Traxler, J. (2010). Will student devices deliver innovation, inclusion, and transformation? *Journal of the Research Center for Educational Technology* (Kent State University), *6*(1), 3–16.

Trucano, M. (2010). *Worst practice in ICT use in education.* Blogpost. World Bank. http://blogs.worldbank.org/edutech/worst-practice.

Trucano, M. (2012). *Separating the hope from the hype.* Blogpost. World Bank. www.worldbank.org/education/ict

Trudell, B. (2016). Language choice and education quality in Eastern and Southern Africa: A review. *Comparative Education, 52*(3), 281–293.

Tshotsho, B. P. (2013). Mother tongue debate and language policy in South Africa. *International Journal of Humanities and Social Science, 3*(13), 39–44.

Tuijnman, A., Kirsch, I., & Wagner, D. A. (Eds.). (1997). *Adult basic skills: Innovations in measurement and policy analysis.* Cresskill, NJ: Hampton Press.

Tutu, D. (2010). The fatal complacency. In Kagawa, F. & Selby, D. (Eds.), *Education and climate change: Living and learning in interesting times.* New York: Routledge. Pps. xv–xvi.

UBS Optimus Foundation. (2014). *Optimus impact: Exploring early education programs in Peri-Urban settings in Africa.* www.educationinnovations.org/sites/default/files/10712_Optimus_Impact_Final%20report_5.pdf. Accessed November 23, 2016.

Ul-Haq, M. (1995). *Reflections on human development.* Oxford: Oxford University Press.

UNESCO. (1953). *The use of vernacular languages in education.* Monograph on Fundamental Education, No. 8. Paris: UNESCO.

UNESCO. (1975). *Declaration of persepolis.* International Symposium for Literacy, Persepolis, 3–8 September. www.unesco.org/education/pdf/PERSEP_E.PDF

UNESCO. (1990). *World declaration on education for all.* Paris: UNESCO.

UNESCO. (2003). *Education in a multilingual world.* Paris: UNESCO.

UNESCO. (2005). *Education for all global monitoring report: The quality imperative.* Paris: UNESCO.

UNESCO. (2006). *Education for all global monitoring report: Literacy for life.* Paris: UNESCO.

UNESCO. (2008). *ICT competency standards for teachers: Policy framework.* Paris: UNESCO. http://unesdoc.unesco.org/images/0015/001562/156210e.pdf

UNESCO. (2009). *Education for all global monitoring report: Overcoming inequality—Why governance matters.* Paris: UNESCO.

UNESCO. (2010). *Education for all global monitoring report: Reaching the marginalized.* Paris: UNESCO.

UNESCO. (2011). *Education for all global monitoring report: The hidden crisis—Armed conflict and education.* Paris: UNESCO.

UNESCO. (2012a). *World atlas of gender equality in education.* Paris: UNESCO.

UNESCO. (2012b). *Education for all global monitoring report: Youth and skills: Putting education to work.* Paris: UNESCO.

UNESCO. (2013a). *Policy guidelines for mobile learning.* Paris: UNESCO. http://unesdoc.unesco.org/images/0021/002196/219641e.pdf

UNESCO. (2013b). *Transversal competencies in education policy and practice: Phase I.* Bangkok: UNESCO.

UNESCO. (2014a). *Education for all global monitoring report: Teaching and learning: Achieving quality for all.* Paris: UNESCO.

UNESCO. (2014b). *Reading in the mobile era: A study of mobile reading in developing countries.* Paris: UNESCO.

UNESCO. (2015a). *Education for all global monitoring report: Education for all 2000–2015: Achievements and challenges*. Paris: UNESCO.

UNESCO. (2015b). *Investing in teachers is investing in learning: A prerequisite for the transformative power of education*. Background paper for the Oslo Summit on Education for Development. Paris: UNESCO.

UNESCO. (2015c). *Rethinking education: Towards a global common good?* Paris: UNESCO.

UNESCO. (2016a). *Education for people and planet: Creating sustainable futures for all*. Global Education Monitoring Report. Paris: UNESCO.

UNESCO. (2016b). *Every child should have a textbook*. GEM Policy Paper 23. Paris: UNESCO.

UNESCO-IIEP. (2010). *SACMEQ III project results: Pupil achievement levels in reading and mathematics* (Authors: Hungi, N., Makuwa, D., Saito, M., Dolata, S., van Cappelle, F., Paviot, L., & Vellien, J.). Paris: UNESCO-IIEP.

UNESCO Institute for Statistics. (2011). *Global education digest, 2011*. Montreal: UIS.

UNESCO Institute for Statistics. (2012). *School and teaching resources in Sub-Saharan Africa: Analysis of the 2011: UIS regional data collection on education*. UIS Information Bulletin 9. Montreal: UNESCO.

UNESCO Institute for Statistics. (2014). *Learning metrics partnership: A capacity support and policy strengthening initiative to develop and use common learning metrics for mathematics and reading*. Montreal: UIS.

UNESCO Institute for Statistics. (2016). *The global and thematic indicators for SDG4-education 2030*. Montreal: UIS.

UNESCO Institute for Statistics and Brookings Institution. (2013). *Toward universal learning: Recommendations for universal learning: Recommendations from the Learning Metrics Task Force*. Washington, DC: Brookings-Unesco-UIS.

UNESCO-Pole de Dakar. (2014). *Education sector analysis methodological guidelines*. Dakar: BREDA-UNESCO.

UNESCO-UIL. (2015). *Learning families: Intergenerational approaches to literacy teaching and learning*. Hamburg: UIL.

UNESCO-UIL. (2016). *Third global report on adult learning and education: The impact of adult learning and education on health and well-being. Employment and the labour market; and social, civic and community life*. Hamburg: UIL.

UNESCO website. (nd). *Themes: Early childhood care and education*. http://en.unesco.org/themes/early-childhood-care-and-education. Accessed November 23, 2016.

UN General Assembly. (1989). *Convention on the rights of the child*. www.unicef.org/crc/. Accessed August 14, 2013.

UNHCR (United Nations High Commission for Refugees). (2011). *Global trends 2011: A year of crises*. Geneva: UNHCR.

UNICEF. (2012). *Inequities in early childhood development: What the data say*. New York: UNICEF.

UNICEF. (2015). *Levels and trends in child mortality: Report 2015: Estimates developed by the UN Inter-Agency Group for Child Mortality Estimation*. New York: UNICEF. https://data.unicef.org/wp-content/uploads/2015/12/IGME-report-2015-child-mortality-final_236.pdf

UNICEF. (2016). *Journeys to scale: Accompanying the finalists of the innovations in education initiative*. See: http://www.educationinnovations.org/sites/default/files/Journeys%20to%20Scale%20-%20Full%20Report.pdf

United Nations. (2000). *United Nations millennium declaration*. Resolution adopted by the General Assembly. United Nations A/RES/55/2. www.un.org/millennium/declaration/ares552e.htm

United Nations. (2015a). *UN development goals report*. New York: United Nations.

United Nations. (2015b). *Transforming our world: The 2030 agenda for sustainable development*. New York: United Nations.

United Nations, Department of Economic and Social Affairs. (2013). *International migration report 2013*. New York: United Nations.

United Nations, Department of Economic and Social Affairs. (2014). *World urbanization prospects 2014*. New York: United Nations.

United Nations, Department of Economic and Social Affairs, Population Division. (2015). *World population prospects: The 2015 revision, DVD edition*. New York: United Nations.

United Nations Development Program (UNDP). (2009). *Human development report 2009: Overcoming barriers—Human mobility and development*. New York: UNDP.

United Nations Development Program (UNDP). (2010). *Human development report 2010: The real wealth of nations: Pathways to human development*. New York: UNDP.

United Nations Development Program (UNDP). (2011). *Human development report 2011: Sustainability and equity: A better future for all*. New York: UNDP.

United Nations Development Program (UNDP). (2013a). *Human development report 2013: The rise of the South: Human progress in a diverse world*. New York: UNDP.

United Nations Development Program (UNDP). (2013b). *ICTs and the Post-2015 agenda: Learning from the sustainable networking programme*. New York: UNDP.

United Nations Development Program (UNDP). (2013c). *Humanity divided: Confronting inequality in developing countries*. New York: UNDP.

United Nations Development Program (UNDP). (2014). *Human development report 2014: Sustaining human progress: Reducing vulnerabilities and building resilience*. New York: UNDP.

United Nations Development Program (UNDP). (2015). *Human development report 2015: Work for human development*. New York: UNDP.

Unwin, T. (2005). Towards a framework for the use of ICT in teacher training in Africa. *Open Learning: The Journal of Open, Distance and e-Learning, 20*(2), 113–129.

Unwin, T. (2009). Development agendas and the place of ICTs. In Unwin, T. (Ed.), *ICT4D: Information and communication technology for development*. London: Cambridge University Press. Pps 7–38.

Unwin, T. (2014). Evaluating communication for development. *Information Technologies and International Development, 10*(2), 63–65.

Upgren, A. R. (2008). *Weather: How it works and why it matters*. New York: Basic Books.

Uwezo. (2011). Are our children learning? In *Uganda annual learning assessment report*. Nairobi: Uwezo. Pps. 1-73.

Uwezo. (2014). Uganda annual assessment report summary. In *Uganda annual learning assessment report*. Nairobi: Uwezo. Pps. 1–50.

Valdiviezo, L. A. (2013). Vertical and horizontal approaches to ethnography of language policy in Peru. *International Journal of the Sociology of Language, 219*, 23–46.

Van Bavel, J. J., Mende-Siedlecki, P., Brady, W. J., & Reinero, D. A. (2016). Contextual sensitivity in scientific reproducibility. *Proceedings of the National Academy of Sciences, 113*(23), 6454–6459.

Van Damme, D. (2014). *How closely is the distribution of skills related to countries' overall level of social inequality and economic prosperity?* OECD Education Working Papers, EDU NAEC Paper Series, No. 1. Paris: OECD.

Van Damme, D. (in press). Is it sustainable to leave the bottom behind in the process of educational expansion? In Wagner, D. A., Boruch, R. F., & Wolf, S. (Eds.), *Learning at the bottom of the pyramid*. Paris: UNESCO-IIEP.

Vavrus, F., & Bartlett, L. (2012). Comparative pedagogies and epistemological diversity: Social and materials contexts of teaching in Tanzania. *Comparative Education Review, 56*(4), 634–658.

Venezky, R. L., Wagner, D. A., & Ciliberti, B. S. (1990). *Toward defining literacy.* Newark, DE: International Reading Association.

Venezky, R. L., & Wagner, D. A. (1996). Supply and demand for literacy instruction in the United States. *Adult Education Quarterly, 46,* 197–208.

Vogel, I. (2012). *Review of the use of 'theory of change' in international development.* Technical Report. London: DFID.

Von Bertalanffy, L. (1968). *General system theory: Foundations, development, applications.* New York: George Braziller.

Von Uexkull, N., Croicu, M., Fjelde, H., & Buhaug, H. (2016). Civil conflict sensitivity to growing-season drought. *Proceedings of the National Academy of Sciences, 113,* 12391–12396.

Vygotsky, L. (1978). *Mind in society: The development of higher psychological processes.* Cambridge, MA: MIT Press.

Wade, R. H. (2004). Is globalization reducing poverty and inequality? *World Development, 32*(4), 567–589.

Wagner, D. A. (1974). The development of short-term and incidental memory: A cross-cultural study. *Child Development, 45,* 389–396.

Wagner, D. A. (1977). Ontogeny of the Ponzo illusion: Effects of age, schooling and environment. *International Journal of Psychology, 12,* 161–176.

Wagner, D. A. (1978). Memories of Morocco: The influence of age, schooling and environment. *Cognitive Psychology, 10,* 1–28.

Wagner, D. A. (Ed.). (1983a). *Child development and international development: Research-policy interfaces.* San Francisco: Jossey-Bass.

Wagner, D. A. (1983b). Special issue editor, 'Literacy and Ethnicity'. *In the International Journal of the Sociology of Language, 42,* 1–121.

Wagner, D. A. (1983c). Rediscovering 'rote': Some cognitive and pedagogical preliminaries. In Irvine, S. & Berry, J. W. (Eds.), *Human assessment and cultural factors.* New York: Plenum. Pps. 179–190.

Wagner, D. A. (1986). Child development research and the Third World: A future of mutual interest? *American Psychologist, 41,* 298–301.

Wagner, D. A. (1989a). *In support of primary schooling in developing countries: A new look at traditional indigenous schools.* World Bank Background Paper Series, Doc. No. PHREE/89/23. Washington, DC: World Bank.

Wagner, D. A. (1989b). Literacy campaigns: Past, present and future. *Comparative Education Review, 33,* 256–260.

Wagner, D. A. (1990). Literacy assessment in the Third World: An overview and proposed schema for survey use. *Comparative Education Review, 33,* 112–138.

Wagner, D. A. (1993). *Literacy, culture and development: Becoming literate in Morocco.* New York: Cambridge University Press.

Wagner, D. A. (1999). Indigenous education and literacy learning. In Wagner, D. A., Venezky, R. L., & Street, B. V. (Eds.), *Literacy: An international handbook.* Boulder, CO: Westview Press. Pps. 283–287.

Wagner, D. A. (2001). IT and education for the poorest of the poor: Constraints, possibilities, and principles. In *TechKnowlogia: International journal for the advancement of knowledge and learning.* Washington, DC. www.techknowlogia.org/TKL_Articles/PDF/304.pdf

Wagner, D. A. (2003). Smaller, quicker, cheaper: Alternative strategies for literacy assessment in the UN literacy decade. *International Journal of Educational Research, 39*(3), 293–309.

Wagner, D. A. (2004). Literacy(ies), culture(s) and development(s): The ethnographic challenge. *Reading Research Quarterly, 39*(2), 234–241.

Wagner, D. A. (Ed.). (2005). *Monitoring and evaluation of ICT in education projects: A handbook for developing countries.* Washington: World Bank/InfoDev.

Wagner, D. A. (2009). Pro-poor approaches to using technology for human development: Monitoring and evaluation perspectives. In Bekman, S. & Aksu-Koc, A. (Eds.), *Perspectives on human development, family and culture: Essays in honor of Cigdem Kagiticibasi.* Cambridge: Cambridge University Press. Pps. 267–380.

Wagner, D. A. (2010a). Literacy. In Bornstein, M. (Ed.), *Handbook of cultural developmental science.* New York: Taylor & Francis. Pps. 161–173.

Wagner, D. A. (2010b). Quality of education, comparability, and assessment choice in developing countries. *Compare: A Journal of Comparative and International Education, 40*(6), 741–760.

Wagner, D. A. (2011a). *Smaller, quicker, cheaper: Improving learning assessments in developing countries.* Paris and Washington: UNESCO-IIEP and EFA Fast Track Initiative of Global Partnership for Education.

Wagner, D. A. (2011b). What happened to literacy? Historical and conceptual perspectives on literacy in UNESCO. *International Journal of Educational Development, 31,* 319–323.

Wagner, D. A. (2014a). *MOOCs for teacher professional development: Moving beyond the cascade method.* Presentation at Mobile Learning Week. Paris: UNESCO. www.unesco.org/new/en/unesco/themes/icts/m4ed/unesco-mobile-learning-week-2014/symposium/breakout-sessions/moocs-for-teacher/

Wagner, D. A. (2014b). *Mobiles for reading: A landscape research review.* Technical Report. Washington, DC: USAID/JBS. https://allchildrenreading.org/resources/mobiles-for-reading-a-landscape-research-review/

Wagner, D. A. (2014c). Learning first: An introduction. In Wagner, D. A. (Ed.). In Wagner, D. A. (Ed.). *Learning and education in developing countries: Research and policy for the post-2015 UN development goals.* New York: Palgrave Macmillan. Pps. 1–25.

Wagner, D. A. (2014d). Conclusion: Toward a learning research agenda. In Wagner, D. A. (Ed.). *Learning and education in developing countries: Research and policy for the post-2015 UN development goals.* New York: Palgrave Macmillan. Pps. 110–117.

Wagner, D. A. (Ed.). (2014e). *Learning and education in developing countries: Research and policy for the post-2015 UN development goals.* NY: Palgrave Macmillan.

Wagner, D. A. (2015b). Review of William Easterly's tyranny of experts. *Comparative Education Review, 59*(2), 361–364.

Wagner, D. A. (2017). Learning, literacy and sustainable development: Inclusion, vulnerability, and the SDGs. In Battro, A., Lena P., Sanchez-Sorondo, M. & von Braun, J. (Eds.), *Children and Sustainable Development: Ecological education in a globalized world.* Rome: Pontifical Academy of Sciences (Vatican)/Springer. Pps. 45–66.

Wagner, D. A. (in press). Technology for education in developing countries: Towards a Post-2015 Agenda. In Lubin, I. (Ed.), *ICT-supported innovations in small countries and developing regions: Perspectives and recommendations for international education.* New York: Springer.

Wagner, D. A., Babson, A., & Murphy, K. M. (2011). How much is learning measurement worth? Assessment costs in low-income countries. *Current Issues in Comparative Education, 14,* 3–21.

Wagner, D. A., Boruch, R. F., & Wolf, S. (Eds.) (in press). *Learning at the bottom of the pyramid.* Paris: UNESCO-IIEP.

Wagner, D. A., Buek, K. W., Adler, A. Castillo, N. M., Zahra, F. T., Lee, J., Chittamuru, D., & Lee, S. (2016). Cognitive dissonance: Psychological theory meets international development: Review of World Bank (2015): Mind, society and behavior. *Comparative Education Review, 60,* 601–603.

Wagner, D. A., & Castillo, N. M. (2014). Learning at the bottom of the pyramid: Constraints, comparability and policy in developing countries. *Prospects, 44,* 627–638.

Wagner, D. A., & Castillo, N. M. (2016). *BFI-South Africa evaluation report to USAID.* Technical Report, International Literacy Institute. Philadelphia: University of Pennsylvania.

Wagner, D. A., Daswani, C. J., & Karnati, R. (2010). Technology and mother-tongue literacy in Southern India: Impact studies among young children and out-of-school youth. *Information Technology and International Development, 6*(4), 23–43.

Wagner, D. A., Day, B., & Sun, J. (2004). *Information technologies and education for the poor in Africa: Recommendations for a pro-poor ICT4D non-formal education policy.* Technical Report. International Literacy Institute. Philadelphia: University of Pennsylvania. www.literacy.org/sites/literacy.org/files/publications/itepa_webrep_may26_jcs5.pdf

Wagner, D. A., & Heald, K. (1979). Carpentered world vs. Piaget: Revisiting the illusions of Segall, Campbell and Herskovits. In Eckensberger, L. H., Lonner, W. J., & Poortinga, Y. H. (Eds.), *Cross-cultural contributions to psychology.* Holland: Swets & Zeitlinger. Pps. 40–44.

Wagner, D. A., & Kaul, I. (2006). *Out-of-school children and youth in the MENA region.* Unpublished Background Paper for the MENA Regional Education Report. Washington, DC: World Bank.

Wagner, D. A., & Kozma, R. (2005). *New technologies for literacy and adult education: A global perspective.* Paris: UNESCO.

Wagner, D. A., & Lotfi, A. (1980). Traditional Islamic education in Morocco: Socio-historical and psychological perspectives. *Comparative Education Review, 24,* 238–251.

Wagner, D. A., & Lotfi, A. (1983). Learning to read by 'rote'. *International Journal of the Sociology of Language, 42,* 111–121.

Wagner, D. A., Murphy, K. M., & de Korne, H. (2012). *Learning first: A research agenda for improving learning in low-income countries.* Washington, DC: Brookings Institution. www.brookings.edu/~/media/research/files/papers/2012/12/learning%20first%20wagner%20murphy%20de%20korne/12%20learning%20first%20wagner%20murphy%20de%20korne.pdf

Wagner, D. A., & Paris, S. G. (1981). Problems and prospects in comparative studies of memory. *Human Development, 24*(6), 412–424.

Wagner, D. A., Sabatini, J., & Gal, I. (1999). *Assessing basic learning competencies among youth and young adults in developing countries: Analytic survey framework and implementation guidelines.* EFA 2000 Assessment Surveys Report. Philadelphia-Paris: International Literacy Institute-UNESCO. ERIC. http://files.eric.ed.gov/fulltext/ED449299.pdf

Wagner, D. A., Spratt, J. E., & Ezzaki, A. (1989). Does learning to read in a second language always put the child at a disadvantage? Some counterevidence from Morocco. *Applied Psycholinguistics, 10,* 31–48.

Wagner, D. A., & Srivastava, A. B. L. (Principal authors). (1989). *Measuring literacy through household surveys.* Doc. No. DP/UN/INT-88-X01/10E. New York: United Nations Statistical Office.

Wagner, D. A., & Stevenson, H. W. (Eds.). (1982). *Cultural perspectives on child development.* New York: WH Freeman.

Wagner, D. A. & Venezky, R. L. (1999). Adult literacy: The next generation. *Educational Researcher, 28,* 1, 21-29.

Wagner, D. A., Venezky, R. L., & Street, B. V. (Eds.). (1999). *Literacy: An international handbook.* Boulder, CO: Westview Press.

Wail, B., Hanchane, S., & Kamal, A. (2012). A new data set of educational inequality in the world, 1950–2010: Gini index of education by age group. In Bishop, J. A. & Salas, R. (Eds.). *Inequality, mobility, and segregation: Essays in honor of Jacques Silber* (Vol. 20). Emerald Group Publishing. Pps. 337–366.

Wali, A. (2012). A different measure of well-being. *American Anthropologist, 114*(1), 12–13.

Wallerstein, I. M. (1992). The West, capitalism, and the modern world-system. *Review (Fernand Braudel Center), 15*(4), 561–619.

Wallerstein, I. M. (2000). Globalization or the age of transition? A long-term view of the trajectory of the world-system. *International Sociology, 15*(2), 249–265.

Wallerstein, I. M. (2004). *World-systems analysis: An introduction.* Durham, NC: Duke.

Wals, A. E., Brody, M., Dillon, J., & Stevenson, R. B. (2014). Convergence between science and environmental education. *Science, 344*(6184), 583–584.

Wals, A. E. J., & Lenglet, F. (2016). Sustainability citizens: Collaborative and disruptive social learning. In Horne, R., Fien, J., Beza, B., & Nelson, A. (Eds.), *Sustainability citizenship in cities: Theory and practice.* London, Routledge. Pps. 52–67.

Walsh, C., & Shaheen, R. (2013). *English in action (EIA): Mobile phones as an agent of change for large-scale teacher professional development and English language learning in Bangladesh.* For American Educational Association Annual Meeting, San Francisco, CA.

Walter, S., & Dekker, D. (2011). Mother tongue instruction in Lubuagan: A case study from the Philippines. *International Review of Education, 57*(5–6), 667–683.

Wang, Y. (2012). *Education in a changing world: Flexibility, skills, and employability.* Washington: World Bank.

Warschauer, M. (2004). *Technology and social inclusion: Rethinking the digital divide.* Boston: MIT press.

Wasik, B. A., & Hindman, A. H. (2015). Talk alone won't close the 30-million word gap. *Phi Delta Kappan, 96*(6), 50–54.

Webster, N., & Engberg-Pedersen, L. (Eds.). (2002). *In the name of the poor: Contesting political space for poverty reduction.* London: Zed Books.

Weisberg, H. I. (2014). *Willful ignorance: The mismeasure of uncertainty.* New York: John Wiley & Sons.

West, A., Ingram, D., & Hind, A. (2006). "Skimming the cream" admissions to charter schools in the United States and to autonomous schools in England. *Educational Policy, 20*(4), 615–639.

Westbrook, J., Durrani, N., Brown, R., Orr, D., Pryor, J., Boddy, J., & Salvi, F. (2013). *Pedagogy, curriculum, teaching practices and teacher education in developing countries.* London: UK Department for International Development.

White, T. H. (1987). *The once and future king.* New York, NY: Ace Books.

Whiting, B. B., & Whiting, J. W. (1975). *Children of six cultures: A psycho-cultural analysis.* Cambridge, MA: Harvard.

Williams, C. (2011). Review of F. Kagawa and D. Selby (Eds.), *Education and climate change: Living and learning in interesting times. British Journal of Educational Studies, 59*(4), 500–502.

Williams, J. H., & Cummings, W. C. (2015). Education from the bottom up: UNICEF's education programme in Somalia. *International Peacekeeping, 22*(4), 419–434.

Williams, T. P., Abbott, P., & Mupenzi, A. (2015). 'Education at our school is not free': The hidden costs of fee-free schooling in Rwanda. *Compare: A Journal of Comparative and International Education, 45*(6), 931–952.

Willis, K. (2011). *Theories and practices of development.* London: Taylor & Francis.

Willms, D., & Tramonte, L. (2014). *Towards the development of contextual questionnaires for the pisa for development study.* Paris: OECD. www.oecd.org/callsfortenders/Annex%20 E%20-%20Contextual%20Questionnaires%20Paper.pdf

Winthrop, R., & McGivney, E. (2015). *Why wait 100 years? Bridging the gap in global education.* Washington, DC: Brookings.

Winthrop, R., & Smith, M. S. (2012). *A new face of education: Bringing technology into the classroom in the developing world* (Pps. 1–52). Working Paper. Washington, DC: Brookings.

Witkin, H. A., Moore, C. A., Goodenough, D. R., & Cox, P. W. (1977). Field-dependent and field-independent cognitive styles and their educational implications. *Review of Educational Research, 47,* 1–64.

Wolff, L. (2007). *The costs of student assessments in Latin America.* Working Paper 38. Washington: PREAL.

Woodhead, M. (2007). *Changing perspectives on early childhood: Theory, research and policy.* Background paper prepared for the Education for All Global Monitoring Report. Paris: UNESCO.

Woodhead, M., Frost, M., & James, Z. (2013). Does growth in private schooling contribute to education for all? Evidence from a longitudinal, two cohort study in Andhra Pradesh, India. *International Journal of Educational Development, 33*(1), 65–73.

Woodhead, M., & Streuli, N. (2013). Early education for all: Is there a role for the private sector? In Britto, P. R., Engle, P. E., & Super, C. (Eds.), *Handbook of early childhood development research and its impact on global policy.* New York, NY: Oxford University Press. Pps. 308–328.

Woolcock, M. (2014). *Culture, politics, and development.* World Bank Policy Research Working Paper, No. 6939. Washington, DC: World Bank.

Wong, G. K. (2014). Engaging students using their own mobile devices for learning mathematics in classroom discourse: A case study in Hong Kong. *International Journal of Mobile Learning and Organisation, 8*(2), 143–165.

World Bank. (2002). *Global economic prospects and the developing countries 2002: Making trade work for the world's poor.* Washington, DC: The World Bank.

World Bank. (2006). *World development report 2006: Equity and development.* Washington, DC: The World Bank.

World Bank. (2011). *Learning for all: Investing in people's knowledge and skills to promote development.* Washington: World Bank.

World Bank. (2012a). *The transformational use of information and communication technologies in Africa.* E-Transform Africa: World Bank.

World Bank. (2012b). *Uganda: Teachers.* SABER Country Report. Washington, DC: The World Bank.

World Bank. (2015a). *World development indicators.* Washington, DC: World Bank.

World Bank. (2015b). *Mind, society and behavior.* World Development Report. Washington, DC: World Bank. www.worldbank.org/content/dam/Worldbank/Publications/WDR/ WDR%202015/WDR-2015-Full-Report.pdf

World Bank. (2016a). *Ending extreme poverty.* www.worldbank.org/en/news/ feature/2016/06/08/ending-extreme-poverty

World Bank. (2016b). *Digital dividends.* World Development Report. Washington, DC: World Bank.

World Information and Technology Services Alliance (WITSA). (2013). *The digital planet 2013 edition.* www.witsa.org

Wu, T. (2016). *The attention merchants: The epic scramble to get inside our heads.* New York: Knopf Publishing Group.

Wundt, W. (1916). *Elements of folk psychology: Outlines of a psychological history of the development of mankind.* New York: George Allen and Unwin.

Yardley, H. (2011). *International Women's Day: Cambodia's pink tech revolution.* Oxfam Southern Africa Blog. www.oxfamblogs.org/southernafrica/?p=2246#sthash.Ip6bbFzf.dpuf

Yoshikawa, H., & Kalil, A. (2011). The effects of parental undocumented status on the developmental contexts of young children in immigrant families. *Child Development Perspectives, 5*(4), 291–297.

Yoshikawa, H., Leyva, D., Snow, C. E., Treviño, E., Barata, M., Weiland, C., Gomez, C. J., Moreno, L., Rolla, A. D'Sa, N., & Arbour, M. C. (2015). Experimental impacts of a teacher professional development program in Chile on preschool classroom quality and child outcomes. *Developmental Psychology, 51*(3), 309.

Young, M. E. (Ed.). (2002). *From early child development to human development: Investing in our children's future.* Washington, DC: World Bank Publications.

Yoza Project. (2009–2013). *Project website.* http://yozaproject.com/about-the-project/

Zahra, F. T. (2017). *Educating farmers in farmers in farmer field schools in Bangladesh: Impact on knowledge, practices and production.* Ph.D. dissertation. Philadelphia: University of Pennsylvania.

Zaval, L., & Cornwell, F. J. (2016). *Effective education and communication strategies to promote environmental engagement: The role of social-psychological mechanisms.* GEM Background Paper. Paris: UNESCO.

Zeiders, K. H., Umaña-Taylor, A. J., Jahromi, L. B., Updegraff, K. A., & White, R. M. (2016). Discrimination and acculturation stress: A longitudinal study of children's well-being from prenatal development to 5 years of age. *Journal of Developmental & Behavioral Pediatrics, 37*(7), 557–564.

Zimmerman, J. (2011). 'Money, materials, and manpower': Ghanaian in service teacher education and the political economy of failure, 1961–1971. *History of Education Quarterly, 51*(1), 1–27.

Zurita, G., & Nussbaum, M. (2004). A constructivist mobile learning environment supported by a wireless handheld network. *Journal of Computer Assisted Learning, 20*(4), 235-243.

INDEX

Page numbers in italics indicate figures and page numbers in bold indicate tables. Page numbers followed by b and n indicate boxes and notes.